AutoCAD 3D

COMPANION

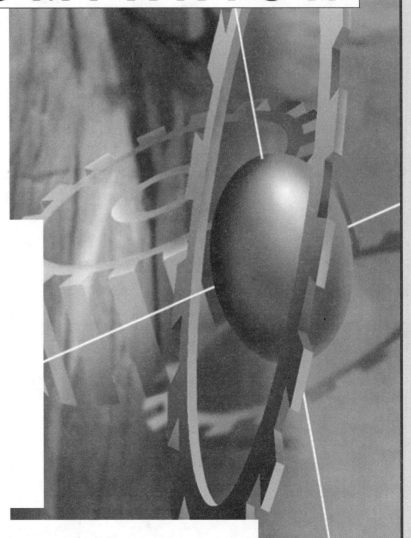

AutoCAD 3D

COMPANION

THE ILLUSTRATED

GUIDE TO

AUTOCAD'S

THIRD

DIMENSION

For Release 13

for Windows

Second Edition

George O. Head

VENTANA
PRESS

AutoCAD Reference Library™

AutoCAD 3D Companion: The Illustrated Guide to AutoCAD's Third Dimension for Release 13 for Windows, Second Edition
Copyright © 1995 by George O. Head

Library of Congress Cataloging-in-Publication Data

Head, George O., 1945-
     The AutoCAD 3D companion : the illustrated guide to AutoCAD's third dimension / George O. Head. -- 2nd ed.
          p.   cm.
     Includes index.
     ISBN 1-56604-142-2
     1. AutoCAD (Computer file) 2. Computer graphics. I. Title.
T385.H374 1995
620'.0042'02855369--dc20   95-1949
                                        CIP

Book design: Karen Wysocki
Cover design: Tom Draper Design
Vice President, Ventana Press: Walter R. Bruce III
Art Director: Marcia Webb
Design staff: Dawne Sherman, Mike Webster
Editorial Manager: Pam Richardson
Editorial staff: Angela Anderson, Tracye Giles, Nathaniel Mund
Developmental Editor: Tim C. Mattson
Project Editor: Jessica Ryan
Print Department: Dan Koeller, Wendy Bernhardt
Product Manager: Clif McCormick
Production Manager: John Cotterman
Production staff: Patrick Berry, Jaimie Livingston
Index service: Richard Evans, Infodex
Proofreader: Laura Wenzel
Technical editor: Brian Matthews, Architectural Technology Dept. Head, Wake Technical Community College

Second Edition 9 8 7 6 5 4 3 2 1
Printed in the United States of America

For information about our audio products, write us at Newbridge Book Clubs, 3000 Cindel Drive, Delran, NJ 08375.

Ventana Press, Inc.
P.O. Box 2468
Chapel Hill, NC 27515
919/942-0220
FAX 919/942-1140

Limits of Liability and Disclaimer of Warranty

The authors and publisher of this book have used their best efforts in preparing the book and the programs contained in it. These efforts include the development, research and testing of the theories and programs to determine their effectiveness. The authors and publisher make no warranty of any kind, expressed or implied, with regard to these programs or the documentation contained in this book.

The authors and publisher shall not be liable in the event of incidental or consequential damages in connection with, or arising out of, the furnishing, performance or use of the programs, associated instructions and/or claims of productivity gains.

Trademarks

Trademarked names appear throughout this book. Rather than list the names and entities that own the trademarks or insert a trademark symbol with each mention of the trademarked name, the publisher states that it is using the names only for editorial purposes and to the benefit of the trademark owner with no intention of infringing upon that trademark.

About the Author

George O. Head is president of Associated Market Research, a business management consulting firm for architects and engineers. He is the developer of A/E Solutions, a project management and financial accounting software package for architects and engineers. He is also author of *AutoLISP in Plain English* and coauthor of *1,000 AutoCAD Tips & Tricks* and *The AutoCAD Productivity Book* (all published by Ventana Press).

About the Technical Editor

Brian Matthews is coauthor for this book and technical editor for all of the books in the Ventana Press AutoCAD Reference Library. He heads the Architectural Technology department at Wake Technical Community College in Raleigh, NC, and directs the college's AutoCAD Training Center. For the past nine years, he has been responsible for organizing and creating AutoCAD and AutoLISP courses, which are taught as part of a two-year engineering technology curriculum. He has also coordinated and taught several AutoCAD Industrial Extension Service programs at North Carolina State University.

Readers with technical inquiries can reach Brian Matthews by phone at 919-662-3476, by fax at 919-779-3360, or by e-mail on the Internet at *bmatt@wtcc-gw.wake.tec.nc.us*.

Contents

SECTION II: INTRODUCTION TO TUTORIALS

SECTION III: PRACTICE TUTORIALS

Section IV: AutoLISP Programs

Section v: Appendices

AutoCAD is no longer just a computer-aided drafting program. In addition to giving you the ability to create a complete model and helping you to communicate better, AutoCAD has truly evolved into the graphics engine used by far more expensive systems.

Working in 3D has become an integral part of the design process. Anyone who has a need to create more than one view of the same object should work in 3D, and anyone who wants to create a first-class presentation should work in 3D. A 3D model is the basis for computer-aided manufacturing. A 3D model also is the basis for a photorealistic rendering. Although the days of 2D drafting are not gone, 3D design enhances your ability to communicate and design.

What's Inside?

The *AutoCAD 3D Companion* is a comprehensive book that equips you with all the tools you'll need to understand and work in 3D. Chapters 1 through 14 take you step by step through all the tools given to you in AutoCAD. Each chapter is a tutorial on one or more of the essential tools, presented in a way that is not discipline-specific.

Chapters 15 and 16 are discipline-specific tutorials designed to walk you through the development of complete models. Both Chapter 15, a mechanical tutorial, and Chapter 16, an architectural tutorial, are carefully designed to give you a practical application of the concepts you learned in the first 14 chapters.

Chapter 17 is the 3D Toolkit, including 53 ready-to-run AutoLISP programs specifically designed to give you the most productivity possible while working in 3D. Not just a series of isolated programs at the end of the book, each of these programs is used as an integral part of the previous chapters. In this way you learn to incorporate each program into your 3D arsenal as you progress.

What Will You Learn?

The *AutoCAD 3D Companion* is designed as a complete 3D tutorial. You'll gain a thorough understanding of how AutoCAD's 3D interface works. You'll also learn how to use the User Coordinate System, how to view your model with DVIEW and VPOINT, how to work with surfaces and much, much more.

More important than just learning the various AutoCAD commands, you'll learn how and when to use these tools. Not only does each of the chapters teach you the specific concepts, but you gain the experience of working on models as you learn. And in Chapters 15 and 16 you have the opportunity to work through two practical applications.

As good a job as Autodesk did in creating the 3D interface for AutoCAD, it isn't complete. Your work in 3D can be enhanced dramatically by adding 3D AutoLISP programs to your system in much the same way you use the built-in commands found in AutoCAD.

How Well Do You Need to Know AutoCAD?

The *AutoCAD 3D Companion* assumes that you have a working knowledge of the basic AutoCAD commands. You should know how to draw lines, arcs and circles, and use object snaps and layers.

You don't have to be an expert at AutoCAD, and you don't have to know how to program in AutoLISP (for you'll use the AutoLISP programs just like regular AutoCAD commands). In short, this book will teach you everything you need to draw effectively in 3D, whether or not you have programming experience.

How to Use This Book

The *AutoCAD 3D Companion* is designed to be used as a hands-on tutorial. You learn by doing. Therefore, the best way to use the book is with Auto-CAD. After you've gone through each of the tutorial chapters, you'll also find that this book will be an invaluable and lasting reference. It will become your number one resource as you work on your own models.

The chapters give you a thorough explanation of the concepts introduced, along with exercises to fully illustrate these concepts. To most effectively learn the concepts, you should work through each of the exercises as it's presented.

Software and Hardware Requirements

Following are the general software and hardware requirements for using The *AutoCAD 3D Companion:*

1. You'll need AutoCAD Release 13. The book is designed to work with and take advantage of all the features of Release 13, and it will work with all versions and platforms of Release 13. If you don't yet have Release 13, you can still benefit from much of the book with Releases 10, 11 and 12.

2. You'll need a computer and operating system capable of running Release 13. A printer or plotter is *not* required to use this book.

3. The Advanced Modeling Extension (AME) is *not* required to use this book as you'll find the Solids command built into Release 13. Choose the Solids toolbar; twelve icons allow you to create 3D objects and also convert AME files to the new Release 13 ACIS format.

Rules of the Road

Following are some general rules to keep in mind while working through The *AutoCAD 3D Companion:*

1. Each time you are to begin an AutoCAD command the available toolbar icon is shown if applicable. Because not everyone will have the appropriate toolbar and icon immediately visible on the screen you are also given the command that may be typed. Therefore to facilitate your use of this book we use a Type: - Response: format. When you see **Type:**, you're to type what follows. This is generally followed by **Response:**, which is the system's response that you see at the Command line.

2. <Enter> means you should press the Enter key. In most cases while in AutoCAD, you can also press the space bar to get the same results.

3. If you see a plus sign at the end of a line of AutoLISP code, it indicates that the line continues. Don't type the plus sign; it's simply there because the code wouldn't fit on one line. When at all possible use the companion disk instead of typing the AutoLISP programs. This not only saves you time, but eliminates typing errors.

4. When directed to use an object snap, make that object snap active for the next pick. You can do this using any of the AutoCAD methods for picking with object snap, such as the cursor menu, the options menu or the Object Snap toolbar.

5. "Confirm the selection set" means press Enter once after you've selected all the objects.

6. You must load each of the AutoLISP programs before it can be executed. You're encouraged to use the AutoLISP program called 3DTOOLS.LSP to load automatically all of the programs found in the 3D Toolkit. The *Companion Disk* is included, complete with all of the programs ready to use. Complete instructions on the use of these programs are located in Appendix A, "AutoLISP & Your 3D Toolkit."

Getting Started

You probably purchased AutoCAD to improve your efficiency, productivity and communication with your associates and clientele. The tools to draw in 3D are available to you at no additional cost; all you have to do is learn how to use them. So let's get started.

— George Head
Warwick, Rhode Island

SECTION I

BASIC
TUTORIALS

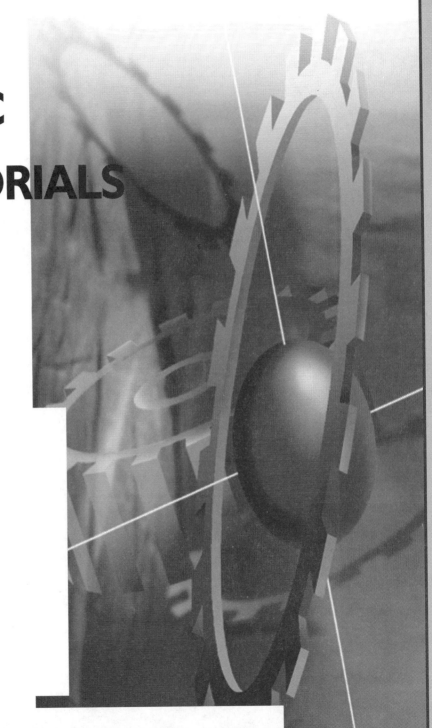

CHAPTER 1

3D Preview

A New Way of Thinking

 AutoCAD Release 13 is a complete 3D database with all its objects expressed as X, Y and Z coordinates. Although the evolution of 3D drawing to this current stage has been a long and arduous road, it wasn't always this way. Let's begin your introduction to 3D with a brief review of this evolutionary process.

A few years ago, Autodesk, the developer of AutoCAD, admitted that AutoCAD was a 2D drafting tool. While other competitors entered the 3D market, AutoCAD languished behind. In a valiant but poor effort, Autodesk tested the 3D water with Release 9, only to find its reception poor at best—not because the world wasn't ready for a good 3D CAD system, but because AutoCAD was not at that time a good 3D CAD system. Release 9 was frequently given the label of 2-1/2D.

With Release 10, 11 and 12 and the ensuing Release 13, the way of working with AutoCAD changed forever. Now, in Release 13, AutoCAD is a completely true 3D database. This means that all objects in AutoCAD are expressed as X, Y and Z coordinates. Even if you think you're drawing in 2D, you're really drawing in 3D—except the Z coordinate is 0. Therefore, when you hear others say they want to convert their drawings to 3D, they don't exactly have it right. What they mean to say is that they want either to add objects somewhere in 3D space or they want to extrude existing objects. Later in this chapter, you'll look at extrusions. But for now think of an extrusion as simply adding height to objects.

As you will see, working in 3D is more a case of viewing your drawing from many different angles and working on one side of a drawing at a time. You'll soon learn you don't really draw in 3D: you draw in 2D on each part of the drawing. Then, as you start to look at the model from different angles, you set up 2D areas of drawing and toggle to each view as you move around the drawing. On your part, this process will require a new way of thinking, but it's not hard and can be quite enjoyable once you know what you're doing. Now you'll draw something quick and easy in 3D.

Quick Draw in 3D

Settings for drawing:

UNITS	Decimal
Precision	2
LIMITS	0,0
Upper right	12,9
GRID	.25
SNAP	.25

Figure 1-1: Object Creation icon from the Object Properties toolbar

In Release 13 for Windows, begin by learning to use the dialog boxes and icons as much as possible. Choose the Object Creation icon from the Object Properties toolbar or from the pull-down menu, pick Data; then pick Object Creation… for the Entity Creation Modes dialog box. You'll see the dialog box shown in Figure 1-2.

Change 0.0000 in the Thickness box to 4; then pick OK.

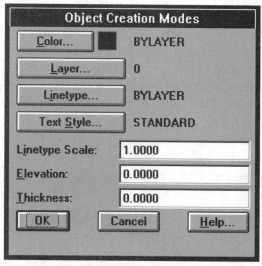

Figure 1-2: Object Creation Modes dialog box

Alternatively, type **THICKNESS** <Enter>; then, at the New value for Thickness prompt, type **4** <Enter>.

You've just set a thickness of 4 units. To see the effect this setting will have, draw an illustration like Figure 1-3. Each line is about 3 units long. Also, eyeball the arc. Later, your drawings will become more precise.

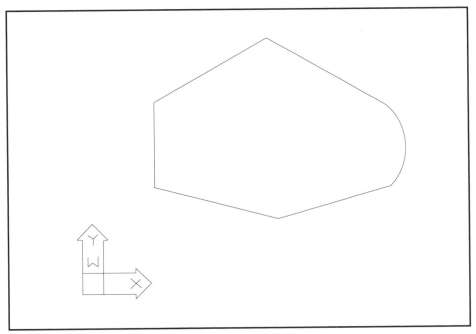

Figure 1-3: Draw the figure with a thickness of 4

Before you proceed any further, set your thickness back to 0:

Pick: Object Creation icon or Object Creation... from the Data pull-down menu.

You'll see the dialog box reappear (see Figure 1-2). Change thickness to 0 and pick OK.

Thus far, you've drawn a few lines in Plan view. For all practical purposes, it looks like a 2D drawing. But because you set thickness to 4 units, you've really drawn the lines and the arc with a height of 4 units.

Figure 1-4: The S. E. Isometric View icon from the View toolbar

Now let's change the viewpoint of the model to illustrate what effect the thickness command produced. First, choose the View toolbar and you notice that 10 of the icons are preset views. They use the VPOINT command to preset views, such as top, bottom, front, back, etc. along with preset isometric views. Later, in Chapter 4, "VPOINT: The Faster Alternative," you'll review this in-depth, but for now choose the View toolbar and pick the S. E. Isometric View icon or in the command prompt window type the command to change your view of the model.

Type: VPOINT <Enter>

Response: Rotate/<Viewpoint><0.00,0.00,1.00>:

Type: 1,-1,1 <Enter>

Look at the difference in Figure 1-5. You actually were drawing in 3D all the time. New ways to view your drawings will be discussed later in this chapter and in following chapters, but next you'll learn about the X,Y,Z coordinates.

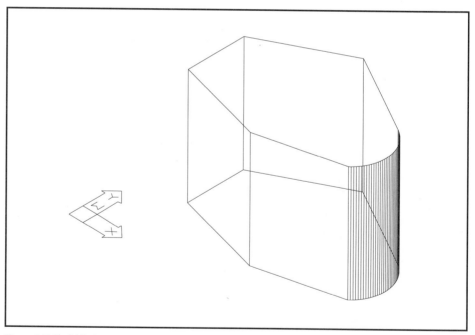

Figure 1-5: Model in Isometric view

Which Way Is Up?

Have you ever looked at television broadcasts of the astronauts on the shuttle? For all practical purposes, they're flying upside down, relative to the earth. But it doesn't seem upside down to them because of the lack of gravity. Up and down are relative terms with no absolute meaning in space nor with much meaning in AutoCAD. Therefore, what is needed is a more precise way of describing things.

When you talk about up and down in 3D, you're really referring to a positive Z coordinate (see Figure 1-6).

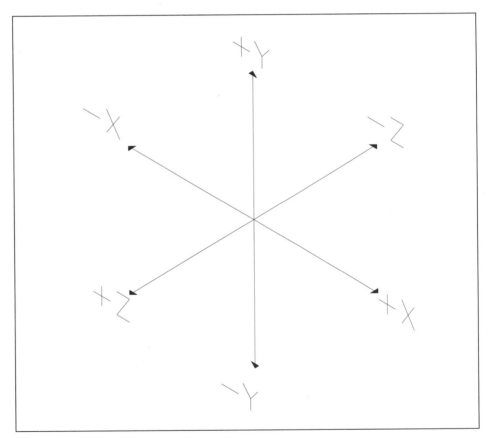

Figure 1-6: X, Y, Z coordinates

X, Y and Z are always at 90 degrees to each other. Imagine your screen where the intersection of all the lines is 0,0. To the right is positive X. At the top of the screen is positive Y. To the left of the screen is negative X, and below the screen is negative Y. Then where is Z? In Figure 1-7 the XY icon sits at the point of origin where the lines intersect.

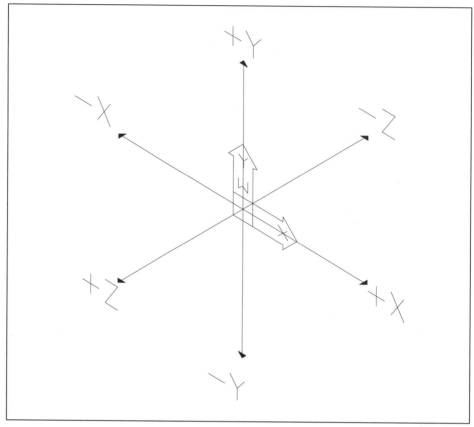

Figure 1-7: The UCS icon in the coordinate system

The X part of the arrow points toward positive X, and the Y part of the arrow points toward positive Y. If you were looking directly at X and Y, then positive Z would be coming straight at you and negative Z would be going away from you.

The *AutoCAD Reference Manual* uses a different analogy that amounts to the same thing. It's called the *right-hand rule* (see Figure 1-8). Take your right hand and point your thumb to the right, your index finger up and the three extended fingers toward you. Your thumb is pointing toward positive X. Your index finger is pointing toward positive Y, and the three fingers pointing at you represent positive Z. If you ever get lost in 3D and are unsure of where the coordinates are, you can always use your right hand to regain your bearings.

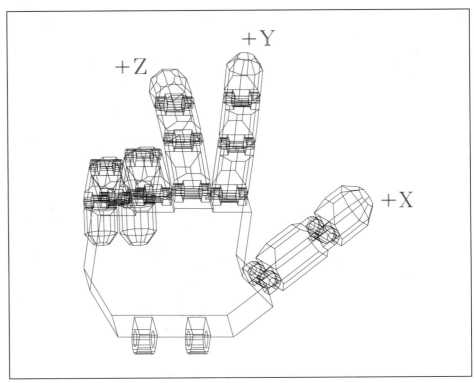

Figure 1-8: Right-hand rule

Look back at the XY icon in Figure 1-5. From this view point, you can see where the original Plan view was. Notice that relative to this view, positive Z is up. Thickness raises the lines that you draw toward the direction of positive Z. This is called an *extrusion*. In AutoCAD extrusion and thickness are the same thing.

Say you want to draw a circle on one side of the model. If you try to draw the circle at this point, it will be on what you might think of as the ground. Try it and see. Then how do you draw on one side? See Figure 1-9.

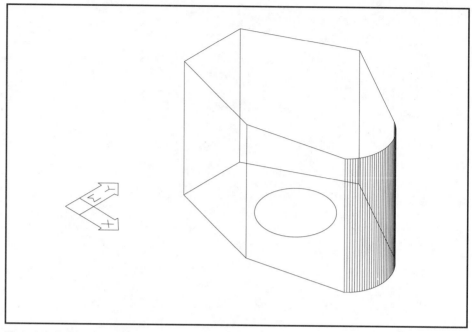

Figure 1-9: Circle at elevation 0

The problem is that your mouse or digitizer puck is a simple 2D device. No matter where you point, the mouse returns only two of the three coordinates. Therefore, the third coordinate is supplied by the coordinate system in effect; the Z value defaults to 0.

Yet what if you had the ability to change the direction of your coordinate system? In fact, you do have the ability to create as many coordinate systems as you want. These coordinate systems collectively are called the User Coordinate System, or UCS for short.

This means that if you point the direction of the X and the Y on the UCS icon to line up with one of the sides on which you want to draw, then you're still drawing and securing coordinates for X and Y when you pick. In addition, you've also determined the direction of that X and Y to match the side on which you want to draw.

Before you try it, you must set the UCS icon to pop to your new origin. Choose UCS from the Options pull-down menu, then Icon Origin. This forces the icon to appear at the origin of the coordinate system. Or in the command prompt window:

Type: UCSICON <Enter>

Response: ON/OFF/All/Noorigin/ORigin<ON>:

Type: OR <Enter>

    Nothing happens that you can see. But, essentially, you set the position of the UCS icon to place itself on the origin—you've not redefined the origin yet, so nothing appears to have happened.

    Now change the coordinate system. *IMPORTANT:* On each of the points you pick below, make certain you set OSNAP to INTersection.

 Figure 1-10: The 3 point UCS icon from the UCS toolbar

    Choose the UCS toolbar and the 3 point UCS icon. Or from the command prompt window:

Type: UCS <Enter>

Response: Origin/Zaxis/3point/OBject/View/X/Y/Z/Prev/Restore/Save/Del/?<World>:

Type: 3POINT <Enter>

Response: Origin point <0,0,0>:

Pick: Point 1 (on Figure 1-11)

Response: Point on positive portion of the X-axis:

    Here, you're pointing toward what will become positive X.

Pick: Point 2 (on Figure 1-11)

Response: Point on positive-Y portion of the UCS XY plane:

    Here, you're pointing toward what will become positive Y.

Pick: Point 3 (on Figure 1-11)

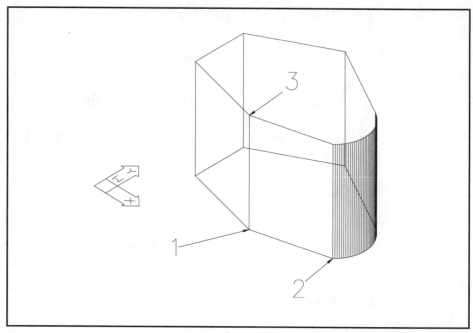

Figure 1-11: UCS 3point

Notice that the UCS icon pops immediately to the new origin you picked. But more important, note the direction of X and Y. You've redefined your own coordinate system. Now draw the circle (see Figure 1-12). Notice that the circle lines up on the correct side of your model.

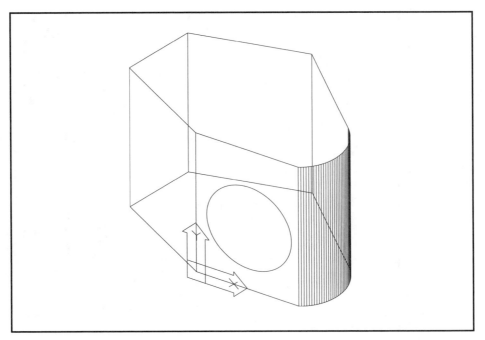

Figure 1-12: Changing the plane

In Figure 1-12 you see a *wireframe.* You can see through the model, so it's difficult to visualize exactly what the model looks like. This is especially true if the model is extremely complex.

 Figure 1-13: The Hide icon from the Render toolbar

But AutoCAD gives you the ability to hide the lines. Choose the Hide icon from the Render toolbar. Or at the command prompt window:

Type: HIDE   <Enter>

See Figure 1-14.

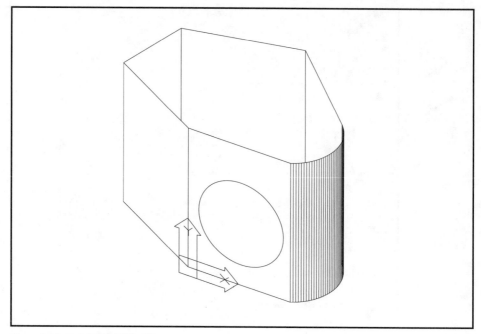

Figure 1-14: Model with hidden lines

To reveal the lines, you must regenerate the drawing:

Type: REGEN <Enter>

Reevaluate your point of view relative to the now current UCS (User Coordinate System). See if you can determine where Z is. If you want to move the circle inside the model, in what direction should it go? Move it in the direction of negative Z, which you'll do easily with the following move.

Figure 1-15: The Move icon from the Modify toolbar

Choose the Move icon from the Modify toolbar, or from the command prompt:

Type: MOVE <Enter>

Response: Select Objects:

Pick: `Select the circle and <Enter>`

Response: `Base point or displacement:`

Pick: `Pick the center of the circle`

Response: `Second point of displacement:`

Type: `@0,0,-1 <Enter>`

From the last point picked—which was your base point—you enter a relative coordinate. The only thing different is the Z coordinate, which is the third coordinate. Relative to the coordinate system in effect at this time, you move the circle 0 in the X direction; 0 in the Y direction; and −1 in the Z direction or 1 unit in the negative Z direction. Notice how the circle jumps inside the box. Now hide your lines. Choose the Hide icon or

Type: `HIDE <Enter>`

The circle has disappeared; it's now inside.

What you've learned here is that the direction in which you move something is relative to the position of the UCS icon or your User Coordinate System. When working in 3D, you must always be fully aware of the position of your coordinate system.

Viewing the Model

There are several tools available for viewing your model. The quickest way is through the VPOINT command. The View toolbar is a new Release 13 viewing tool for your 3D models. It uses the VPOINT command preset to 10 different views, such as top or bottom or S. E. Isometric View. You used this command to secure an Isometric view when you typed **VPOINT 1,–1,1** and then press Enter. Later in Chapter 4, "VPOINT: The Faster Alternative," the viewpoint options will be explained in-depth.

Figure 1-16: The View toolbar

The most visual method of changing the point of view of your model is with the DVIEW command. Try it just to get the flavor of this command. At the command prompt window:

Type: DVIEW <Enter>

Response: Select Objects:

Type: ALL <Enter> <Enter>

You now have quite a few options available for viewing your model. Just look at one; you'll change the camera position relative to the model you've created in this chapter. AutoCAD uses the metaphor of a camera always pointing toward a target to create an angle of view in 3D. (Remember, you should still be in DVIEW.)

Response: ***Switching to WCS***
            CAmera/TArget/Distance/POints/PAn/Zoom/TWist/CLip/Hide/Off/Undo/<eXit>:

Type: CA <Enter>

Notice how your model whirls around on the screen. Move your crosshairs up and down and/or left and right. These moves control the elevation of the camera on the up and down move and the rotation of the camera around the model on the left and right move. You don't need to analyze it; you can just see it. But you can also type in first your angle of elevation and then the angle of rotation:

Response: Toggle angle in/Enter angle from XY plane <35.26>:

Type: 45 <Enter>

Response: Toggle angle in/Enter angle from XY plane from XY axis <-45.00>:

Type: 60 <Enter>

Response: CAmera/TArget/Distance/POints/PAn/Zoom/TWist/CLip/Hide/Off/Undo/<eXit>:

Type: <Enter>

Response: ***Returning to UCS***

This procedure rotates your view of the model (see Figure 1-17). The final <Enter> exits you from the DVIEW command and makes your chosen view of the model permanent.

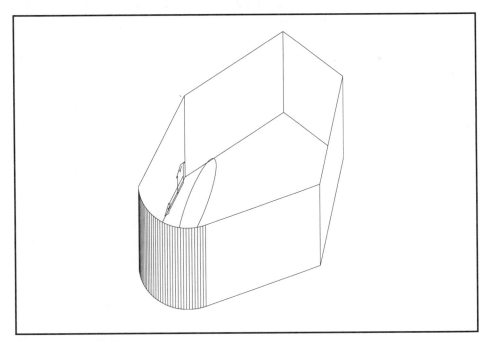

Figure 1-17: Rotated view

You don't have to keep rotating around your drawing to get to each side. With AutoCAD you can set up and use multiple viewports. A viewport is a separate window containing your window. In each viewport, you can create a different view of your drawing. Viewports are easy to create. From the View pull-down menu, choose Tiled Viewports. Or in the command prompt window:

Type: VPORTS <Enter>

Response: Save/Restore/Delete/Join/Single/?/2/<3>/4:

Type: 4 <Enter>

The VPORTS command creates four viewports on your screen. As you pick in each of the viewports, your crosshairs appear. At the same time in the other viewports, there's an arrow. When the crosshairs appear, the viewport is active. Otherwise, the viewport is inactive.

By making each viewport active one at a time, you can change your view of the model in that viewport. You also can begin a command in one viewport and continue that command in any of the others. Figure 1-18 illustrates four different views.

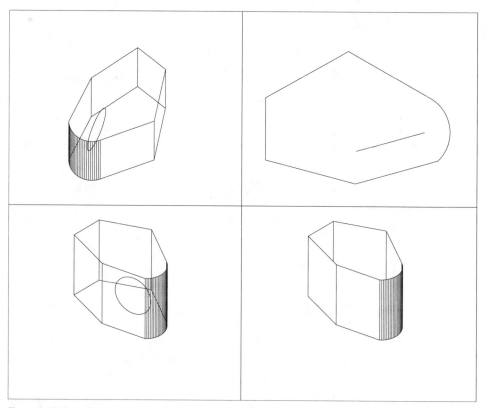

Figure 1-18: Four viewports

Clearing Up Familiar Terms

Many terms in regard to 3D have different meanings depending on who uses them. Clearing up what AutoCAD means is important, so you'll understand the same concepts. In the following sections, you'll learn some familiar terms and what AutoCAD means by them.

Plan

Plan is a common term used by most architects and engineers. Yet it doesn't always mean the same thing to different people. In AutoCAD 3D, plan is a view point in 3D space. The view point is at a positive Z. Positive X points to the right on the screen, and positive Y points toward the top of the screen. This view point is considered to be Plan view.

How many Plan views can you have? Because the definition of plan is so precise, it would seem obvious that you could have only one Plan view. AutoCAD has created a whole new dimension to the term *plan*. The idea that you can have only one Plan view is based on the assumption that you can have only one coordinate system. Because in AutoCAD you can create an infinite number of User Coordinate Systems—that is, the differing directions of X, Y and Z—then you could be plan to any one of these differing coordinate systems. Therefore, just as you can have an infinite number of User Coordinate Systems, you can have an infinite number of Plan views relative to each coordinate system.

One of the tricks that you will learn later in the book is how to change your view point quickly to a precise angle. This trick involves positioning your User Coordinate System to an angle from which you want to view. Then you use the AutoCAD command, PLAN, to position your view point as plan to that User Coordinate System. This is one of the quickest ways to rotate a view.

Elevation

An architect uses the term *elevation* to designate a specific view point of the model. To understand this view point, begin with a plan view and rotate 90 degrees around X to create an elevation view. The view point, therefore, is no longer at Z with X to the right and Y toward the top of the screen. The view point is at negative Y. Positive X is still to the right, but positive Z points toward the top of the screen. If you want this view, you'll learn how to create a coordinate system reflecting this view and then produce a plan to that coordinate system.

The preceding explanation is not what AutoCAD means by elevation. Elevation in AutoCAD is not a view. *Elevation* in AutoCAD is the value of the Z coordinate. In any given User Coordinate System, the intersection of X, Y and Z is a 0 elevation. An entity drawn with an elevation of 5 units has a Z value of 5. In plain English, elevation really means how high Z is off the ground, where the ground is considered to be 0 elevation. But the problem here is that the ground is never stable. Elevation is always relative to the current User Coordinate System.

The point to remember here is that elevation in AutoCAD is not a view; it's a coordinate in 3D space. More precisely, ELEVATION is an AutoCAD command that controls the default value of the Z coordinate relative to the current User Coordinate System. If you set the elevation to 5, as you draw by picking X and Y, the Z will be set to 5 for each point picked automatically.

Plane

Plane has to be one of the most confusing terms in 3D. In AutoCAD it has a simple definition. If you remember, the definition of the User Coordinate System is the right angle made by the direction of positive X, Y and Z at any point in space. As any two of the X, Y and Z directions are moved, then the other axis must also move at the same right angle relative to the first. This positive direction of X, Y and Z defines a 3D plane. Therefore, the User Coordinate System is the plane. The term *plane* is rarely used in the *AutoCAD Reference Manual*. Instead, the manual uses the concept of the User Coordinate System.

Parallel to the Current UCS

Parallel to the current UCS is a tricky term. If you refer to Figure 1-7, you see that the User Coordinate System is defined by the positive direction of X, Y and Z, each at right angles. When you create an entity or object (they are the same) in AutoCAD, the UCS in effect at the time that object was created is saved along with the object. This is known as the *Object Coordinate System*, or OCS. This is also known as the *Entity Coordinate System*, or ECS.

Many times AutoCAD requires that the two coordinate systems—the current UCS and the OCS—be parallel. This does not mean that the object must have exactly the same coordinates. It can have any value of X, Y and Z. But if you were to take the angle of the X, Y and Z of the OCS and line it up with the current UCS, then the direction of positive X of both coordinate systems would be parallel to each other, and the direction of positive Y of each coordinate system would be parallel. Once you have any two axes that are parallel with the corresponding axis of the other coordinate system, then the two coordinate systems are said to be parallel.

This concept is so important that AutoCAD gives you an easy way to make certain that the two coordinate systems are parallel. Because you can't change the Object Coordinate System, AutoCAD gives you the ability to quickly line up the current User Coordinate System with the Object Coordinate System. This process is discussed in more detail later in this chapter.

Thickness & Extrusion

First and foremost, *thickness* and *extrusion* are synonymous. If you understand one term, you will understand the other. For now, begin with thickness.

If you draw a line in AutoCAD with a zero thickness, then the line has no height. Look at Figure 1-19. On the left is a rectangle drawn with zero thickness. On the right is the same rectangle drawn with a thickness of 4. Notice that because each line has a thickness, it produces a cube even though it was drawn from Plan view as only four lines. Thickness is one of AutoCAD's primary tools for drawing in Plan view and 3D at the same time.

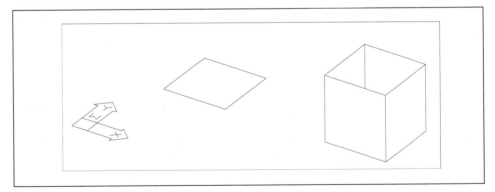

Figure 1-19: Without and with thickness

Beginning with AutoCAD Release 10, Autodesk decided to change the term *thickness* to *extrusion*. This change was necessary because thickness can be used only as a noun. For a precise term, AutoCAD needed a noun, an adjective and a verb. Thickness did not fit the bill. Therefore, the noun thickness was changed to extrusion. By using extrusion, it now becomes much easier to use it as a verb and an adjective and say that the line *extrudes* in the Z direction or that it is an *extruded* entity.

Coordinate Systems

So far I've tried to give you the flavor of the coordinate systems available with AutoCAD. Now I'll define these coordinate systems for you.

When creating a model, you always need a starting point—a base to which you can return and from which you can measure changes. This arbitrary starting point is called the *World Coordinate System,* or WCS. The UCS icon arrow always indicates that you're in the World Coordinate System by displaying a W on the icon. Any other coordinate system that you create is called the User Coordinate System, or UCS.

The World Coordinate System and the User Coordinate System are the only two coordinate systems over which you have any control. Obviously, when you use the term *User Coordinate System,* you're referring to an infinite number of coordinate systems that you may create. It doesn't refer to only a single coordinate system.

A third coordinate system is called the Object Coordinate System, or OCS. You have no direct control over the Object Coordinate System. It's strictly the coordinate system that was in effect at the time the entity was created. This OCS is saved with the entity in the AutoCAD database. Therefore, you can restore the OCS as the current User Coordinate System by simply picking the entity at the appropriate time. When the OCS is restored as the UCS, it's the same as any other UCS in effect at any time.

Relative to the Current UCS

As you've now become aware, you can have an infinite number of User Coordinate Systems available to you. Once X, Y and Z are pointing in whatever direction you've chosen, then everything that AutoCAD does is relative to the User Coordinate System in effect at that time.

Examine this concept using ELEVATION. Remember that elevation is defined as the value of the Z coordinate. But it is the Z coordinate relative to the current UCS. Furthermore, the Z coordinate in one coordinate system might be the Y coordinate in another coordinate system.

Type: ELEV \<Enter\>

Response: New Current Elevation \<0.00\>:

Type: 5 \<Enter\>

Response: New Current Thickness \<0.00\>:

Type: 0 \<Enter\>

You've just set the current elevation to 5. Now draw a line; then use the LIST command to list it:

Type: LIST \<Enter\>

Pick the line and press Enter.

Notice that your Z has a value of 5 as you would expect. Now change your UCS. Choose the UCS X Axis Rotate icon or:

Type: UCS \<Enter\>
            X \<Enter\>
            90 \<Enter\>

Here, you've rotated your current UCS 90 degrees around the X axis. Now list the same line:

Type: LIST \<Enter\>

Pick the line and press Enter.

As you'll notice, the value of Z for 5 now has changed to be the value of Y for 5. In reality, the Y and Z have swapped values. The value of Z is now relative to the current UCS. Notice one other thing: Your UCS icon changed dramatically to what is known as a *broken pencil*. This occurs when you can't see the X and the Y icon. This is AutoCAD's warning that picking is not always apparent.

In summary, the values of X, Y and Z are not absolute. They are always relative to the current UCS in effect at any time.

Moving On

This first chapter provided you with a flavor of some of the tools and techniques available to you with AutoCAD 3D. As you've seen, the User Coordinate System is the key to working successfully in AutoCAD 3D. A mistake in the UCS can cause errors other places in your drawing.

You're now going to go step by step into each of the AutoCAD 3D tools. In the next chapter, you'll work extensively with the User Coordinate System and see how it's put together, review its uses and learn how you can best use it to get the job done.

CHAPTER 2

The User Coordinate System

The purpose of this chapter is to give you an in-depth look at the User Coordinate System (UCS) and to discover not only the mechanics involved, but some of the tricks that you can use to help you in your work.

As you saw in the preceding chapter, the User Coordinate System is important to working on any model in 3D. The first chapter gave you a flavor of the concepts. Here you'll get the full taste. The User Coordinate System is vital to your successfully working in 3D. This complex command in AutoCAD involves more than 12 subcommands, each having a specific purpose and requiring an understanding of how and why it is used.

The UCS toolbar is a new Release 13 tool for your 3D model and it includes more than 12 subcommands to let you set up and use the multiple UCS options. In "The UCS Command" section, you'll work through the subcommands.

Figure 2-1: The UCS toolbar

To understand the User Coordinate System, take a look at how and why it came about in the first place. Long before AutoCAD introduced its first full 3D program with Release 10, other programs on the market made an attempt at using three-dimensional capability. Each of these had one basic problem: the hardware was limited to working with only two coordinates at a time.

This point is best illustrated by using your mouse or digitizer puck. When you pick a point on the screen, the mouse returns the two coordinates: generally, the X and Y. Therefore, a CAD developer must find an easy and acceptable way to include the third, or Z, coordinate.

Look also at the limitation of your screen. Although a model may appear 3D on the screen, it really is an optical illusion. The screen is still a 2D device. There's no way you can physically get into the screen and pick depth. So how does a 3D CAD system know the depth you want to pick? This is the basic problem that all 3D CAD systems' developers have had to face.

There have been many attempts to solve this problem. Some systems line up the view of the object with the plane. As you draw on the plane, the Z coordinate is held constant. Other CAD systems (AutoCAD Release 9 included) required that you input from the keyboard the third coordinate after you picked the XY. Incidentally, AutoCAD still uses this method—not as the primary method of input, but as a valuable tool that you'll use later.

AutoCAD, beginning with Release 10, came up with an ingenious method that enabled you to view your model independently of your drawing plane. It was the User Coordinate System.

The User Coordinate System is unique in that it is a built-in coordinate translator. As you saw in Chapter 1, all coordinates are relative to the UCS in effect at the time. This means that once a User Coordinate System is established, the point of origin in the XY plane has an elevation of zero. Relative to the World Coordinate System, this XY plane may be five units of elevation. Therefore, you can establish a User Coordinate System and draw on a 2D plane on any side of your model. Then you can revert to the World Coordinate System, and all coordinates relative to the World Coordinate System will be accurate. This frees you from trying to key in and keep track of Z all the time. In fact, you don't have to really think in 3D at all.

Drawing Setup

For this chapter's example, begin a new drawing with the following setup. After you enter the settings, issue a ZOOM All command as the final step.

Settings for drawing:

UNITS	Decimal
Precision	2
LIMITS	0,0
Upper right	12,9
GRID	.25
SNAP	.25
ZOOM	All

Next, set your thickness to 1:

Type: `THICKNESS <Enter>`
        `1 <Enter>`

Now set up your UCS icon:

Type: UCSICON <Enter>
       or <Enter>

Draw the rectangle as illustrated in Figure 2-2. Do not draw the dimensions. They only show you the approximate size of the rectangle.

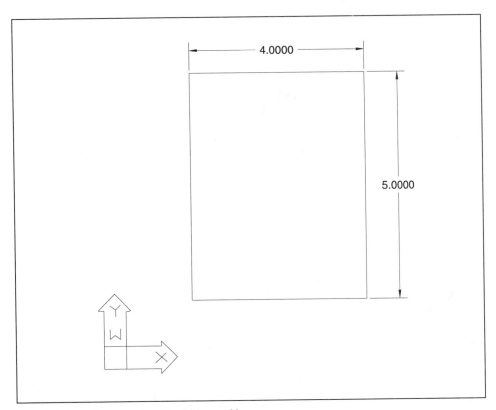

Figure 2-2: Draw the rectangle with a thickness of 1

You've now drawn a rectangular cube because of the thickness settings. As you'll learn later in "The Edge Command" section of Chapter 7, the sides of the extrusion have a surface or hiding capability. For this exercise, you're going to add a surface to the top and bottom, using 3DFACE.

Figure 2-3: The 3DFACE icon from the Surfaces toolbar

Choose the 3DFACE icon from the Surfaces toolbar or from the Draw pull-down menu, choose Surfaces then 3DFACE, or in the command line window:

Type: 3DFACE <Enter>

Using object snap intersection, pick each of the four intersections on your rectangle. After you've picked all four, then press Enter. Pressing the ESC key cancels out the command.

Where do you think the 3D face is, on the top or on the bottom of the rectangular cube? It's on the bottom because the elevation of the World Coordinate System is zero. That's where the plane is. Now you need to copy the face to the top of the cube.

Figure 2-4: The Copy icon from the Modify toolbar

From the Modify toolbar, choose the Copy flyout icon. Or in the command prompt window:

Type: COPY <Enter>

Response: Select Objects:

Type: L <Enter> <Enter>

(This is the last object drawn.)

Response: Base point or displacement>/Multiple:

Type: @ <Enter>

(The base point is the last point picked.)

Response: Second point of displacement:

Type: @0,0,1 <Enter>

Relative to the World Coordinate System, you copied the face from where it was to 1 unit in the Z direction. Now it's located on top of the rectangle.

Next, work on the front of the rectangle. The easiest way to do this is to rotate the UCS. Choose the UCS X Axis Rotate icon or in the command prompt window:

Type: UCS <Enter>

Response: Origin/ZAxis/3point/OBject/View/X/Y/Z/Prev/Restore/Save/Del/?/<World>:

Type: X <Enter>

Response: Rotation angle about X axis:

Type: 90 <Enter>

Don't worry about what happens to the UCS icon; it turns into a broken pencil. Now you want a Plan view relative to this current UCS:

Type: PLAN <Enter>

Response: <Current UCS>/Ucs/World:

The current UCS is the default.

Type: <Enter>

Your model now should look like Figure 2-5.

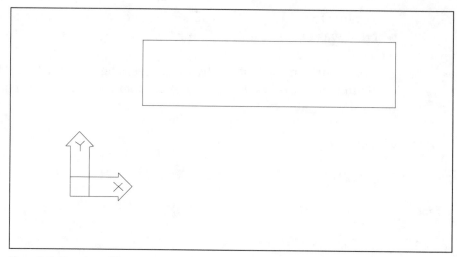

Figure 2-5: Plan view of front

From time to time you might need to make your zoom level smaller in order to center the model. You can do that as follows:

Type: ZOOM <Enter>
         .6x <Enter>

You're now plan to the front of the model.

Type: THICKNESS <Enter>
         .25 <Enter>

Move your origin so that it sits squarely on the lower-left corner of the apparent rectangle. Remember to use OSNAP INTersection.

    Figure 2-6: The UCS Origin icon

Choose the UCS Origin icon or in the command prompt window:

Type: UCS <Enter>

Response: Origin/ZAxis/3point/OBject/View/X/Y/Z/Prev/Restore/Save/Del/?/<World>:

Type: 0 <Enter>

Response: Origin point <0,0,0>:

Pick the lower-left corner, as shown in Figure 2-7. The front of this rectangle is now the drawing plane.

Figure 2-7: Change of origin

Draw a second rectangle on the front of the model, as shown in Figure 2-8.

Figure 2-8: Connector with 0.25 thickness

The next step is to fillet the corners using a .125 fillet radius.

   Figure 2-9: The Fillet icon

From the Modify-Feature flyout, choose the Fillet icon. Or in the command prompt window:

Type: FILLET <Enter>
          R <Enter>
          .125 <Enter>

This sets up Fillet with a .125 radius. Now use it as follows:

Type: FILLET <Enter>

Pick two adjacent lines that form the intersections on the inside rectangle. Repeat the FILLET command and continue picking adjacent intersections until your model looks like Figure 2-10.

Figure 2-10: Fillet corners

Finally, place a few circles with an approximate radius of .06 across the front, as shown in Figure 2-12. Remember, your thickness is still set to .25. What do you think is going to happen to the circles? You'll see shortly.

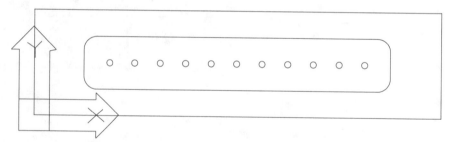

Figure 2-11: Connector pins

As a matter of practice, you should always set the thickness back to zero when you're through—just so you won't be surprised later on:

Type: THICKNESS <Enter>
       0 <Enter>

Also, change back to the World Coordinate System.

Figure 2-12: The World UCS icon

Choose the World UCS icon, or in the command prompt window:

Type: UCS <Enter> <Enter>

To make working on the model in 3D easier, turn off your snap and grid. You can generally do this by pressing the F7 and F9 function keys until snap and grid are off.

Now take a look at your model. Using the VPOINT command is a quick way to get to an Isometric view. You'll analyze this command later.

 Figure 2-13: The S. E. Isometric View icon

Choose the S. E. Isometric View icon from the View toolbar, or in the command prompt window:

Type: VPOINT <Enter>
        1,-1,1 <Enter>

Your model should now look like Figure 2-14.

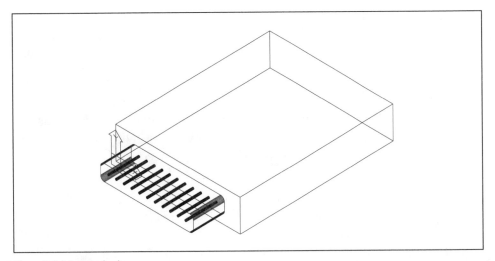

Figure 2-14: Isometric view

If you hide the lines, your model should look similar to Figure 2-16.

Figure 2-15: The Hide icon from the Render toolbar

Choose the Hide icon from the Render toolbar, or in the command prompt window:

Type: HIDE <Enter>

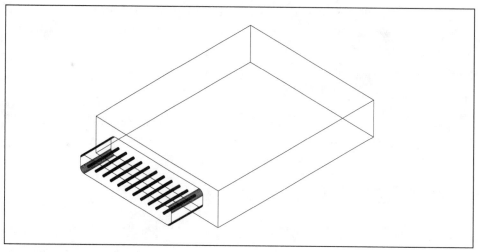

Figure 2-16: Model with hidden lines

If you want to unhide the lines, you must regenerate your drawing:

Type: REGEN <Enter>

Now that you've created a model, you can use it. In case something goes wrong, save the drawing now as MODEL1.DWG. In this way, you can get back to this spot easily if you need to.

The UCS Icon

To help you visually with any existing UCS, AutoCAD constantly points the direction of X and Y. Remember that once you know the proper direction of X and Y, with the right-hand rule you know the direction of positive Z. Before you look at all of the options of the UCS command, you should properly set up your UCS icon so that you can see the results of the operation.

There are two major controls for the UCS icon. You can control its visibility and whether or not it is attached to the origin. Because you're going to move the origin around on your model, attaching the UCS icon to the origin is the same as attaching the icon to the model itself. By attaching the icon to the model (the origin), you can see the UCS plane much easier.

The AutoCAD command you use to control the UCS icon is UCSICON. The following are your options:

ON

OFF

All

Noorigin

ORigin

Changing the UCS Icon

Before you can see any changes in the UCS icon, change the point of origin on your drawing.

Figure 2-17: The UCS Origin icon

Choose the UCS Origin icon or from the View pull-down menu choose Set UCS, then Origin. Or in the command prompt window:

Type: UCS <Enter>
         O <Enter>

Now use object snap intersection and pick point 1 shown on Figure 2-18. You've moved the origin from the lower left-hand corner of the screen to the right side of the model. Now see what you can do with the UCSICON command. From the Options pull-down menu, choose UCS then Icon. Or in the command prompt window:

Type: `UCSICON <Enter>`

Response: `ON/OFF/All/Noorigin/ORigin<ON>:`

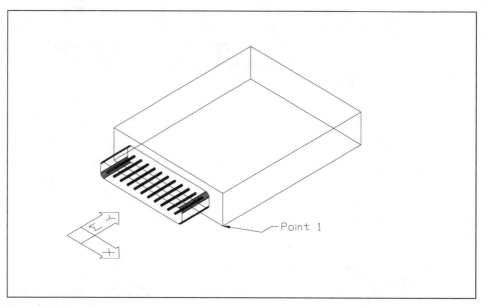

Figure 2-18: Changing point of origin

Notice that as you choose UCS from the Options pull-down menu the Icon command may or may not have a check mark. If UCS Icon has a check mark, it is ON. See Figure 2-25.

If you enter the UCS icon at the keyboard, the simplest of the commands are ON and OFF:

Type: `OFF <Enter>`

Notice that after issuing each one of these commands—except All—you return to the AutoCAD Command line. By typing OFF, the UCS icon completely disappears.

To bring back the UCS icon, do the following:

Type: `UCSICON <Enter>`

Response: `ON/OFF/All/Noorigin/ORigin<OFF>:`

Type: `ON <Enter>`

You can place the UCS icon back to the lower left-hand corner of your screen using Noorigin:

Type: `UCSICON <Enter>`

Response: `ON/OFF/All/Noorigin/ORigin<ON>:`

Type: `N <Enter>` (this stands for no origin)

Use ORigin to place the UCS icon on the origin of your model:

Type: `UCSICON <Enter>`

Response: `ON/OFF/All/Noorigin/ORigin<ON>:`

Type: `OR <Enter>`

Because you moved the origin with the UCS command, the UCS icon pops to the model itself (see Figure 2-19).

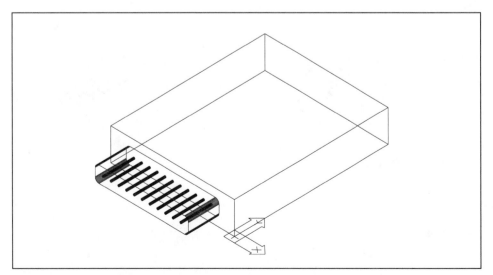

Figure 2-19: UCS icon on origin

The UCS icon will not always attach itself to the origin even though you have told it to. It attaches itself to the origin only if the UCS icon can appear 100 percent on the screen. If the origin is too close to one of the edges of the screen, you can't see all of the icon. If this becomes the case, then the icon places itself in the lower left-hand corner, regardless of the setting.

Now you've come to the final setting of the UCSICON command: All. To see the effects of this setting, you'll need to create multiple viewports.

From the View pull-down menu, choose Tiled Viewports, then 4 Viewports. Or in the command prompt window:

Type: VPORTS <Enter>
        4 <Enter>

Your screen should now look like Figure 2-20.

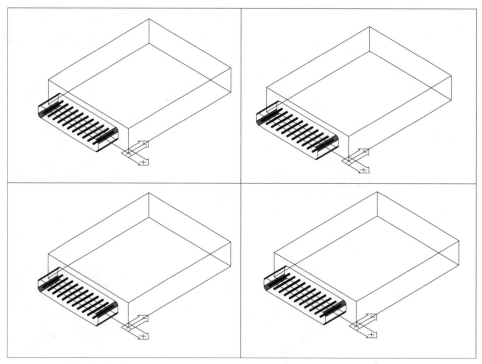

Figure 2-20: Four viewports

There is a UCS icon in each one of the viewports. Without any other instructions, the UCSICON command will affect only the active viewport. Pick and make active the viewport in the upper right-hand corner of your screen. You should now have crosshairs in that viewport and an arrow in each of the other three.

Choose UCS then Icon from the Options pull-down menu to turn OFF the UCSICON, or in the command prompt window:

Type: `UCSICON <Enter>`

Response: `ON/OFF/All/Noorigin/ORigin<ON>:`

Type: `OFF <Enter>`

Here you have turned off the UCS icon only in the upper right-hand corner viewport, which was the active viewport. See Figure 2-21. This is where the All option comes in.

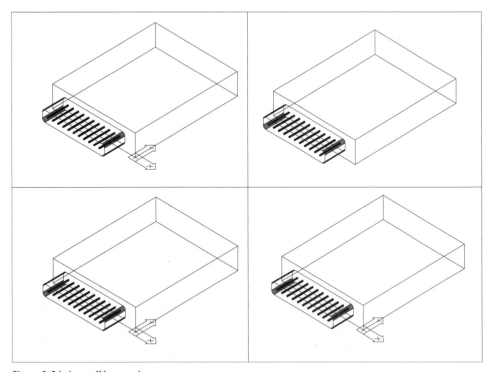

Figure 2-21: Icon off in one viewport

The All option determines whether the UCSICON commands issued affect all of the viewports or just the currently active viewport. It is important to remember that the All option is not a toggle. You must issue it each and every time you issue a UCSICON command for it to affect all viewports:

Type: UCSICON <Enter>

Response: ON/OFF/All/Noorigin/ORigin<OFF>:

Type: ALL <Enter>

Response: ON/OFF/All/Noorigin/ORigin<OFF>:

Type: OFF <Enter>

The UCS icon is now gone from each of the viewports. Before continuing, put it back:

Type: UCSICON <Enter>

Response: ON/OFF/All/Noorigin/ORigin<OFF>:

Type: ALL <Enter>

Response: ON/OFF/All/Noorigin/ORigin

Type: ON <Enter>

Now the icon is turned back on in all of the viewports. Set your viewports back to single:

Type: VPORTS <Enter>
            SI <Enter>

This command should return you to a single viewport screen.

Getting Clues From the UCS Icon

Many times when you work with a 3D wireframe model, it's difficult to tell exactly what you're looking at. Depending on the number of entities involved, the wireframe creates an optical illusion. In fact, many times it's difficult to tell if you're on top of or below the object. Of course, you can use the HIDE command to determine your position relative to the model. But this can be a time-consuming process if you only want to orient yourself to the view of the model. In this case, the UCS icon can come to the rescue (see Figure 2-22).

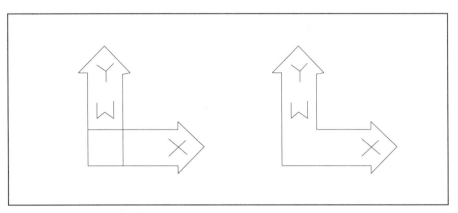

Figure 2-22: Top and bottom icons

The UCS icon indicates whether you are looking at the model from the top down or if you're looking at the model from the bottom up. Notice the difference in the icons in Figure 2-22. The one on the left is crisscrossed where the X and Y come together. The icon on the right doesn't have the crisscross lines. When the icon lines cross, you're looking at the object from top down. If the icon lines don't cross, you're looking at the model from bottom up. This piece of information can save you a lot of time.

CAUTION: One of the options with the DVIEW command is Twist. If you have twisted the model 180 degrees, it is really upside down. The UCS icon has no way of knowing this. The information contained in the UCS icon indicates only your vantage point relative to that current UCS. If your model itself has been rotated or twisted upside down, then the icon will still indicate that you're looking from top down, even though you're looking from bottom up.

Look at two other pieces of information that you can learn from the icon. The icon on the left in Figure 2-23 has a *W* below the Y arrow, whereas the icon on the right does not. The W indicates that you are in the World Coordinate System (WCS). Remember that the WCS is an arbitrary coordinate system used as the base from which all other coordinate systems are measured. Because of the importance of the World Coordinate System, AutoCAD gives you an easy way to always return to the WCS. The UCS icon will always have a W to tell you when you are there. Also remember that any time you change any aspect of the UCS, even if it's a simple change of origin, you're no longer in the World Coordinate System; thus, the W will disappear.

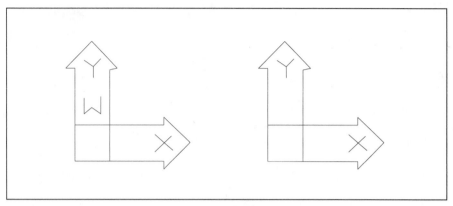

Figure 2-23: World Coordinate System icon and UCS icon

The third piece of information that you can learn from the icon is illustrated in Figure 2-24. Notice that neither of these two icons has a W. This indicates that with each one you're in a User Coordinate System. And notice that the icon on the left has a cross where the X and Y arrows come together, whereas the icon on the right does not. If this cross appears, the icon is attached to the origin. If the cross does not appear, then the icon is not attached to the origin.

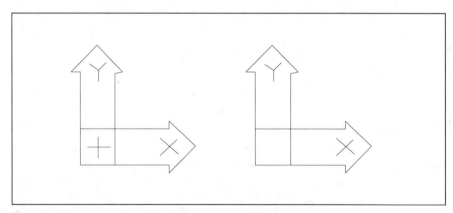

Figure 2-24: Icon attached to origin and icon not attached to origin

NOTE: To make certain your UCS icon is acting properly, make sure it's set to Origin.

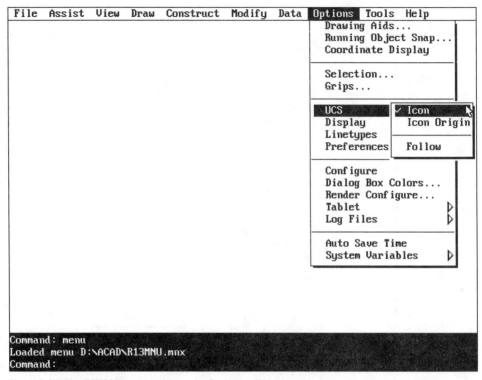

Figure 2-25: The UCSICON command from the Options pull-down menu

The UCS Command

The User Coordinate System is one of the major keys to working with AutoCAD 3D. Release 13 provides three types of tools to activate UCS subcommands. First is the UCS toolbar (see Figure 2-26). Second is the Set UCS command from the View pull-down menu (see Figure 2-27). And finally the UCS commands from the command prompt window. Now look at the command itself and go through the options that are available to you.

Figure 2-26: The UCS toolbar

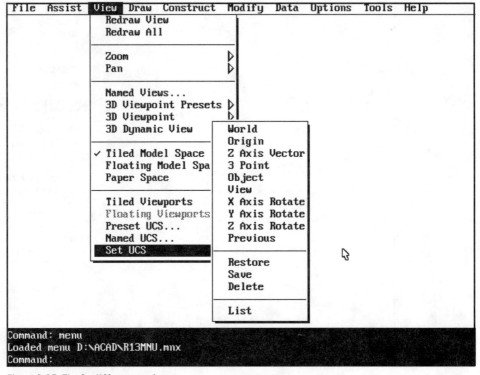

Figure 2-27: The Set UCS commands

Type: UCS <Enter>

Response: Origin/ZAxis/3point/OBject/View/X/Y/Z/Prev/Restore/Save/Del/?/<World>:

It seems overwhelming at first, but remember that each one of these subcommands is really a tool to help you properly position the UCS for your required purpose. You'll look at the subcommands in the following sections.

Type: <Enter>

<World> is the first option available with the UCS command. Notice that the default <World> is at the end of the response. Therefore, simply pressing Enter will put you back to the World Coordinate System.

Establishing the UCS Origin (Origin)

Now use one of the easiest of the options to place the origin by itself without changing the direction of X, Y or Z. You're simply going to move the origin from one place to another. Choose the UCS Origin icon or in the command prompt window:

Type: UCS <Enter>

Response: Origin/ZAxis/3point/OBject/View/X/Y/Z/Prev/Restore/Save/Del/?/<World>:

Type: O <Enter>

Response: Origin point <0,0,0>:

Using object snap intersection, pick point 1 as indicated in Figure 2-28. If your icon is set to Origin, notice how the icon attaches itself to the point that you picked. Also notice the cross at the bottom of the icon indicating that the icon is indeed on the new origin.

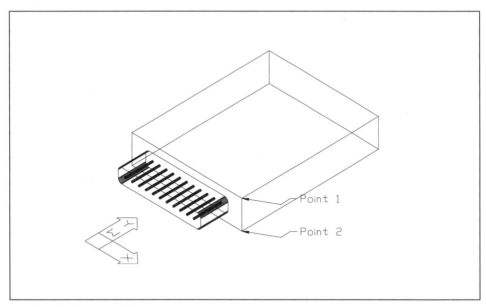

Figure 2-28: Placement of origin

One of the primary reasons for moving the origin without changing the direction of X, Y or Z is to change the elevation and still maintain a parallel UCS. If the X, Y or Z are not changed and only the origin is changed, then the X, Y and Z arrows of the new UCS will remain parallel with the X, Y and Z of the previous coordinate system.

Type: UCS <Enter>

Response: Origin/ZAxis/3point/OBject/View/X/Y/Z/Prev/Restore/Save/Del/?/<World>:

Type: O <Enter>

Response: Origin point <0,0,0>:

Using object snap intersection, pick point 2, as indicated in Figure 2-28. You should move the origin from point 1 to point 2. The plane thus moves 1 unit in the negative Z direction. This will now become the new zero elevation relative to the new UCS.

Now draw a circle, as indicated in Figure 2-29. The circle you've just drawn in the middle of the model is 1 unit below the previous plane, even though the elevation is still set to zero. Therefore, moving the origin without adjusting the direction of X, Y or Z is another way to change elevation and still be parallel to the previous coordinate system.

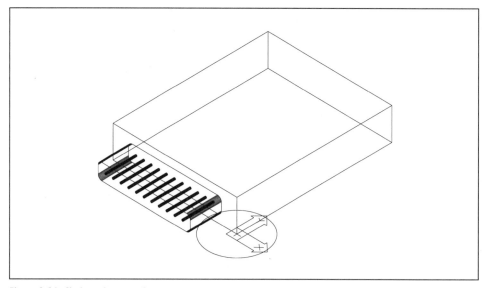

Figure 2-29: Circle on bottom plane

Now erase the circle. I'll provide another reason for moving the origin after you've learned a few more of the UCS commands.

Defining the Plane Using 3Point (3Point)

The 3Point subcommand is probably the most used of all of the UCS command options. With this command you have the flexibility of designating the absolute coordinate of your origin point along with the direction of X and Y. The three points you pick will define the plane.

Try one and see how it works. With each point you pick, make certain that your object snap is set to intersection. Don't try to eyeball because it will not work. In 3D what you see is not necessarily what you get because of your viewing angle.

Figure 2-30: The 3point UCS icon from the UCS toolbar

Choose the 3point UCS icon or in the command prompt window:

Type: `UCS <Enter>`

Response: `Origin/ZAxis/3point/OBject/View/X/Y/Z/Prev/Restore/Save/Del/?/<World>:`

Type: `3 <Enter>`

Response: `Origin point <0,0,0>:`

Pick the origin at point 1 in Figure 2-31 and press Enter:

Response: `Point on positive portion of the X-axis:`

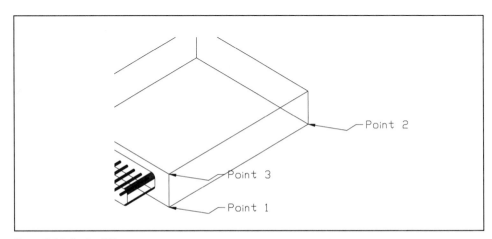

Figure 2-31: 3point UCS

Although the response may seem strange, AutoCAD is actually asking you to pick a point that will define the direction of positive X.

Now pick point 2, as indicated in Figure 2-31 and press Enter:

Response: `Point on positive-Y portion of the UCS XY plane:`

Now AutoCAD is asking you to pick a point that defines the direction of positive Y. Because point 3 and the intersection above point 2 in Figure 2-31 are parallel to each other, you don't have to pick one point over the other. For this example, pick point 3.

Your UCS icon now pops to the User Coordinate System defined by the three points. As a recap, the 3Point option will ask you for three things: the origin, a point defining the direction of positive X and a point defining the direction of positive Y.

Now that you've set up this User Coordinate System, try an experiment to show how the UCS is used. First, draw a circle on the side of the current UCS, as indicated in Figure 2-32. Because the UCS is defined squarely on the side of the model, you can draw the circle easily across this plane. Next, hide the lines:

Type: `HIDE <Enter>`

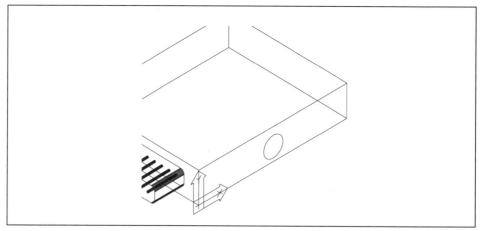

Figure 2-32: Circle on right-side plane

The circle appears because it's even with the outside of the side of the model. The only way to unhide the lines is by regenerating your drawing:

Type: `REGEN <Enter>`

Assume now that you want to move the circle inside the model by 1 unit. Begin with the MOVE command:

Type: `MOVE <Enter>`

Response: `Select Objects:`

Pick the circle and press Enter.

Response: `Base point of displacement:`

Type: `@ <Enter>`

(The base point is the last point picked.)

Response: `Second point of displacement:`

Type: `@0,0,-1 <Enter>`

Notice how the circle pops inside the model. You can prove this by hiding the lines:

Type: `HIDE <Enter>`

This procedure works because the UCS icon is at elevation zero: the point of origin. If you use the right-hand rule, then Z comes out from the model. Therefore, to go in the model, you must go to a negative Z. When you issued the MOVE command using relative absolute coordinates, you were moving it zero in the X direction, zero in the Y direction and negative 1 in the Z direction.

Type: `U <Enter>`

Type U <Enter> and REGEN enough times to return you to the model that looks like Figure 2-32 so that you can repeat this process.

Rotate around X, Y & Z (X) (Y) (Z)

Now look at an alternative method of using the UCS. Assume that you want your point of origin to stay the same as it is now. You want X to point in the same direction, but Y to lie flat against the bottom of the model. AutoCAD gives you three methods of doing this—called X, Y and Z. What each of these means is to rotate around X, rotate around Y or rotate around Z. If you find this difficult to imagine, use your right hand and pretend that X does not move and rotate Y and Z counterclockwise around X. Remember that the axis you're rotating around does not move.

Type: UCS <Enter>

Response: Origin/ZAxis/3point/OBject/View/X/Y/Z/Prev/Restore/Save/Del/?/<World>:

Type: X <Enter>

Response: Rotation angle about X axis:

Type: −90 <Enter>

Notice that in Figure 2-33 the point of origin has remained constant. X still points in the same direction. But now Y has rotated 90 degrees clockwise. This has the effect of placing Y flat against the bottom of your model.

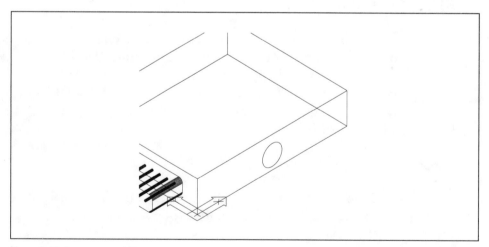

Figure 2-33: Rotate around X

With the UCS icon in this position, you have another alternative in moving the circle inside the model:

Type: MOVE <Enter>

Response: Select Objects:

Pick the circle and press Enter.

Response: Base point of displacement:

Type: @ <Enter>

(The base point is the last point picked.)

Response: Second point of displacement:

Type: @0,1,0 <Enter>

The circle now is inside as before because the direction of the icon has changed. You're now moving it in the Y direction.

Type: U <Enter>

This returns the circle to its previous location.
There is still another way to move the circle:

Type: MOVE <Enter>

Response: Select Objects:

Pick the circle and press Enter.

Response: Base point of displacement:

Type: @ <Enter>

(The base point is the last point picked.)

Response: Second point of displacement:

Type: @1<90 <Enter>

Why do you think this method works? Remember that you're still using all of AutoCAD's 2D functions. You've simply created a 2D coordinate system somewhere in 3D space. Once that coordinate system is created, you're still using the 2D commands and are under the same 2D rules as always.

One of these 2D functions is called *relative polar coordinates.* You can move an object relative to its base point at a distance and angle. Remember that the angle of X is always zero, and the angle of Y is always 90. The angle of negative X is 180, and the angle of negative Y is 270. These rules have not changed. Now that Y is pointing in the direction you want to go, you can still use the relative polar coordinates to move your object @1<90—that is, 1 unit in the direction of 90 degrees.

Personally, I like to call this *point and shoot.* This means that you find a way to point the icon in the direction you want to go by pointing the X or Y and then moving it at an angle of 0 or 90. As long as you can keep track of which way the X and Y are going, then the regular AutoCAD commands are still available to you.

3D Tools

As I mentioned in the introduction, this book is unique in that it not only supplies you with many AutoLISP programs in the AutoLISP section, but throughout the tutorial I'll show you when, where and how to use these tools in actual applications. You'll also use these tools as you actually construct the model because they'll save you time and should be part of your 3D AutoLISP arsenal.

If you have installed the companion disk per its instructions, load the file called 3DTOOLS.LSP as follows:

Type: `(load "3DTOOLS") <Enter>`

This AutoLISP program enables you to simply type in the name of each tool you'll be using, and it automatically loads and executes the programs as if they were AutoCAD commands (see Appendix A, "AutoLISP & Your 3D Toolkit.").

You'll use RX.LSP, RY.LSP and RZ.LSP now. You should load each one of these files. For example, type the following:

```
(load "rx") <Enter>
(load "ry") <Enter>
(load "rz") <Enter>
```

Take the time now to read Appendix A. There is a shortcut to loading each of these AutoLISP tools; you can create your own 3DTOOLS.LSP file to automatically load and execute the programs.

The *Companion Disk* will save you a lot of time, typing, and debugging and let you get right to work. And, you will be using these tools all the time.

Now that you have loaded the RX, RY and RZ functions, see how they work. Rather than go through the UCS command, these tools rotate around their corresponding X, Y and Z by 90 degrees each time the program is run. Because these are AutoCAD command-line programs, you can type them from the Command line:

Type: RX <Enter>

Notice how the icon rotates 90 degrees around X. If this is not enough, press Enter and the command will be repeated. Continue to press Enter until the icon is pointing in the correct direction.

Try each of these functions by typing RY and then RZ. You'll be surprised how often you can correctly line up the icon by simply using these three commands. Play with them until you get the feel of how they work. They are much simpler than their UCS counterparts. Also, they rotate exactly 90 degrees at a time. There'll be times you need a more precise angle, but these tools can be most helpful, and you'll use them throughout this book.

Defining a Plane With One Known Coordinate (ZAxis)

Although working with 3Point is convenient in defining the UCS, it is not the end-all of the tools necessary to align the plane. From time to time you will discover geometry that doesn't lend itself to 3Point. Consider on the example model that you want to place the UCS squarely on the top of the connector. As you can see, a fillet there does not lend itself to an origin, X axis and Y axis. At best, you can probably find an origin to snap onto and maybe one other point. This is where the ZAxis option comes in.

The ZAxis option permits you to define an origin and pick only one additional point to define the plane. Obviously, this may or may not define the correct plane, but it will give you a starting place. Try it to see what happens.

Figure 2-34: The ZAxis Vector UCS icon

Choose the ZAxis Vector icon or in the command prompt window:

Type: `UCS <Enter>`

Response: `Origin/ZAxis/3point/OBject/View/X/Y/Z/Prev/Restore/Save/Del/?/<World>:`

Type: `ZA <Enter>`

Response: `Origin point <0,0,0>:`

With your object snap set to nearest, pick the point somewhere along the line defined as point 1 in Figure 2-35. Make sure the point is on the line and not the fillet. (Some of the pins are erased in the figure to give you a better view of the icon.)

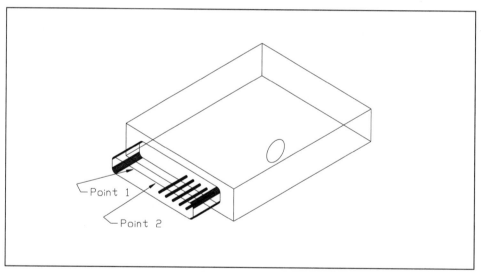

Figure 2-35: Using ZAxis on connector

Response: `Point on positive portion of the Z-axis:`

Set your object snap again to nearest and pick a point on the same line approximately at point 2, as illustrated in Figure 2-35.

Notice now that the UCS icon in Figure 2-36 is positioned on your model. You've defined the origin and the direction of the Z axis.

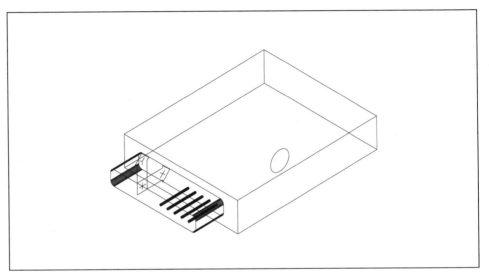

Figure 2-36: Icon aligned along Z axis

The ZAxis option is really a rotation around X, but it's different from the X, Y and Z rotation options in that the X, Y and Z require a number of degrees and do not let you choose the origin. Many times using ZAxis is more convenient and sometimes the only way for you to establish a plane on an irregular shaped object.

AutoCAD could have provided you with an XAxis and YAxis command as well as the ZAxis command, but that's not necessary. Once a plane is defined as it's done here, even though it isn't exactly the correct plane, you now can use your RX, RY and RZ commands to rotate the icon easily to the correct plane.

Assume that you want to draw across the top of the connector, for example. At this point you've defined a plane across the top, but unfortunately the X and Y are going in the wrong direction. The X looks all right, but the Y must rotate 90 degrees around the X. Simple, isn't it?

Type: RX <Enter>

Now by using what you've learned before and the new 3D tools at your disposal, you can type RX, RY and RZ and press Enter or the spacebar as needed. So, as you can see, there is no real need for an XAxis or a YAxis command when you have these other tools. See Figure 2-37.

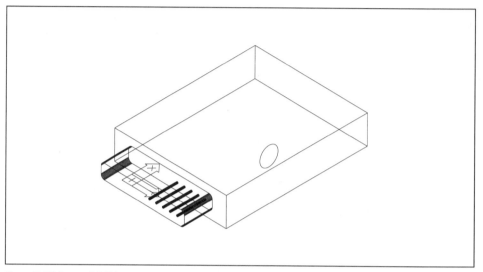

Figure 2-37: Rotated UCS icon

Parallel to an Entity or Object (OBject)

You'll recall from Chapter 1, "3D Preview," that there are really three coordinate systems: the WCS, UCS and OCS. The OCS is the Object Coordinate System. You really don't have any control over the Object Coordinate System. Whenever an object is created, AutoCAD saves the UCS in effect at that time. You can't change the OCS, but you can change the current UCS to be the same as the OCS.

This capability especially comes in handy when you receive an error message in AutoCAD indicating that you can't perform a specific command because the object is not parallel to the current UCS. Because you can't make the object parallel to the current UCS, you need to make the current UCS parallel to the object. This procedure will become important when dimensioning and placing text in 3D:

Type: `UCS <Enter>`

Response: `Origin/ZAxis/3point/OBject/View/X/Y/Z/Prev/Restore/Save/Del/?/<World>:`

Type: `OB <Enter>`

Pick any object on the model to which you want to be parallel. Notice how this moves the UCS icon to be parallel with the object selected. Admittedly, the X and Y might not be going in the correct direction, but by now you know how to change that with the 3D tools you have.

TIP: From time to time, you get several error messages while working in 3D. The most common of these is that the object is not parallel with the current UCS. Immediately on getting that error, issue a UCS Object command and pick the object in question. You'll then be parallel. Perform the operation as necessary. When that operation is finished, use the UCS Previous option, which returns you to the UCS you were previously working in. This way, the UCS Object command is really a temporary command to bypass the error messages in AutoCAD and then return to the previous UCS.

AutoCAD treats UCS Previous the same as all other Previous options in other commands such as ZOOM Previous. The previous UCSs are saved only during the current drawing. You can back up through previous UCSs as long as they are available. Anything in AutoCAD that would disrupt a previous selection set or zoom might have the same effect on the UCS. Therefore, if a UCS is important to you, you should save it with a name before you leave it. This way, you can always get it back, even after the drawing is saved.

Working With Text

One of the problems that you will constantly come up against is the alignment of text and dimensions. Later, you'll look in-depth at dimensioning. For now, concentrate on the alignment of text. What you learn here you will use in dimensioning as well.

The problem with text is really twofold. The first thing you have to ask yourself is what you want the text to look like. There are really two different types of text in 3D. One is text aligned with the object, and the other is labeling text.

If you place text in a drawing arbitrarily, it may look all right from the initial view point. That doesn't mean, however, that if you change your view point of the drawing, you will even be able to see the text. There is no telling where the text is really located. Most of the time you'll probably want to align your text with the object. That way, the text will be readable (albeit as a mirror image at times) from any view point.

The one major thing to remember about text is that unless the style is set to write the text upside down and backwards, all text goes in the direction of positive X. Therefore, it is imperative that you make the UCS icon line up with the X arrow going in the direction you want the text to go.

Your first step is to use the UCS Object command and choose the object to which you want the text to be aligned. Assume, for example, you want the text to be aligned with the model as indicated by point 1 in Figure 2-38:

Type: UCS <Enter>

Response: Origin/ZAxis/3point/OBject/View/X/Y/Z/Prev/Restore/Save/Del/?/<World>:

Type: OB <Enter>

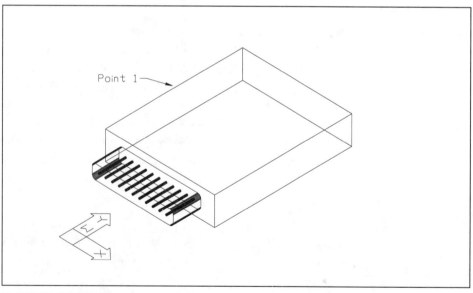

Figure 2-38: Pick UCS Object

Now pick the line as indicated by point 1 in Figure 2-38. Notice that the icon immediately becomes parallel with that object. The problem is that the X arrow may not be going in the correct direction. This direction is totally dependent on how you drew the lines to begin with and the angle from which you're currently viewing the drawing. Use the RX, RY or RZ command until the icon is facing the direction shown in Figure 2-39. The position of the origin is not important. If your icon moves off the origin, it couldn't fit. Issue ZOOM .8x until it's back on the model.

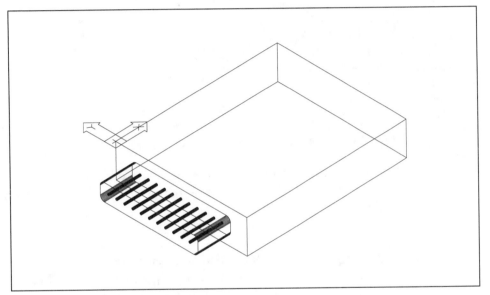

Figure 2-39: Align X arrow for text direction

Using the DTEXT command, type in a line of text, picking a starting point near the object in question. Notice in Figure 2-40 how easy it is to read the text that is aligned with the object at the bottom of your model.

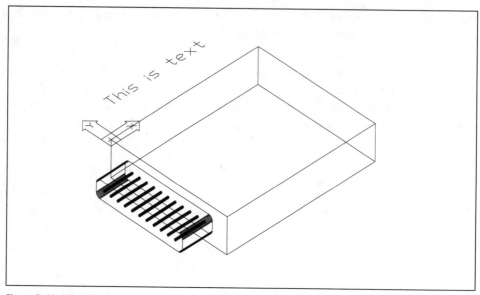

Figure 2-40: Aligned text

The important thing to remember about adding text is that the text will remain aligned with the object no matter the angle from which you view it. It will not get lost in space.

Aligning the UCS With the Screen (View)

The other type of text is labeling text—the kind of text you'd use on a drawing where you don't want to align the text with the object. Actually, you want to align the text with the screen itself so that it appears flat against the screen or the plotted sheet, regardless of the viewing angle of the model.

For this approach to work, you first must align the current UCS with the screen itself. To do this, you use the View option of the UCS command.

Figure 2-41: The View UCS icon

Choose the View UCS icon or in the command prompt window:

Type: UCS <Enter>

Response: Origin/ZAxis/3point/OBject/View/X/Y/Z/Prev/Restore/Save/Del/?/<World>:

Type: V <Enter>

The icon at this point is totally parallel with the screen. Now type your text as shown in Figure 2-42.

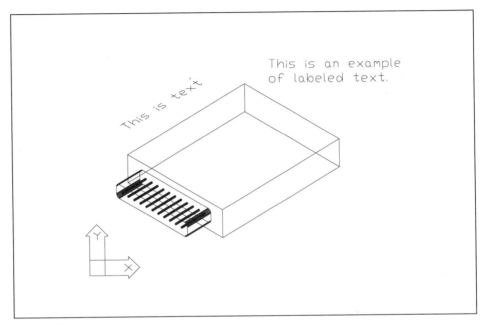

Figure 2-42: Label text

There's a major caution necessary here. It's very important that, if you use this alignment for your text, you make sure the text is placed on a specific layer so it can be turned on and off as necessary. It's also a good idea to create a named view by the same name as the layer on which you placed the text. Finally, you should save the UCS—in effect using the same name.

All this is necessary because the text currently does not have a fixed point in space that you can rely on. If you were to rotate your view of the object, the text could be anywhere. Therefore, if you use a different view of the object, later on you may want different labeling text. And if you ever want to return to this view so that you can turn on the proper text layer, you'll need to make certain you can restore the view at the same time. This way, the name of the view, the name of the layer and the name of the UCS will be the same.

To make this procedure as easy as possible, you can use the three AutoLISP programs in the AutoLISP section of the book. The first program is USLVIEW, which stands for UCS Save Layer View. This program asks you the name of the view and then creates a view layer and saves the UCS by the same name. It also sets you to the layer, ready for the text. The accompanying program is URVIEW, which stands for UCS Restore View. The third program, USVIEW, is the same as USLVIEW, but it doesn't create and set you to the layer. You'll use this program often for purposes other than labeling text.

As with the RX, RY and RZ programs, make certain that USLVIEW, USVIEW and URVIEW are properly loaded. If you're using the *AutoCAD 3D Companion Disk*, installed properly and with 3DTOOLS.LSP loaded, all you need do is type in the name of the program.

The AutoLISP section of the book explains the programs USLVIEW, USVIEW and URVIEW. Make certain that these files are loaded and ready to use. Complete instructions on creating and loading these programs are found in Chapter 17 and Appendix A.

Type: USLVIEW <Enter>

Response: Name of view, UCS and layer to save:

Type: V1 <Enter>

Here you have the option of naming your view and UCS anything that you want. Notice that the program first makes a layer called V1 if one doesn't already exist and then sets you to that layer. It then saves the current UCS as V1 and saves the current view also as V1.

Now that you are in a UCS view, feel free to type anything on the screen that you want. The text that you are typing is on layer V1.

Change both the view and your UCS and see how the URVIEW program works:

Type: PLAN <Enter>

Response: <Current UCS>/Ucs/World:

Type: W <Enter>

You've now changed to Plan view relative to the World Coordinate System.

Type: `UCS <Enter>`

Response: `Origin/ZAxis/3point/OBject/View/X/Y/Z/Prev/Restore/Save/Del/?/<World>:`

Type: `<Enter>`

The preceding series of operations changes you directly to the World Coordinate System. Now test the URVIEW command:

Type: `URVIEW <Enter>`

Response: `Name of view and UCS to restore:`

Type: `V1 <Enter>`

The UCS and the correct view are restored at the same time. The program doesn't set you to the V1 layer. This you'll need to do on your own because you may not always want to be set to that layer. Remember that you can use this program for many other purposes. Normally, the URVIEW and the USVIEW are used generically in pairs.

Saving & Restoring the UCS (Save) (Restore)

As the importance of the UCS becomes more apparent, you'll discover that you'll be creating more coordinate systems to work on your model. It's not time-effective to create the same UCS over and over again as you move around. Therefore, AutoCAD gives you the ability to save a UCS under a user-defined name. Later, as you need to work with this same UCS again, you can restore it. This method is similar to saving and restoring views, styles or dimstyles, except that the UCS is not necessarily tied to the view.

Saving a UCS is very simple. Begin by setting up any UCS you want:

Type: `UCS <Enter>`

Response: `Origin/ZAxis/3point/OBject/View/X/Y/Z/Prev/Restore/Save/Del/?/<World>:`

Type: S <Enter>

Response: ?/Desired UCS name:

Type: sideplate <Enter>

 Figure 2-43: The Save UCS icon

Alternatively, use the Save UCS icon.

Naturally, "sideplate" is a made-up name. You can give the UCS the name of your choice.

Change now to UCS World:

Type: UCS <Enter>

Response: Origin/ZAxis/3point/OBject/View/X/Y/Z/Prev/Restore/Save/Del/?/<World>:

Type: <Enter>

Restore the UCS "sideplate":

Type: UCS <Enter>

Response: Origin/ZAxis/3point/OBject/View/X/Y/Z/Prev/Restore/Save/Del/?/<World>:

Type: R <Enter>

Response: ?/Name of UCS to restore:

Type: sideplate <Enter>

 Figure 2-44: The UCS Restore icon

Alternatively, use the UCS Restore icon.

The UCS is restored to the UCS called "sideplate." It's important to remember that just because the UCS is restored, the view that was in effect at the time the UCS was created isn't necessarily restored along with it. This is why you have the two programs USVIEW and URVIEW, which stand for UCS Save View and UCS Restore View, respectively. They save the UCS and the view under the same name. When you use URVIEW, the UCS and the view are also restored at the same time.

These programs can be very useful if you want to work on one side of your model and at the same time automatically have the correct UCS restored.

As you can see, the UCS command is complex. But each of the options just discussed serves an important purpose. Each option in its own way helps you to adjust the UCS quickly to the correct plane.

Working With Dialog Boxes

Now that you understand the options available to you with the UCS, it's time to see how you can use a few of these options with the standard AutoCAD pull-down menus and dialog boxes.

Go to the pull-down menus and pick View. On the View pull-down menu, you will see Named UCS..., Preset UCS... and Set UCS.

Named UCS...

Begin this exercise by setting a UCS totally different from any UCS you have set before. Now pick Named UCS...—either choose the Named UCS icon (see Figure 2-45) or use the View pull-down menu. This is the first of several dialog boxes and menu options that give you access to the UCS. With this dialog box, you primarily have the ability to set a previously named UCS, to name the UCS, to delete the UCS and to ascertain relative coordinates of the UCS settings (see Figure 2-46).

Figure 2-45: The Named UCS icon

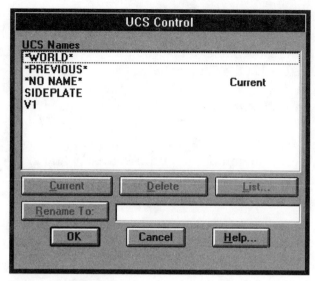

Figure 2-46: UCS dialog box

Begin with how you name a UCS. Notice in Figure 2-46 that one of the UCSs is NO NAME. This UCS generally is the current UCS if it has no name. (This is why you created a UCS you've never created before.) If you want to use the dialog box to save the current UCS under a user-defined name, then begin by tagging NO NAME. To tag a UCS, pick anywhere along the line where NO NAME appears. Look down at the text box where Rename To: is to the side; NO NAME is now in the text box. Change NO NAME in this text box to BACKSIDE. Then pick the Rename To: box. In the list of UCSs that are now available, NO NAME has been changed to BACKSIDE. Naming the UCS is not permanent until you pick OK in the dialog. But don't do that yet; you're not through.

Now tag SIDEPLATE. Once this UCS is tagged, the boxes Delete, Current, and List... are active. Pick Current to make SIDEPLATE the current UCS, and the UCS will be shifted to SIDEPLATE as soon as you pick OK in the dialog box.

Choosing Delete will, of course, delete the tagged UCS, and choosing List... will give you the directional coordinates of the UCS.

Pick OK. The UCS is then changed to SIDEPLATE.

As you can see, using this dialog box to name a UCS is rather cumbersome. It's easier to establish a UCS and then to type **UCS <Enter> S <Enter>** and give it a name. Where this dialog box comes in handy is your ability to change to a new UCS by visually picking from the available UCSs on the screen. Many times you may have a lot of named UCSs, and it's difficult to remember just what you called them.

Presets...

When things are confusing and difficult to understand, it's generally not because the concept is difficult to understand, but because the program and/or feature is not well thought out. This is the case with the Presets... dialog box.

One of the major problems here is that there are precious few instructions. But of course that's why you have this book, isn't it? The AutoCAD developers are attempting to permit you to pick one of the icons here and change your UCS in a preset manner.

But the Presets... dialog box has some big problems. It's main problem is that it doesn't have any base from which to rotate the UCS. There is also a problem with the name *Presets* itself; this is misleading. The UCSs aren't really preset. They are various 90-degree relations from the last UCS or absolute to the world coordinate system. Therefore, if the UCS is on the side of the model and you pick right side, then the UCS could move below the model. This is extremely difficult to visualize.

Apparently, Autodesk was trying to start you with some base, the top, and from that base to create constants so that you could always move the UCS parallel to the right side, left side, bottom, etc. But because each UCS is relative to the last UCS, using this dialog box becomes very convoluted and confusing for the average user. This is even more true when coupled with the lack of documentation.

 Figure 2-47: The Preset UCS icon

Now try the Presets dialog box for yourself. Pick the View pull-down menu and pick Presets... or use the Preset UCS icon (see Figure 2-47). This dialog box is not much more than a series of rotations around X, Y and Z, relative to the current UCS (see Figure 2-48). Look at the following list of options and the corresponding commands you can use to achieve the same effect.

Top	Stays the same
Right	RX RY
Left	RX RY RY RY
Front	RX
Bottom	RX RX

Current View	View
World (Arrows)	World
Previous	Previous

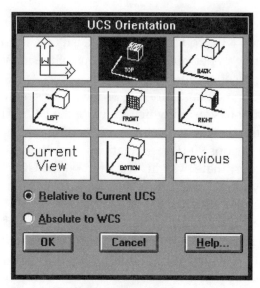

Figure 2-48: UCS Orientation dialog box

From this chart the only options that are really self-evident to the user are Current View, World and Previous. Using the RX and RY AutoLISP programs to quickly rotate 90 degrees around X and Y, you can see from the chart that picking Right in this dialog box is the same as typing RX and then RY.

The Left option is a little more complicated because it actually turns around 180 degrees after rotating around X. Using Left is equivalent to typing RX followed by RY three times. Of course, you could enter the three RYs by pressing Return or the spacebar.

As you can see, even if this is as far as it goes, it's easier to visualize where you want to go by using the RX, RY and RZ tools to rotate 90 degrees each time. But I'm not going to stop here. The concept that Autodesk was trying to put together was good. They just didn't go far enough. The key here is that you have absolutely no base from which to begin and establish a constant for your model. This means that there is no consistent top. Therefore, each UCS you choose is relative to the last current UCS. So let's see if we can't improve on what AutoCAD was trying to do with Presets.

In the AutoLISP section of this book are several AutoLISP programs that you can use instead of the Presets.... They are

UBASE

RSIDE

LSIDE

FSIDE

BSIDE

TSIDE

These programs should be loaded and ready to use in accordance with all AutoLISP programs in this book. See Appendix A.

Here's how these programs work. To begin with, you must have a constant base from which to begin. To use the programs, you must first establish this base. Begin by creating a UCS on the top of the model; create a 3Point UCS as in Figure 2-49. Once this is done, you can use the LISP programs to find your way around the model:

Type: UBASE <Enter>

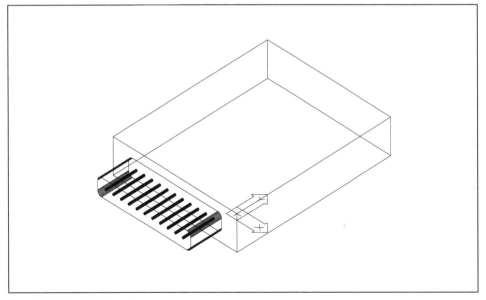

Figure 2-49: Establishing a base

That's all there is to it. This program creates a UCS named BASE out of your current UCS. This base UCS is what RSIDE, LSIDE, FSIDE, and BSIDE use.

Type: RSIDE <Enter> (Right side)

From the base, the UCS icon is rotated to the right side of the model.

Type: LSIDE <Enter>   (Left side)

Even though you're coming from the right side, the program begins back at the base to give you the left side UCS. Therefore, the X arrow is pointing toward the front.

Type: FSIDE <Enter> (Front side)

Now the Y is pointing up, and the X is pointing to the right.

Type: BSIDE <Enter> (Bottom side)

This represents the bottom of the model.

Type: TSIDE <Enter>   (Top side)

This takes you back to the base, which should have been the top of the model. Do you see how easily this works?

One final note. These programs work nicely in orienting the right, left, front, top and bottom of the model. These programs create a parallel UCS to those sides. They don't actually move the origin. If you want to move the origin, you'll need to use the regular UCS Origin option. But the programs are smart enough to remember the last origin and maintain that origin while at the same time maintaining themselves at right angles to the base and parallel to the current side. This makes it very easy to set a base with an origin to begin with and then to move the origin and have the new origin the constant until it is moved again.

Using 2D Commands in 3D

Virtually all AutoCAD commands are really 2D commands, not 3D commands. In reality, there are only a handful of 3D-specific commands in AutoCAD such as UCS, DVIEW and some surface commands. Therefore, the vast number of AutoCAD commands are exclusively 2D. But this doesn't mean that you can't use them in 3D. Remember that the purpose of a UCS is to create a 2D plane. Once this 2D plane is created, then all 2D commands in AutoCAD work as before, relative to the current UCS.

Now try one example. First, create a UCS parallel to the right side of the model (see Figure 2-50). Then draw a small circle on the right side of the model.

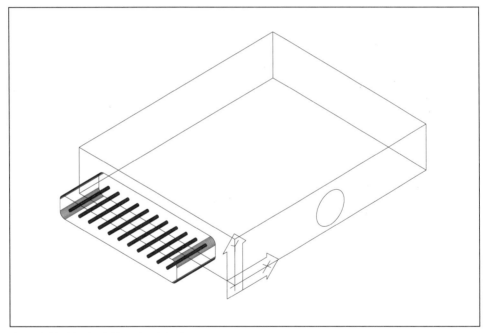

Figure 2-50: Aligning UCS on the right side

Think how the AutoCAD ROTATE command works. This command asks you to select an object, pick a base point and enter the angle of rotation. When AutoCAD rotates an object, it rotates either clockwise or counterclockwise around Z in the direction of X and Y when looked at from Plan view.

Look at the UCS icon as it is now in Figure 2-50. If you were to use the ROTATE command to rotate that circle using the center of the circle as the base point, what would happen? The circle would rotate, but you wouldn't see very much. Why? Because the circle rotates about the center in an XY direction.

What if what you really wanted to do was to spin the circle into the model—that is, rotate the circle around XZ. The AutoCAD ROTATE command is strictly a 2D command in that it rotates only in the XY direction. Then how do you solve your problem? You solve the problem not by changing the ROTATE command, but by changing the UCS:

Type: RX <Enter>

Notice now that the icon points toward a new plane that is in a Y direction inside/outside the model (see Figure 2-51). Go ahead and try the ROTATE command.

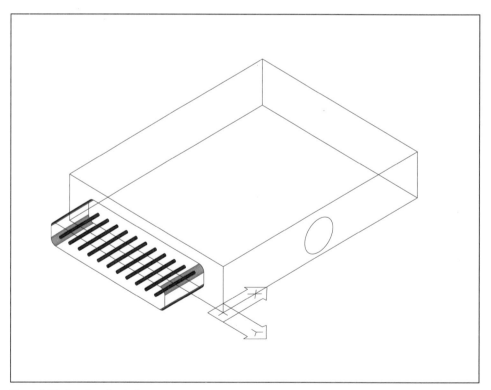

Figure 2-51: Rotating the circle

Type: ROTATE <Enter>

Response: Select Objects:

Pick the circle and press Enter to confirm the selection.

Response: Base point:

Using object snap center, pick the center of the circle.

Response: <Rotation angle>/Reference:

Drag the rotation and see what happens. See how easy it is to spin it into the model (see Figure 2-52).

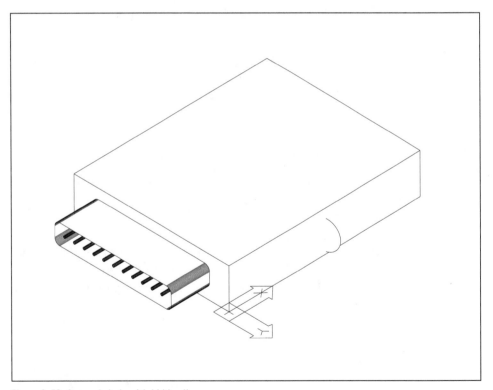

Figure 2-52: Rotated circle with hidden lines

This is a classic example of how to use regular AutoCAD commands in 3D. The key to almost all AutoCAD 2D commands lies with the UCS. Remember that the purpose of the UCS is to create a 2D plane infinitely in 3D space; then your only job is to line up the UCS icon correctly.

2D Uses for UCS

In the preceding section you learned how to use 2D AutoCAD commands in 3D. This section deals primarily with how to use the UCS as a 2D tool. You'll look at a few examples of how the UCS can be of help in these 2D applications. You will see how easy it is to extend a line at an angle, be perpendicular to an object, change a 2D origin and change the direction of text.

For these examples, start a new drawing with the same setup parameters you used at the beginning of this chapter.

I. Extend a line at an angle

Draw a diagonal line across your screen. You want to extend this line 2 units at a specified end. The problem is that you don't know the angle of the line.

Type: `UCS <Enter>`

Response: `Origin/ZAxis/3point/OBject/View/X/Y/Z/Prev/Restore/Save/Del/?/<World>:`

Type: `OB <Enter>`

Pick the line. Notice that the crosshairs and the UCS change to align themselves with the object. Make certain that grips are enabled. Now without issuing any other command, pick the line. This will select the line and turn on the grips (see Figure 2-53).

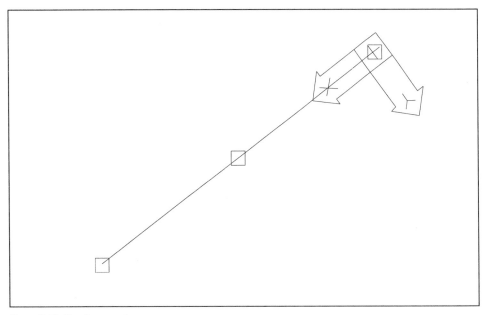

Figure 2-53: Turning on grips

Pick the grip at one end of the line. The grip that you pick should change color; this is your base point (see Figure 2-54). Notice the direction of your icon; it may or may not be pointing in the same direction as the one shown in the figure because the direction of the icon is dependent on the direction that you drew the line. For the example, extend the line in a negative X direction 2 units:

Type: @2<180 <Enter>

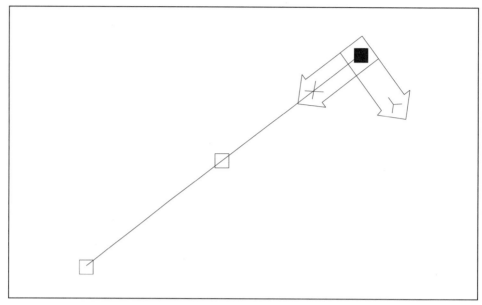

Figure 2-54: Pick your grip base point

As you can see, the line extends 2 units in the direction of negative X. If you want to extend the line at the other end, then you could choose the other grip and type **@2<0**. Remember that positive X is 0 degrees, positive Y is 90, negative X is 180 and negative Y is 270. You, of course, have to keep your eye on the direction of the UCS.

To return to the UCS World:

Type: UCS <Enter> <Enter>

2. Perpendicular to an object

You can use the same concept as the diagonal line method to draw a line perpendicular to another object. When you use the UCS Object option and pick the object to which you wish to be perpendicular, the crosshairs change to be perpendicular with that object. At this point, using ORTHO you can align at 90 degrees to the object. Now it's a simple case of drawing a line with ortho on.

3. Changing Origin in 2D

You can use the UCS Origin option to change the origin anywhere, even in 2D. This way, you can use absolute coordinates from this origin without having to concern yourself with the last point picked and the @ option.

This approach is especially helpful if you're using ordinate dimensioning. One of the problems with ordinate dimensioning is that the *AutoCAD Reference Manual* never mentions how to establish a base origin. The ordinate dimensioning routine creates the XDATUM and YDATUM, but they are always based on the origin. If your origin stays at World 0,0,0 then you have no way of creating the base point on your model—even in 2D—from which the XDATUM and YDATUM are computed. This also causes a problem if you want to change the base point on the same model for a different set of ordinate dimensions.

The answer is incredibly simple. Use the UCS Origin option to establish the base point. From then on, the ordinate dimensions will be absolute X and YDATUM from that origin. If you need a second base point on your model, just move the origin.

4. Change direction of text

There are many ways to change the direction of text, but here's a very easy one. If you want to control the direction of the text without changing the rotation of the text or even to write the text backwards without creating a backwards style, simply adjust the UCS icon to point X in the direction you want the text to go. If you want the text to be written backwards, make sure that the X arrow of the icon points to the left. At this point, begin the TEXT, DTEXT or MTEXT command. The text always follows the direction of positive X.

Moving On

By now you have a good handle on how to manipulate the User Coordinate System. But AutoCAD gives you much, much more. You're not restricted to viewing your model from only one plane. The UCS and the view point are separate. Dynamically moving anywhere in 3D is visually exciting. Just as with the UCS, there is a wealth of tools at your disposal. As you move to the next chapter and take an in-depth look at DVIEW, your drawings will really come alive.

CHAPTER 3

Dynamic Views

A three-dimensional view is visually exciting. From the days of early film history, 3D conjured up the feeling of being a part of the action. This chapter looks at AutoCAD's primary tool for viewing a model—DVIEW. With it you will learn how to set up your camera and target angles, move inside and around your model, create perfect perspectives, perform real-time pan and zooms, clip away unwanted areas and hide lines.

Even though animation in Release 13 is not a part of basic AutoCAD as yet, what you'll learn with DVIEW is the basis for all walk throughs and fly bys. Still, on a computer it's hard to imagine anything more impressive than walk throughs, fly bys and moving around and about in a model on the screen in real time.

There are limitations to Release 13; by itself AutoCAD is not equipped to create first-class animations, but it does enable you to move easily and intuitively around in your drawing. So, it's time to get started with your next drawing.

Setting Up Your Drawing

Begin a new drawing with the following settings:

UNITS	Architectural
Precision	1/16
LIMITS	0,0
Upper right	144',96'
GRID	3'
SNAP	3'

After you make the settings:

Type: ZOOM <Enter>

Type: All <Enter>

Begin with the PLINE command and draw a basic outline similar to Figure 3-1. Do not draw the dimensions. It's not necessary that your drawing look exactly like Figure 3-1; the dimensions given are meant only to provide you with some idea of the size and scale of the drawing.

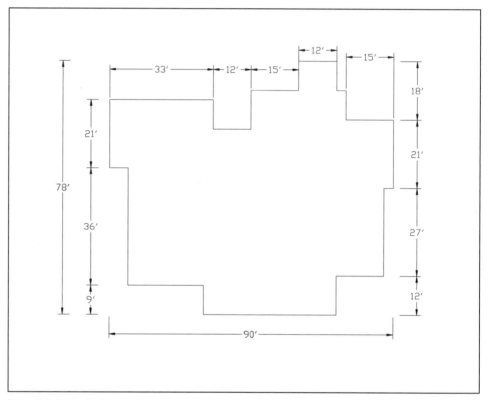

Figure 3-1: Beginning base plan

In this chapter you use an architectural model as an example because it affords the most flexibility in working with each of the DVIEW commands. Don't worry about exact measurements. In fact, you can be a little more creative if you like. The only important part here is to make certain that you do draw your model using a *closed* polyline.

What you've drawn is the basic outline for your floor plan. At this point I haven't asked you to set a thickness for the walls because you're going to use the basic floor plan to create the ceiling also. Therefore, once you draw the outline, before you add any walls or thickness, you will copy the outline to another layer. The only problem with this step is that AutoCAD does not have a copy layer command that lets you copy objects from one layer to another. You're therefore going to use a program called CPLAYER.LSP.

You can find CPLAYER.LSP in the AutoLISP section of the book. This program asks you the name of the target layer where you want to copy the objects. If the layer doesn't exist, then it's created for you.

As with the 3D programs, make certain that CPLAYER.LSP is properly loaded. Complete instructions on creating and loading these programs are found in Chapter 17 and Appendix A "AutoLISP & Your 3D Toolkit."

Type: CPLAYER <Enter>

Response: Enter target layer name:

Type: Ceiling <Enter>

Response: Select objects:

Pick the polyline representing the base plan and press Enter to confirm the selection.

You have made a copy of the base plan and placed it on a layer called Ceiling. Now change the elevation of the copy that is on the ceiling layer to 14':

Type: CHANGE <Enter>

Response: Select Objects:

Type: L <Enter> <Enter>

(This is the last object created.)

Response: Properties/<Change point>:

Type: P <Enter>

Response: Change what property (Color/Elev/LAyer/LType/ltScale/Thickness)?

Type: E <Enter>

(This stands for elevation.)

Response: New elevation <0'-0">:

Type: 14' <Enter> <Enter>

Because the polyline forming the ceiling is the last object created, it is then moved to an elevation of 14'.

For now, issue the FREEZE command to freeze the ceiling layer so that you're working only with the polyline representing the base plan:

Type: `LAYER <Enter>`

Type: `F <Enter>`

Type: `Ceiling <Enter> <Enter>`

The ceiling layer is now frozen.

Next, change the extrusion of your base plan polyline to 14' so that the top of the walls match the ceiling:

Type: `CHPROP <Enter>`

Response: `Select objects:`

Pick the base plan polyline and

Type: `<Enter>`

Response: `Change what property`
           `(Color/LAyer/Ltype/ltScale/Thickness)?`

Type: `T <Enter>`

(This stands for thickness.)

Response: `New thickness <0'-0">:`

Type: `14' <Enter> <Enter>`

The walls now have an extrusion of 14'. At this point you should draw the interior walls. And because you're not going to use them for any other purpose, you might as well set thickness to 14':

Type: `THICKNESS <Enter>`

Response: `New value for THICKNESS <0'-0">:`

Type: `14' <Enter>`

Using the PLINE command, draw the interior walls similar to those shown in Figure 3-2.

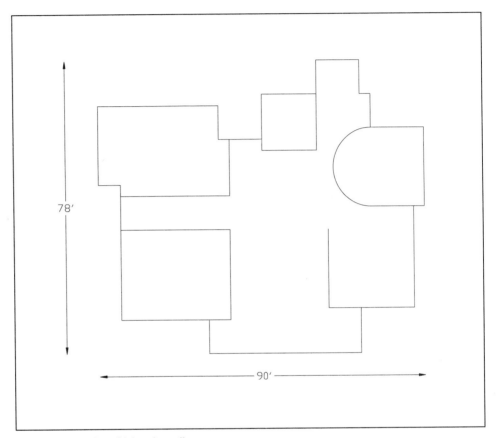

Figure 3-2: Base plan with interior walls

You draw each of the rooms with a polyline. The only part that might give you a problem is the curved wall area. You do it by beginning with a polyline and picking the endpoint of the upper wall. Immediately after picking this point, type **A** (which stands for Arc) and press Enter, then pick the endpoint of the bottom wall to form a polyarc.

Now that you have your interior walls, use the Break command and simply pick two points to break openings into the walls, as shown in Figure 3-3. Be sure to put a large opening in the lower-left room and the main entrance.

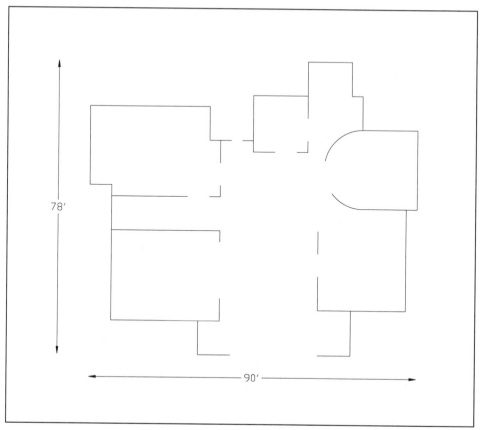

Figure 3-3: Breaking openings in the walls

To add something interesting inside your structure, add a fountain in the center and set the thickness of the base of the fountain to 4':

Type: THICKNESS <Enter>

Response: New value for THICKNESS <0'-0">:

Type: 4' <Enter>

Now draw a circle, as shown in Figure 3-4.

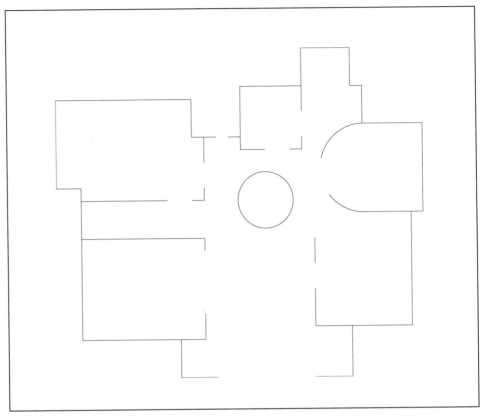

Figure 3-4: The fountain base

To make this a three-tier fountain, you're going to draw two other circles with the same center. Therefore, do this in two steps. First, set the thickness for the second tier to 2':

Type: THICKNESS <Enter>

Response: New value for THICKNESS <0'-0">:

Type: 2' <Enter>

Now your second circle will have an extrusion of 2', but you want it to sit on top of your fountain base. The second step you must do is to raise the elevation to the top of the base, which is 4':

Type: ELEV <Enter>

Response: New current elevation:

Type: 4' <Enter>

Response: New current thickness <2'-0">:

Type: <Enter>

Notice that the elevation command (ELEV) also enables you to set the thickness at the same time. But because you already set the thickness using the THICKNESS system variable, you only have to press Enter at this prompt.

Now draw a second circle using the same center point as the first (see Figure 3-5).

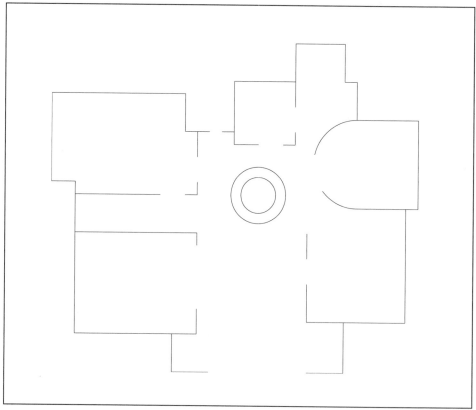

Figure 3-5: The second tier of the fountain

Then draw a third circle inside the first two. This time, let the elevation command do the work for both changing the elevation and the thickness at the same time:

Type: ELEV <Enter>

Response: New current elevation <4'-0">:

Type: 6' <Enter>

Response: New current thickness <2'-0">:

Type: 1' <Enter>

With this single ELEV command, you have set both the new elevation and the new thickness for the final circle.

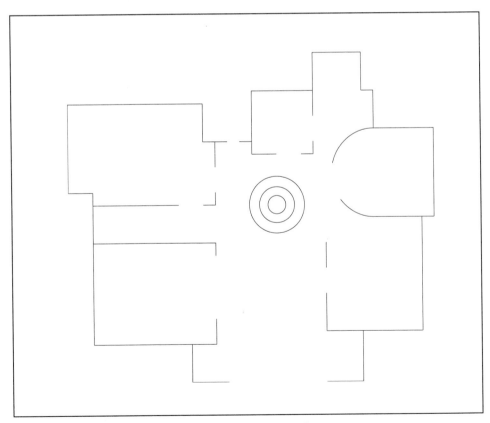

Figure 3-6: The third tier of the fountain

Before you forget, remember to set both the thickness and elevation back to 0:

Type: `ELEV <Enter>`

Response: `New current elevation <6'-0">:`

Type: `0 <Enter>`

Response: `New current thickness <1'-0">:`

Type: `0 <Enter>`

Now that you have your drawing in place, you can take a look at how the DVIEW command works.

Starting the DVIEW Command

DVIEW is an AutoCAD command that enables you to dynamically view your drawing from any angle. The term *dynamic* in AutoCAD means that you actually see the object on the screen as it's supposed to appear while you perform the command.

Type: `DVIEW <Enter>`

Response: `Select Objects:`

Type: `All <Enter> <Enter>`

Response: `CAmera/TArget/Distance/POints/PAn/Zoom/TWist/CLip/Hide/Off/Undo/<eXit>:`

Type: `CA <Enter>`

(CA stands for camera.)

Move the crosshairs around your screen. Every so often stop and let the image refresh itself on the screen. As you can see, you dynamically have control of the view of the object. Moving the crosshairs up and down is the equivalent to raising the camera relative to the target. As you move the crosshairs straight down, you're lowering the camera. Look at the word Angle in your status line. It indicates your camera's vertical angle above or below the target. Moving the crosshairs left and right has the effect of moving around the target 180 degrees each way. This way, you can completely move around the model. Remember though that the angle displayed at the top of the screen only reflects the vertical camera angle, not the horizontal revolution around the target.

Response: `Toggle angle in/Enter angle from XY plane <90.00>:`

AutoCAD really has a way with words, doesn't it? What it is trying to say here is that you can pick your viewing angle both in the vertical and horizontal, or you may type first the vertical angle of your camera. See what happens if you simply type the vertical angle:

Type: `30 <Enter>`

Response: `Toggle angle from/Enter angle in XY plane from X axis <-90.00>:`

This response makes about as much sense to the average person reading it as the first response does. But now look at the angles shown at the status line. Because you've typed in the vertical angle, it is now held constant. You no longer can use your cursor to point to a vertical angle. Now you can move your crosshairs only left and right in a horizontal rotation. This expresses an angle from –180 to +180 degrees, enabling you to go completely around your target. You can either pick this angle dynamically on the screen or you can type it in at this prompt. For now, type in the angle:

Type: `-130 <Enter>`

You're now back at the DVIEW options. If you were to press Esc at any time, you would cancel anything you had done while in this DVIEW session. To make this view permanent one final time:

Type: `<Enter>`

Look at the wireframe in Figure 3-7. If you were to hide the lines, the model would look more interesting.

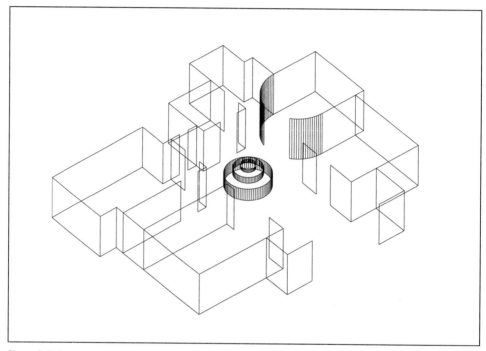

Figure 3-7: Rotated model

Type: HIDE <Enter>

Figure 3-8 illustrates the model with the lines hidden.

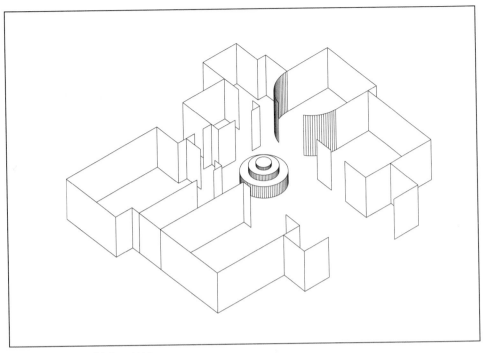

Figure 3-8: Model with lines hidden

DRAGP1

The number of objects that you manipulate can determine the ease of use of the DVIEW command. If you have a relatively slow machine and select a large number of objects, then dynamically moving around in your drawing can become slow and time consuming. One of the choices that you make up front when you begin the DVIEW command is the number of objects you choose to be affected dynamically by the command. You're not required to select every object in your model. You may select only those objects in the area that you're viewing. You can put a window around only those objects that might be representative of the model. This way, as you're dynamically viewing the model, only those objects are dragging on the screen. If your computer is slow or there are many objects, you can help speed things up by selecting only a few objects when you're asked to select objects.

Even though you might have selected only a few objects and you can see only those objects selected during the DVIEW command, this doesn't mean that all of the objects in the drawing are not being rotated into the proper view. When you press Enter one final time and return to the Command line, the drawing will regenerate one additional time. Here all of the objects will reflect the proper viewing angle, regardless of the number of objects that were first chosen.

On the other hand, there is the possibility that your computer is extremely fast or that the number of objects that you're selecting is not that numerous. In this event, by using the All option of select objects, you can select all of the objects in the drawing.

One of the problems you will initially encounter when you're using a fast computer is that even though your computer is capable of it, you will not see all of the object dynamically as you move it around with your crosshairs. This happens because AutoCAD has a system variable setting that controls the number of objects that are painted on the screen during any form of drag operation. This system variable is called DRAGP1. The default of AutoCAD out of the box is set to 10. As you increase DRAGP1, this permits more of the model to be displayed as you move your crosshairs around the screen.

If you're running a fast computer, you might want to set DRAGP1 very high. This is, of course, totally dependent on the number of objects that you're manipulating and the speed of your machine.

Type: DRAGP1 <Enter>

Response: New value for DRAGP1 <10>:

Type: 200 <Enter>

DRAGP1 is global for all drawings once set. For a drawing this size, this setting is about right for a 486/33 Megahertz machine. You might want to experiment with your computer by raising the value to see whether it gives you a sluggish feel. As your drawing becomes larger, you need to lower DRAGP1. Adjust these settings depending on the size of your drawing and the speed of your machine until you can get as many objects to refresh as often as possible without feeling like you're dragging a ton of bricks along with it.

Using the Camera

Now take a more in-depth look at how AutoCAD uses the metaphor of a camera and a target to move around in the model. Return now to the DVIEW command.

Type: DVIEW <Enter>

Response: Select Objects:

Type: All <Enter> <Enter>

Response: CAmera/TArget/Distance/POints/PAn/Zoom/TWist/CLip/Hide/Off/Undo/<eXit>:

The camera options use the metaphor of a camera and a target. Figure 3-9 represents a vertical angle view of camera to target. This figure represents the model that is in the center with a camera toward the top and bottom.

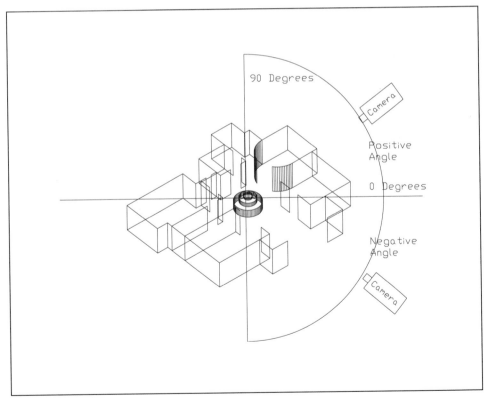

Figure 3-9: Vertical angle of camera to target

The horizontal line going across the model represents zero degrees. If the camera were fixed at exactly zero degrees, then you would be looking at the model from the side. This is what architects refer to as an *Elevation view*. Remember though that the word *elevation* has a completely different meaning in AutoCAD.

You can continue to move the camera upward around the arc until it's at 90 degrees directly over the model. This is a Plan view. At the same time you could move the camera below zero degrees and go into a negative angle relative to the model. From there you would be viewing the object from the bottom up. See what this would look like:

Type: CA <Enter>

Response: Toggle angle in/Enter angle from XY plane <30.00>:

Type: -40 <Enter>

Response: Toggle angle from/Enter angle in XY plane from X axis <-130.00>:

Type: <Enter>
         H <Enter>

(This is to hide the lines.)

Even without leaving the DVIEW command, you can hide lines so that you can better see where you are relative to the model. Even though it's difficult to determine visually without hiding the lines whether you're on top looking down or below looking up, remember that you can look at the UCS icon. In Figure 3-10, which shows a view of the model from the bottom up, the lines do not crisscross where the X and the Y meet on the UCS icon. Therefore, you know that you're below the model.

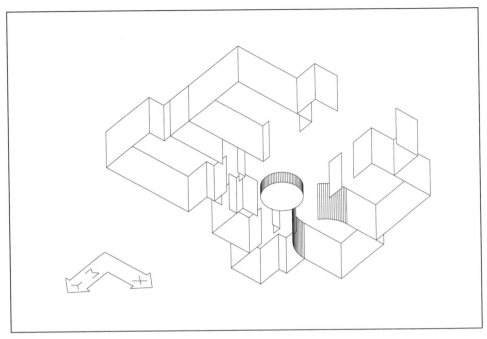

Figure 3-10: Model from bottom up

AutoCAD has a built-in Undo option as part of the DVIEW command to permit you to undo errors as they occur:

Type: U <Enter>
        U <Enter>

(This returns you to your original angle.)

Figure 3-11 represents a horizontal view of the angle of camera to target. After you type the vertical angle, you're asked for the horizontal angle rotation. This figure shows a circle going 360 degrees around the model. As you can see, you can type up to a maximum of +/− 180 degrees. Thus, you can go all the way around the object.

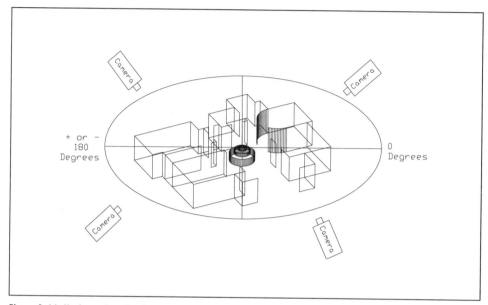

Figure 3-11: Horizontal angle of camera to target

The difference between typing and picking an angle may be confusing at first. Actually, you have only three alternatives:

1. When you choose the camera option, you can move the crosshairs in any direction. Moving them vertically controls the vertical angle, and moving them horizontally controls the horizontal angle. At any point when the model looks right on the screen, then pick and both the vertical and horizontal angles will be chosen automatically.

2. After you type the vertical angle, your cursor is only controlling the horizontal angle. When you get to the point where you are on the correct side of the model, then pick.

3. You can type in the vertical angle and then type in the horizontal angle instead of picking it.

Moving the Target

Continuing the metaphor of the camera and the target, AutoCAD gives you the ability to maintain the camera stationary and move the target above or below and around the camera. Visually on the screen, it looks the same, but the angle that you type in is inverted. Compare Figure 3-9 with Figure 3-12; notice that it compares vertical angles using the TArget option.

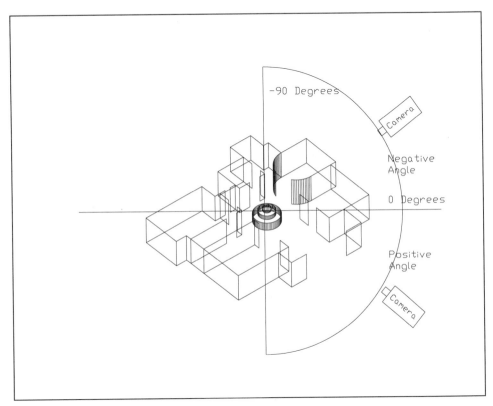

Figure 3-12: Vertical angles using TArget

The only difference in Figure 3-12 is that the positive and negative angles are reversed. Remember that the angle is represented relative to the target, not the camera. Therefore, if the target is moved to a positive angle, then the target has been moved above the camera. Thus, you're looking from bottom up. On the other hand, if the target has been moved to a negative angle relative to the camera, then the target is below the camera. You are therefore looking from top down.

Why would AutoCAD give you two ways to do the same thing? There is no real reason for this except that Autodesk wanted to give you the flexibility of moving the target relative to the camera as well as moving the camera relative to the target.

There is one thing you should always keep in mind: you're not really moving the objects themselves. This is only the angle from which you view the model. The TArget option is similar to ZOOM. When you zoom in or out on an object, the coordinates of that object are not really moved. Only your view of the object changes.

Adjusting the Object on the Screen

There are three primary commands to DVIEW that you use to adjust the model on the screen: TWIST, ZOOM and PAN. In reality these three work together to fully adjust where the object appears. Therefore, you might zoom in a little and then pan it over. If the object is not straight, then twist it to get a better look. In the following sections, you'll see how each of these commands works.

Twisting the Object On-Screen

From time to time your model may not be at the angle you want it. With the TWIST option, AutoCAD gives you the ability to rotate the object on the screen without actually moving the objects' coordinates:

Type: TW <Enter>

Notice that because the first two letters of TWist are uppercase, you must type both letters if you're typing the commands because both TArget and TWist begin with a T.

Response: New view twist <0.00>:

Here you can dynamically rotate the object until it is at the angle you desire. Or you can type in a rotated angle:

Type: 30 <Enter>

The model is now rotated 30 degrees counterclockwise. See Figure 3-13 for a view of the twisted model.

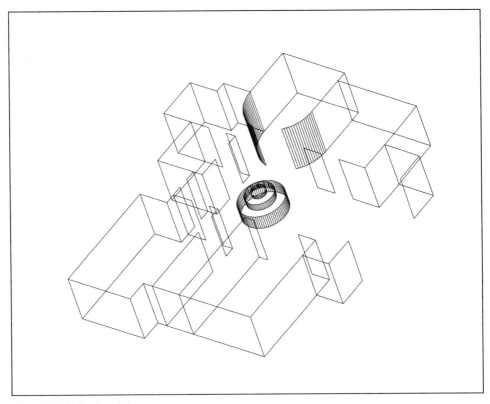

Figure 3-13: Twisted model

Use the Undo option at this point because you really don't want to twist your model:

Type: U <Enter>

Notice that you're still in the DVIEW command and the last option has been reversed.

Zooming In & Out

You can zoom dynamically in and out in real time. The purpose of ZOOM is to give you the tools to enable you to focus on an area of your drawing and to center that area on the screen. See how this works:

Type: Z <Enter>

Response: Adjust zoom scale factor <1>:

Notice the horizontal slider bar at the top of your screen. It should be sitting at 1x. Depending on where your cursor happened to be when you executed the ZOOM command, you might be anywhere from a tight zoom to a far away zoom where your model appears as a microscopic image on your screen. Move the cursor to the right until it reaches approximately 4x on the slider bar.

In the pull-down menu area, you'll see the exact scale factor as you move the slider bar. Continue to move the slider bar to 9x. You're now nine times the original zoom. Notice that the maximum factor is 16x. But 16x is not an absolute maximum; it is only the maximum with a single pick. Move the slider bar now to 16x; this should be to the far right.

You can also dynamically zoom out. Move the slider bar to the left of 1x. As you approach 0x, the model gets smaller and smaller. But what if you want to zoom in more than 16x? At the Command line, you always have the alternative to simply type in the zoom scale factor. Do not include the "X" after your scale.

But if you really want to dynamically zoom to a factor of more than 16x without typing it in, this becomes a two-step operation. First, move the slider bar to 16x and pick. You should now be in a very tight zoom. If you want to go even further, repeat the ZOOM command:

Type: Z <Enter>

Now the 1x is where the 16x left off. Next, move the slider bar left or right until you can comfortably see the entire image on the screen and then pick.

Centering the Model With PAN

Zooming in and out of your model is only one of the tools you have to adjust the object on your screen. Just because you've zoomed in, the object may not be completely centered. But you can use a dynamic pan:

Type: PA <Enter>

Notice here that you have to type both the P and the A because there are two commands that begin with a P: they are PAn and POints.

Response: Displacement base point:

Pick any point on the screen as though you were picking up the model to move it:

Response: `Second point:`

Now move your crosshairs around. Notice that the model follows as you move so that you can dynamically center it on the screen.

In a limited form you can also use this operation to pan horizontally and vertically when you get inside the model. But for now, use the PAN command to center the model and then pick.

With the careful use of ZOOM, TWIST and PAN, you can move the model anywhere on the screen.

Setting Perspective

Reality is not always what the eye sees. A distortion of reality may often appear the most real. Using CAmera and TArget, you can view your model from any angle, but to the mind's eye, this is not reality.

Reality is when you look down a long straight pair of railroad tracks and know that the tracks are parallel. But what does your mind's eye tell you? It shows the tracks coming together until their individual endpoints vanish or merge completely. If you were to draw the reality of the tracks, it would look like a child's drawing with parallel lines going up the page. What you're missing is called *perspective.*

Perspective is what the mind's eye sees relative to distance. If you were to look at real railroad tracks and add a railroad station down the line close to the point where the lines come together, you would notice that as you get closer to the station, the tracks separate and become more parallel. The degree of convergence is directly dependent on your distance to the object. This point of convergence or lack thereof is called the *vanishing point.*

The good news is that with AutoCAD you don't have to worry about the vanishing point. AutoCAD does it all for you. When you're constructing your model, you don't want to draw in perspective. You draw using real-world dimensions. When you're ready to add perspective, you don't determine distance by the amount of perspective, but you determine the amount of perspective by the distance. This means that you don't have to concern yourself at all as to how to draw an object in perspective. Just make certain that the dimension and the proportions of the object are correct in reality. When you're ready, you then add perspective using the DVIEW command by indicating to AutoCAD the distance of the camera to the target. Once AutoCAD knows the distance, it can apply the correct perspective.

Now see how this process works:

Type: D <Enter>

Response: New camera/target distance <0'-1">:

There are two ways you can give AutoCAD the distance you are from the object. Notice the slider bar at the top of the screen. The bar goes from 0x to 16X. These are factors times your current distance from the object. 1x is the distance you are now.

Slide the bar back and forth. Either the object will move in and out wildly, appearing extremely small or very large, or the object will barely move at all. When the object doesn't appear to move at all as you go back and forth along the slider bar, you are too close. If you're only one inch from the target, then the best you can do is move 16 inches. If you move to 16x and pick, you can choose Distance again. Now the object will begin to move. The slider bar will move you from 16 inches to 16 X 16 inches. Pick and do this a third time, and you will have total control of the object with your cursor.

There is an easier way to apply distance. When you choose the Distance option, you may give the distance at the Command line. If the Command line says one inch, simply change it by typing the correct distance to the target. The distance will be applied immediately.

Once you're in the distance or perspective mode, you'll notice that your UCS icon has changed from the XY arrow to an oblong box. This icon indicates that you're in perspective. So that you won't be confused, there is no perspective command. Also the word *perspective* doesn't appear as one of the DVIEW options and is not mentioned except in the *AutoCAD Reference Manual*. In AutoCAD, Distance is the command that turns on perspective.

Now that perspective is on, how do you turn it off? In DVIEW there is an option called OFF; there is no option called ON. The OFF command turns off distance or perspective. If you want to turn perspective back on again without changing the distance, simply choose the Distance option and press Enter through all the defaults, and perspective will be turned back on at the same distance as previously set.

Tips to Working With a Perspective

Several things can go wrong when working with perspective on. You'll need to watch out for these potential problems. The first major restriction is that you can't use a pointing device to pick while perspective is turned on. With most of the commands, you may choose points by typing coordinates. Some commands like ZOOM simply won't work at all. This is only true if you are outside of the DVIEW options. The Zoom option within DVIEW works while perspective is on.

The second concern that you need to be aware of is that there is an interactive relationship between the Zoom option of DVIEW and the Distance option. The easiest way to explain this relationship is to return to the railroad tracks metaphor. As you physically move closer to the railroad station, the tracks tend to come apart again; that is, you lose your perspective. But assume that you're not physically moving closer to the station. You're standing in the same spot, but now you're looking toward the station with a pair of high-powered binoculars. What now is the perspective effect? The answer is that you would see the tracks the same as if you were standing as close to the railroad station as the binoculars made it appear.

This is what happens with the Zoom option of DVIEW. The Zoom option of DVIEW works differently from the regular ZOOM command in AutoCAD and differently from the Zoom option of DVIEW, depending on whether perspective is on or off. As you just learned, using the Zoom option of DVIEW is similar to the ZOOM by factor command outside of DVIEW. But if perspective is turned on, then you're no longer dealing with a zoom factor.

The metaphor changes to a lens length. Imagine that the ZOOM command is a pair of binoculars. The larger the millimeter lens length, the more powerful are the binoculars and the closer the objects appear to be. If you enter 50, this is what you should see if you were looking at the object with a 50mm telephoto lens on a 35mm camera. Decreasing the size of the lens makes the object seem smaller and puts it farther from the camera.

Notice the effect changing the millimeter lens has on Distance. You may still be physically 100 feet from the object. But the perspective appearance will change if you change the lens length of the ZOOM command. You may appear to be closer, and thus the perspective is adjusted. This means that the perspective is not fully controlled solely by the Distance option.

The third problem you should watch out for is to always have some standard lens length that you can consider to be absolute. This means a lens length setting as though you're not using those binoculars. This setting is something you can come back to and depend on. It really doesn't matter what standard lens length you choose. This way, you can add some degree of meaning to Distance so that 100' can be relative to 150'. If you arbitrarily change the ZOOM lens length, then you can't depend on the appearances of the relative distances.

Try the Distance option to see how it works. If you're not in the Distance option, then

Type: D <Enter>

Response: New camera/target distance <0'-1">:

If this is the first time that you've used the Distance option, then you're probably set to 1". Begin by typing 100' to get a relationship that makes sense for the size of model that you're working on:

Type: 100' <Enter>

Now you can see most of your model. Repeat the Distance option:

Type: D <Enter>

Response: New camera/target distance <100'-0">:

As you move the slider bar left and right, notice that as it goes toward 0x you tend to be closer to your model. Toward 16x the model is set farther away. Remember that the slider bar is working with factors times your current view, which is set at 100'. Move the slider bar left and right to get the feel of it.

Type: 200' <Enter>

Figure 3-14 shows perspective on at a distance of 200'. Notice in this figure that the lines are no longer parallel. Depending on your angle of view and the distance of your target and camera from each other, these parallel lines will begin to converge and make your model look more real.

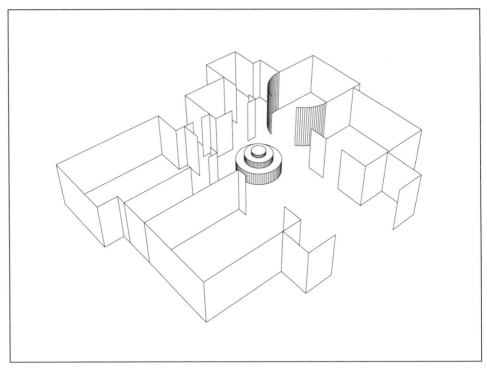

Figure 3-14: Perspective on at 200'-00"

Turn off perspective before moving on to the next example:

Type: OFF <Enter>

Going Inside the Model

Using a DVIEW subcommand called POINTS, you can actually set the coordinate points for your target and camera. If you don't understand all the rules of POINTS, you might wonder what's going on in the next exercise.

Type: PO <Enter>

Response: Enter target point:

The coordinates of the target point are given as the default. For this example, place the target point at about Point 1, as shown in Figure 3-15, to show changing target and camera points.

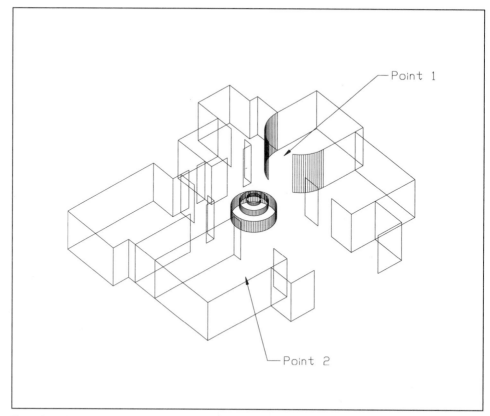

Figure 3-15: Changing target and camera points

Because you haven't changed your User Coordinate System and your elevation is still at zero, if you pick a point for your target at Point 1, then that point will be on the ground. Say you really want your target point to be 7' in elevation. You will need to use a point filter command:

Type: .XY <Enter>

Response: of

            Pick Point 1 (in Figure 3-15).

Response: (need Z):

The (.XY) point filters that you typed are enabling you to pick a point in the XY plane without your using the current Z value of the current User Coordinate System. After you pick the point in the XY plane, then it asks you for the Z value:

Type: `7' <Enter>`

Response: `Enter camera point:`

      AutoCAD defaults to the last coordinates of the camera. You'll want to place the camera at a 9' elevation. So as before, you'll use the .XY filters:

Type: `.XY`

Response: `of`

      Pick Point 2 (in Figure 3-15).

Response: `(need Z):`

Type: `9' <Enter>`

      Here your camera should be above your target to create a slight angle. What a mess! See Figure 3-16 to see how your view point was thrown outside the model.

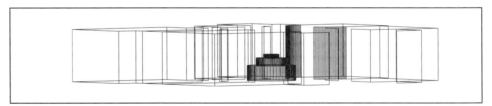

Figure 3-16: Points thrown outside the model with distance off

      This angle of view is not at all what you expected to see. What went wrong? Well, nothing went wrong. You just didn't understand all of the rules. You probably expected to be inside the model at an angle and distance that you had picked. If the distance is not turned on, then the POINTS command only creates an angle relative to the points. It does not change the original distance. Do you remember what your last distance was set for? It was set for 200'. Therefore, your target and camera points created an angle of view, but you were still left 200' away from the target.

      Then how do you get to where you really want to be? Just make certain that distance is turned on. It doesn't matter what distance you're set to. If distance is turned on when you issue the POINTS command, then not only will the angle be adjusted, but also AutoCAD will measure and change the distance between the two points picked.

First, undo the last command and perform the Points option differently:

Type: U <Enter>

Now turn on distance:

Type: D <Enter> <Enter>

This procedure maintains your distance at 200' because all you actually needed to do was to turn on distance. You don't have to set a new distance first. The POINTS command does that for you:

Type: PO <Enter>

Now repeat the steps as before:

Response: Enter target point:

Type: .XY <Enter>

Response: of

Pick Point 1 (in Figure 3-15).

Response: (need Z):

Type: 7' <Enter>

Response: Enter camera point:

Type: .XY

Response: of

Pick Point 2 (in Figure 3-15).

Response: (need Z):

Type: 9' <Enter>

What a difference this change makes. Now see Figure 3-17 for a more complete view inside the model.

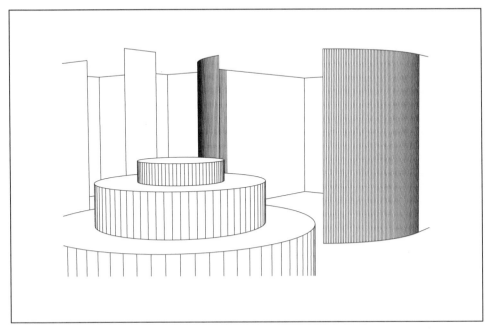

Figure 3-17: Inside the model

You also have some limited pan capabilities here. If you issue the PAN command while in DVIEW, even though you're in perspective you can pan up and down and left and right. Although you originally used this command to help you center your image on the screen, as long as you don't need to change the angle of view, you can pan left and right and up and down.

Before you leave perspective, why don't you add a little more class to your view and make it look more interesting? Remember the ceiling that you put on your drawing at the beginning of this chapter? That ceiling was really a copy of the polyline of the base plan placed on a layer called ceiling. You froze that layer, but see what you can do with it.

However, you don't want to lose what you have before you proceed. Because you're still in the DVIEW command, you'll need to make your view permanent.

Type: `<Enter>`

This Enter takes you back to the Command line. Save this view. Remember USVIEW and URVIEW from the preceding chapter. USVIEW saves the UCS and the view at the same time. Even if you're not interested in saving the UCS, you can still use it as a quick way to save your view. To use these programs, make sure that either they are loaded or that 3DTOOLS.LSP is loaded. See Appendix A.

Type: `USVIEW <Enter>`

Response: `Name of view and UCS to save:`

Type: `V1 <Enter>`

Now change to Plan view:

Type: `PLAN <Enter> <Enter>`

Your drawing may now be a little off the center of the screen. Use ZOOM All to get it back:

Type: `ZOOM <Enter>`

Type: `A <Enter>`

Notice that the UCS icon has now returned. You're no longer in Perspective view. You can't be in Perspective view when you are plan to the current UCS.

Now thaw the ceiling layer, set your current layer to the ceiling layer and freeze all other layers. Following is one way:

Type: `LAYER <Enter>`

Type: `T <Enter>`

Type: `Ceiling <Enter>`

Type: `S <Enter>`

Type: `Ceiling <Enter>`

Type: F <Enter>

Type: * <Enter> <Enter>

The outline of the floor plan, which is really the ceiling, should now be the only thing that is visible. And you should be set to the ceiling layer.

Next, hatch the ceiling layer. You can use any method and pattern that you want. Here is an example:

Type: HATCH <Enter>

Response: Pattern:

Type: AR-PARQ1 <Enter>

Response: Scale for pattern:

Type: 10 <Enter>

Response: Angle for pattern:

Type: <Enter>

Response: Select Objects:

Pick the polyline on your screen.

Type: <Enter>

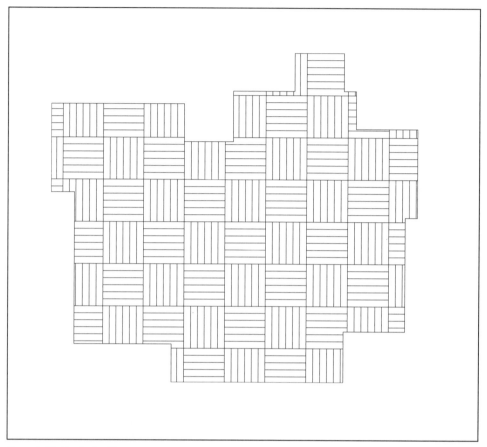

Figure 3-18: Hatched ceiling

At this point your ceiling should look something like Figure 3-18. It doesn't look like much now, but it will. But where did you put the hatch pattern? Is it at the 14' elevation of the ceiling or is it lying on the ground? To see, first you have to thaw your other layers:

Type: LAYER <Enter>

Type: T <Enter>

Type: * <Enter> <Enter>

Using the URVIEW program, restore as V1 the view you saved with USVIEW:

Type: URVIEW <Enter>

Response: Name of view and UCS to restore:

Type: V1 <Enter>

The mystery is solved. The hatch pattern was placed on the floor. See Figure 3-19 for a view of the pattern on the floor. What went wrong? Well, to begin with, the URVIEW program did restore the proper view, and you're in a perspective. This status was restored along with the view.

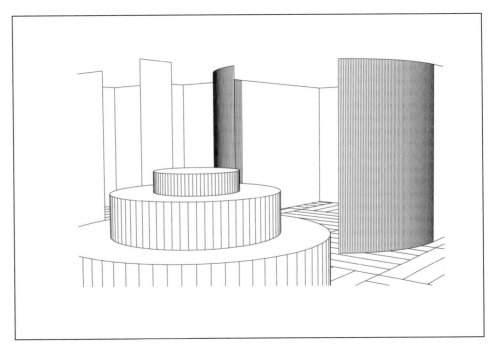

Figure 3-19: The ceiling pattern on the floor

Yet, in Figure 3-19, why didn't the hatch pattern take on the same elevation as the ceiling polyline that was hatched? The answer is that the polyline was used only as a boundary for the hatch. The hatch doesn't actually attach itself to the boundary. Therefore, because the UCS was still at zero elevation, the hatch was placed on the floor. For this example to work as you wanted, you could have done two things before the hatch was created. You could have moved the origin of the UCS to an elevation of 14'.

Or you could have changed the elevation with the ELEV command to 14', relative to that coordinate system before the hatch. Either of these two methods would have worked.

But what can you do now? By using the CHANGE command, you can change the current elevation of the hatch pattern after the fact.

Type: `CHANGE <Enter>`

Response: `Select Objects:`

Pick the hatch pattern, being very careful not to pick other objects:

Type: `<Enter>`

(This confirms the selection.)

Response: `Properties/<Change point>:`

Type: `P <Enter>`

Response: `Change what property`
          `(Color/Elev/LAyer/Ltype/ltScale/Thickness)?`

Type: `E <Enter>`

Response: `New elevation <0'-0">:`

Type: `14' <Enter> <Enter>`

Now you have your ceiling. See Figure 3-20 for a view of the ceiling at a 14' elevation. It's beginning to look like a real office, isn't it?

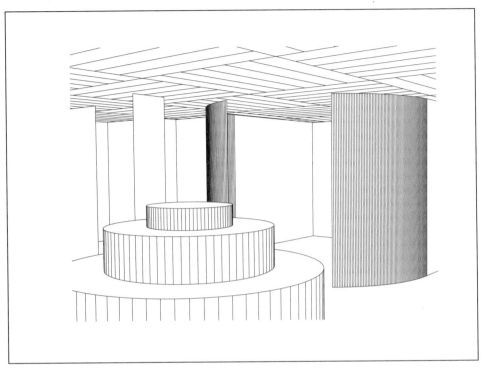

Figure 3-20: Ceiling view at 14' elevation

Working With Perspective On

As you've seen, some of the major problems of working while perspective is on are (1) you can't zoom at all, and (2) you can't pick a point in many of the AutoCAD commands. The primary reason that you can't pick points is easy to understand. Perspective is really a distortion of reality. Where the objects appear on the screen is not where their coordinates really are. Therefore, AutoCAD doesn't have the capability to permit you to select by picking.

But there are some tricks that will enable you to work while perspective is on. For this example, get the drawing back to where it was originally:

Type: DVIEW <Enter>

Response: Select Objects:

Type: <Enter>

What is that on your screen? You must press Enter instead of selecting objects. Whenever you don't select objects, AutoCAD brings up the outline of a house. These minimal objects give you some idea of where you are. It doesn't look very much like a house here because perspective is on, and you're at a close distance. But as you can see from the Command line, all of your responses are available.

Response: CAmera/TArget/Distance/POints/PAn/Zoom/TWist/CLip/Hide/Off/Undo/<eXit>:

Type: OFF <Enter>

Now you can plainly see the house.

AutoCAD brings up a house to give you some idea of where you are relative to your own drawing without having to actually select the objects. This is a fast way to make changes where you don't actually need a visual image of your drawing on the screen. Using this process can save a lot of time when you're working with many objects.

For example, in this case it doesn't matter whether your image is on the screen or not. You're going to turn perspective off and then you're going to set your fixed camera angle at 30 degrees in the vertical and −130 degrees in the horizontal. You don't have to see your image to make these changes.

Response: CAmera/TArget/Distance/POints/PAn/Zoom/TWist/CLip/Hide/Off/Undo/<eXit>:

Type: CA <Enter>

Response: Toggle angle in/Enter angle from XY plane:

Type: 30 <Enter>

Response: Toggle angle from/Enter angle in XY plane from X axis:

Type: −130 <Enter>

Response: CAmera/TArget/Distance/POints/PAn/Zoom/TWist/CLip/Hide/Off/Undo/<eXit>:

Type: <Enter>

Now your model is exactly as it was before, but it has the ceiling.

As a side note here, because this chapter deals primarily with viewing, I took a shortcut when showing you how to create the model. If you were to hide the lines now, you could see the hatch pattern, but you could also see through the holes in the pattern; also, the lines representing the rooms and the fountain would be visible. A hatch pattern in and of itself doesn't create a surface. If you had wanted to create a surface where you could not see through the top of the model, you could have used one of the surface meshes or faces. You did that in Chapter 2, "The User Coordinate System," when you placed a top and bottom cover on your connector.

Now set the drawing to the 0 layer and again freeze the ceiling layer. It will also save time when you hide lines:

Type: LAYER <Enter>

Type: S <Enter>

Type: 0 <Enter> (zero layer)

Type: F <Enter>

Type: Ceiling <Enter> <Enter>

When you work in perspective, you'll find yourself turning perspective on and off many times. Therefore, you should create two AutoLISP programs that will do that for you: PON and POFF. PON turns perspective on, leaving your distance set as it is—assuming that you have set the distance at least once—and POFF turns perspective off.

You can find PON and POFF in the AutoLISP section of the book. As with all 3D programs, make certain that PON and POFF are properly loaded. If you installed the *AutoCAD 3D Companion Disk* properly and loaded 3DTOOLS.LSP, all you need do is type in the name of the program.

Type: PON <Enter>

This is the only command you need. Wherever the distance was previously set, the distance will be turned on. Remember that your distance was probably 50' from your target.

Type: POFF <Enter>

This quickly turns perspective off. With these two commands, you have better control over when perspective is on or off.

Now quickly set your distance to 200':

Type: `DVIEW <Enter> <Enter>`

Type: `D <Enter>`

Type: `200' <Enter> <Enter>`

    Naturally, when you need to issue an AutoCAD command and perspective is on, you can always turn it off with the POFF command and then restore it with the PON command as needed. Although this is an acceptable method, it does require you to issue a REGEN of your drawing each time. There is a way you can have your cake and eat it too. That is, you can have perspective on and see what you are doing in perspective and at the same time pick in 3D.

    To do this, you'll have to have at least two viewports. You'll get an in-depth look at viewports later, but for now simply create two viewports:

Type: `VPORTS <Enter>`

Response: `Save/Restore/Join/SIngle/?/2/3/4:`

Type: `2 <Enter>`

Response: `Horizontal/Vertical:`

Type: `V <Enter>`

    Pick the viewport on the right and make it active. Although the viewport on the right is now active, both viewports have perspective on. Next, turn perspective off:

Type: `POFF <Enter>`

    You see the same view in both viewports, but the one on the left has perspective on and the one on the right has perspective off.

    Draw a couple of lines in your drawing on the right. Notice that you have no trouble picking points. Also notice that as you draw these lines, you can see them appear in the left viewport in perspective. This way, by splitting your screen in at least two viewports, you can keep perspective on in one of the viewports while working and manipulating objects in the other.

Erase the lines that you've just drawn and return to a single viewport:

Type: VPORTS <Enter>

Response: Save/Restore/Join/SIngle/?/2/3/4:

Type: SI <Enter>

Type: ZOOM <Enter>

Type: A <Enter>

Now that you're back in a single viewport, turn perspective back on:

Type: PON <Enter>

As you can see, perspective is a powerful visualization tool, but it does require understanding and control to use it properly and not let it get in the way.

Clipping

Sometimes it's difficult to get exactly where you want to be on your object because there are other parts of the model in the way. Or for one reason or another, you simply want to create a view where some of the objects are peeled back. AutoCAD gives you a command in DVIEW called CLIP. Using this command, you can create a view where you can peel back the front or the back of the model or both:

Type: DVIEW <Enter>

Response: Select Objects

Type: All <Enter> <Enter>

Response: CAmera/TArget/Distance/POints/PAn/Zoom/TWist/CLip/Hide/Off/Undo/<eXit>:

Type: CL <Enter>

(This stands for Clip.)

Response: `Back/Front/<Off>:`

(Think of clipping as peeling back.)

Type: `F <Enter>`

A slider bar appears at the top of the screen. As you move it left, all of the drawing appears. As you move it to the right, the front of your drawing begins to peel away and disappear. Figure 3-21 shows a front clipping view. This figure was created with perspective on and produced with hidden lines.

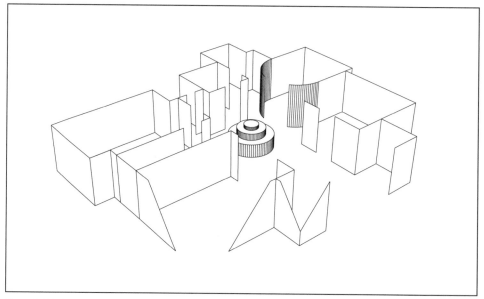

Figure 3-21: Front clipping

Turn the front clipping plane off and turn the back clipping plane on:

Type: `CL <Enter>`

Response: `Back/Front/<Off>:`

Type: `Off <Enter>`
`CL <Enter>`
`B <Enter>`

Response: `ON/OFF/<Distance from target>:`

You can clip from the back forward in the same manner all the way up to the fountain. Figure 3-22 shows a view of a back clipping. Remember, you also can clip both the back and the front simultaneously or turn one or the other off.

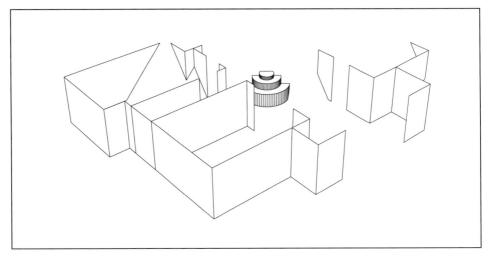

Figure 3-22: Back clipping view

Type: `CL <Enter>`

Type: `Off <Enter>`

Hiding Lines

As you know by now, hiding lines gives you a more realistic view of your model than working totally in wireframe. Without hiding, visualizing a complex model is difficult.

There are two primary places where you give AutoCAD the HIDE command. The first is the Command line, and the second is an option within DVIEW. Within DVIEW you can hide lines so that you can see where you are without having to exit.

There is one final thing to remember concerning hidden lines: objects on an off layer will continue to hide lines. If the objects are on a frozen layer, then they will not hide lines.

Moving On

In this chapter you saw how AutoCAD gives you some very dramatic and exciting tools for dynamically viewing your model from anywhere in 3D space. Just because the DVIEW command is available and gives you an intuitive way of moving about in your drawing, that doesn't mean it is the best or easiest way to create a view.

Beginning with Release 9, AutoCAD had another way of viewing your model: the VPOINT command. Although it's more difficult to understand and is not visual, it's a faster command to use. Chapter 4, "VPOINT: The Faster Alternative," will take the mystery out of the VPOINT command, as well as teach you how to use the icon dialog boxes provided by Release 13 to create set points of view in 3D. You also will learn some more 3D tools to help you set Isometric and other views instantly.

VPOINT: The Faster Alternative

In this chapter you'll learn the ins and outs of the VPOINT command so that you'll have a thorough understanding of it. As you know from the preceding chapter, DVIEW is not the only command you can use in AutoCAD to establish a view. There are several other ways that you can create views.

VPOINT is one of those commands. But it carries with it some problems. With Release 9, AutoCAD had its beginnings in 3D. In that release, the only way you could establish a 3D view was through the VPOINT command. If you've ever tried to use the VPOINT command without any instruction, you could go crazy trying to figure out where you'll be thrown in 3D space. And to make matters worse, if you looked up the command in the documentation, you would become even more confused than you were before.

Some people refer to this command as the bull's eye command because one of the options of VPOINT is an image that is made up of two concentric circles that resembles a bull's eye. To the left of the bull's eye are the three right-angle lines representing the coordinates. As you move the cursor around the bull's eye, the X, Y and Z move. But try to figure out where you are!

Some people who use this command without understanding it might find a few points that seem to get them where they want to go, and they use these points over and over. And there's nothing wrong with that. Or they might remember reading somewhere that if they type **1,–1,1** at the VPOINT prompt, they'll somehow get an Isometric view of their model. And they use that procedure from then on. But remarkably enough, very few people really understand what's going on with this command, much less how to use it.

Now Release 13 has corrected that problem with a new set of VPOINT tools (see Figure 4-1).

Figure 4-1: The View toolbar

The View toolbar is a new quick access viewing tool for your 3D models. It uses the VPOINT command preset to ten different views. They are: Top view, Bottom view, Left view, Right view, Front view, Back view, S. W. Isometric view, S. E. Isometric view, N. W. Isometric view and N. E. Isometric view.

The first icon of Figure 4-1 provides access to Named Views and the View Control dialog box. You may use this to access any named views you create.

You'll notice that Figure 4-2 explains the ratio numbers in order for you to use the VPOINT command at a glance without having to remember the top or bottom views or how the isometrics are set up.

This chapter is all about how to use the VPOINT command properly. The VPOINT command is probably the most under-used command in AutoCAD. Using this command can be one of the fastest ways to get to where you want to be and is the basis of most AutoLISP programs that help you with your views. I'll also show you some other AutoCAD features that will permit you to create any view you want quickly, without having to go through DVIEW.

Remember that VPOINT is not meant to take the place of DVIEW in its entirety. Unlike DVIEW, VPOINT does not give you the opportunity to set distance, twist, zoom, pan or create any perspective. VPOINT only establishes a target and camera angle; distance is not a consideration.

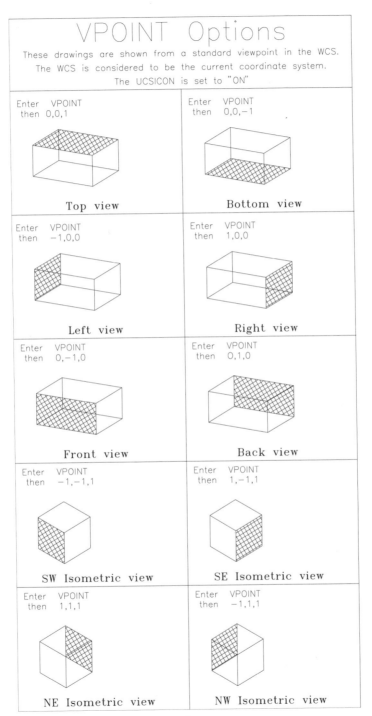

Figure 4-2: Using the **VPOINT** command

Setting Up Your Drawing

For this chapter's example, begin a new drawing with the following parameters:

UNITS	Decimal
Precision	2
LIMITS	0,0
Upper right	12,9
GRID	.5
SNAP	.5

After you make the settings:

Type: ZOOM <Enter>

Type: All <Enter>

One of the primary purposes of the exercises in this chapter is to create a number of view points relative to camera and target and to explore what happens each time a view point is changed. To do that, you need a model where there is no doubt as to which side you are on. Therefore, to accomplish this goal, you will draw a simple oblong cube. Begin by setting your thickness to 2:

Type: THICKNESS <Enter>

Response: New value for THICKNESS:

Type: 2 <Enter>

Figure 4-3: 3 x 2 rectangle

Draw a 3 by 2 rectangle, as indicated in Figure 4-3. The next step is to place a number outside of each side of the rectangle. Make the text height about .5 (see Figure 4-4).

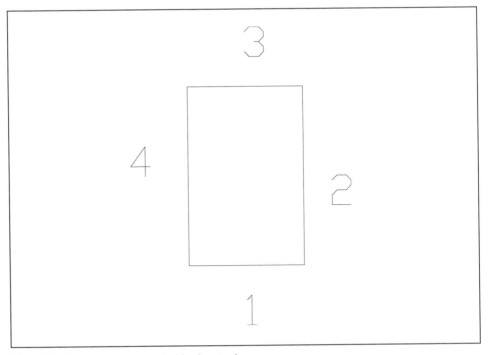

Figure 4-4: Placing numbers on each side of rectangle

To reduce confusion, also place a number against the side of each of the walls of the cube. To do that, first set the UCS icon to pop to the origin:

Type: `UCSICON <Enter>`

Type: `OR <Enter>`

Now move the origin:

Type: `UCS <Enter>`

Response: `Origin/ZAxis/3point/OBject/View/X/Y/Z/Prev/Restore/Save/Del/?/<World>:`

Type: `O <Enter>`

Response: `Origin point <0,0,0>:`

Using object snap intersection, pick Point 1, as shown in Figure 4-5. The UCS icon should now snap to that origin. You are going to use the RX and RY command to rotate the UCS as you go around the cube.

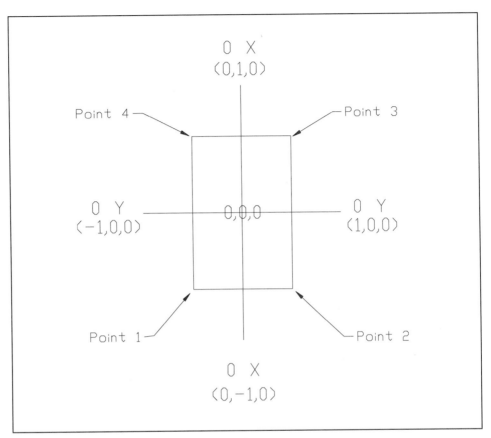

Figure 4-5: VPOINT coordinates

You can find the RX and RY programs in the AutoLISP section of the book. As with all 3D programs, make certain that they are properly loaded. If you have installed the *AutoCAD 3D Companion Disk* properly and loaded 3DTOOLS.LSP, all that you need to do is type in the name of the program.

Type: RX <Enter>

This rotates the UCS 90 degrees around X.

Type: PLAN <Enter> <Enter>

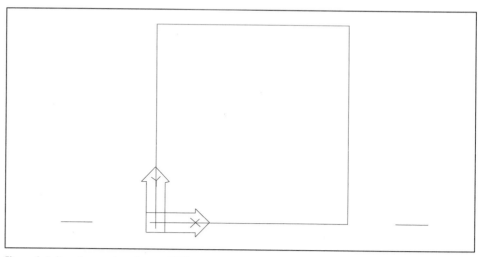

Figure 4-6: Changing to plan of rotated UCS

This places your plan to side 1 of the cube (see Figure 4-6). Using the TEXT or DTEXT command, put a "1" on this side of the cube (see Figure 4-7).

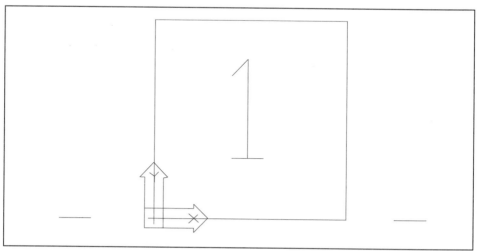

Figure 4-7: Placing a 1 on side 1

Now return to the original Plan view. You can change to Plan view without changing the UCS by typing **W** (for World) at the PLAN prompt:

Type: PLAN <Enter>

Type: W <Enter>

You may need to issue ZOOM All to center the number on the screen. Now move the origin to side 2:

Type: UCS <Enter>

Response: Origin/ZAxis/3point/OBject/View/X/Y/Z/Prev/Restore/Save/Del/?/<World>:

Type: O <Enter>

Response: Origin point <0,0,0>:

Using object snap intersection, pick Point 2, as indicated on Figure 4-5. Then rotate 90 degrees around Y:

Type: RY <Enter>

Go PLAN to this UCS (enter the PLAN command to move to a Plan view for this UCS):

Type: PLAN <Enter> <Enter>

Using DTEXT, place a "2" on this side, as shown in Figure 4-8.

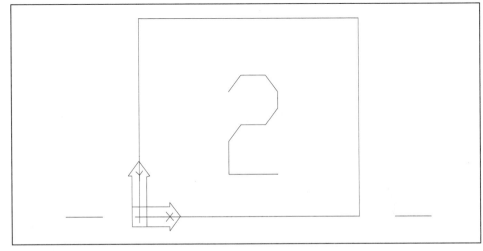

Figure 4-8: Placing a 2 on side 2

Now return to the original Plan view:

Type: PLAN <Enter>

Type: W <Enter>

You may need to issue ZOOM All to center the number on the screen. Now move the origin to side 3:

Type: UCS <Enter>

Response: Origin/ZAxis/3point/OBject/View/X/Y/Z/Prev/Restore/Save/Del/?/<World>:

Type: O <Enter>

Response: Origin point <0,0,0>:

Using object snap intersection, pick Point 3, as indicated on Figure 4-5. Then rotate 90 degrees around Y:

Type: RY <Enter>

Go PLAN to this UCS:

Type: PLAN <Enter> <Enter>

Using DTEXT, place a "3" on this side, as shown in Figure 4-9. Don't worry if it looks like you're writing over the mirror image of the "1." You're not.

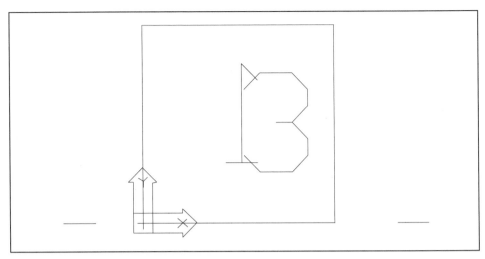

Figure 4-9: Placing a 3 on side 3

One more time, return to your original Plan view:

Type: PLAN <Enter>

Type: W <Enter>

You may need to issue ZOOM All to center the number on the screen. Now move the origin to side 4:

Type: UCS <Enter>

Response: Origin/ZAxis/3point/OBject/View/X/Y/Z/Prev/Restore/Save/Del/?/<World>:

Type: O <Enter>

Response: Origin point <0,0,0>:

Using object snap intersection, pick Point 4, as indicated on Figure 4-5. Then rotate 90 degrees around Y:

Type: RY <Enter>

Go PLAN to this UCS:

Type: PLAN <Enter> <Enter>

Using DTEXT, place a "4" on this side, as shown in Figure 4-10.

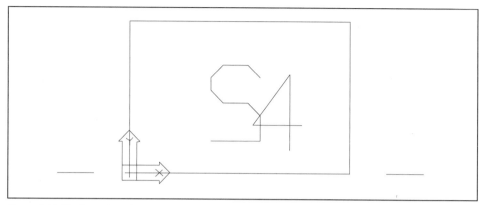

Figure 4-10: Placing a 4 on side 4

Type: PLAN <Enter>

Type: W <Enter>

Change back to the World Coordinate System:

Type: UCS <Enter> <Enter>

Now take a look at the drawing you've set up. From the UCS toolbar, choose the S. E. Isometric View icon, or:

Type: VPOINT <Enter>

Response: Rotate/<View point><0.00,0.00,1.00>:

Type: 1,−1,1 <Enter>

In Figure 4-11 you can plainly see all four numbers, so you can determine during the exercise in the following sections which side of the cube you're on.

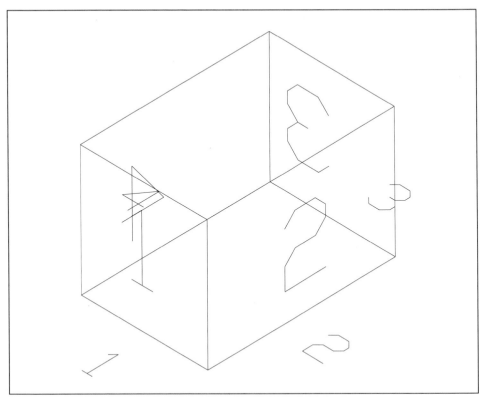

Figure 4-11: VPOINT 1,–1,1

The **VPOINT** Command

There are really three parts to the VPOINT command. The first part deals with ratios of X, Y and Z. The second tries to give you a visual cue as to where you're picking. And the third is a quick rotation angle similar to DVIEW. You'll learn more about these parts in the following sections.

Ratios

Remember that VPOINT does not deal with distance. All you're working with is the ratios of X, Y and Z to each other, meaning that the ratios of these three coordinates determine the angle of view. The size of the numbers is of no significance; for example, a 1,1,1 creates an equal X, Y and Z view point and gives you the exact same result as an 8,8,8 or even a 500,500,500. Each of these responses gives you exactly the same view because you're working with ratios, not the numbers themselves. And because distance is not even part of the equation, it makes no sense to necessarily talk in terms of size of the numbers.

Then what do these numbers mean? Well, I'll start with the most obvious, which is 0,0,1. Refer back to Figures 4-2 and 4-5, which shows that view—a Plan view. Keep Figure 4-5 handy; you will reference those four points as opposed to sides.

AutoCAD doesn't permit you to use 0,0,0, but that is where the camera always begins. Even though the number 1 is small, think of the smallest number that you use as a large enough movement to create a view that is a ZOOM All so that you can see the entire drawing. Also, no matter what side of the model the camera is on, it always looks toward the model. Therefore, the camera always begins at 0,0,0. If you move the camera 0,0,1, then you are moving it 0 units in the direction of X, 0 units in the direction of Y and 1 unit is the direction of Z. Thus, you're directly overhead, which is the definition of Plan view. Try it and see for yourself.

 Figure 4-12: The Top View icon

Choose the Top View icon from the View toolbar. Or in the command prompt window:

Type: `VPOINT <Enter>`

Response: `Rotate/<View point><0.00,0.00,1.00>:`

Type: `0,0,1 <Enter>`

This sequence leaves you in Plan view. What if you were to type **1,1,1**? Look at Figure 4-5 again. Begin the camera at 0,0,0 and move it 1 unit to the right, then move it 1 unit toward point 3, which is the Y direction, and finally raise it 1 unit in the air, which is the Z direction, and turn the camera around looking at the model. You should be out from point 3 in the air looking at the model.

Figure 4-13: The N. E. Isometric View icon

Choose the N. E. Isometric View icon from the View toolbar. Or in the command prompt window:

Type: `VPOINT <Enter>`

Response: `Rotate/<View point><0.00,0.00,1.00>:`

Type: `1,1,1 <Enter>`

Look at Figure 4-14 to see if you're right. I must point out one thing here: the positions that you use are absolute, not relative to where you are when you type the ratios. AutoCAD always creates these views relative to the World Coordinate System. This is why you see the brief message "Switching to the world coordinate system" before the prompt. This view is controlled by the system variable WORLDVIEW. If yours is not acting right, make sure that WORLDVIEW is set to 1. If it's set to 0, then it will not switch before the prompt and will be relative to the current UCS. Although this setting might be desirable, it will be very confusing for this exercise. AutoCAD comes with WORLDVIEW set to 1 out of the box.

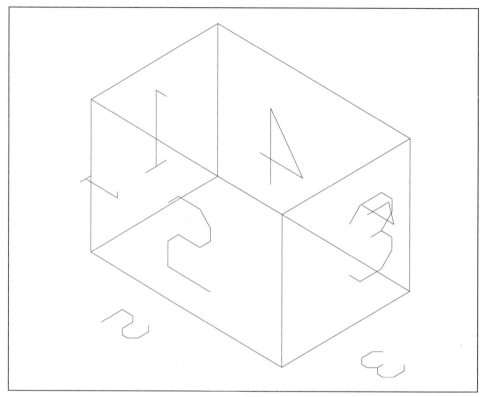

Figure 4-14: VPOINT 1,1,1

What happens if one of the numbers is negative? Where does –1,1,1 put you? In Figure 4-5 refer to position 0,0,0 again. First, move to the left 1 unit because the X direction is negative. Then move 1 unit toward Point 4 in the Y direction and 1 unit in the air, positive Z.

Figure 4-15: The N. W. Isometric View icon

Choose the N. W. Isometric View icon from the View toolbar. Or in the command prompt window:

Type: VPOINT <Enter>

Response: Rotate/<View point><0.00,0.00,1.00>:

Type: –1,1,1 <Enter>

Figure 4-16 illustrates where you're looking from Point 4. Side 3 is on your left, and side 4 is on the right.

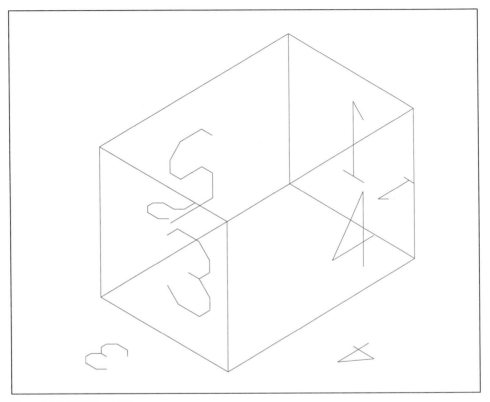

Figure 4-16: VPOINT −1,1,1

To move to Point 1, move 1 unit to the left (–1 X), 1 unit in the negative Y direction and 1 unit in the Z direction (–1,1,1).

 Figure 4-17: The S. W. Isometric View icon

Choose the S. W. Isometric View icon from the View toolbar. Or in the command prompt window:

Type: VPOINT <Enter>

Response: Rotate/<View point><0.00,0.00,1.00>:

Type: −1,−1,1 <Enter>

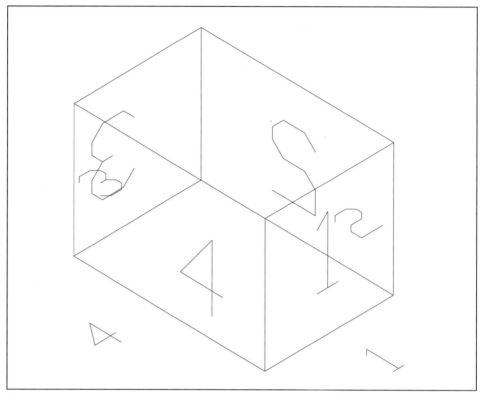

Figure 4-18: VPOINT −1,−1,1

See Figure 4-18. Why wouldn't this setting have worked as −1,0,1? That's a good question and is why there's much confusion. Look closer at Figure 4-5. Position 0,0,0 is at the intersection of the axes lines. Remember that the view point is always projected out so that you can see the entire model. Therefore, zero Y can be two places depending on the value of X. It can be at (1,0) and at (−1,0). Also, a zero X can be two places depending on the value of Y: (0,1) and (0,−1).

For example, if you create a −1,0,1 value, you would be looking from side 4 because starting at 0,0,0, −X takes you to the left, but Y does not move and then Z goes up in the air. Therefore, to get to an angle at Point 1, you use −1,−1,1. You start at 0,0,0 and move to the left −1, then down −1 and then in the Z direction +1.

Now see what it looks like to keep one of these coordinates at zero:

Type: VPOINT <Enter>

Response: Rotate/<View point><0.00,0.00,1.00>:

Type: 0,1,1 <Enter>

Figure 4-19 looks strange, doesn't it? That's because you haven't moved off X at all. In Figure 4-5, refer to coordinates 0,0,0 and follow the axis line straight up to 0,1,0 and then move 1 unit in the Z direction. You're now facing side 3, but from the air. The lines look strange because X is 0.

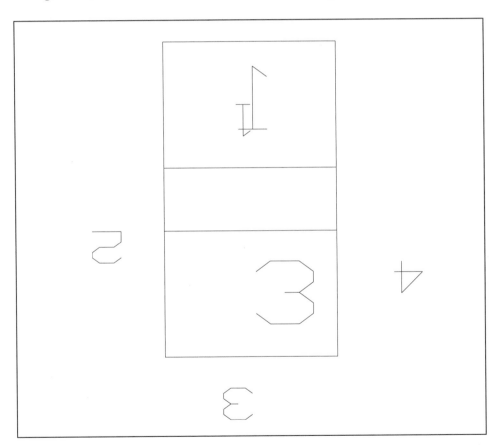

Figure 4-19: VPOINT 0,1,1

Now change X just a fraction to get some perspective of where you are:

Type: VPOINT <Enter>

Response: Rotate/<View point><0.00,0.00,1.00>:

Type: .1,1,1 <Enter>

In Figure 4-20, X is moved just a fraction to make the sides of the cube not line up exactly for easier viewing. What happens if the ratios are not equal? Notice that there is just enough movement in X to move the view of the cube a little off center in the X direction.

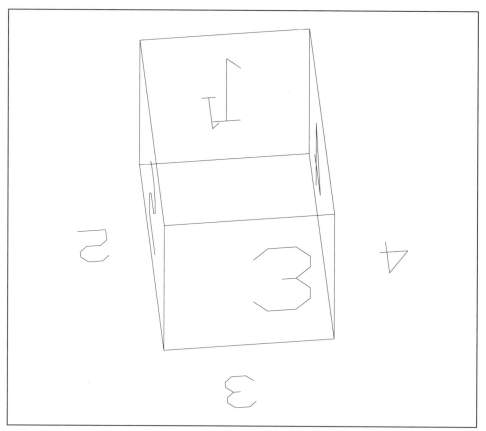

Figure 4-20: VPOINT .1,1,1

Now make more of a drastic move to Z:

Type: VPOINT <Enter>

Response: Rotate/<View point><0.00,0.00,1.00>:

Type: 1,-1,.5 <Enter>

Here instead of Z being equal in ratio to X and Y, you moved Z only half as much. Notice that in Figure 4-21 the elevation is not as steep.

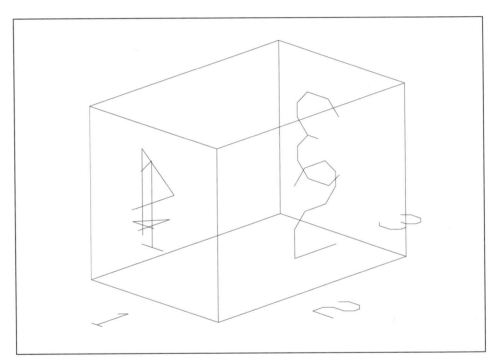

Figure 4-21: VPOINT 1,-1,.5

Now triple the elevation:

Type: VPOINT <Enter>

Response: Rotate/<View point><0.00,0.00,1.00>:

Type: 1,-1,3 <Enter>

See Figure 4-22. Don't confuse movement in elevation with distance. Z is simply a view point further away, relative to the movement of X and Y. There is no absolute distance.

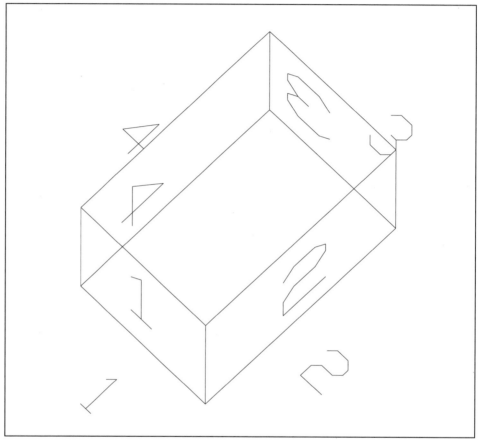

Figure 4-22: VPOINT 1,—1,3

Look at one final example. How do you become plan to only one side? Assume you want to look square to side 2. Look at Figure 4-5 again. You need to move 1 unit in the X direction and 0 units in the Y direction. You don't want to go above the model; therefore, Z would be zero.

Figure 4-23: The Right View icon

Choose the Right View icon from the View toolbar. Or in the command prompt window:

Type: VPOINT <Enter>

Response: Rotate/<View point><0.00,0.00,1.00>:

Type: 1,0,0 <Enter>

This will take you plan to side 2 (see Figure 4-24).

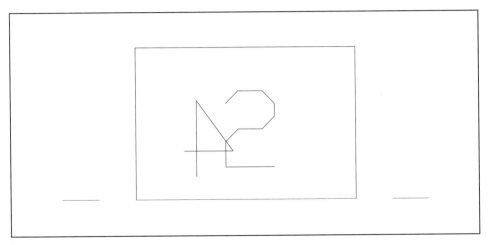

Figure 4-24: VPOINT 1,0,0

As you can see, once you get the hang of how these numbers work together, you can move around much faster with VPOINT than with DVIEW.

The Bull's Eye

The second part of the VPOINT command is often referred to as the bull's eye. Here's how you get there:

Type: VPOINT <Enter>

Response: Rotate/<View point><0.00,0.00,1.00>:

Type: <Enter>

This time instead of typing the three coordinates, press Enter and take the default, which is the <View point>. See Figure 4-25.

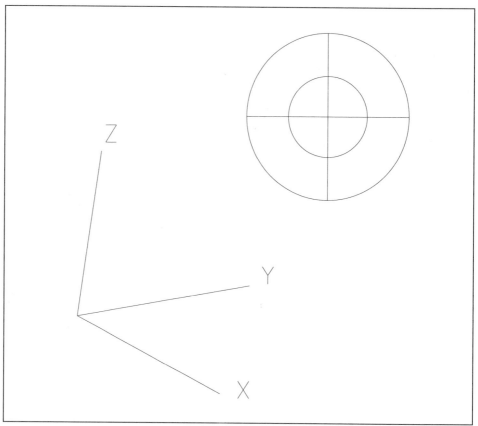

Figure 4-25: VPOINT bull's eye with X, Y, Z axes

What you see in Figure 4-25 are two concentric circles with the cross axes drawn through them. To the left is a representation of the X, Y and Z axes. These axes are meant to give you a clue as to where you will be when you pick a point. But that's very difficult to control. You're better off keeping your eye on the bull's eye.

AutoCAD uses the earth as a metaphor for the two concentric circles. Notice the crosshairs in the bull's eye. These are similar to the crosshairs used to illustrate Figure 4-5. The intersection of these crosshairs represents 0,0,1. These coordinates are similar to your Figure 4-5 except that Z is 1 unit in the air. On the earth this position would be the north pole. If you were to pick exactly at these crosshairs, that intersection would be the same as 0,0,1 or Plan view.

Begin on the intersection and move to the right along the X line. The farther you move to the right, the smaller is the value of Z until you reach the first concentric circle. This first circle from the center represents the equator or a Z value of zero. Continue along to the right until you get to the second circle, and the value of Z continues to decline into the negative. Once it reaches the outer circle, Z has a positive value again. If you continue outside the outer circle, the value declines again. Because you are moving across the line on the X axis, while you are decreasing the value of Z, you are simultaneously increasing the value of X.

In Figure 4-26, Point 1 is the equivalent of 0,0,5. Remember that these are ratios; the absolute numbers don't matter. As you move to the left and down, you may move 2 units to the left of center and 2 units down. Because you're moving toward the inner circle, the value of Z decreases. Therefore, Point 2 might be –2,–2,2. Z has come down from +5 to +2. Point 3 continues as this angle moves X and Y each to –4. Because this point is on the first circle, Z is now absolute zero. Continue at the same angle at Point 4, and X and Y continue to increase in the negative direction. As Z moves to the next circle, it decreases in value until it actually touches the outer circle where it has a positive value.

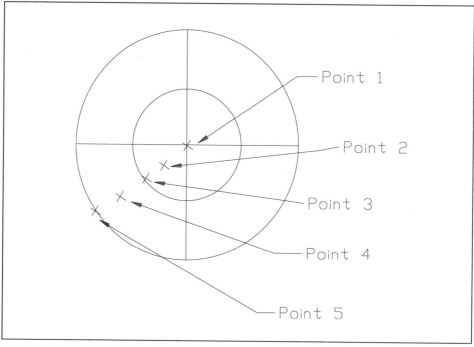

Figure 4-26: Points on the bull's eye

This exercise is meant to be visual, not academic. What it means to your view is that you pick a point along one of the quadrants and that is your XY viewing angle. How close you come to the inner or outer circle determines the Z angle. It's really that simple. If you try to pick a point that has a specific ratio, you'll go crazy. The bull's eye was never meant for that. That's why you can type in the X, Y and Z ratios. The bull's eye is a quick graphic representation of your angle of view.

VPOINT Rotate

Now take a look at the last of the three options available with VPOINT. Rotate is actually the easiest to use because it's the closest to the DVIEW option, even though it's not dynamic.

Type: VPOINT <Enter>

Response: Rotate/<View point><0.00,0.00,1.00>:

Type: R <Enter>

(This stands for Rotate.)

Response: Enter angle in XY plane from X axis:

Here, AutoCAD prompts you for the number of degrees the camera is to rotate around the model.

Response: –130 <Enter>

Response: Enter angle from XY plane:

Now AutoCAD prompts you for the number of degrees of camera elevation.

Type: 30 <Enter>

Notice this procedure is similar to DVIEW camera except that it's not dynamic and the order of the questions is reversed. AutoCAD asks for the rotation around the object first and then the elevation of the camera.

VPOINT Presets...

Now that you have a basic idea of how the VPOINT command works, take a look at one of the easier aspects of VPOINT in AutoCAD: the Presets... dialog box. Go to the View pull-down menu and pick 3D Viewpoint then Rotate…

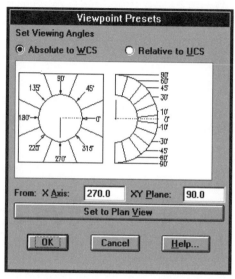

Figure 4-27: The Viewpoint Presets dialog box

The Viewpoint Presets dialog box shown in Figure 4-27 not only permits you to pick the proper view points, but also shows you what your current view point is set to. Notice the line in the center; this line in the figure is pointing toward 225 on the left and 30 degrees on the right. This setting indicates that your camera is currently at an elevation of 30 degrees and in a horizontal rotation of 225 degrees.

The Viewpoint Presets is the same as the VPOINT Rotate option. In the "from X axis and XY plane" text box, you can type in any degrees you want. But if you need to type degrees, it would be easier to type **VPOINT R** and type them in there. The real usefulness of this dialog box is getting a quick view, not necessarily an absolutely accurate view of your model.

To try this procedure, first pick at approximately 315. Notice how the line points to the 315 box. Then pick 45 degrees in the camera elevation. The line on the right points to 45 degrees. Then pick OK. That's all there is to it.

System Variables

There are a number of system variables that either maintain the value of the view point or are in some way related to creating your angle of view. You need to be aware of these variables.

TARGET   A read-only system variable that represents the coordinates of the target point. This point is either preset by AutoCAD as the center of your object if you haven't set it or you set it using the POints option of DVIEW.

LENSLENGTH   A read-only system variable that maintains the zoom lens length that is set in the Zoom option of DVIEW. Remember that you can set the lens length only if distance is on. If, for example, the number in LENSLENGTH is 50, then it represents the metaphor of a 50mm lens on a 35mm camera.

UCSFOLLOW   A system variable that can be either 0 or 1. If UCSFOLLOW is set to 0, then AutoCAD will act as it has during these exercises. On the other hand, you have the option of setting it to 1. When it's set to 1, any time you change the UCS, AutoCAD automatically changes your angle of view to plan of that current UCS. This can be helpful as a temporary setting if you want to move around the object in a manner similar to the way you did when you were putting the numbers on each side of the cube. Otherwise, it can be disconcerting if you aren't aware of what is happening and UCSFOLLOW has been inadvertently set to 1.

VIEWDIR   A read-only system variable that maintains the coordinates of VPOINT. You can test this variable by typing VPOINT 1,–1,1 and then checking the VIEWDIR system variable. You will see that it contains the coordinates 1,–1,1.

WORLDVIEW   A system variable that is set by AutoCAD out of the box to 1. This means that whenever VPOINT is active or you go into DVIEW, you automatically are switched to the World Coordinate System. This way, you can maintain some degree of consistency with your coordinates and angles. If, on the other hand, WORLDVIEW were set to 0, then switching to the World Coordinate System would not take place, and the angles of DVIEW and coordinates of VPOINT would be relative to the current User Coordinate System.

Other Viewing Tools

Before leaving this chapter, take a look at seven AutoLISP programs that will help you move quickly around your model. They are

- BSVIEW

- RVIEW

- LVIEW

- FVIEW

- BVIEW

- VPD

- ISO

The first five programs are similar to the ones found in Chapter 2, "The User Coordinate System." Remember that RSIDE moved your UCS to the right side of the model by 90 degrees. You first had to establish a base; then all of the sides were available to you. These programs work the same way.

Start with a top view. Then type **BSVIEW** to establish a view called BASEVIEW. Then you can move your view around your model with RVIEW (right view), LVIEW (left view), FVIEW (front view, which returns you to your base view) and BVIEW (back view).

One of the best parts about VPOINT is the Rotate option because it lets you get right to the place you want to be without issuing an extra REGEN that DVIEW requires. Wouldn't it be nice if you combined the VPOINT Rotate option with one additional prompt concerning distance? The VPD program asks you the angle of rotation and the angle of elevation just like the VPOINT Rotate option; then it asks you for the distance. If you want the angles to remain the same and all you want to do is set the distance, it can do that too. Just press Enter through either or both of the angle of rotation questions, and it will leave that part alone; then you can just set the distance.

The final program is one that will set you to an isometric view. It's just a real quick way to issue VPOINT 1,–1,1. All you have to do is type **ISO** and press Enter.

You can find these programs in the AutoLISP section of the book. As with all 3D programs, make certain that they are properly loaded. If you have the *AutoCAD 3D Companion Disk* installed properly and have loaded 3DTOOLS.LSP, all that you need to do is type in the name of the program.

Assume that the view that you are looking at now should be the Base view:

Type: BSVIEW <Enter>

The Base view has been established, and you can now move around your model by typing each of the other program names.

Now try the VPD program:

Type: VPD <Enter>

Response: Angle of rotation:

Type: 45 <Enter>

Response: Angle of elevation:

Type: 30 <Enter>

Response: Distance: <Enter>

Type: 20 <Enter>

Finally, try the simplest one of them all, ISO:

Type: ISO <Enter>

That's all there is to it. This program takes you directly to an Isometric view.

Moving On

As you learned in this chapter, VPOINT and its various options can be extremely fast and convenient. Unfortunately, it has been a very under-used command. Hopefully, this chapter has taken the mystery out of this command.

Before leaving this chapter, I want to recap why you should use VPOINT at times in lieu of DVIEW and when it can't take the place of DVIEW. For DVIEW to be effective, you must select objects. On a large model selecting objects requires time to create the selection set and confirm the objects by pressing Enter; then there is the first REGEN as you enter the DVIEW command and the objects are displayed. AutoCAD requires one additional REGEN when you exit DVIEW. This can be time consuming. As long as you don't need some of the features of DVIEW and can work without seeing the object itself to create the view, using VPOINT in any of its modes is much faster. VPOINT is not useful for zooming, panning, clipping or setting perspective—although the VPD program can help you greatly with that one.

In Chapter 5, "Establishing Coordinates," you will consolidate some of the information that you've learned so far to clear up any confusion you might have on coordinates in 3D space and how you determine and pick them. You'll learn the relationships of the UCS with extrusions, object snaps, filters and elevation settings. Chapter 5 can help bring much of what you've learned so far into focus.

Establishing Coordinates

This chapter will bring into focus the numerous ways the Z coordinate is affected and the order of priorities that affect how coordinates are entered. One of the things that can be most confusing is how coordinates come to be in spite of the User Coordinate System rather than because of it. Many concepts have been introduced in the previous four chapters. And although some of you may have a good handle on what has been presented thus far, others may be a little fuzzy understanding the concept of coordinates and how they relate in 3D. That's because the User Coordinate System is not the end-all of how the Z coordinate is supplied. The end purpose, therefore, of this chapter is to consolidate concepts.

Setting Up Your Drawing

Begin a new drawing with the following parameters:

UNITS	Decimal
Precision	2
LIMITS	0,0
Upper right	12,9
GRID	.5
SNAP	.5

After you make the settings:

Type: ZOOM <Enter>

Type: All <Enter>

Begin drawing by setting elevation to 0 and thickness to 4:

Type: ELEV <Enter>

Response: New current elevation <0.00>:

Type: <Enter>

Response: New current thickness <0.00>:

Type: 4 <Enter>

Now draw a 5-by-5 unit square as indicated in Figure 5-1.

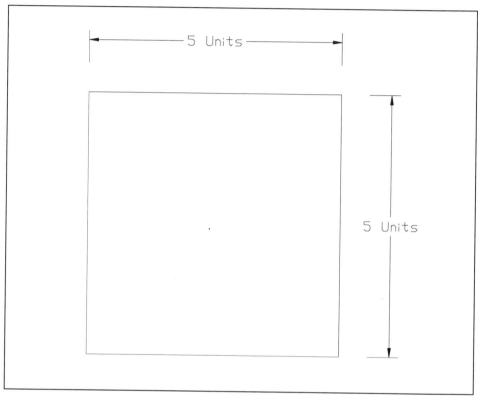

Figure 5-1: 5 unit square (elevation 0, thickness 4)

Now change the elevation and thickness as follows:

Type: ELEV <Enter>

Response: New current elevation <0.00>:

Type: 4 <Enter>

Response: New current thickness <4.00>:

Type: 2 <Enter>

Now, as indicated in Figure 5-2, draw a 3-by-3 unit square inside the first square.

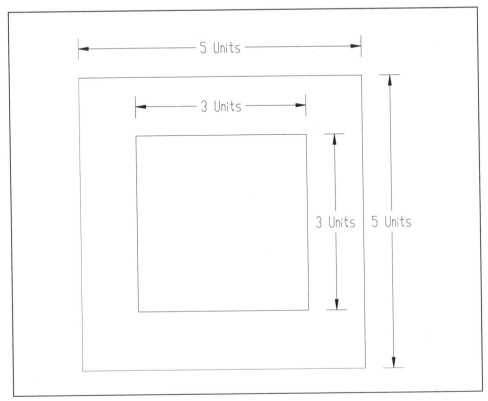

Figure 5-2: 3 unit square (elevation 4, thickness 2)

Change your elevation and thickness one last time, as follows:

Type: `ELEV <Enter>`

Response: `New current elevation <4.00>:`

Type: `6 <Enter>`

Response: `New current thickness <2.00>:`

Type: `1 <Enter>`

Now draw a 2-by-2 unit square as indicated in Figure 5-3.

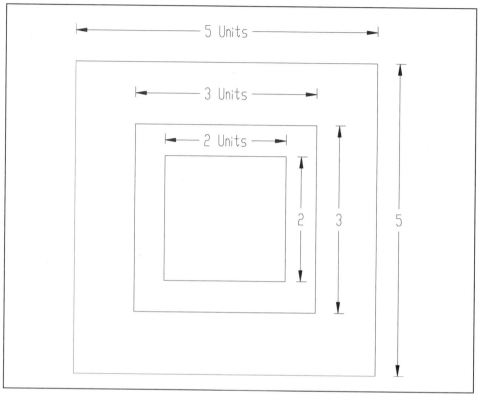

Figure 5-3: 2 unit square (elevation 6, thickness 1)

Turn off your snap, grid and ortho. Depending on your computer, you might use function keys F7, F8 and F9. Now see what you've created. Begin by setting your view point as 1,–1,1.

 Figure 5-4: The S. E. Isometric View icon from the View toolbar

From the View toolbar choose the S. E. Isometric View icon. Or in the command prompt window:

Type: VPOINT <Enter>

Response: Rotate/<View point><0.00,0.00,1.00>:

Type: 1,–1,1 <Enter>

Figure 5-5 shows an Isometric view of the finished drawing.

Figure 5-5: Isometric view of finished drawing

So that you can see exactly how these cubes fit on top of each other, turn the view point into a Plan view of a side.

 Figure 5-6: The Front View icon from the View toolbar

From the View toolbar choose the Front View icon. Or in the command prompt window:

Type: VPOINT <Enter>

Response: `Rotate/<View point>:`

Type: `0,-1,0 <Enter>`

For a Plan view of one side, see Figure 5-7. Notice how neatly the cubes stack.

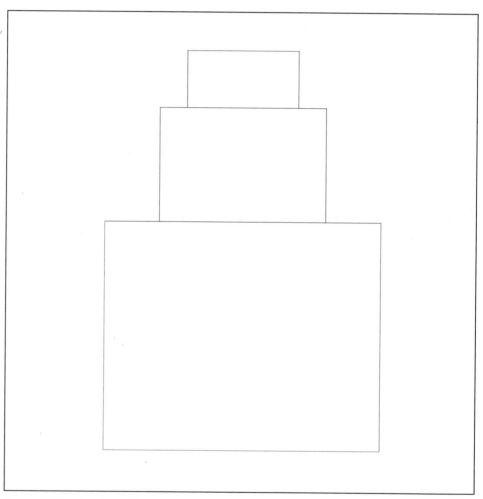

Figure 5-7: Plan view of one side

Extrusion & Elevation

As I mentioned in Chapter 1, "3D Preview," the biggest problem that developers of 3D programs have is attempting to express all three of the coordinates with the limitations of the 2D devices available, such as the digitizer and the screen. Developers have created all kinds of innovative techniques trying to overcome this problem. And in setting up your drawing for this exercise, you've used two of those techniques: elevation and extrusion.

But now, first begin by analyzing what is meant by the X, Y and Z coordinates and where those coordinates are in any coordinate system. Figure 5-8 illustrates a simple 2D Coordinate System.

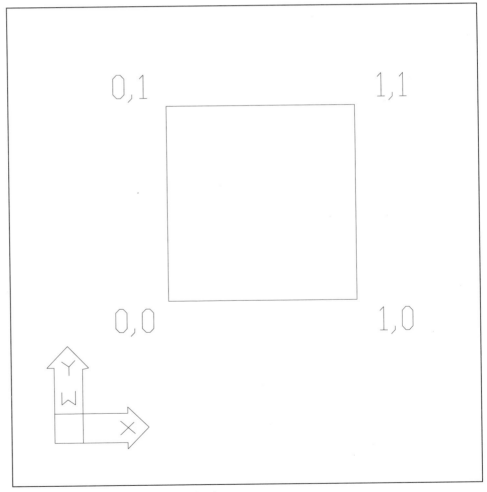

Figure 5-8: 2D Coordinate System using a 1 unit square

2D Versus 3D Coordinates

In a simple 2D world you see the coordinates as they exist in Figure 5-8. Assume that the lower left-hand corner of this 1 unit square is 0,0 (X,Y); then move straight up the screen in the Y direction. The next coordinate is 0,1. This movement is self-explanatory to anyone with experience with AutoCAD in 2D drafting.

Yet where is Z? Remember, the simple 1 unit square was drawn also with a 1 unit extrusion. So turn it into a VPOINT of –1.25,1,1, as you learned in Chapter 4. Now keep your eye both on the UCS icon in Figure 5-8, which is 2D, and the 3D Coordinate System in Figure 5-9.

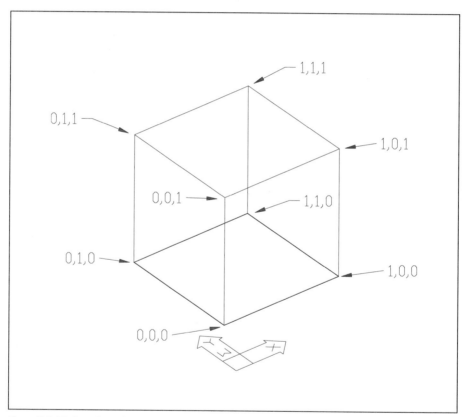

Figure 5-9: 3D Coordinate System

In Figure 5-9 the Z coordinates are added. (Look at the base of the square as it existed before. The base has been drawn a little darker so that you can see it better.) The only thing different with the coordinates is that an extra zero is added. That's because the original coordinates had a Z value of zero. Look at each of the four corners above your original square.

The XY coordinates of these points are exactly the same as the ones below them, but they now have 1 as their Z value.

In a simple world you would have no problem working with this coordinate system. If you think absolutely in terms of 3D coordinates, developing CAD systems for 3D would be relatively simple, and you wouldn't need the vast array of tools developed by Autodesk.

In the final analysis, what you see here is the way the computer must think and eventually translate whatever coordinates you use into those that are absolute. The tools and techniques Autodesk created are specifically for the purpose of aiding human beings and creating an interface that would be easier to work with.

2D to 3D Database of Objects

Now go back to the model that you constructed earlier. You began your initial lines with an elevation of zero and a thickness of 4 units. When you're in any coordinate system (and now you'll concentrate only on the World Coordinate System), setting the elevation is a primary technique for the inclusion of the Z coordinate. As you began, the elevation was set to zero, and for each point that you picked, AutoCAD automatically included a zero value for Z. I must emphasize here that even though you might be drawing exclusively in 2D and elevation is set at zero, AutoCAD at all times includes that zero as the Z coordinate for every object. Thus, even in 2D, AutoCAD constructs a 3D database of objects.

In the second rectangle you drew, you changed your elevation to 4 units and thickness to 2 units. In essence you're using these rectangles to draw something similar to the fountain that you drew in Chapter 3, "Dynamic Views." But here you won't confuse the issue with curved lines.

Even though you were in Plan view and it clearly seemed that you were drawing the second rectangle inside the first, you set the elevation of the second to 4 units. This elevation was the same as the extrusion of the first. It will suffice to say that for every point you picked for your second rectangle, AutoCAD automatically placed in the Z coordinate the value of 4. Therefore, your only concern was to pick the XY points as usual.

Finally, look at the third rectangle. Here you set the elevation to 6 and the thickness to 1. Thickness and extrusion are taken up together and AutoCAD has included thickness as a second option in the ELEV command because there is a direct relationship between the two, as you can plainly see.

In the first and second rectangle, the extrusion determined the height of the lines. That is, as you drew the first lines, the height of the lines was 4 units. You set the height of the second rectangle's lines to 2 units. Because the second rectangle began at the height of the first and then added 2 units of height, you set the elevation of the third at 6 units, which is the sum of the first two heights, and thus the third rectangle sits squarely on top of the second. This rectangle has its own extrusion of 1. This concept of tiering and setting elevation equal to the extrusion of another object is common in AutoCAD.

The Entity or Object Database

Now back up a second. Where are the actual coordinates of the lines? You might think that this exercise is relatively self-explanatory and that you've used these same concepts in the previous four chapters, and you would be correct. But there are some nuances that need further explanation. This has to do with the objects themselves. Whenever you're dealing with an extrusion, the object itself doesn't actually have the coordinate of the top of the extruded line. The actual coordinate of the extruded line is the base of the extrusion or the line at the lower elevation.

If you'll recall, the object database maintains the User Coordinate System in effect at the time the object was created; it is called the Object Coordinate System. The line has information concerning only the X, Y and Z coordinates of the beginning and ending point of any line. In another associative field of the object database is stored the information concerning the extrusion. From this information AutoCAD can construct the line and the extrusion. But AutoCAD can't find the actual coordinates of the top of the extrusion.

In summary, the elevation command (ELEV) creates a default elevation used by AutoCAD any time an object is created in order to supply the Z value. This elevation is always relative to the current UCS in effect at the time. An extrusion always extrudes in the direction of positive Z relative to the User Coordinate System. If you want to set the extrusion to extrude in a negative direction, enter a negative number at the thickness prompt.

After the fact, you can change thickness with the CHPROP command or the CHANGE command. You can only change elevation using the CHANGE command, and the object must be parallel to the current UCS at that time. Otherwise, you can't change the object. In fact, that's why CHPROP was invented. Because CHPROP doesn't include elevation as an option, you can perform the other property changes without the object being parallel to the current User Coordinate System.

As an alternative to using the CHANGE elevation option, you can always issue the MOVE command to move the object anywhere in 3D space.

Object Snap

If you don't remember anything else in this chapter, remember this: *the coordinates provided by an object snap will override any other coordinate development system in AutoCAD.*

What I mean by this statement is simple: Regardless of your elevation or UCS, when you lock onto an object with an object snap intersection, for example, the X, Y and Z coordinates of that intersection are fully known by AutoCAD. And because, by definition, when you use object snap, you're snapping to those exact coordinates, then AutoCAD chooses all three of the coordinates.

This means that if you have objects in 3D space sufficient to secure the coordinates at any time, you don't have to change the User Coordinate System. While drawing, make certain that you're object snapping to every point that you pick.

Assume, for example, that you want to draw a line from Point 1 to Point 2, as illustrated in Figure 5-10. You don't have to concern yourself by setting a UCS across another plane that would define that line. In fact, that line may have its endpoints on two different planes, thus forming its own plane. All you have to do is to set your object snap to intersection and pick the point while in the LINE command, and the line will be drawn perfectly.

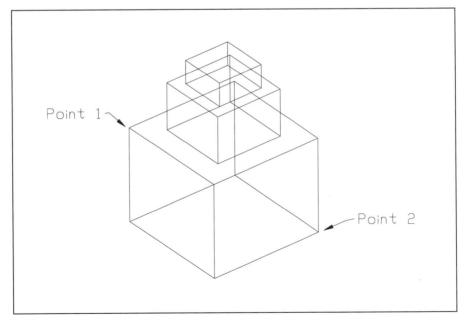

Figure 5-10: Drawing a diagonal line from Point 1 to Point 2

See Figure 5-11 for a view of a diagonal line drawn by object snap intersection.

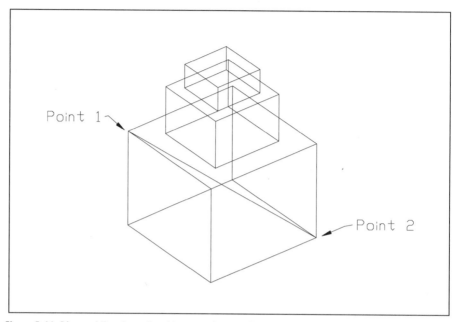

Figure 5-11: Diagonal line drawn by object snap intersection

Tips for Using Object Snap

When using object snap, there are several caveats that you have to watch out for, as outlined in the following list. Object snap doesn't always work as perfectly as you might imagine.

1. Watch out for object snap nearest. As you're aware, viewing and picking in 3D freehand can be a tricky matter. Just be careful; you don't always get the coordinate that you think you're getting by a simple object snap of nearest. You think an object is nearest to you, but Auto-CAD may have other ideas.

2. Make certain that the aperture box is small enough or that you're zoomed in close enough to pick only one intersection. The algorithm in AutoCAD will choose the closest intersection to your crosshairs if there is more than one from which to choose. What AutoCAD knows is closest and what you think is the closest may not be the same intersection.

3. You must understand the definition of an intersection: It's the point where two or more objects have exactly the same coordinates. Apparent intersections are not necessarily intersections. Look at Figure 5-12 for a view of apparent intersections. In the figure, it looks as though there are numerous intersections to the diagonal line at Points 1, 2, 3 and 4, but these lines don't intersect.

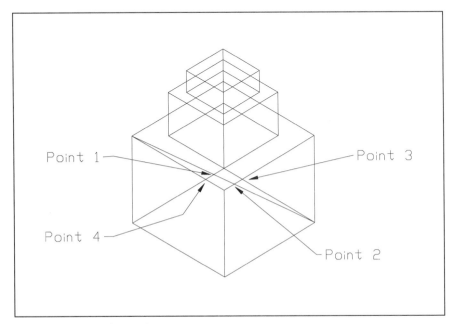

Figure 5-12: Apparent intersections

It's entirely possible from a given angle of view for it to appear that two lines truly do intersect when in reality they are far apart. Thus, an object snap intersection will not snap onto the apparent intersection that is created only from your angle of view. The apparent intersection will be as long as all objects are true lines, not extrusions.

4. What about extrusions? Can you object snap onto the intersections formed by the extrusion—meaning can you snap onto the intersection of 1,1,1 in Figure 5-9? Remember, you learned earlier in this chapter that AutoCAD doesn't actually save this coordinate as part of the database. Beginning with Release 10, the answer is yes. When AutoCAD came out with its first 3D package as Release 9, the answer was no. With Release 10 and all later versions, you can object snap onto these extruded parts. Again, beware of object snap nearest.

XYZ Filters

With AutoCAD Release 9 there was no User Coordinate System. To draw in 3D, you had to use extrusion, elevation, absolute coordinates and filters. In this section you'll learn about filters and how you use them to draw in 3D in AutoCAD's current release. *Caution:* Do not confuse XYZ filters with the Release 13 Filter command which finds objects by color or linetype.

XYZ filters are a simple concept. Because the mouse is capable of returning only two of the three coordinates in the UCS, it doesn't make any difference to AutoCAD which two of the three coordinates the mouse sends. Therefore, you only have to tell AutoCAD that you're going to pick two of the three coordinates and then type in the third coordinate from the keyboard. You activate an XYZ filter by placing a period (.) before the letter representing the one or two coordinates you want the mouse to pick. The remaining coordinates you type in. Alternatively, use the XYZ filters from the standard toolbar.

Figure 5-13: The XYZ filters from the standard toolbar

If you want to pick the XY coordinates and type in the Z coordinate, for example, then you type **.XY** before you pick. AutoCAD responds with "of." Then you pick the point, and AutoCAD responds with "needs Z." Finally, you type in the value of Z. The point that you've picked now has the three coordinates.

You're not restricted to using simply .XY. You can filter .XZ and type in the Y coordinate. Any combination of X, Y and Z is a valid filter: .XY, .XZ,

.YZ. In addition, you can use a single filter. You can type **.X**, for instance, then pick a point and AutoCAD will ask you for the YZ.

Why would you want use an XYZ filter now that you have the UCS available to you? The answer to that is simple. AutoCAD provides you with a variety of tools for any given circumstance. You may find it easier to use one tool over another. As long as using the XYZ filter options is not your primary way of entering points, XYZ filters make useful tools.

Using XYZ Filters as Tools

Look at a simple XYZ filter variation. Figure 5-14 shows a view of a second point 3 units in Z. Assuming that the elevation is set at zero, drawing on the established plane will maintain the zero value relative to the User Coordinate System. Say you want to draw a line that begins 3 units in the direction of Z. Pick your first point without a filter. But for the second point of the line, use the .XY filter and pick the point on the zero elevation. Then type **3** as the Z value. These filters give you one more method to move around in 3D space without changing the UCS.

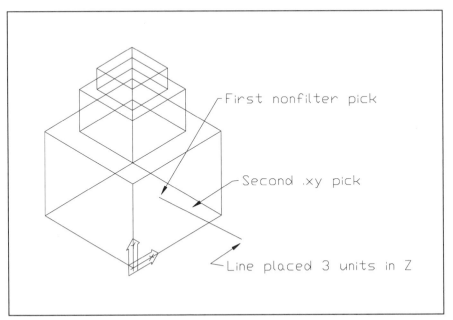

Figure 5-14: Second point 3 units in Z

In this situation an XYZ filter is the best tool for the job. Remember in Chapter 3 you changed the points of your camera and target. Having to create a plane that is at an angle created by a camera with an elevation of 9' and a target point of 7' is tedious indeed. When you're in a command that requires you to pick two or more points with different Z values is an ideal situation for using filters.

Here's a trick you can perform using XYZ filters in a 2D environment. If you need to find the exact center of a rectangle, for example, here's the traditional way to do it. Draw two construction lines from the midpoints of each side. Where they intersect is the center of the rectangle. Draw whatever you needed to draw at this center point and then erase the construction lines.

Now here's a better way of finding the center using XYZ filters. Your problem is that you want to draw a circle whose center point is in the center of the rectangle. Begin with a rectangle as indicated in Figure 5-15. Now start the CIRCLE command.

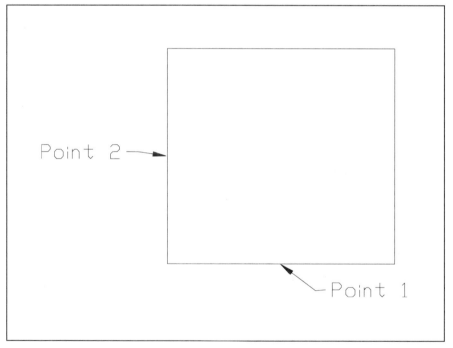

Figure 5-15: Beginning with a simple rectangle

Type: CIRCLE <Enter>

Response: 3P/2P/TTR/<Center point>:

Figure 5-16: The .X filter from the XYZ Filter flyout of the Standard toolbar

From the XYZ Filter flyout of the Standard toolbar choose the .X filter. Or in the command prompt window:

Type: .X <Enter>

Response: of

Using object snap midpoint, pick the midpoint of the bottom line at Point 1 (as shown in Figure 5-15).

Response: (need YZ):

Using object snap midpoint, pick the midpoint of either side of the rectangle at approximately Point 2 (as shown in the Figure 5-15). As you can see, AutoCAD finds the center of the rectangle. See Figure 5-17 for a view of the circle in the center of the rectangle.

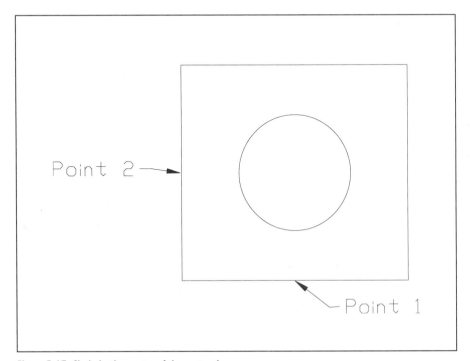

Figure 5-17: Circle in the center of the rectangle

The XYZ filter option sometimes provides not only a convenient mechanism for supplying the Z value, it is many times the only way. When you use it at the appropriate time, it can be a powerful tool.

UCS: The Coordinate Translator

If you could visualize your entire model by absolute coordinates, you wouldn't need all the tools discussed in the previous sections. Regardless of how you think of your model, the computer must eventually translate all points as absolute coordinates. As such, you can use the UCS as a coordinate translator. When you pick a point relative to the current coordinate system—such as 1,0,1, for example—in the World Coordinate System it may be a completely different coordinate point.

Now go back to the original drawing. Change your view point to 1,–1,1 and set the UCS icon to Origin.

See how the coordinates are affected.

Figure 5-18: The Origin UCS icon from the UCS toolbar

From the UCS toolbar choose the Origin UCS icon. Or in the command prompt window:

Type: UCS <Enter>

Response: Origin/ZAxis/3point/OBject/View/X/Y/Z/Prev/Restore/Save/Del/?/<World>:

Type: O <Enter>

Response: Origin point <0,0,0>:

Using your object snap intersection, pick Point 1, as shown in Figure 5-19.

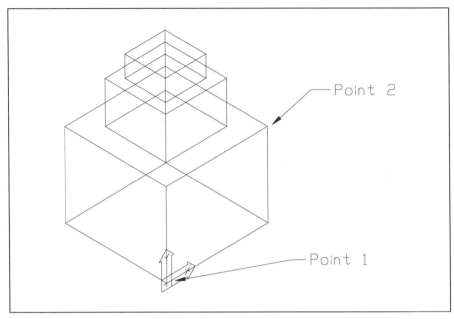

Figure 5-19: Setting UCS Origin and ID point

Now ID another point:

Type: ID <Enter>

Using your object snap intersection, pick Point 2, as shown in Figure 5-19, and write down this coordinate. Now change to the World Coordinate System:

Type: UCS <Enter> <Enter>

Type: ID <Enter>

Again using your object snap intersection, pick Point 2 of Figure 5-19 and write down the coordinates. Compare the two. Of course, they're different. AutoCAD translated the same coordinate relative to the two different coordinate systems.

This method has a practical 2D application as well. Civil engineers often need to enter points as coordinates based upon one origin and list those points by coordinates relative to another origin. The UCS, thus, is tailor-made for this kind of operation. By using UCS Origin, you can establish two origins. Points you enter under one UCS can later be listed relative to another UCS; point coordinates will be translated automatically.

Moving On

This chapter taught you how you handle coordinates using the various options and tools afforded you by AutoCAD. The purpose of these tools is to make the interface between you and the computer intuitive and easy to understand and work with.

One of the benefits a CAD system has over manual drafting is accuracy. Just as in 2D drafting, you should never eyeball anything. You should always be as accurate as possible using object snap, relative polar coordinates, and relative and absolute coordinates.

If these rules are necessary in 2D drafting, then they are ten times as important in 3D. Eyeballing objects in 3D space is an unforgivable no-no. Although you might get by with it from time to time in 2D, eyeballing is downright sinful in 3D. The absolute coordinates of objects in 3D and where they appear can be skewed dramatically by your viewing angle. What you think you're picking when you eyeball it on the screen is a complex combination of all features that are set at any time, UCS, elevation, etc. Therefore, it's imperative that you attempt to draw as accurately as possible while working in 3D, using the entire arsenal at your disposal.

Even when you do the very best you can, trying to be as accurate as possible, you'll make mistakes. From your viewing angle, these mistakes won't always be apparent. Therefore, AutoCAD gives you another viewing tool, viewports, which you'll learn about in the next chapter.

In Chapter 6, "Viewports," you will learn how to use viewports, not only for presentation, but also for error checking. You'll also learn how to move around in your drawing without a single regeneration caused by DVIEW and VPOINT. Viewports make working in 3D effortless and enable you to get the job done fast. As you draw you'll see the drawing come to life from each angle at once.

Viewports

This chapter will take the confusion out of viewports. Two main aspects of viewports will be reviewed; first, the mechanics of viewports—how they are are created and subdivided, how to move from one to the other, and how to save and restore their configurations as well as regenerations and redraws; second, how to develop and compose a drawing using the versatility of viewports.

A unique aspect of AutoCAD is that you can define a plane independently of the viewing angle. This means that the *angle of view* and the *defined plane* don't have to be the same, which gives rise to some interesting possibilities. What if you could view your model dynamically from virtually an unlimited number of points of view, and as you drew you could see your model created for you visually on the screen.

That's exactly what AutoCAD viewports do. They let you see your model created for you visually on the screen, all from multiple viewing angles.

Why Use Viewports?

There are three main reasons to use viewports, as follow:

- *Error Checking.* No matter how good you are at drafting or how careful, mistakes occur. Many times these mistakes aren't obvious at first. Depending on your angle of view, the mistake may not be apparent. By having multiple views of the model available at the same time, identifying and correcting mistakes is much easier. Some mistakes aren't always the result of drafting—sometimes they are in the design. By being able to see and measure from different angles of view, you can readily catch mistakes of design.

- *Modeling.* You have a viewing choice in AutoCAD. You either can go around the model, or you can have different angles of the model stationary on the screen in multiple viewports. Moving around the model with the VPOINT or DVIEW command can be time-consuming. If you need to work on one side of the model or the other, then it's much easier to have each side visible in a separate viewport and toggle to that viewport to work on the side in question. This way, there aren't any regens, and you can even begin a command in one viewport and continue that same command in another, thus going from the back of the model to the front.

- *Presentation.* You don't necessarily want to present only one view of the model. It's much easier to create a presentation if you have all of the component views available to you at the same time. This will especially be true when you get to the chapter on Paper Space. You can put together all kinds of presentations, orthographic projections, assembly drawings, etc. Having more than one viewport on the screen at a time is the basis of any of these presentations.

You'll find a detailed discussion on Paper Space in Chapter 10, "Paper Space," and a further discussion on composition and presentation in Chapter 13, "The AutoCAD Solid Modeler."

Dividing Views as Tiles

At this time, you won't actually work with a drawing. That will come later in the chapter. Instead, look now at the simple mechanics of dividing the screen into viewports. To do that, you'll start with a blank screen, the VPORTS command and its options:

Type: VPORTS <Enter>

Response: Save/Restore/Delete/Join/SIngle/?/2/<3>/4:

In the following sections, you will look at the individual options Save/Restore/Delete/Join/SIngle/?/2/<3>/4: in detail. You may use the Tiled Viewports command from the View pull-down menu or type the VPORTS command as outlined below.

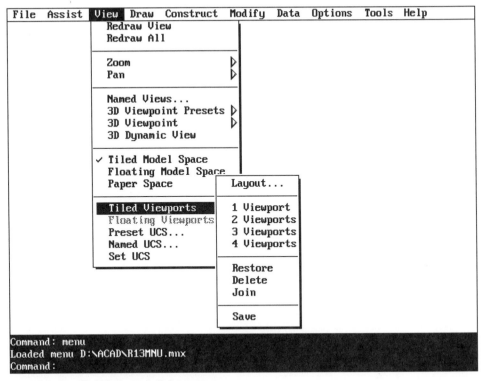

Figure 6-1: The Tiled Viewports pull-down menu

Two Viewports (2)

To create two viewports, simply type **2** after entering the VPORTS command:

Type: VPORTS <Enter>

Response: Save/Restore/Delete/Join/SIngle/?/2/<3>/4:

Type: 2 <Enter>

Response: Horizontal/<Vertical>:

You can now create two viewports on your screen either horizontally or vertically. Look at Figure 6-2 for a view of two horizontal viewports and Figure 6-3 for a view of two vertical viewports. To determine which viewport you want, type either **H** or **V** and press Enter.

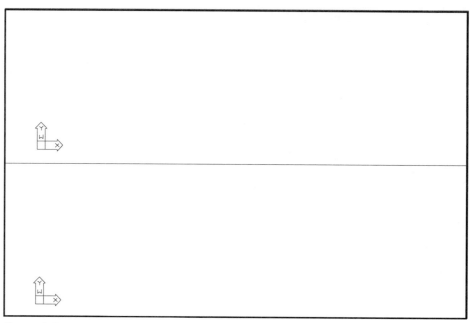

Figure 6-2: Two horizontal viewports

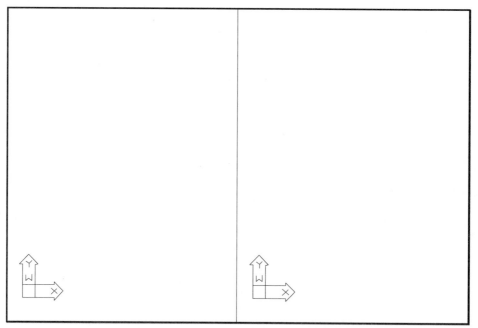

Figure 6-3: Two vertical viewports

Three Viewports (3)

As with two viewports, you also have the option of creating three view-ports horizontally or vertically:

Type: VPORTS <Enter>

Response: Save/Restore/Delete/Join/SIngle/?/2/<3>/4:

Type: 3 <Enter>

Response: Horizontal/Vertical/Above/Below/Left/<Right>:

See Figure 6-4 for a view of three horizontal viewports and Figure 6-5 for three vertical viewports.

Figure 6-4: Three horizontal viewports

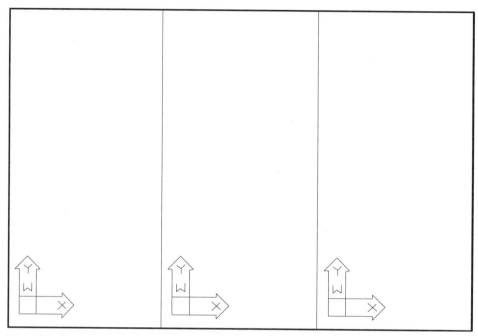

Figure 6-5: Three vertical viewports

If your three viewports aren't evenly spaced, then AutoCAD will create two smaller viewports and one large viewport. The only question that you have to answer is where you want AutoCAD to place the largest of the viewports.

Figures 6-6, 6-7, 6-8 and 6-9 show you viewports in a variety of configurations. Figure 6-6 shows the three viewports with the largest above. Figure 6-7 shows the largest viewport below. Figure 6-8 shows the largest on the left, and Figure 6-9 has the largest on the right.

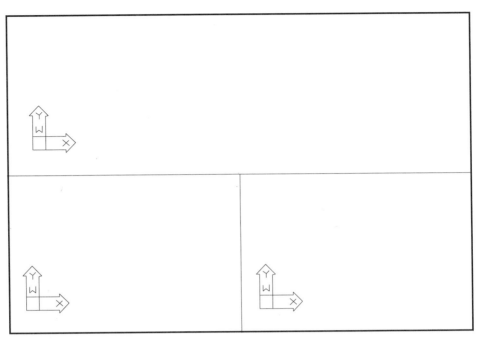

Figure 6-6: Three viewports with largest above

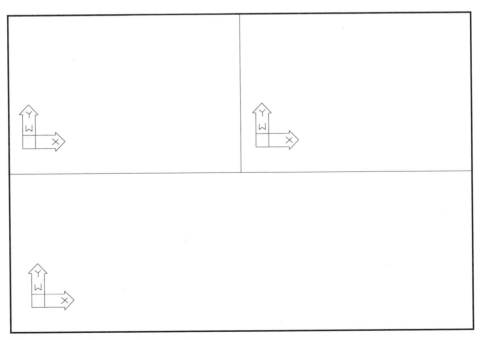

Figure 6-7: Three viewports with largest below

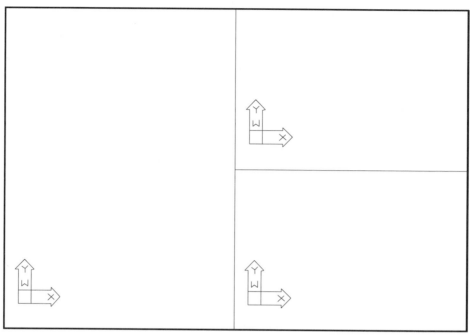

Figure 6-8: Three viewports with largest left

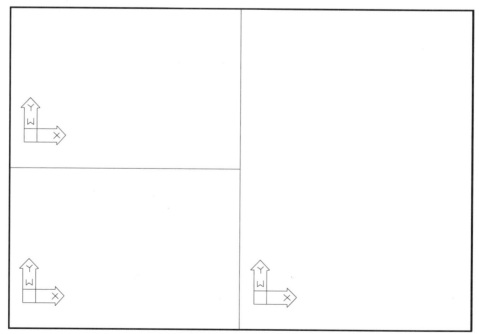

Figure 6-9: Three viewports with largest right

Four Viewports (4)

There are no special placement options when you choose four viewports.
AutoCAD simply divides your screen into four equal views.

Type: VPORTS <Enter>

Response: Save/Restore/Delete/Join/SIngle/?/2/<3>/4:

Type: 4 <Enter>

See Figure 6-10 for a view of four viewports.

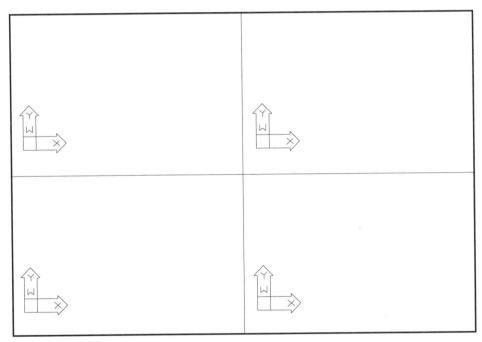

Figure 6-10: Four viewports

Subdividing Viewports

AutoCAD gives you a maximum of 64 viewports. To create more than the
four, which is the maximum option, you must subdivide an existing
viewport. Simply pick one of the viewports and make it active. You can
determine whether a viewport is active by moving your crosshairs around
the screen. One viewport will have crosshairs (the active viewport) and the
remaining viewports will have an arrow instead (inactive). To make an

inactive viewport into an active viewport, simply pick the viewport the arrow is in; the arrow then changes into crosshairs.

Once a viewport is active, all you need to do is to repeat the viewports command. Repeating the command will further subdivide that viewport. You can continue this operation until the viewports are too small to create another one.

Because AutoCAD gives you the ability to create 64 viewports doesn't mean that the objects in those viewports will all be visible at the same time. If you want to make the objects all visible at one time, you may. However, there is a lot of overhead work involved. AutoCAD out of the box defaults with 16 viewports visible at one time.

The System Variable MAXACTVP

Although you can always see the multiple viewport boxes themselves, the models in the viewports may or may not be visible. A system variable called MAXACTVP is saved with the drawing. This variable determines the maximum number of viewports visible at one time. See Figure 6-11 for a view of subdivided viewports.

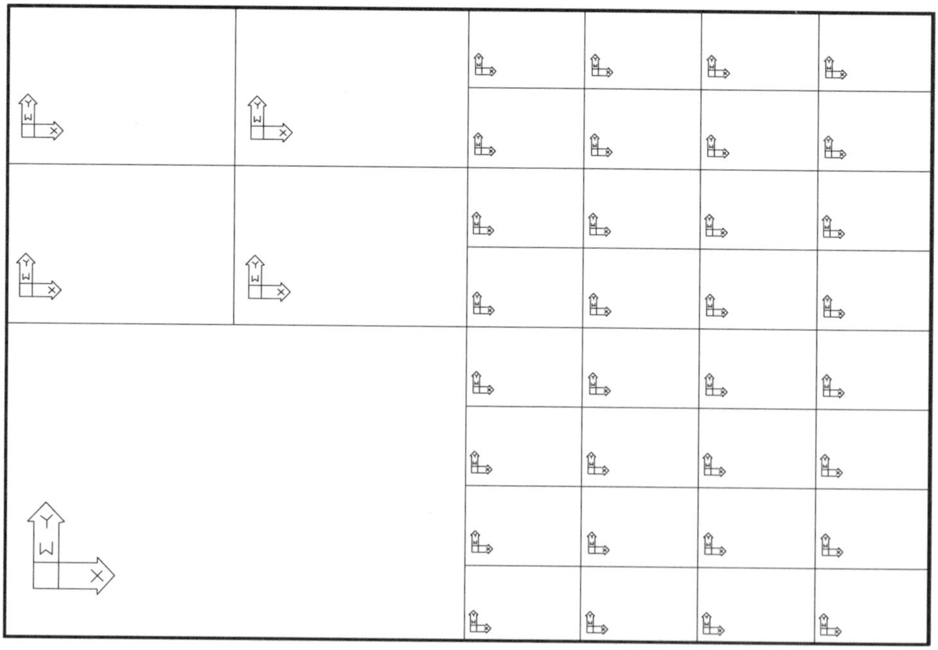

Figure 6-11: Subdivided viewports

Getting Back to One Viewport (SIngle)

To go back to a single viewport, use the SI option of the VPORTS command:

Type: `VPORTS <Enter>`

Response: `Save/Restore/Delete/Join/SIngle/?/2/<3>/4:`

Type: `SI <Enter>`

When you're in the VPORTS command, SI stands for Single and will return you to a single viewport. The SI is in uppercase in the prompt to indicate that you have to type both of the letters.

If your screen were divided into three viewports and each viewport had a different angle of view of the drawing, then when you returned to the single viewport, which view would you have filling the screen? The answer is the viewport that was active at the time when you returned to a single viewport.

Saving & Restoring Viewports (Save) (Restore)

You can have an unlimited number of viewport configurations available to you. Therefore, you might want to save your configuration under a user-defined name for the following reasons. First, all aspects of a viewport are saved with the configuration. That means the angle of view of each one of the viewports and the settings within the viewports, such as snap, grid, ortho, etc., are saved with the configuration. You may, therefore, set up several configurations in your prototype drawing—not just the number of viewports, but also the angle of view for each even before anything is drawn. At any time you may restore the saved viewport to the screen:

Type: `VPORTS <Enter>`

Response: `Save/Restore/Delete/Join/SIngle/?/2/<3>/4:`

Type: `S <Enter>`

Response: `?/Name for new viewport configuration:`

Type: `V1 <Enter>`

Now return to a single viewport:

Type: `VPORTS <Enter>`

Response: `Save/Restore/Delete/Join/SIngle/?/2/<3>/4:`

Type: `SI <Enter>`

Now restore the V1 viewport:

Type: `VPORTS <Enter>`

Response: `Save/Restore/Delete/Join/SIngle/?/2/<3>/4:`

Type: `R <Enter>`

Response: `?/Name of viewport configuration to restore:`

Type: `V1 <Enter>`

The second reason to save a viewport configuration is that the viewports that are created in Model Space (which is what you're in right now) can be transferred over to Paper Space, but only if you first have a viewport configuration saved in Model Space.

Regens, Redraws & Settings

Most of the drawing aid settings, such as snap, grid and ortho, can be set independently in each one of the viewports. This means that one viewport can have snap and grid set to one increment or even turned off, and another viewport can be set to something else.

Regens and redraws are also independent in each of the viewports. Therefore, if you simply pick REDRAW or REGEN, then only the active viewport will be regenerated or redrawn. You also can regenerate or redraw all the viewports at one time using REGENALL or REDRAWALL.

One thing you can't do is issue FREEZE to freeze a layer on one viewport independently of another while in Model Space. This, by the way, is possible in Paper Space (discussed in Chapter 10)—but not with the VPORTS command.

View Menu Image Tiles

Alternatively, AutoCAD gives you a visual way to create the various viewports available to you. You find this method in the View pull-down menu under Tiled Viewports then Layout…. You then see the image tiles of the possible viewport configurations from which you may pick.

Now that you've seen the mechanics of how the viewports are put together and how you can toggle from one to another, I'll show you how you can use the viewports in creating an actual model.

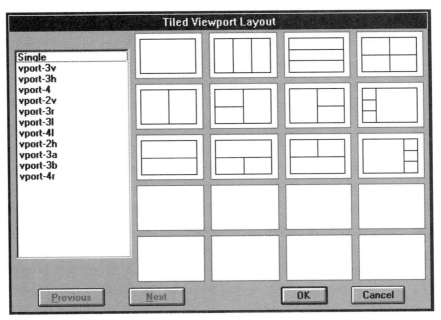

Figure 6-12: Tiled Viewport Layout dialog box

Designing With Viewports

Begin a new drawing with the following parameters:

UNITS	Decimal
Precision	2
LIMITS	0,0
Upper right	12,9
GRID	.25
SNAP	.25

After you make the settings:

Type: ZOOM <Enter>

Type: All <Enter>

Begin with four viewports, as shown in Figure 6-9. Pick and make active the upper-left viewport:

Type: PLAN <Enter>

Type: W <Enter>

This step guarantees that the upper-left viewport is in Plan view to the World Coordinate System.

Next, pick and make active the upper-right viewport. Change the view point of this viewport to 1,–1,1.

Figure 6-13: The S. E. Isometric View icon from the View toolbar

From the View toolbar, choose the S. E. Isometric View icon. Or in the command prompt window:

Type: VPOINT <Enter>

Type: 1,–1,1 <Enter>

Pick and make active the bottom-left viewport. Change the view point of this viewport to 1,0,0.

Figure 6-14: The Right View icon from the View toolbar

From the View toolbar choose the Right View icon. Or in the command prompt window:

Type: VPOINT <Enter>

Type: 1,0,0 <Enter>

Pick and make active the bottom-right viewport. Change this view point to –1,1,1.

Figure 6-15: The N. W. Isometric View icon from the View toolbar

From the View toolbar choose the N. W. Isometric View icon. Or in the command prompt window:

Type: VPOINT <Enter>

Type: –1,1,1 <Enter>

Now pick and make active the upper-left viewport, which is your Plan view.

The model that you're going to draw for this example is your digitizer puck or mouse. Although your digitizer puck or mouse may look different than the one shown in the following figures, follow along with the general concepts.

Before starting your drawing, make sure that your elevation is set to zero and your thickness is set to 2.75:

Type: ELEV <Enter>

Response: New current elevation:

Type:　0 <Enter>

Response:　New current thickness:

Type:　2.75 <Enter>

Begin by drawing from left to right a line 3 units long. Now draw down .75 unit, to the left 3.25 units and then close the shape. See the upper-left viewport in Figure 6-16 on how to begin the drawing.

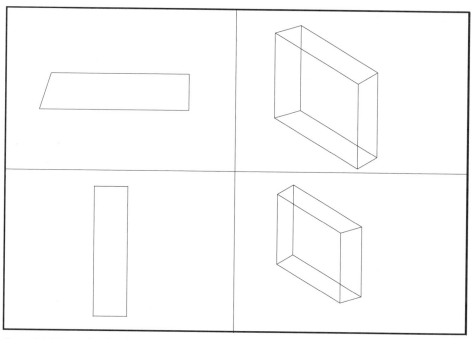

Figure 6-16: Beginning drawing

Pick each one of the viewports in turn, use ZOOM Extents and then reduce the ZOOM Extents by .9x. This series of commands is used often to maximize the size of the object within a viewport yet at the same time not make the objects so large that they completely fill the viewport without leaving you room to work.

To make your life a little easier, a program called ZX.LSP is included to maximize the object within 90 percent of the extents of the viewport. You'll find ZX.LSP in the AutoLISP section of the book. As with the other 3D programs, make certain that ZX.LSP is properly loaded. If you have the

AutoCAD 3D Companion Disk installed properly and have loaded 3DTOOLS.LSP, all you need to do is type in the name of the program.

Pick and make active one at a time each of the four viewports. When the viewport is active:

Type: ZX <Enter>

Your drawing should look similar to Figure 6-16.

Because you made the extrusion lengthwise across the digitizer puck rather than vertically, it might be a good idea to turn the puck around 90 degrees so you can conveniently work on the top. Rotating the puck will give you an Isometric view in the other two viewports.

The easiest way to rotate the puck is to attach the UCS icon to the model and then position it correctly to rotate around Z in the direction of XY. Of course, you must make sure that the UCS icon is attached to the origin in all four viewports:

Type: UCSICON <Enter>

Response: ON/OFF/All/Noorigin/ORigin<ON>:

Type: All <Enter>

Response: ON/OFF/Noorigin/ORigin<ON>:

Type: OR <Enter>

Pick the upper-right viewport and make it active. Now, using the 3Point UCS command, create the UCS as indicated in Figure 6-17. The figure shows how to change ORigin.

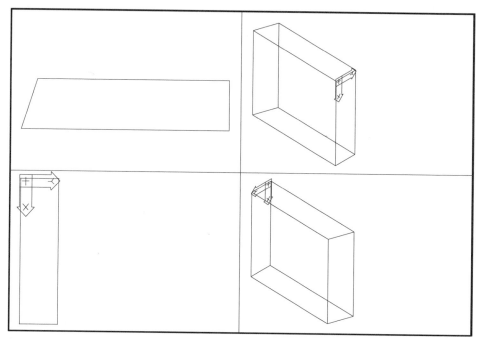

Figure 6-17: Changing ORigin

Now pick and make active the lower-left viewport. Change the UCS to be parallel with the view.

Figure 6-18: The Rotate flyout of the Modify toolbar

From the Modify toolbar, choose the Rotate flyout. Or in the command prompt window:

Type: ROTATE <Enter>

Response: Select objects:

Type: All <Enter> <Enter>

Response: Base point:

Now use the trick you learned in Chapter 5, "Establishing Coordinates," for finding the center of a rectangle; use the .X filter:

Type: .X

Response: of

Using object snap midpoint, pick the bottom side of the rectangle:

Response: (Need YZ):

Using object snap midpoint, pick the right side of the rectangle. This procedure correctly finds the center of the rectangle.

Response: <Rotation angle>/Reference:

Type: 90 <Enter>

Pick and make active the upper-right viewport. The rotation caused your origin to be in the wrong place. You may want to move your origin back to the lower-left viewport after the rotation, but it's not required for this drawing because you will move it again anyway.

Now fix each one of the viewports. Pick and make active each viewport one at a time and type the **ZX** command, which will make the model as large as possible in the viewports. Figure 6-19 shows the rotated model.

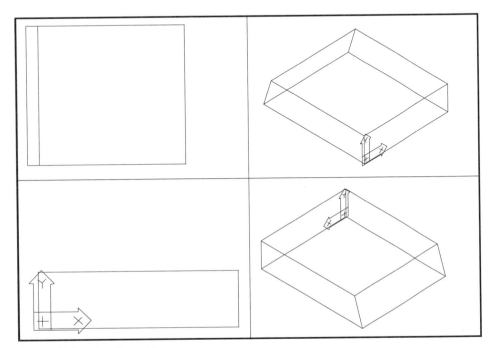

Figure 6-19: Rotating the model

You now have a Plan view from the top of your model. The upper-right viewport is a back-side Isometric view of the model. The lower-right viewport is a front-side Isometric view. The lower left is a Plan view of the back of the digitizer puck.

Now put some buttons on the top. Pick and make active the lower-right viewport. Use the UCS command and place the UCS icon on the top of the digitizer puck, as indicated in Figure 6-20.

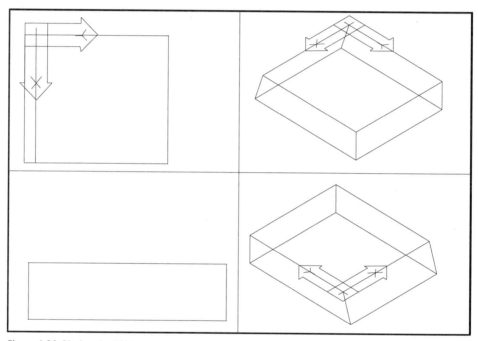

Figure 6-20: Placing the UCS icon on top of the puck

Now set your elevation to −.125 and thickness .25:

Type: ELEV <Enter>

Response: New current elevation:

Type: −.125 <Enter>

Response: New current thickness:

Type: .25 <Enter>

Pick and make active the upper-left viewport—the one that is your Plan view. It's easier at this point to work in plan. Place the buttons using the CIRCLE command. Place as many circles across the top as you like, using a radius of .15.

HINT: After you place one circle, then you can either use the ARRAY command or a multiple copy. If you use the ARRAY command, be careful which way the X and Y point.

Every time you place a circle, you can see it in each of the other viewports at the same time (see Figure 6-21).

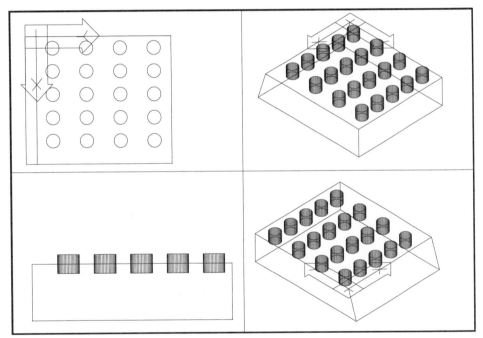

Figure 6-21: Making buttons

Although you probably won't use REGENALL much because you don't want drawings to regenerate any more than necessary, you'll find using REDRAWALL is very common. Therefore, I've included a program called RD.LSP. This program will redraw all of the viewports, and it's easier to type than REDRAWALL.

You will find RD.LSP in the AutoLISP section of the book. As with the other 3D programs, make certain that RD.LSP is properly loaded. If you have the *AutoCAD 3D Companion Disk* installed properly and have loaded 3DTOOLS.LSP, all you need to do is type in the name of the program.

Type: RD <Enter>

Now put in the pointer. The easiest way to do that is to continue to work in Plan view. If you look at the UCS icon in the lower-right viewport, it looks like it's on the correct plane. But your pointer should start about a third of the way down from the top of the puck. Rather than move the UCS icon, however, it's simpler to change the elevation:

Type: ELEV <Enter>

Response: New current elevation:

Type: -.40 <Enter>

Response: New current thickness:

Type: .125 <Enter>

To give yourself room to draw, make the size of the drawing in that viewport half the size that it is now:

Type: ZOOM <Enter>

Type: .5x <Enter>

Now draw a trapezoid as shown in the upper-left viewport in Figure 6-22.

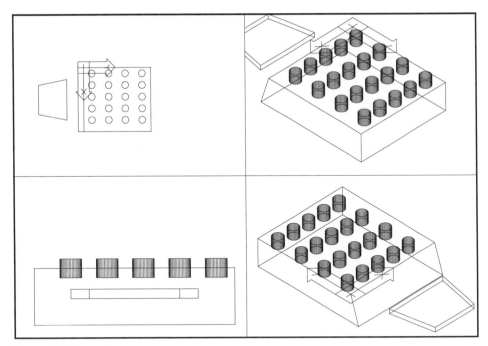

Figure 6-22: Draw pointer area

For the circle and crosshairs, change the elevation to –.35 and the thickness to 0:

Type: ELEV <Enter>

Response: New current elevation:

Type: –.35 <Enter>

Response: New current thickness:

Type: 0 <Enter>

Draw a circle and cross lines in the pointer area as indicated in Figure 6-23.

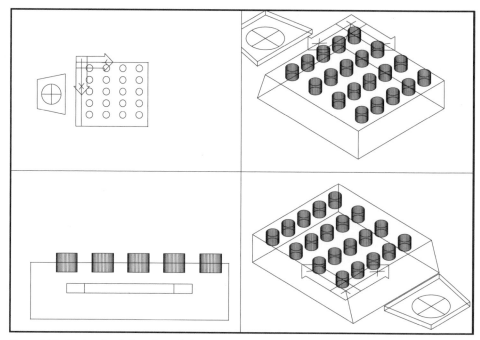

Figure 6-23: Placing the circle and crosshairs

HINT: Change the UCS to View and use the .X trick you learned in Chapter 5 to center the circle. Remember to change the UCS back to UCS Previous.

Now move the pointer area back inside the main area of the puck.

Figure 6-24: The Move icon from the Modify toolbar

From the Modify toolbar, choose the Move icon. Or in the command prompt window:

Type: `MOVE <Enter>`

Response: `Select objects:`

Put a window around the pointer group of objects and press Enter to confirm:

Response: `Base point or displacement:`

Type: @ <Enter>

Response: Second point of displacement:

Type: @.75<90> <Enter>

The angle is 90 degrees because of the direction of the UCS. The distance you move it is determined by how far out you drew it in the first place. Now make the upper-left viewport model the same size as the rest:

Type: ZX <Enter>

Figure 6-25 shows how to move the pointer inside the puck.

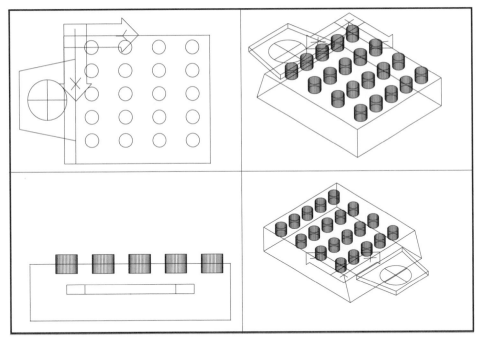

Figure 6-25: Moving the pointer inside the puck

Now pick and make active the lower-left viewport. Turn from the back side to the left side of the model. The easiest way to do this is with an RX and then an RY:

Type: RX <Enter>

Type: RY <Enter>

Type: PLAN <Enter> <Enter>

The model is now plan to the current UCS.

Type: ZX <Enter>

You now see a side view of the model. See Figure 6-26, which shows a bottom left-side Plan view.

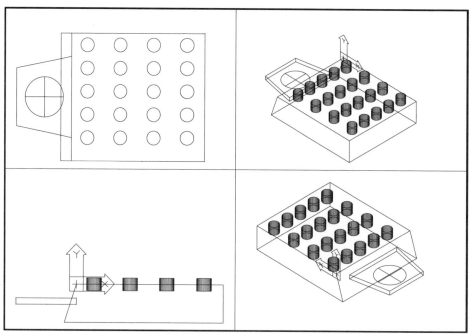

Figure 6-26: Bottom left-side Plan view

Now that you are plan to the side, put a fillet on the right side.

Figure 6-27: The Fillet icon feature from the Modify toolbar

From the Feature flyout of the Modify toolbar choose the Fillet icon . Or in the command prompt window:

Type: FILLET <Enter>

Type: R <Enter>

Type: .25 <Enter>

This step sets the fillet radius.

Type: FILLET <Enter>

When you pick any two adjacent lines on the right side of the model, the fillet is created. Repeat the command for the other two lines on the right side. Figure 6-28 shows the fillet of the back side.

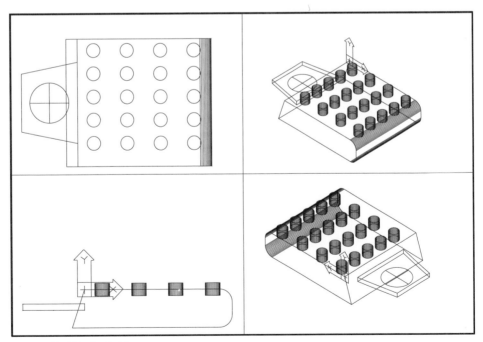

Figure 6-28: Fillet back side

Figure 6-29 shows the final drawing with hidden lines. In it, you'll see the finished digitizer puck with one of the viewports hidden.

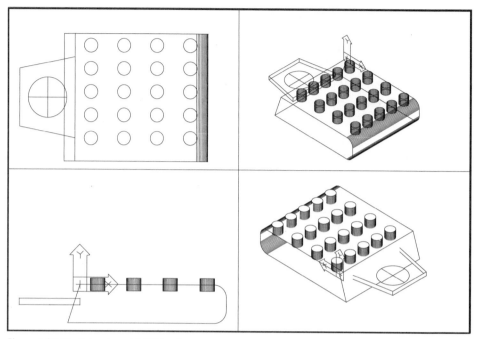

Figure 6-29: Final drawing with hidden lines

This exercise shows you how you can use viewports to move around the drawing as you create the model. Save this drawing, as you will use it in another chapter.

Moving On

As you can see, viewports play an important, if not integral, part in the development of a model in 3D. To recap, you can work on each side of the model without having to constantly rely on DVIEW or VPOINT.

It also permits some error checking. As in the case of the puck, you might discover that the buttons are too close to the fillet at the back of the puck. That might be a design flaw or it might be an error in drafting. Go back and look at Figure 6-29 to see how this error is plainly visible in both the Plan view and the side Plan view of the model. You might not catch errors like this unless you can see all views at one time.

But the model still has a problem. Creating an extrusion is not the only way to put a surface on a model. Because of the way you drew the model to begin with, the top of the puck is covered with the extrusion, but the sides are not. That's why AutoCAD gives you a variety of surfaces.

In Chapter 7, "Surfaces," you will look at the different ways you can place faces, meshes and extrusions so that you can properly hide lines or render a model. The concepts you learn in Chapter 7 will form the basis of what is required in most surface modeling to render a model in any package.

Surfaces

In this chapter you'll learn how to work with the most fascinating part of AutoCAD 3D: Surfaces. They are also the most complex and what most users find the most difficult. After reading this chapter, you'll find surfaces are still the most fascinating part of AutoCAD 3D and not nearly as difficult as you once thought. The Release 13 Surfaces toolbar is a new quick access tool for all the surface commands you'll need. The fifteen icons provide basic shapes such as box, cone, wedge and torus through to 3D meshes and revolved, extruded and edge surfaces.

Figure 7-1: The Surfaces toolbar

What Are Surfaces?

While working with a civic organization years ago, I had the opportunity to be responsible for the committee putting together a float for the local Christmas parade. We formed our figure on the float with chicken wire. Then we filled in the holes with colored tissue paper. The chicken wire and tissue paper made a gorgeous float, and we won first prize.

What has a Christmas float got to do with AutoCAD? Well, a lot actually. When the float was in the chicken wire stage, we had created a wireframe in the most literal sense. In fact, you could hardly tell what the form was. Then, when we began filling in the holes in the wire, the figure began to take form. At that point, we were adding surfaces.

The process is the same with AutoCAD. Most of what you draw is done in wireframe. And unless you put some form of surface on it, you can see right through the model. This means that nothing will happen when you type HIDE or SHADE. Also, if you send the drawing to other rendering packages, there'll be nothing there to render because the drawing has no surface, only a bunch of lines.

Types of Surfaces

Without a surface, nothing will hide, shade or render. It's as simple as that. Then what kind of surfaces do you have? There are only four: *extrusions, faces, meshes* and *regions*. In the following sections you'll look at all of the possibilities with each of these surface types.

Extrusions

By now you should be familiar with extrusions. (Remember that extrusion is the same as thickness.) Most objects can be extruded to form a surface that will hide lines and shade or render.

If you're going to use extrusions as surfaces, you have to decide which way you want the extrusion to point. This decision can determine how much you will have to surface later on. It doesn't make much sense to extrude in a short direction when you could extrude the model in a more complex and larger direction. Generally, the rule is: *extrude the part that will be the most difficult to surface later on.*

In the preceding chapter, you created a mouse or digitizer puck. You drew it from the side and extruded it toward you because it was easier to draw the outline of the side. Therefore, the top and the bottom were automatically surfaced. Remember, the extrusion is always in the direction of positive Z.

There are disadvantages to using extrusions. Sometimes the extrusion can be a crutch that can get in the way. This is especially true if you need to put a hole where the extrusion is. Remember that you can't cut a hole in an extrusion. There are ways to get a hole in a surface, but not an extrusion. Therefore, if you want to cut a hole, then you should not draw your model with extrusions; you should draw it as individual lines and then apply a different type of surface.

But it's difficult to draw some things in 3D. It's much easier to draw in Plan view than to create the 3D with an extrusion. I have the perfect answer for you. It's a program called TCOPY (which stands for Thickness Copy). It works very much like thickness.

Begin by drawing in Plan view. After you've drawn a model, begin the TCOPY program. It will ask you to select objects, and you select and confirm all of the objects you want to be copied "up." The program will ask for the thickness distance. Then you pick each intersection for the connecting lines. That's all there is to it. The finished product will look much like extruded lines, but you won't have any surfaces at all.

You can find TCOPY.LSP in the AutoLISP section of the book. As with the other 3D programs, make certain that TCOPY.LSP is properly loaded. If you have the *AutoCAD 3D Companion Disk* installed properly and have loaded 3DTOOLS.LSP, all you need to do is type in the name of the program.

Now see how TCOPY.LSP works. Begin with a 2D drawing that you must copy. Figure 7-2 shows a drawing to be copied "up." You want to make your drawing look as though it had been extruded without the actual extrusion.

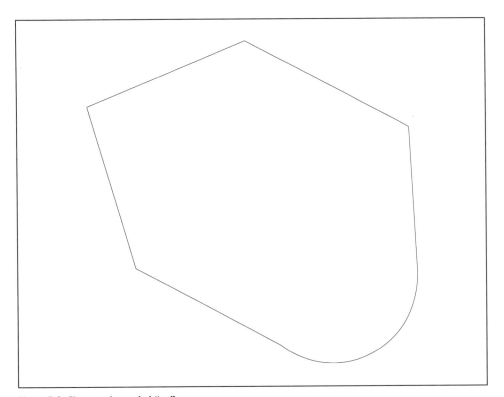

Figure 7-2: Figure to be copied "up"

Type: TCOPY <Enter>

Response: Select objects:

Select the objects to be copied and press Enter to confirm.

Response: Enter distance:

Type: 4 <Enter>

Response: Pick all intersections then <Enter> to quit:

Object snap intersection is now turned on. Pick each intersection in the drawing. After you've picked all intersections, then press Enter. The objects will be copied up, and connecting lines will be automatically drawn (see Figure 7-3).

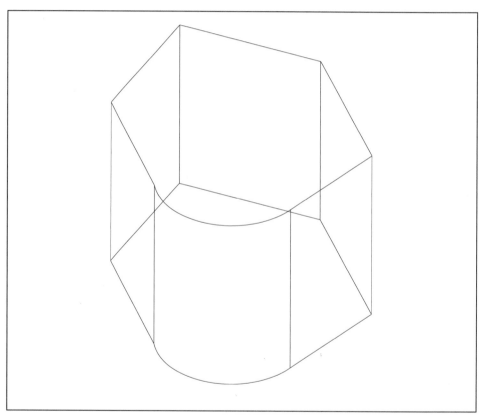

Figure 7-3: Copied "up" figure with connecting lines

As you can see, Figure 7-3 has a similar appearance and is as easy to work as an extrusion.

Faces

One of the easiest ways to put a surface on an area is with a face. Faces are basically large, multisided linear areas that are generally connected at intersections. Although you can use faces on curved areas, they would have to be so small and there would have to be so many of them that they would be too tedious to construct by hand because all faces are formed by a series of straight lines. Therefore, the real purpose of faces is to put a surface on large linear areas.

There are two main types of faces, one is a *3D face* and the other is a *pface*. Pface stands for polyface. You'll learn about these faces in the following sections.

3D Face

A 3D face requires a minimum of 3 points. Thus, a 3D face can be in the form of a triangle. For example, in Chapter 2, "The User Coordinate System," you used a 3D face on the User Coordinate System when you put a top and bottom face on the connector. That example made the perfect opportunity for a 3D face because you were covering a four-sided object.

The following is an example of the structure of the 3DFACE command:

Figure 7-4: The 3Dface icon from the Surfaces toolbar

From the Surfaces toolbar, choose the 3Dface icon. Or in the command prompt window:

Type: 3DFACE <Enter>

Response: First point:

            Pick Point 1.

Response: Second point:

            Pick Point 2.

Response: Third point:

            Pick Point 3.

Response: Fourth point:

Pick Point 4.

Response: Third point:

Type: <Enter>

This last Enter terminates the 3DFACE command. See Figure 7-5.

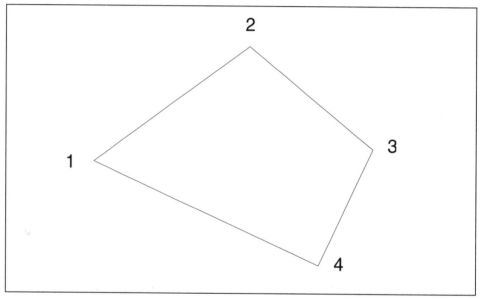

Figure 7-5: Four-sided 3D face

You can continue with the 3DFACE command. Notice that with the fourth pick a 3D face is created and AutoCAD continues to ask you for another *third* point. You can continue to add points to a 3D face, but each time you do, AutoCAD will add cross lines. (Figure 7-6 shows Multiple 3D faces.) Therefore, 3DFACE is not the optimum command to use when you have a multisided form to cover.

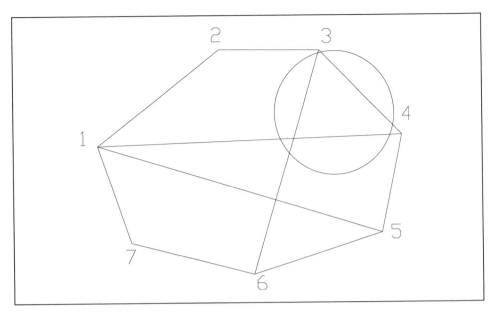

Figure 7-6: Multiple 3D faces

PFACE

As a result of the restriction of 3DFACE for multisided forms, PFACE was invented to provide a polyface mesh similar to a 3Dmesh. It's constructed vertex by vertex and allows you to create irregular surface shapes.

The command gives you the ability to place irregular shaped faces easily. For this example, start with the same irregular shaped area. Figure 7-7 shows the area before using PFACE. The circle is drawn at a negative elevation so that you can see it hidden if you are successful in putting the face on the area.

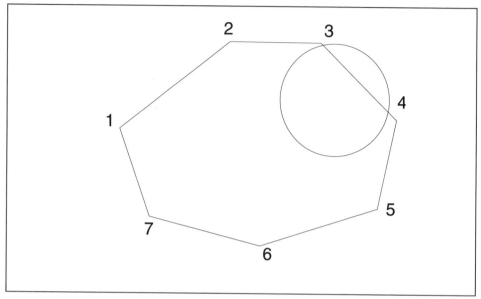

Figure 7-7: Area before using PFACE

Type: PFACE <Enter>

Response: Vertex 1:

           Vertex 2:

           Vertex 3:

           Vertex 4:

           Vertex 5:

           Vertex 6:

           Vertex 7:

Each time AutoCAD responds with a vertex number, you should pick Points 1 through 7, as shown in the figure. Be sure to pick them with an object snap intersection. AutoCAD first asks you to identify by number each one of the vertices of the area. When you are through identifying the vertices, then press Enter on the last vertex question:

Response: Vertex 8:

Type: <Enter>

    This is part one. You have identified by number each one of the vertices. Now you can place as many faces on the object as you want by telling AutoCAD to draw the face from one vertex number to the next. In this case, you'll put on only one face. In reality, the order of the vertex numbers will be the direction of the perimeter of the face.

Response: Face 1, vertex 1:

Type: 1 <Enter>

Response: Face 1, vertex 2:

Type: 2 <Enter>

Response: Face 1, vertex 3:

Type: 3 <Enter>

Response: Face 1, vertex 4:

Type: 4 <Enter>

Response: Face 1, vertex 5:

Type: 5 <Enter>

Response: Face 1, vertex 6:

Type: 6 <Enter>

Response: Face 1, vertex 7:

Type: 7 <Enter>

Response: Face 1, vertex 8:

Type: <Enter>

Response: Face 2, vertex 1:

Type: <Enter>

After you place the seventh part of the face, AutoCAD asks for the eighth vertex of face 1. When you press Enter, AutoCAD assumes you're through with face 1 and wants to know about face 2. Pressing Enter a second time tells AutoCAD you have no more faces to place.

You have now placed a single face on the entire form. When AutoCAD asked you for face 1, vertex 1:, it was really saying that you previously identified the vertices by number in the first part of the command. Now it wants to know which vertex is the first vertex of the pface (polyface). You answer with 1, and you continue around the entire form. Obviously, using the same point number with the same vertex number is convenient. But you could have drawn a face from any vertex to any other vertex. You even could have overlapped them if necessary.

Now see how you did:

Type: HIDE <Enter>

See Figure 7-8 with the pface added, and you will see that the circle is hidden.

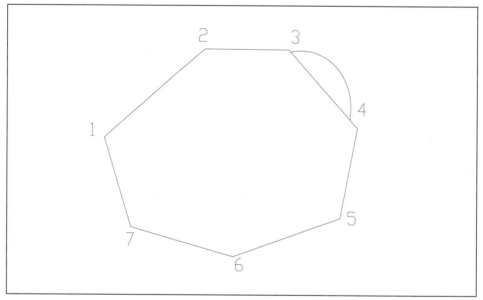

Figure 7-8: The pface added

You also can make the pfaces different colors or place them on different layers. At any time when asked for face 1, vertex 1:, you can type **COLOR** or **LAYER** and then change the color or layer for the upcoming face.

There is one caution. People often think of a face the same as a mesh. With a mesh you can change the vertex point of any part of the mesh. This is not true with a pface. Once it is on, you can't edit it. You edit a polyface mesh as a single entity.

Making 3D Faces Invisible

When creating a 3D face, you may not want the overlapping lines formed by the face to be visible. In Release 13 you can make the lines of a 3D face invisible in one of two ways, first by typing **i** before picking the point as you use the 3DFACE command; second, by using the edge command. You can even make all the lines of the 3D face invisible. If you do, the face will not appear in the wireframe, but it will hide lines as required and will do its job in shaded renderings.

AutoCAD enables you to make the lines of a 3D face invisible while you are drawing it. But many times you will want to make the lines invisible after they are drawn. In fact, this is probably the way you will want to do it all the time; it's easier. I have created two AutoLISP programs to help you make lines invisible. The first is called IFACE for invisible face, the second, SFACE. The IFACE program will make invisible any combination of four sides of a 3D face. Look at the following chart. The code numbers will be used by the program to determine which side(s) will be made invisible.

Code numbers	Side
1	Side 1
2	Side 2
4	Side 3
8	Side 4

Notice that the code numbers in the chart double each time. That is to leave room for the combination of the sums. For example, if you want to make sides 1 and 2 invisible, you would use code 3. Code 3 is the sum of the codes for sides 1 and 2. If you want to make sides 2 and 4 invisible, then you would use the code 10. Side 2 is code 2, and side 4 is code 8. The sum of 2 and 8 is 10. Do you get the idea? If you want all four sides to be invisible, then you would add all of them to get 15. Using 0 would make all sides visible.

If you are interested in AutoLISP and the object associative code being changed, Associative 70 in the object list contains this information about a 3D face.

If you need to know which side to make invisible, how do you know which of the four sides it is? You usually can't tell just by looking at them. Therefore, the SFACE program will go along with IFACE to help you find which side is which. SFACE stands for Side of the 3D face.

To use the program, pick the 3D face you want to know about. Side 1 will disappear. Press Enter and side 2 will disappear. Press Enter again and the 3D face will return to its normal state. Once you know sides 1 and 2, sides 3 and 4 continue in the same direction.

You can find IFACE.LSP and SFACE.LSP in the AutoLISP section of the book. As with the other 3D programs, make certain that IFACE.LSP and SFACE.LSP are properly loaded. If you have the *AutoCAD 3D Companion Disk* installed properly and have loaded 3DTOOLS.LSP, all you need to do is type in the name of the program.

To see where the invisible 3D face lines really are after you have made them invisible, change the system variable SPLFRAME. If it's set to 1, then the invisible 3D face lines will be visible again. If it's set to 0, then the invisible 3D face lines will not be visible. You must regen after the change to see the effect. Obviously, if you're going to make any of the lines permanently visible again with the IFACE.LSP program, then you will first have to make them visible temporarily with SPLFRAME in order to choose them. Then you can set their sides to 0 to start over again.

Edge Command

The edge command is an easier method of creating invisible faces or edges. Simply use the 3DFACE command to make your object, then use the edge command to choose which faces need to be invisible. You then use the SPLFRAME variable to either turn the invisible edges ON or OFF.

Figure 7-9: The Edge icon

The edge command changes (hides) the visibility of 3D faces.
Let's look at how to use the command. You'll create a simple 3D model
then hide the edges.

What you'll do is create a 3D wireframe using the 3DFACE command,
then use the edge command selecting edges to make invisible, and finally
use the SPLFRAME variable set to 0 to turn off the display of invisible
edges.

Follow the prompts below:

First, set your viewpoint to -1,-1,1. From the Views toolbar choose the
S.W. Isometric View icon, or in the command prompt window:

Type: VPOINT

Response: Rotate/<View point><0.0000,0.0000,1,0000>:

Type: -1,-1,1

From the Surfaces toolbar select the 3Dface icon, and create a 3D face. Or
in the command prompt window:

Type: 3DFACE

Response: First point: 5,5,6 <Enter>
            Second point: 6.0261,2.1809,0 <Enter>
            Third point: 7.5981,3.5000,0 <Enter>
            Fourth point: 5,5,6 <Enter>
            Third point: <Enter>

You've created a simple 3D triangular face, now let's array it in 3D.
Choose the 3Darray icon from the Copy flyout of the Modify toolbar, or
use the 3DARRAY command at the command prompt:

Type: 3DARRAY
            Select objects: L (for last object)
            Rectangular or Polar (R/P): P
            Number of items: 9
            Angle to fill <360>: <Enter>
            Rotate objects as they are copied <Y>: Y

```
Center point of array: 5,5,6
Second point on axis of rotation: 5,5,0
```

A simple 3D Tepee model is created; now let's issue the edge command picking the back faces of the Tepee.

Type: EDGE

Response: `Display/<Select edge>:`

Select the back faces you want to hide. You'll see the faces are hidden. The end result is that the back edges of the 3D model are now invisible. But what if you needed to work with the edges you just hid. How would you redisplay them to work on?

If you wish to display them use the edge command again.

Type: EDGE

Response: `Display/<Select edge>:`

Type: D (for Display)

Response: `Select/<All>:`

Type: A

Response: `**Regenerating 3DFACE objects....done.`

Response: `Display/<Select edge>:`

Now choose some of the edges you previously hid and they are displayed for you to work with.

Response: `Display/<Select edge>: <Enter>`

There is also a variable that may be used: Splframe.
You may also use the SPLFRAME variable set to 1 to turn ON the display of invisible edges.

Type: SPLFRAME <0> 1

Type: Regen

Meshes

What is a mesh? Remember that a face is generally limited to linear areas. Not all surfaces are straight lines; they have curves and contours. Therefore, AutoCAD has provided a group of meshes that will automatically place a series of faces around the curvature and form a surface. You could do this by hand. If you could make the face small enough and place enough of them around the curve, then you could do the same thing as a mesh. But who wants to? That's why you have meshes.

Because of the number of faces created, a mesh is expressed as a single object in AutoCAD, thus making it easy to delete or move. Technically a mesh is a mesh, not a face, but if you were to explode a mesh, it would explode back to what could literally amount to thousands of tiny faces. You can't explode a face back any farther.

M & N Direction

AutoCAD provides four basic meshes: RULESURF, TABSURF, REVSURF and EDGESURF. Two of these meshes, RULESURF and TABSURF, create their meshes as faces that go in only one direction called the *M direction*. The other two meshes, REVSURF and EDGESURF, create the faces as a cross grid going in two directions. The REVSURF and the EDGESURF also require the grid pattern and have an M direction. But the second direction is called the *N direction*. See Figure 7-10 with the M & N Direction.

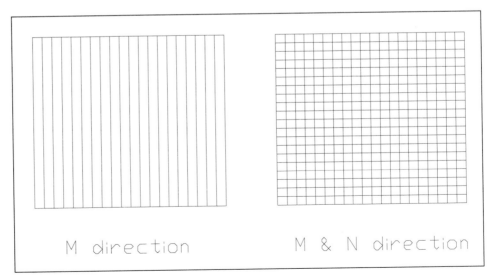

Figure 7-10: M & N Direction

There is no magic in the terms *M* and *N*. AutoCAD uses them only to express the fact that the meshes go in two different directions.

SURFTAB1 & SURFTAB2

AutoCAD must know the density of the faces that will form the mesh. How many faces in the M direction and how many in the N direction will be drawn over a fixed surface? This density is controlled by the SURFTAB1 and SURFTAB2 system variables.

AutoCAD out of the box has these system variables set to only six. This refers to six faces across the surface. This number is generally too low. As long as there is very little curvature to the model, you could live with this number, but you should raise it. Twenty for each direction is a good place to start to fully describe an arc with a mesh. But the size of the area being meshed will determine the optimum number for each of these variables.

SURFTAB1 controls the density of the M direction; SURFTAB2, the N direction. You don't have to set these two variables the same. Depending on your pattern on a REVSURF, for example, the M direction may be much larger than the N direction of SURFTAB2. Be very careful with these system variables. The higher the density, the longer the regenerations, shading and rendering. At the same time, the smoothness around an area without facets depends on the density of this mesh.

Some rendering programs give you the option of curve smoothing. This feature of the rendering program will smooth out the curves, even if the density of the mesh is not very great. If this is the case, you can get by with a lower density and still render the model adequately.

One final point on SURFTAB1 and SURFTAB2. Once these two system variables are set, you may change them at any time without affecting any of the meshes previously drawn under another setting. Therefore, a mesh drawn with a density of 20 cannot be changed later to a density of 60. All you can do is erase the mesh, change the density of the variable and then reapply the mesh with the new density.

RULESURF

SURFTAB1 controls the number of faces provided by RULESURF. RULE-SURF is a basic mesh that connects any two objects. In Figure 7-11 both objects are straight lines.

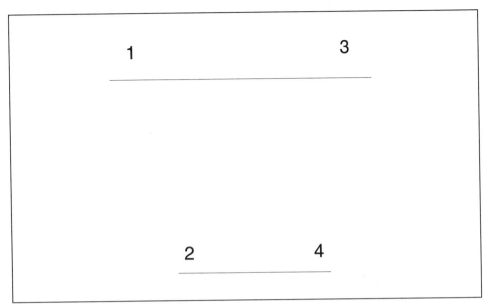

Figure 7-11: Two objects for RULESURF

Here's how you apply a RULESURF to these two lines. First, start by setting SURFTAB1 to at least 20:

Type: SURFTAB1 <Enter>

Type: 20 <Enter>

   Figure 7-12: The Ruled Surface icon from the Surfaces toolbar

From the Surfaces toolbar choose the Ruled Surface icon. Or in the command prompt window:

Type: RULESURF <Enter>

Response: Select first defining curve:

Pick Point 1 as shown in Figure 7-11:

Response: Select second defining curve:

Now pick the second object at Point 2 as shown in Figure 7-11. The result should look like Figure 7-13.

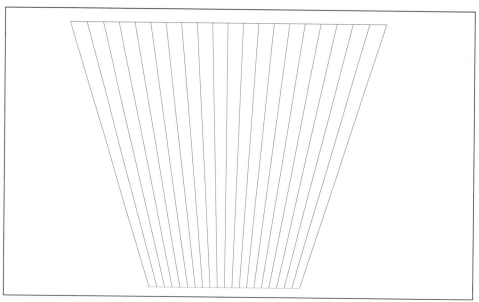

Figure 7-13: Objects with RULESURF

Notice that both picks of the two objects were on the same side of each object relative to the other. If you pick on the left side of one, then you must pick on the left side of the other. If you make a mistake and pick Points 1 and 4 in Figure 7-11, then the result will be a bow-tie effect as shown in Figure 7-14.

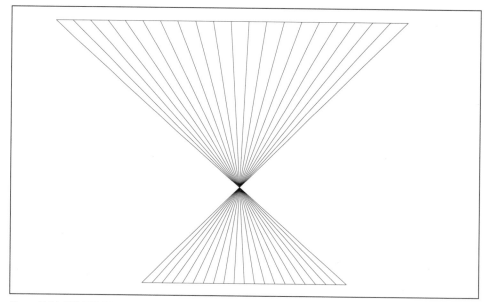

Figure 7-14: RULESURF bow tie

The first response for most of these meshes asks you to pick the first defining curve. This response is misleading because the object doesn't have to be—and many times isn't—a curve at all, as in this case. But of course it could be.

See what would happen if you set SURFTAB1 too low on a curved area. Look at Figure 7-15.

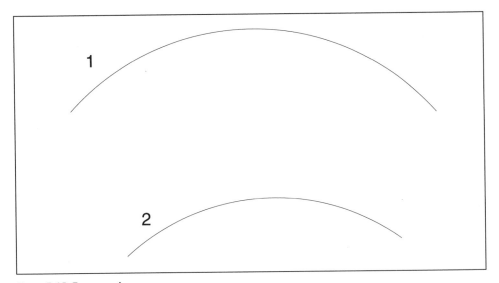

Figure 7-15: Two curved areas

Type: SURFTAB1 <Enter>

Type: 2 <Enter>

Repeat the RULESURF on the arc and the line. See Figure 7-16 with the SURFTAB1 set at 2 for the result. In the figure you can plainly see the two faces that were created. As SURFTAB1 is increased, the density is increased so that it follows the curvature more closely.

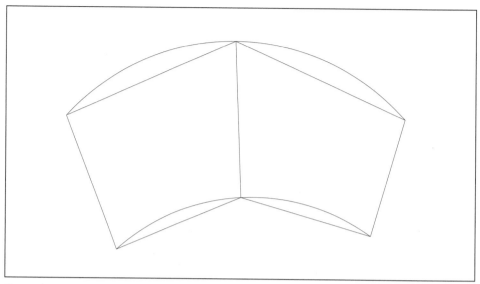

Figure 7-16: SURFTAB1 set at 2

Figure 7-17 represents the same figure with the density set at 60. But even here if you zoom in closely (as in Figure 7-18, which shows the zoomed-in area), you can see that there is still some gap along the curve. You will never get the surface exact. The surface is still made up of straight lines. But you can raise the density to where the little difference doesn't matter.

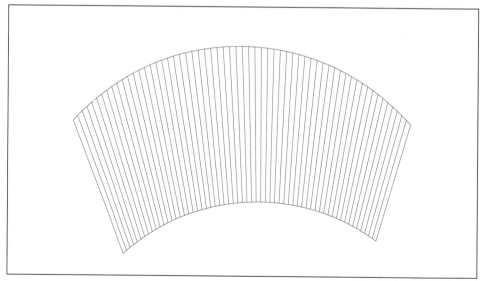

Figure 7-17: SURFTAB1 set at 60

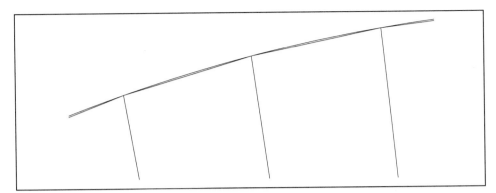

Figure 7-18: Zoomed-in area

Now take an example in 3D and see how RULESURF will be applied. Look at Figure 7-19 to see a box with a curved area. This drawing was created with an extrusion so that the surface is formed on the side, but the top is still open and needs to be covered. The problem with RULESURF is deciding which two objects to choose. In this example you have four objects from which you can choose.

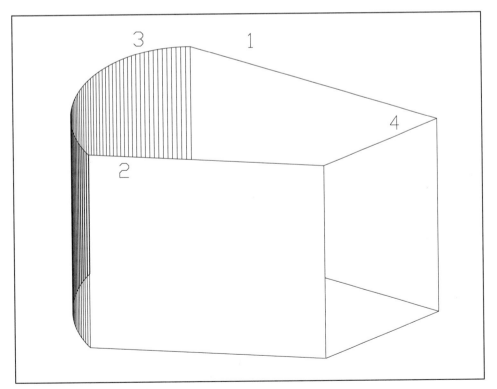

Figure 7-19: Box with a curved area

In the next figure, when the mesh is formed, it is created at zero elevation because that is the elevation of the extruded line. Once you create the
mesh, you will move it to the top of the box.

Figure 7-20 shows what happens if you pick Points 1 and 2, and Figure
7-21 shows what happens when you pick Points 3 and 4. Obviously, Points
3 and 4 should be the ones you pick with RULESURF.

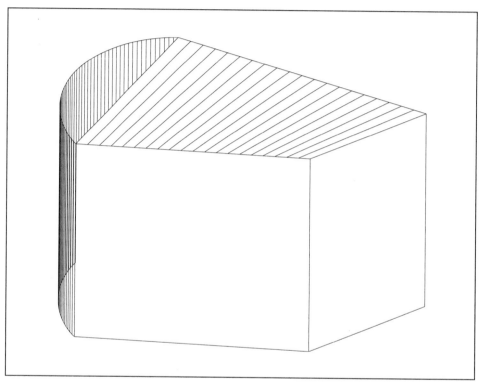

Figure 7-20: The wrong choice

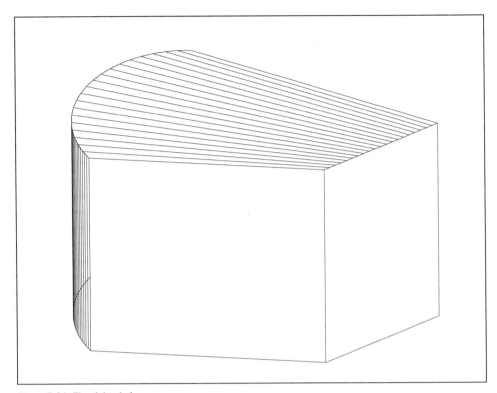

Figure 7-21: The right choice

Virtually any single object can be a defining object for RULESURF. And if it's not, AutoCAD will tell you. You can even use a point. Figure 7-22 shows a circle with a point in the center. As long as the point and the circle are at the same elevation, you can put a surface on the circle by picking the point and the circle with RULESURF. See Figure 7-23 for a view of RULE-SURF with circle and point at the same elevation.

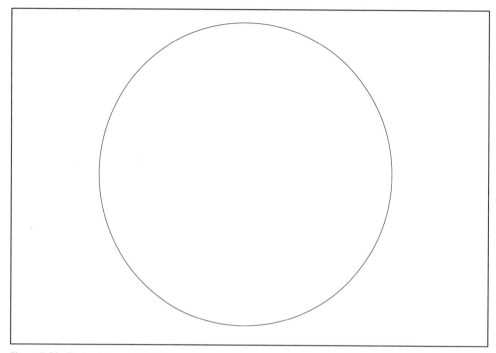

Figure 7-22: Circle with a point in the center

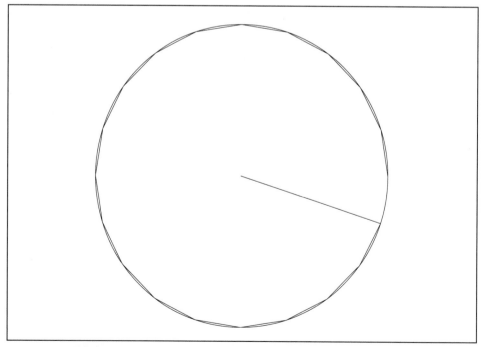

Figure 7-23: RULESURF with a circle and a point at the same elevation

If you change the elevation of the point, you can create a cone. See Figure 7-24 for a view of RULESURF with the circle and point at different elevations. If you had two circles, you could make the bottom of the cone open. Figure 7-25 shows a view of RULESURF with a circle and another circle creating an open end.

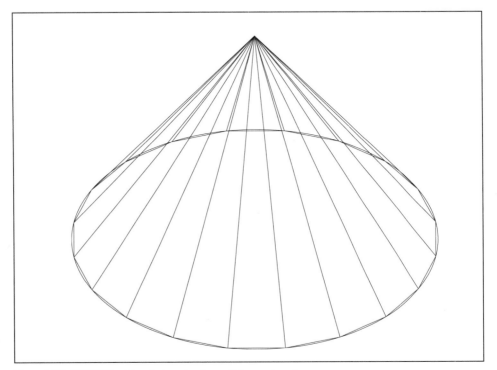

Figure 7-24: RULESURF with a circle and point at different elevations

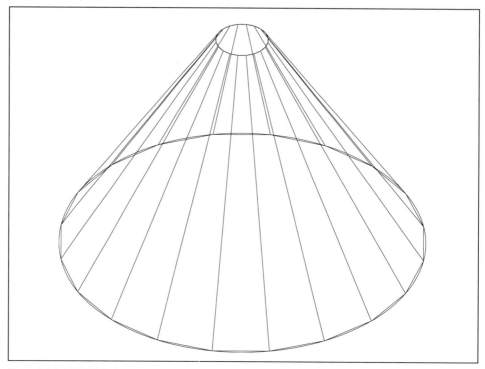

Figure 7-25: RULESURF with a circle and another circle creating an open end

Although one of the primary reasons for meshes is to create a surface that will hide lines and shade objects, it also serves another purpose—that is, to give a form or shape to the model itself.

TABSURF

TABSURF is similar to RULESURF in that it uses SURFTAB1 only in the M direction. But it differs in that it doesn't require two objects. Look at Figure 7-26 to see the polyline that is labeled as 1. Assume you want to place a mesh along the polyline. There is also another object in this drawing. This object can be any place in the drawing; it may be a permanent object that is part of the model or a temporary object that was drawn just for this purpose and then will be erased. It is called the *direction vector*.

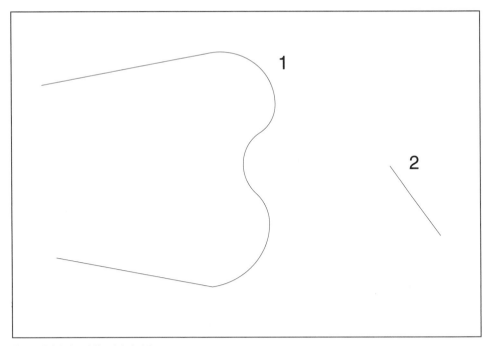

Figure 7-26: A polyline labeled 1

Make a mesh in the size and direction extruding from the polyline labeled 1. The size and direction will be that of the direction vector. Remember that the direction vector is just another object that you use to show AutoCAD how to draw the mesh. The polyline labeled 1 will be your defining curve. Object 2 will be your direction vector.

When AutoCAD creates a TABSURF, it will place object 2 in its size and direction along the path of object 1, extruding from the direction depending on which side of the direction vector you pick. Now see how this process works:

 Figure 7-27: The Extruded Surface icon

From the Surfaces toolbar choose the Extruded Surface icon. Or in the command prompt window:

Type: TABSURF <Enter>

Response: Select path curve:

Pick object 1.

Response: `Select direction vector:`

Pick the direction vector at Point 2.

See Figure 7-28 for a view of the polyline with TABSURF. Notice how the direction vector was placed in the form of a mesh along the path of the defining curve. It still maintains the size and direction of the direction vector. The direction vector doesn't have to be a part of the defining curve. It can be anywhere in the drawing; it is simply used as the model for the size and direction of the mesh.

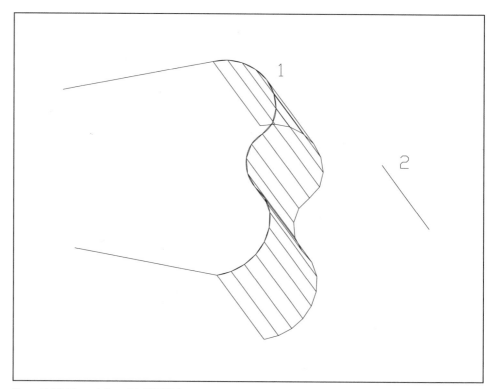

Figure 7-28: The polyline with TABSURF

REVSURF

REVSURF is perhaps the most fascinating of all of the meshes because of all the things that you can do with it. It also presents a challenge because to use it effectively you have to be able to visualize what the object will look like after it has been revolved around a given axis.

Create a simple REVSURF just to get the feel of the mechanics. Look at Figure 7-29 and see the axis and curve path for REVSURF.

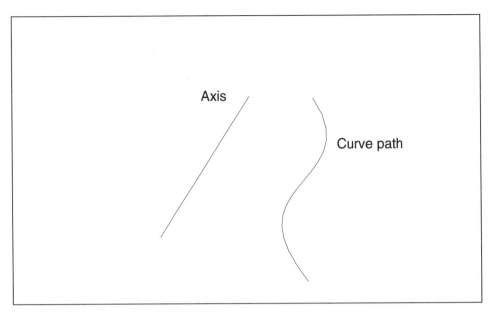

Figure 7-29: Axis and curve path for REVSURF

In Figure 7-29 a straight line represents the axis, and a curved line represents the object that you'll revolve around the axis. REVSURF will use the M and N direction. Therefore, you must make certain that SURFTAB1 and SURFTAB2 are properly set before you begin:

Type: SURFTAB1 <Enter>

Type: 60 <Enter>

Type: SURFTAB2 <Enter>

Type: 60 <Enter>

If your computer is slow, you might want to begin by setting these variables a little lower, say at 40.

 Figure 7-30: The Revolved Surface icon

From the Surfaces toolbar choose the Revolved Surface icon. Or in the command prompt window:

Type: REVSURF <Enter>

Response: Select path curve:

            Pick the curve.

Response: Select axis of revolution:

            Pick the axis line.

Response: Start angle <0>:

Type: <Enter>

Response: Included angle (+=ccw, -=cw)<Full circle>:

Type: 200 <Enter> <Enter>

In this case you only revolved around 200 degrees so that you can see exactly what the effect was. You also can start the revolution at any degree you want.

With the DVIEW command and the model tilted, look at the results of your drawing to see an Angle view of REVSURF (see Figure 7-31).

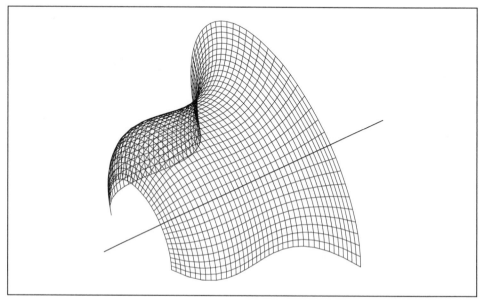

Figure 7-31: Angle view of REVSURF

The real problem with REVSURF is in visualizing what it will look like after it is revolved. Or better stated, what shape should you use for the defining curve and the axis because this will determine the final outcome. To further illustrate this idea, create two more objects as examples, as shown in Figures 7-32 through 7-35. Figure 7-32 and Figure 7-34 show the defining curve and axis, and Figure 7-33 and Figure 7-35 show the finished item with hidden lines removed. In these figures the axis is erased after it is used, leaving only the revolved defining curve.

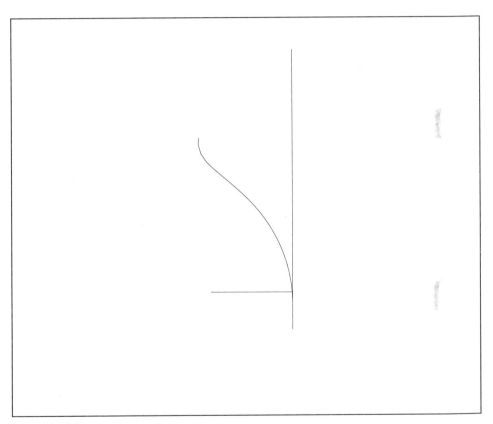

Figure 7-32: Wine glass framework

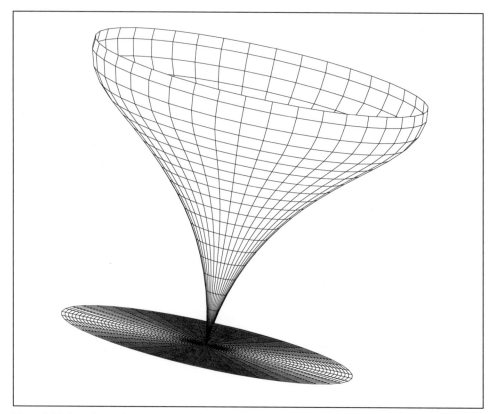

Figure 7-33: Completed wine glass

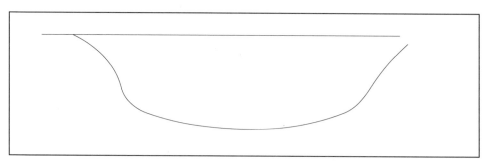

Figure 7-34: Boat framework

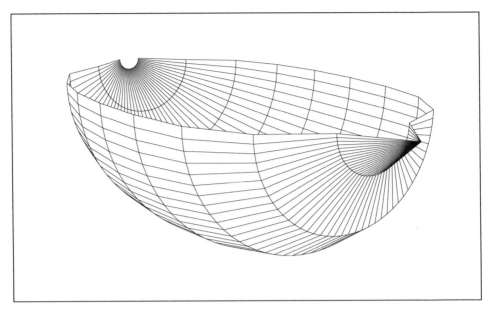

Figure 7-35: Completed boat

As you can see, anything that can be revolved is a candidate for REVSURF.

EDGESURF

There are two things to be aware of when using EDGESURF. First, EDGE-SURF requires you to use exactly four sides. Second, the mesh that is created by EDGESURF follows the contour of the defining curves. One of the biggest problems that most people have when using EDGESURF is not knowing when to use EDGESURF and when to use RULESURF.

Figure 7-36 shows four objects labeled sides 1 through 4. Depending on what you want the mesh to look like, you could use either RULESURF or EDGESURF. Figure 7-37 indicates the four objects were created using RULESURF by picking sides 1 and 3.

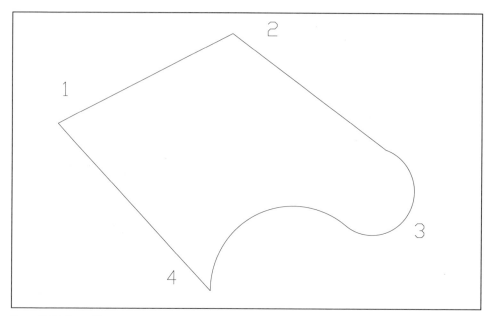

Figure 7-36: Four objects

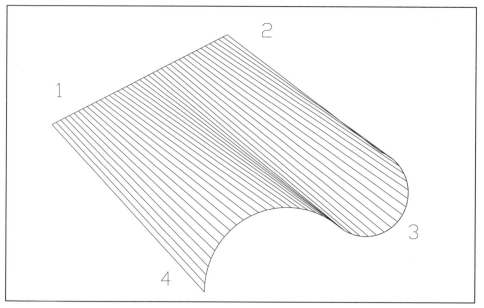

Figure 7-37: Using **RULESURF**

With EDGESURF you pick all four sides. You must pick them in a clockwise or counterclockwise order and relatively on the same side of each. If you skip around, you can get some very unusual results.

 Figure 7-38: The Edge Surface icon

From the Surfaces toolbar choose the Edge Surface icon. Or in the command prompt window:

Type: EDGESURF <Enter>

Response: Select edge 1:

            Pick line 1.

Response: Select edge 2:

            Pick line 2.

Response: Select edge 3:

            Pick line 3.

Response: Select edge 4:

            Pick line 4.

Figure 7-39 indicates the results of using EDGESURF on the four objects.

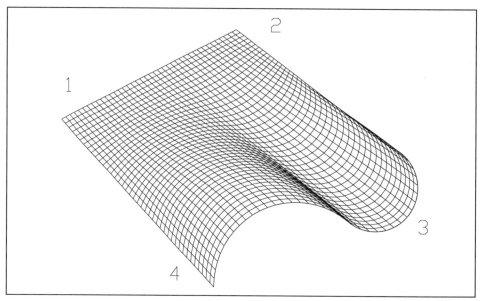

Figure 7-39: Using EDGESURF

Notice the difference in Figures 7-37 and 7-39. The EDGESURF followed the contour of the curve as well as used a mesh in the M and N directions. The vertices of the mesh will also follow the same contour if the points are on a different elevation.

Making Meshes Invisible

As you can see, meshes are invaluable. Their basic problem is that they are ugly. Remember that the purpose of meshes is to hide lines and provide a surface for shading and rendering and also to give shape to the model itself. If you're not planning on rendering or shading the surface and want it only for a hidden line view, then you might want to make your meshes invisible.

You saw previously how you could make 3D faces invisible, but making meshes invisible is a different operation altogether. There are two ways you can do this. The first is by far the easiest. If the mesh is on a layer that is turned off, then you won't be able to see the mesh. Therefore, make sure that all meshes are on at least one separate layer and then turn that layer off. The mesh will still hide the lines, but you won't be able to see the mesh. The major problem with this method is that the mesh will not shade or render. And, of course, if you can't see the mesh, then it has no form or shape. If that was your purpose, you obviously shouldn't be hiding a REVSURF.

The second method is more effective. I have included a program called HIDEMESH.LSP. All you have to do is pick the mesh when asked. Then the mesh lines become invisible. The program explodes the mesh into faces and then makes each face in the selection set invisible. By using this program, you make the mesh invisible, but it still has its shading and rendering characteristics. But you shouldn't use this program if the purpose of the mesh was to give form and shape to the model.

You can find HIDEMESH.LSP in the AutoLISP section of the book. As with the other 3D programs, make certain that HIDEMESH.LSP is properly loaded. If you have the *AutoCAD 3D Companion Disk* installed properly and have loaded 3DTOOLS.LSP, all you need to do is type in the name of the program.

Surfacing Complex Shapes

One of the ironies of meshes is that if the shape were simple, then the application of the mesh would be simple. Unfortunately, most of the shapes that you will encounter are not simple; they are relatively complex. There is, on the other hand, something that you can do to make them simple. You can divide the model into two objects so that you can use RULESURF.

Figure 7-40 illustrates a series of multiple objects. The lines of side 1 and the fillet were originally separate. By using PEDIT, you can make these lines and fillets into a polyline or arc and then join them together, thus creating a single object for the purpose of applying the mesh. Once they are a single object, you can use RULESURF. Figure 7-41 uses RULESURF for the complex shape.

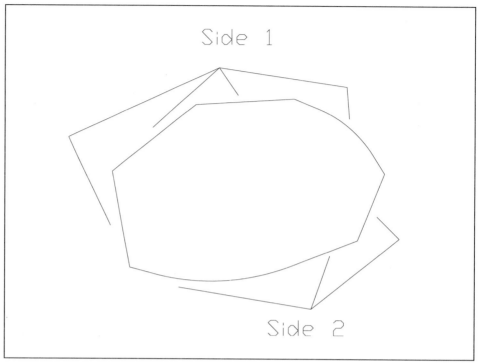

Figure 7-40: Multiple objects

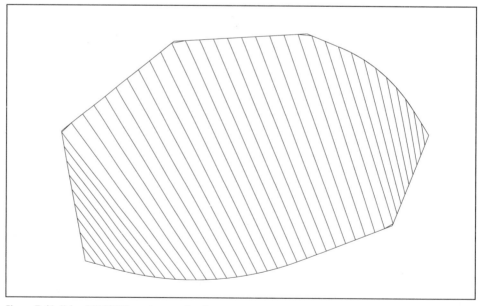

Figure 7-41: Using RULESURF on the complex shape

The following is a method available for Release 12 only. It has *totally* been replaced by the REGION command in Release 13. See the next section for details.

Now take a look at a feature of Release 12 called the *region modeler.* The Release 12 region modeler enables you to identify any complex shape, no matter how many entities are in a single region. Once a region is identified, you'll then use the Release 12 SOLMESH command and AutoCAD will find the boundaries and mesh the region automatically.

It is important that the region modeler be installed. Remember this is not in Release 13. If you receive an error message that the region modeler is not installed, see your *AutoCAD Extras Manual* and the *AutoCAD Installation Manual* for information on its installation for your system.

Now I'm going to show you what has to be the neatest trick I've seen since AutoCAD 3D was released. Let's see exactly how it works. Figure 7-42 represents a box with an irregular shape. You must figure out a way to put a top on the model. Notice that the sides are already extruded; therefore, they form their own surface. But the top of the box (as indicated in Figure 7-43) shows that a top surface must be created. Trying to create a surface mesh for this box can be very difficult.

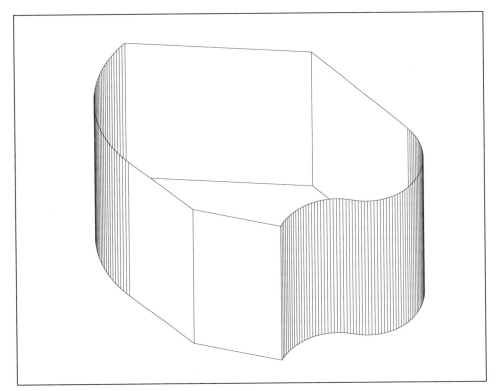

Figure 7-42: Irregular box

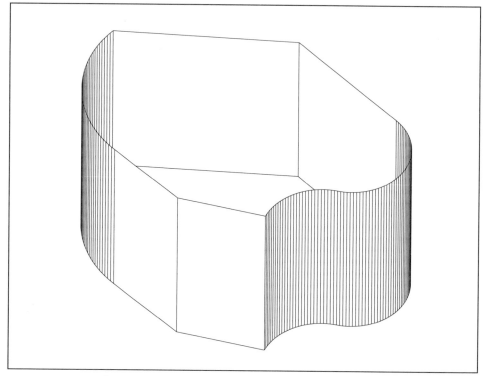

Figure 7-43: Before region mesh

To use the region modeler, you must follow certain rules. The main one is that the objects you are making into a region can't be extruded. This means you have a problem here. This figure is extruded. So how do you get around that?

You'll use the boundary command.

Boundary

There is also a command called boundary (in Release 12 it's called BPOLY).

Figure 7-44: The Boundary icon.

Choose the Boundary icon from the Polygon flyout of the Draw toolbar. See Figure 7-44. This activates the Boundary Creation dialog box (see Figure 7-45). The command is similar to the boundary hatch. Boundary just creates the boundary used by the boundary hatch and lets you keep it without hatching. The boundary it creates can be a polyline or a region.

If you can get the boundary command to create a boundary in the shape of the top of your model, then you can use that boundary as your region because it's not extruded. Then you can mesh the region. Now look at the details.

First, make certain that the UCS is parallel with the object you want to mesh:

Type: UCS <Enter>

Type: OB <Enter>

Pick some place on the top of the model. Then the UCS is made parallel with the object.

Next, change the elevation to be equal to the top of the model. Don't use the ELEV command because you don't know where the top of the model is. An easier way to do this is to change the UCS origin to one of the intersections on the top of the model:

Type: UCS <Enter>

Type: O <Enter>

Now, using object snap intersection, pick an intersection on the top of the model.

You're now ready to issue the boundary command:

Type: BOUNDARY <Enter>

A dialog box appears (see Figure 7-45). If you're lucky enough that other lines don't confuse the BOUNDARY, then you can get away with simply picking Pick Points and then picking somewhere close to the inside edge of one of the top lines.

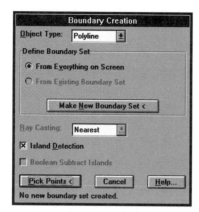

Figure 7-45: The Boundary Creation dialog box

On the other hand, other lines from your angle of view may confuse the boundary command. But you can isolate only the lines you want the BOUNDARY to consider. To do this, pick Make New Boundary Set <. Then pick only the lines you want the BOUNDARY to consider and press Enter. Now pick Pick Points and pick somewhere close to the inside edge of one of the top lines and press Enter. Then pick OK in the dialog box.

Check the boundary:

Type: SELECT <Enter>

Type: L <Enter>

Your polyline will highlight. Check to make sure it forms the correct boundary. If it does not, then erase it with ERASE Last and begin again.

Now that you have a polyline that represents the top of your form, if you're using Release 12, your next step is to create a mesh using the SOLMESH command or if you're using Release 13, use the BMESH13 program included on the companion disk.

Type: SOLMESH <Enter>

Response: Select Objects:

Type: L <Enter> <Enter>   (The last object is the polyline you just created.)

At this point you have the mesh, perfectly formed around the top of the model. Now you can return the UCS to its original settings. If your mesh doesn't completely cover the edges, you can increase the SOLWDENS variable, which acts similarly to SURFTAB1 and SURFTAB2. The values range from 1 to 12. The higher the value, the denser the mesh.

Now try this method:

Type: HIDE <Enter>

Figure 7-46 shows the results of the region mesh.

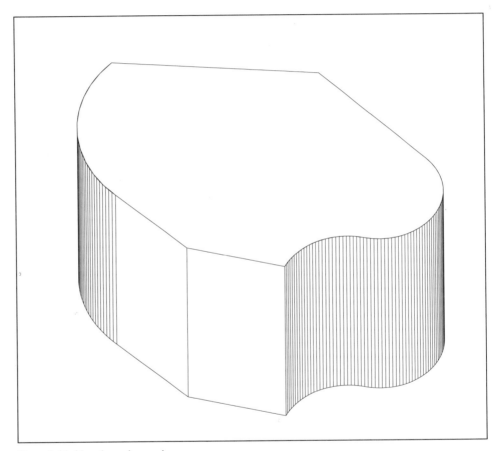

Figure 7-46: After the region mesh

The only problem with this method is that it has many steps. Therefore, I've simplified it for you with two AutoLISP programs to add to your 3D tools. They are BMESH.LSP, which stands for boundary mesh, and the other is RMESH.LSP, which stands for region mesh. The BMESH.LSP program is the simpler of the two. With a little luck, you can use it to create a mesh with only three picks. Your first pick selects an object that sets the UCS for you. The second pick determines the elevation, and your third pick determines the interior boundary. This program won't work on all areas because the UCS may be parallel, but the X and Y may not be going in the correct direction. This possibility is especially true when you try to mesh the side of an object that was created with the TCOPY.LSP program. You might need to rotate the UCS around X. The second problem occurs if the angle of view doesn't permit the BOUNDARY to correctly identify the exact boundary you need.

The RMESH.LSP program will work in all cases. RMESH uses the UCS 3Point option to set your origin and UCS. Once this is done, then RMESH asks you to select objects that bound the area you want to mesh. Then you pick an interior point. This program requires only a few more steps, and it works well.

You can find BMESH.LSP and RMESH.LSP in the AutoLISP section of the book. As with the other 3D programs, make certain that BMESH.LSP and RMESH.LSP are properly loaded. If you have the *AutoCAD 3D Companion Disk* installed properly and have loaded 3DTOOLS.LSP, all you need to do is type in the name of the program.

Now take a look at the mouse or digitizer puck that you created in Chapter 6, "Viewports." Reload the drawing you saved in Chapter 6. Remember that it wasn't quite finished. As you can see in Figure 7-47, there's no surface on either side. The upper-right viewport is one side of the model, and the lower-right viewport is the other side.

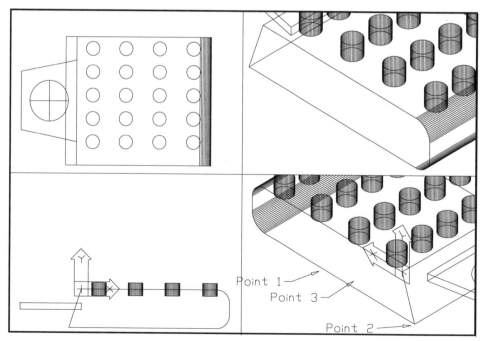

Figure 7-47: Unfinished sides

Pick and make active the lower-right viewport. Then use the BMESH command:

Type: BMESH <Enter>

Response: Pick the object to be meshed
Select object:

Pick Point 1, as shown in Figure 7-47.

Response: Pick endpoint or intersection that represents the elevation

Using object snap intersection, pick at Point 2.

Response: Pick inside area

Pick at Point 3.

That's all there is to it. Repeat the command for the upper-right viewport and see Figure 7-48 for a view of the finished mouse.

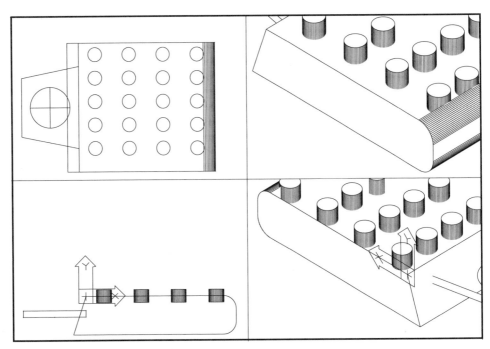

Figure 7-48: Finished sides with BMESH

Cutting Holes in Surfaces

The following is the only method to cut holes in surfaces in Release 12. It is valid in Release 13, but there is a better way in Release 13 using the REGION command.

In this chapter you've learned there are only three ways that you can create a 3D model where lines will be hidden with the HIDE command. They are extrusions, faces and meshes. If you don't have one of these three over the surface of your drawing, then lines behind the surface will not be hidden or shaded.

For this next example, you'll cut a hole in one side of the model. Look at the surface in Figure 7-40. You'll cut a hole through the surface so you can see through it. So that you can see if this example is going to work, I have placed a line at the negative elevation across the area in the figure.

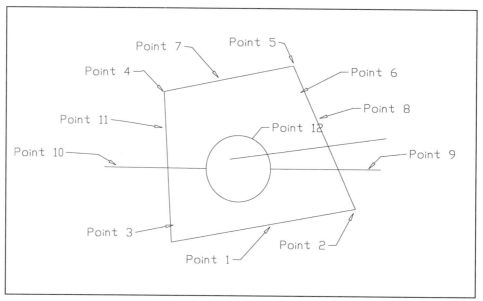

Figure 7-49: Circle with construction lines

If the shape of the opening is formed by a series of straight lines, working with it is easier. Working with a circular opening is the hardest. Therefore, you will use the circle to form the hole you're going to cut.

There is really no way you can cut a hole into an extrusion, a face or a mesh using AutoCAD. But just because you can't actually cut a hole into the surface doesn't mean that you can't build the surface around the hole.

That's exactly what you're going to have to do. Therefore, you won't be able to use an extrusion or a face, such as 3D face or pface to accomplish this task. The only thing that's going to work effectively is a mesh.

Your object here is to place a mesh on all parts of the interior of the rectangle except for the circle. First, draw a construction line from one quadrant of the circle across and then from the other quadrant of the circle across.

Now use the BMESH program and pick Points 1, 2 and 3, as shown in Figure 7-49. For the upper half, you will need to use the RMESH program because the line you drew at the negative elevation will get in the way of the BOUNDARY part of the command. For the Origin and X directions, pick Points 4 and 5. Then choose only the sides that are to be considered by picking Points 7 through 12. Finally, pick Point 6 inside the line.

Now erase the two construction lines and hide the lines (see Figure 7-50). That's all there is to it.

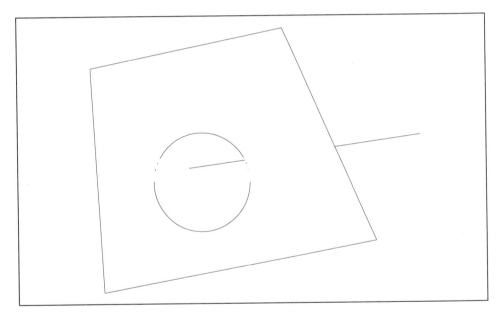

Figure 7-50: Surface with hole

You also could have used RULESURF to create a hole in the surface. But then the exercise becomes a little tricky. For the RULESURF mesh you can have only two objects. If you choose the top line of the rectangle and the bottom line of the rectangle, you will get a surface mesh, but it will go completely through the circle. This won't accomplish your goal. Therefore, you must divide the circle into two arcs.

Dividing a circle into two arcs is not a straightforward process. But I have provided you with a program called DIVCIR.LSP. By picking any two points on the circle, you can divide it into two arcs.

You can find DIVCIR.LSP in the AutoLISP section of the book. As with the other 3D programs, make certain that DIVCIR.LSP is properly loaded. If you have the *AutoCAD 3D Companion Disk* installed properly and have loaded 3DTOOLS.LSP, all you need to do is type in the name of the program.

You are almost ready to proceed. But remember that the RULESURF command requires only two sides. The top side is easy to visualize. But the bottom side is the left line, the top arc and the right line that cuts through the rectangle.

The problem is that you have three objects here, not one. You must therefore join them as a single polyline. To do this, use the PEDIT command:

Type: PEDIT <Enter>

Pick one of the lines. AutoCAD will tell you that it's not a polyline and ask if you want to turn it into one. Answer <Y>.

Type: Join <Enter>

You are now going to join the left line, the top arc and the right line by picking each and then exit the PEDIT command.
Now use RULESURF:

Type: RULESURF <Enter>

Pick the top line of the rectangle and the top arc that has been joined. The RULESURF will create a mesh on the top portion of the rectangle.
Now explode the top arc:

Type: EXPLODE <Enter>

Pick the top arc and press Enter. Then the joined set of polylines will be exploded and separated. You must now join the bottom arc and the two adjacent lines:

Type: PEDIT <Enter>

Pick one of the lines. AutoCAD will tell you that it's not a polyline and ask if you want to turn it into one. Answer <Y>. Remember that the line was exploded with the arc.

Type: Join <Enter>

You are now going to join the left line, the bottom arc and the right line by picking each and then exit the PEDIT command.
Repeat the RULESURF command:

Type: RULESURF <Enter>

This time pick the bottom line of the rectangle and the bottom arc. The RULESURF will form a mesh on the bottom portion of the rectangle. Notice that all of the rectangle except the circle has a mesh around it.
Isn't the BMESH command a lot easier?
If you're using Release 12, there's a third way to cut a hole in the surface using the region modeler—that is to subtract the circle from the rectangle.
Remember that only 2D polylines, circles, 2D solids, donuts and traces can be solidified. Begin with the rectangle by itself and then use the BOUNDARY to create a polyline in the shape of the rectangle as before. Then draw a circle in the center and subtract the circle from the rectangle:

Type: SOLSUB <Enter>

Response: Select Objects:

Type: L <Enter> <Enter>   (Last refers to the polyline just created.)

Response: Objects to subtract from them...
             Select objects:

Pick the circle to form a region. Now you can apply the mesh with the SOLMESH command.
As you can see, I've shown you three ways to cut a hole in a surface. As with most things in AutoCAD, there are many ways to do the same thing. Your task is to gain the experience and discover the right technique for the right situation.

Regions

Beginning with Release 13 AutoCAD changed dramatically the concept of regions. All of the commands beginning with SOL are gone. They have been replaced with REGION, SUBTRACT and UNION. The REGION command creates a region. The SUBTRACT command removes one region from another. And the UNION command joins one region with another. The following is an easy way to create a hole in a surface. Instead of using a mesh or 3DFACE to create the surface, use the REGION command. Begin by drawing a rectangle with a polyline and place a line at a lower elevation behind it as we did before. See Figure 7-51.

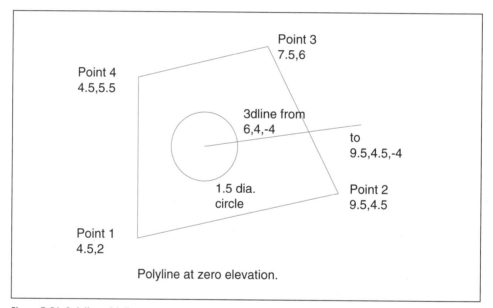

Point 3
7.5,6

Point 4
4.5,5.5

3dline from
6,4,-4

to
9.5,4.5,-4

1.5 dia.
circle

Point 2
9.5,4.5

Point 1
4.5,2

Polyline at zero elevation.

Figure 7-51: Polyline with line

Type: REGION <ENTER>

Response: Select Objects:

Pick the polyline and press Enter.

The polyline is now a region. If you hide the lines you will see that the single line is hidden. Now draw a circle in the middle of the region and over the line. You will now need to make a region of the circle.

Type: REGION <ENTER>

Response: Select Objects:

> Pick the circle and press Enter.
> The circle is now a region. Next subtract from the polyline region, the circle region.

Type: SUBTRACT <ENTER>

Response: Select solids and regions to subtract from...

> Select objects:

> Pick the polyline and press Enter.

Response: Select solids and regions to subtract...

> Select objects:

> Pick the circle and press Enter.
> Now hide the lines. As you can see you now have the same results. See Figure 7-52.

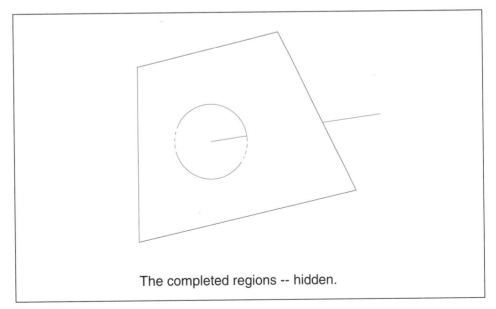

The completed regions -- hidden.

Figure 7-52: Hole cut into region

BMESH13

Because of the differences in the way AutoCAD Release 13 and Release 12 handle regions, the BMESH and the RMESH programs have both been replaced simply by the BMESH13 program. The BMESH and RMESH programs are still part of the disk for those who are still using Release 12. Those programs will not work with Release 13. The REGION command and the BMESH13 program will cover most any of the situations that you find.

For more information on Solid Modeling see Chapter 13.

Moving On

Surfaces are an integral, but complex, part of AutoCAD. Without them you can't effectively work in 3D. You won't really understand all of the aspects of this chapter by reading it one time. Go back and read it again. Then begin by practicing. This way, you will begin to work through the various surfacing problems that you will encounter. Remember to use the AutoLISP programs presented in this chapter; they will make your task much easier.

The next chapter shows you how to dimension in 3D. It may seem simple, but there are some real "gotchas" if you're not careful. As you will see, AutoCAD can lie to you if you don't use it correctly.

CHAPTER 8

Dimensioning in 3D

How sure are you that your dimensions are correct? Now that's a scary question. Even the thought of it should send chills down your spine. Why wouldn't your dimensions be correct in AutoCAD? Well, that's what this chapter is all about. You're going to look at one of the biggest "gotchas" in AutoCAD—when dimensions aren't what they seem.

And you're also going to look at what you can do to assure your dimensions are correct when working in 3D, as well as how to dimension in perspective. To make things simpler, I've created three AutoLISP programs to help you out.

The Problem With AutoCAD

There are only a few things in this life that you can really depend on, and one of them has always been that if you play by AutoCAD's rules, dimensions in AutoCAD are correct. If you draw a line 10 feet long, dimension it and don't play any games, then that line will always be 10 feet long—not 9 feet, not 11 feet and especially not 0 feet. Another truism is that if you inquire using the DIST command in AutoCAD and dimension the same line, then you'll get the same answer. And as long as Associative Dimensioning is on and you've picked correctly, you can bank on the dimensions on your drawings.

But what if you find that dimension and DIST give you different answers on the same line and that the dimension is the wrong one? What makes this problem worse is that you don't necessarily know when AutoCAD is lying to you. There are no error messages, and there is nothing to indicate that something has gone wrong.

The problem lies with the User Coordinate System. I'll offer a couple of examples to help illustrate the point. In Figure 8-1 a rectangular cube is drawn, 7 units by 4 units with an extrusion of 5 units.

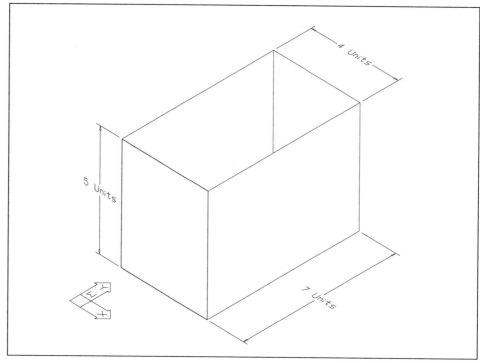

Figure 8-1: 7 x 4 cube

There is nothing unusual about this drawing. The figure was kept purposely simple. Notice the UCS icon in the lower left-hand part of the figure indicating that you're in the World Coordinate System.

First, check the distance to verify that the cube is exactly as it was drawn.

Figure 8-2: The Distance icon from the Inquiry flyout of the Object Properties toolbar

From the Object Properties toolbar, choose the Inquiry flyout then pick the Distance icon. Or in the command prompt window:

Type: DIST <Enter>

Response: First point:

Using object snap intersection, pick one of the intersections.

Response: `Second point:`

Using object snap intersection, pick the other intersection along the long side of the cube.

Response: `Distance=7.0000, Angle in XY Plane=90, Angle from XY Plane=0, Delta X=0.0000, Delta Y=7.0000, Delta Z=0.0000`

This type of information is exactly what you would expect. But start changing a few things around. First, change the UCS with a 3Point as indicated in Figure 8-3 (which shows how to align the UCS icon with the side).

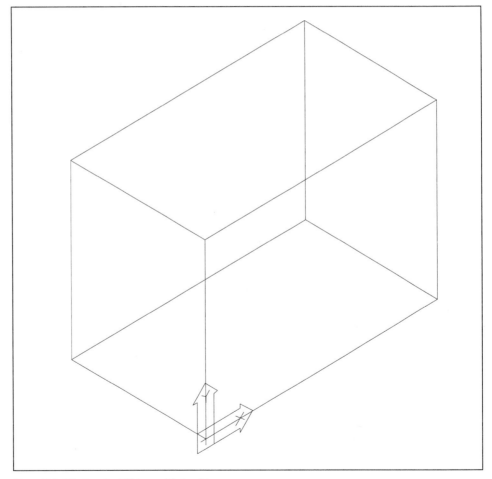

Figure 8-3: Aligning the UCS icon with the side

Now rotate the UCS around an X of 37 degrees and then around a Y of 40 degrees.

Type: UCS <Enter>
        X <Enter>
        37 <Enter>
        UCS <Enter>
        Y <Enter>
        40 <Enter>

This process gives you an angled UCS. Figure 8-4 illustrates a view of the highly skewed UCS.

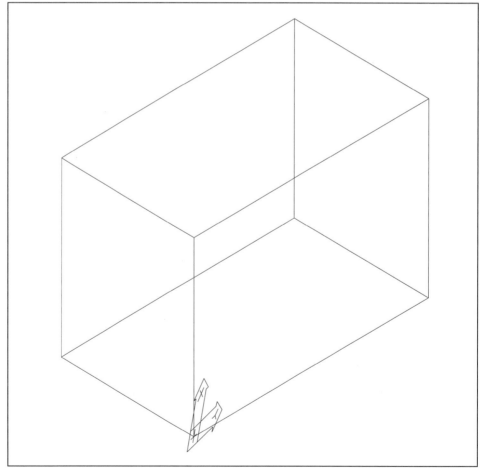

Figure 8-4: Highly skewed UCS

Just to make certain that nothing is wrong—even though the UCS obviously is not parallel with any of the objects in your drawing—check it out again with the DIST command. From the Object Properties toolbar choose the Distance icon. Or in the command prompt window:

Type: `DIST <Enter>`

Response: `First Point:`

Using object snap intersection, pick the same corner as before.

Response: `Second Point:`

Figure 8-5: The Dimensioning toolbar

Again using object snap intersection, pick the other corner indicating the long side of the cube as you did before.

As you can see, the response is still the same. Nothing has changed even though the UCS changed. The length of the line is still 7.0000. So far there is obviously no problem with AutoCAD, and you're getting exactly what you thought you should be getting. In fact, regardless of the direction of the UCS, the DIST command returns the correct distance from any point in 3D space to any other point in 3D space as long as the coordinates themselves are known. And in this case because you're using object snap intersection, you don't have a problem.

Now dimension the line. From the Dimensioning toolbar choose the dimlinear command. Or in the command prompt window type the new DIMLINEAR command. It allows you to create horizontal, vertical and rotated linear dimensions with a single command.

Type: `DIMLINEAR <Enter>`

Response: `First extension line origin or <Enter> to select:`

Pick exactly the same two points using object snap intersection.

Response: `Second extension line origin:`

Pick the other intersection using object snap intersection.

Response: `Dimension line location (Text/Angle):`

It really doesn't matter where you pick because your dimensions will be wrong! Pick any point on the screen.

Response: `Dimension text <5.2020>:`

There isn't any line in the drawing that has this dimension. You checked carefully with the DIST command before you changed the UCS and after you changed it, and it was 7.0000 in each case. Now when you do a dimension command using the Horizontal option, picking the same intersections, the dimension text that is about to be placed in the drawing is 5.2020.

What went wrong? Well, you might say the problem is that the line doesn't really form a horizontal dimension angle. Try to dimension with the only other two options that it could be, Vertical or Aligned. When you retry the operation with Aligned using the same two points, you again get the 5.2020 instead of the 7.0000, which it is supposed to be. When you try using Vertical, the response gets even worse. But at least it's so farfetched that you know something is wrong. The dimension text becomes 0.0000.

Now try one more thing. Rotate several times around X and Y using random angles and then repeat the three dimension options on the same intersections. As you can see, the dimension text keeps changing.

Setting Your UCS for Accurate Dimensions

It doesn't take a nuclear scientist to figure out that the problem with inaccurate dimensions lies with the current UCS in effect at the time you issue the dimension command. In these examples I purposely made the UCS at an odd angle relative to the object being dimensioned to illustrate the point. You wouldn't purposely do this because the angle of the dimension lines would be highly skewed and would not make the kind of dimension you want to make. I purposely created the UCS grossly out of synch with the line that you're dimensioning to illustrate the point that even a slight change in the UCS not parallel with the line being dimensioned could cause unpredictable problems. The last thing that you want is to have a dimension on your drawing that isn't correct—even if the error is small.

The problem is that if the UCS is not completely parallel with the object and is only off by just a little bit, then your dimension might be off by just a little bit. But it might be close enough that, from your angle of view, you wouldn't know it just by looking.

It may be obvious that to have correct dimensions in 3D your UCS must be parallel with the object you're dimensioning. This is going to be necessary to not only line up the dimension with the object, but also to assure that you're going to get the correct dimensions. And once you're aware that there is a problem, then you are alert that there is a proper way to dimension when working in 3D. And if you don't follow some simple principles, then you're at risk of having an undetectable error.

What is the solution? The answer to this question is simple. The UCS has to be parallel with the object you're dimensioning.

Try your dimension again, but first make sure that the current UCS is parallel to the object. The easiest way to do this is by using the UCS Object command.

 Figure 8-6: The Object UCS from the UCS toolbar

From the UCS toolbar choose the Object UCS. Or in the command prompt window type:

Type: UCS <Enter>

Type: OB <Enter>

Response: Select object to align UCS:

This time pick one of the shorter lines in the model. Then the UCS icon rotates, as indicated in Figure 8-7. The figure gives a view of the UCS parallel with a line.

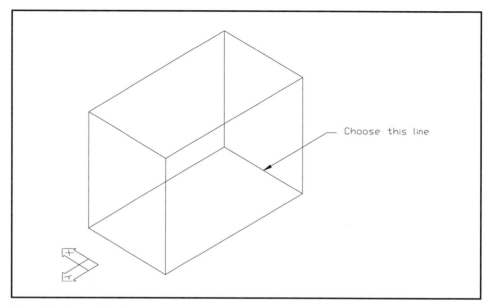

Figure 8-7: UCS parallel with a line

Notice that the UCS is parallel with the object that you're dimensioning. Now dimension the line horizontally.

  Figure 8-8: The Dimlinear icon

From the Dimensioning toolbar choose the Dimlinear icon. Or in the command prompt window:

Type: `DIMLINEAR <Enter>`

Response: `First extension line origin or <Enter> to select:`

Using object snap intersection, pick one of the intersections.

Response: `Second extension line origin:`

Using object snap intersection, pick the other intersection.

Response: `Dimension line location (Text/Angle):`

Pick an area where you want the dimensions to appear.

Response: `Dimension text <4.0000>:`

Type: `<Enter>`

Figure 8-9 shows the correct dimension. You know it's correct because the UCS is properly aligned.

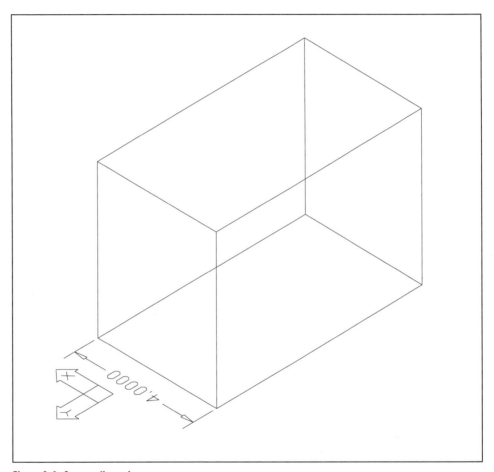

Figure 8-9: Correct dimension

But wait. Do you still have trouble in River City? Look at the dimension. It's possibly upside down; the text is going in the wrong direction. Text goes in the direction of positive X unless you use a style that is upside down or backwards.

Setting the Direction

Because all text, including dimension text, goes in the direction of positive X, you must adjust the direction of the UCS icon so that the X arrow is going in the direction you want the dimension text to go. You could do that with the RY or RX programs. Using either of these programs would assure that as you change the direction of the X arrow, you remain parallel to the object. But I have provided you a simpler program called UCSX.LSP.

UCSX works very simply. It sets you to object snap intersection and asks you to pick the point of origin. Then it asks for a point in the direction of positive X. At this point it leaves you parallel but adjusts the X arrow. See Figure 8-10 for a view of X going in the right direction.

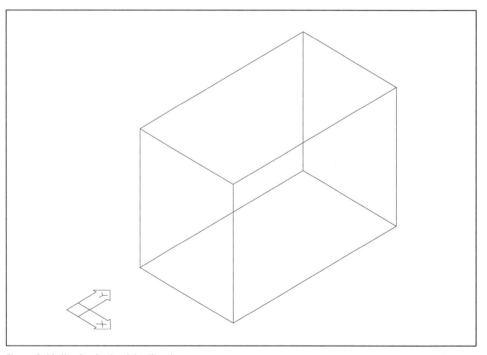

Figure 8-10: X going in the right direction

You can find UCSX.LSP in the AutoLISP section of the book. As with the other 3D programs, make certain that UCSX.LSP is properly loaded. If you have the *AutoCAD 3D Companion Disk* installed properly and have loaded 3DTOOLS.LSP, all you need to do is type in the name of the program.

If you dimension once again now that the X arrow is heading right, you see that the dimensions come out correctly. See Figure 8-11 for the correct dimensions view.

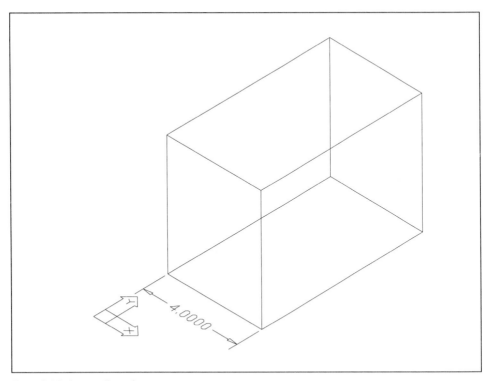

Figure 8-11: Correct dimensions

One further question may come to mind: Do you have to make the UCS parallel for every line in the drawing that you're dimensioning? The answer is not necessarily. Remember that the definition of parallel to the current UCS does not mean that it has to have the exact same X, Y and Z coordinates. The direction of X, Y and Z of one object must be parallel to the direction of X, Y and Z of another.

For example, the top and bottom line of each part of the cube are along the same plane. So if you're sure that the objects lie parallel to the same plane and that they're all parallel to the current UCS, then you can proceed to dimension them as a group. But if any of the dimension objects lie along another plane, then you must repeat the procedure for each group before they can be dimensioned.

Repeating the procedure can obviously be a chore, so wouldn't it be nice if there were a program that would automatically set your UCS and the direction of the X arrow while dimensioning? At the end the program would return you to your previous UCS. That's exactly what 3DDIM.LSP does.

You can find 3DDIM.LSP in the AutoLISP section of the book. As with the other 3D programs, make certain that 3DDIM.LSP is properly loaded. If you have the *AutoCAD 3D Companion Disk* installed properly and have loaded 3DTOOLS.LSP, all you need to do is type in the name of the program.

Here's how the program works:

Type: 3DDIM <Enter>

Response: Select object:

Pick the line you want to dimension.

Response: First point

Pick the first point of the line being dimensioned.

Response: Second point

Pick the second point of the line being dimensioned. Remember to pick these points in the direction you want the text to go.

Response: Dimension line location

Pick a point where you want the dimension to be located. Then the proper dimensions are placed. Figure 8-12 shows automatic 3D dimension.

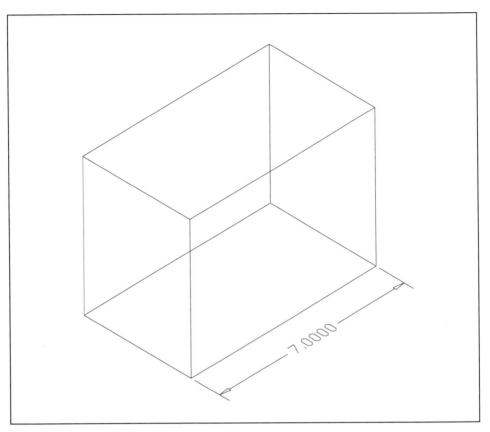

Figure 8-12: Automatic 3D dimension

Dimensioning in 3D is not difficult, especially with the 3DDIM command and the UCSX program. But you must be careful. You can make mistakes no matter how careful you are. The best thing to do is to check all of your dimensions with the DIST command. Because the DIST command never gives you a problem as you go from object snap intersection to object snap intersection, it should be routine that after you place the dimensions, you check them.

To make checking go faster, I have included a quick AutoLISP program called QDIST, which sets you automatically to object snap intersection and asks you to pick two points. It then tells you what the real distance is. This way, you can quickly go around the drawing checking out the dimensions. Each time you want to repeat the command just press Enter.

You can find QDIST.LSP in the AutoLISP section of the book. As with the other 3D programs, make certain that QDIST.LSP is properly loaded. If you have the *AutoCAD 3D Companion Disk* installed properly and have loaded 3DTOOLS.LSP, all you need to do is type in the name of the program.

Dimensioning With Perspective

Is it possible to dimension in perspective? The answer is yes, but there are some challenges. And there are several techniques that you can use. The basic problem is the fact that you can't point and pick while in perspective. If this is the case, then how are you going to pick the dimension line or the points of intersection?

Here's one technique that works nicely. Remember the USVIEW.LSP and URVIEW.LSP programs that you used previously? The USVIEW program saves the view and the current UCS by the same name. The URVIEW restores the UCS and the view of the same name. Get ready to use these programs again.

First, establish the perspective you want before you begin dimensioning. Figure 8-13 shows the model in perspective.

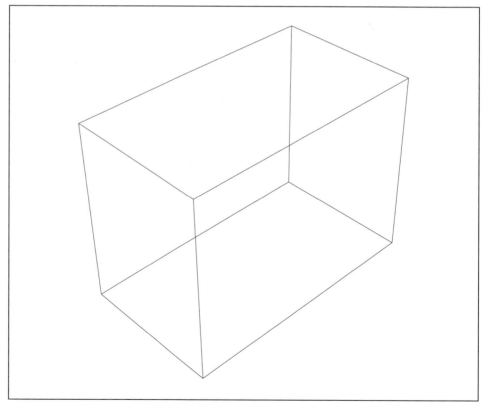

Figure 8-13: Model in perspective

Your next step is to run the USVIEW program:

Type: USVIEW <Enter>

Response: Name of view and UCS to save:

Type: DIM <Enter>

DIM is just a made-up name. Now use the POFF program to turn the perspective off. Proceed to dimension using the 3DDIM command. While you're using the 3DDIM command, you can rotate the model or change the UCS as needed to properly dimension. In this case two of the sides are dimensioned.

You can feel free to move around the model or change the UCS because the URVIEW command will restore both the view and the UCS at one time.

Type: URVIEW <Enter>

Response: Name of view and UCS to restore:

Type: DIM <Enter>

Now, as you can see in Figure 8-14 (which shows the dimension in Perspective view), not only is the model in perspective as it was before, but the dimensions that are correctly dimensioned and aligned with the model are also in perspective as well.

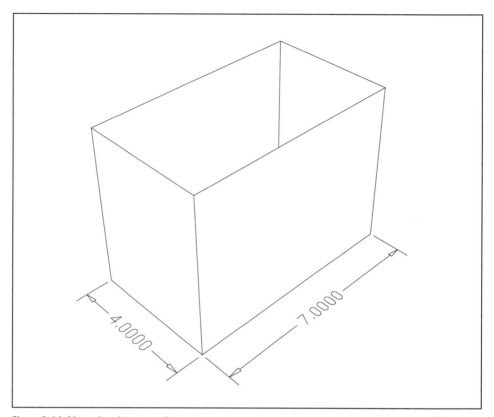

Figure 8-14: Dimensions in perspective

There is another technique that you can use while in perspective. You could, of course, have multiple viewports with one view in perspective and the other not. If you dimension in the one that isn't in perspective, for example, you will see them appear in perspective in the other.

Moving On

In other chapters you will encounter the problem of objects that you want to work with not being parallel with the current UCS. The example used in this chapter is, however, the only time that the results can be so disastrous if you aren't aware of what is going on.

Using the techniques in this chapter to align the current UCS with objects, you will overcome a variety of problems while working in 3D. You'll use these same techniques over and over.

In Chapter 9, "Blocking," you'll look at blocking and inserting in 3D. As with 2D drafting, creating blocks and inserting them is the essence of increased productivity. Understanding how to make blocks in 3D and insert them is crucial. But as with many AutoCAD procedures, you're going to have choices when the blocks are created and again when they're inserted.

As you might imagine, the important UCS is also discussed in Chapter 9.

Blocking

Creating blocks in 3D has the same importance as creating blocks in 2D. No one wants to draw the same items over and over again, and that is the primary reason for blocks in the first place. If you draw a block once, you can use it in as many drawings as you need. In fact, because 3D models are more complex, using 3D blocks is even more essential. But what is vitally important is that all of the blocks fit with each other.

In 2D you learned that you should always draw blocks at 1-to-1 scale so that you could create a parts library that you could insert into any drawing. And if everything were created 1-to-1, then the parts would fit together. This is also true in 3D, but there are other considerations. Parts not only have to be drawn at 1-to-1 scale, but their orientations must also be aligned.

In this chapter you'll learn not only how to create blocks in 3D, but also the relationship of the User Coordinate System to how that block is inserted. If you're not aware of the effect of the User Coordinate System not only at the time the block is created but also when it's inserted, you can get some very strange results.

At the same time you'll also learn how using differing User Coordinate Systems and some plotting tricks can enable you to do some novel things with blocks in both 3D and 2D drawings.

UCS & Blocking

If you can remember one basic rule when blocking in 3D, you'll have learned most of what this chapter has to teach you. The first rule is easy to remember: *The UCS you are using when you block an object has to be the same UCS you use when you insert back that same object. Therefore, use the World Coordinate System.*

This rule means that whatever UCS is set at the time you block, you have to somehow re-create that exact same UCS when you insert the block. If you can re-create the UCS, then the object will be inserted exactly as it was blocked.

This rule might have a shot if the block is inserted into the same drawing. But what about all those blocks that you wrote out to disk with the WBLOCK command? How will you ever keep the UCSs straight from drawing to drawing? The practical answer is that you can't. And if you make a mistake and use a different UCS than that used when the file was written, the block will be inserted at some strange angles.

But you can make blocking easy for yourself if you remember rule number two: *always make sure you are in the World Coordinate System when you block and when you insert.* The World Coordinate System is the only coordinate system that you can be sure is the same from drawing to drawing and from block to block.

The angle of view of the object at the time it is blocked is of no importance except for one trick that I'll show you later in this chapter. This means that if you create a block while in the World Coordinate System, it doesn't matter what your target/camera view point is at the time. The block will be created correctly and, if inserted while in the World Coordinate System, it will be inserted correctly.

One of the biggest misconceptions about blocking in 3D is that just because you're in an Isometric view when you create the block, it will be the same Isometric view when you insert it. In the next section you'll see how to make inserting the same Isometric view possible, but it isn't something that will automatically occur.

Inserting the Block

When you insert a block, not only do you have to concern yourself with the coordinate system in effect at the time you created the block, but you also have to worry about the coordinate system in effect when you insert the block. But if you remember rule number two—use the World Coordinate System when blocking and inserting—then you won't go wrong.

Here's a quick example. Figure 9-1 shows a table in Isometric view, and Figure 9-2 shows the hidden line view of the same table. Notice that the UCS is the World Coordinate System at the time of blocking. Now block the table as you would any other block in AutoCAD. The angle of view at the time the drawing is blocked and the angle of view at the time it's inserted don't matter as long as the coordinate systems are the same.

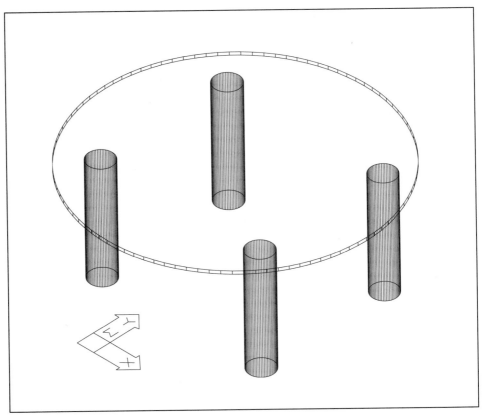

Figure 9-1: Isometric view of table

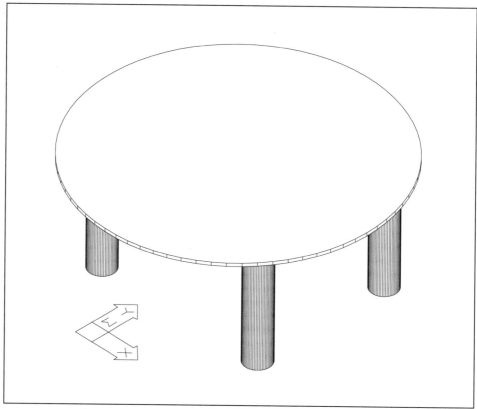

Figure 9-2: Hidden line view

But in this case, you want to prove a point. Rotate the coordinate system 90 degrees around X. Now insert the table. See Figure 9-3, which shows the table inserted and the UCS rotated 90 degrees about X. Notice how the table is now also rotated. If you were to change to a Plan view relative to the current coordinate system, the drawing would look just like the table you drew in Plan view of the World Coordinate System. Figure 9-4 shows the table plan to the UCS.

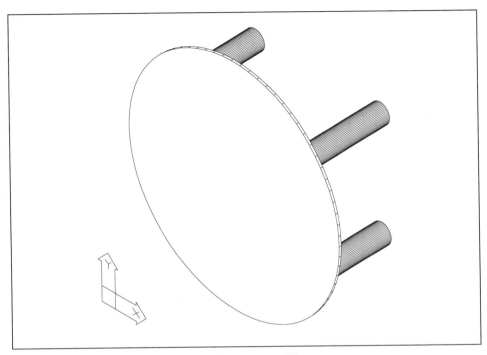

Figure 9-3: Table inserted at UCS and rotated 90 degrees around X

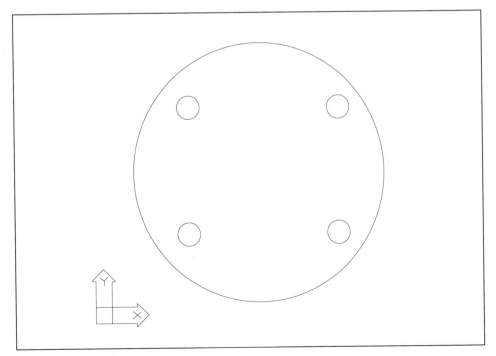

Figure 9-4: Plan to UCS

But you're not in the World Coordinate System. Here, you've learned that blocks are always inserted as Plan view to the current User Coordinate System relative to the coordinate system in effect when the block was created. If this sounds like double-talk, it probably is. So if you start really messing around with the coordinate systems when the block is created and inserted, you won't know which way is up. If you were to change to Plan view of the World Coordinate System, your view would look like Figure 9-5. The figure gives you a view of the inserted block but plan to the WCS.

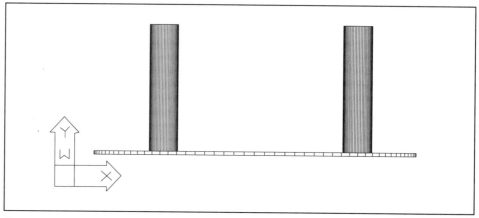

Figure 9-5: Inserted block plan to the WCS

You could go crazy trying to keep all this information straight. There-fore, keep it very, very simple. *Always block while in the World Coordinate System. Always insert while in the World Coordinate System.*

Inserting 3D Blocks at Different Scales

How do you change the scale of the block in 3D? Unless you have read the *AutoCAD Reference Manual* very carefully, this task is not extremely self-apparent. If you have no intention of changing the Z scale factor, then you don't have to do anything differently while inserting a 3D object. On the other hand, you might want to make the X and Y a different scale ratio than the Z or make each different from the other. Normally, AutoCAD asks you for only the X and Y scale factors. If you want to give AutoCAD separate X, Y and Z scale factors, type **XYZ** and press Enter at the first scale question. This way, AutoCAD knows to ask you for the X, Y and Z scale factors separately.

Inserting 3D Blocks in 2D Drawings

There is one major exception to rule number two about inserting blocks. That rule assumes that you want the block to be inserted as it was drawn. There might come a time when you really want the block to be inserted as it was viewed, not as it was drawn.

For example, assume you're in an Isometric view, and you simply want that view inserted in a 2D Plan view, looking isometric. Here's how you do that. Assume that you want the drawing in Figure 9-1 to be inserted at that angle of view in the Plan view of your 2D drawing in the World Coordinate System. This is the one time that you would change the UCS at the time you block the object. You'll have to make the UCS parallel with the screen using the UCS View option.

Figure 9-6: The View UCS icon from the UCS toolbar

From the UCS toolbar choose the View UCS icon. Or in the command prompt window type the command as follows:

Type: UCS <Enter>

Type: V <Enter>

Now the UCS is parallel to the screen. Block the table. Then change to the World Coordinate System and change to Plan view to test it.

Figure 9-7: The World UCS icon from the UCS toolbar

From the UCS toolbar choose the World UCS icon. Or in the command prompt window type the command as follows:

Type: UCS <Enter> <Enter>

This changes you to the World Coordinate System.

Type: Plan <Enter> <Enter>

This changes you to the Plan view of the World Coordinate System.

Now insert the table. It comes in at the same viewing angle it was at the time that it was blocked. If you try to change your view point, the table will look funny. Remember, you wanted a 3D view in a Plan 2D drawing. See Figure 9-8 for a view of how this drawing looks.

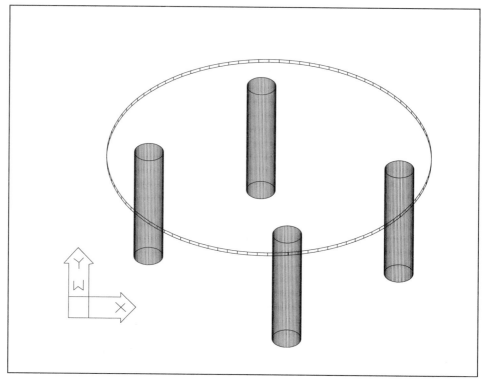

Figure 9-8: 3D drawing in Plan view in the World Coordinate System

Creating a 2D Representation of a 3D Block

For this next example, assume that you want your table to be a hidden line view as a block to be inserted into 2D drawings, but as a simple 2D line drawing with the lines already hidden at that angle of view. Further assume that you want it to be a Perspective view.

To perform this exercise, you must have a 2D representation of the 3D view. You don't want the block to be in 3D. All you want is a 2D line drawing that looks 3D. You will need to create a plotter configuration called a DXB plotter, as follows.

Begin by going into the AutoCAD Configuration menu.

Type: `CONFIG <Enter>`

Press Enter until you get to the Configuration main menu. Then set up a new plotter.

Type: `5 <Enter>`

This number is the Configure Plotter option of the Configuration menu.

Response:
```
Plotter configuration menu
0.  Exit to configuration menu
1.  Add a plotter configuration
2.  Delete a plotter configuration
3.  Change a plotter configuration
4.  Rename a plotter configuration
Enter selection, 0 to 4 <0>:
```

Here you're going to add a plotter configuration.

Type: `1 <Enter>`

AutoCAD then shows you the plotter drivers available to you. The number beside each plotter driver available is different depending on your machine setup and its devices. The one you're looking for is

```
AutoCAD file output formats (pre 4.1) - by Autodesk
```

After you pick this line, you have the following choices:

```
1. ASCII file
2. AutoCAD DXB file
3. Binary plotter file
4. Binary printer-plotter file
5. CAD/Camera file
```

Pick item number 2, DXB file. Then accept all of the defaults and name the plotter configuration DXB file when asked. Continue to press Enter until you're back in your drawing. Now try it. You are now ready to plot your hidden line view to a DXB file.

Type: Plot <Enter>

    From the dialog box, pick plotter devices and choose the DXB plotter that you just created. Make sure that hidden lines is checked. The DXB plotter can plot only to a file. That's why it's grayed out. But you can name the file; for this example, name it TABLE. You might take this opportunity to do a full preview of the plot. When everything is as you want it, pick OK and AutoCAD will begin plotting to the file.

    You can bring the DXB file into your current drawing, but it would be best to start a new drawing without a prototype.

Type: NEW <Enter>

    At the New Drawing dialog box, check no prototype and pick OK. When the new drawing is begun.

Type: DXBIN <Enter>

    Pick or type in **TABLE** from the File dialog box. Your hidden line 2D drawing will appear. It may be a small drawing at the bottom of the screen because it's only the size of the plotted paper that you chose. You'll have to make it larger with the SCALE command.

    Your drawing is no longer a 3D drawing; it looks 3D, but it's not. Figure 9-9 shows a 2D line representation. This really is a 2D line drawing that can be saved as a DWG file or blocked for future insertions in other 2D drawings.

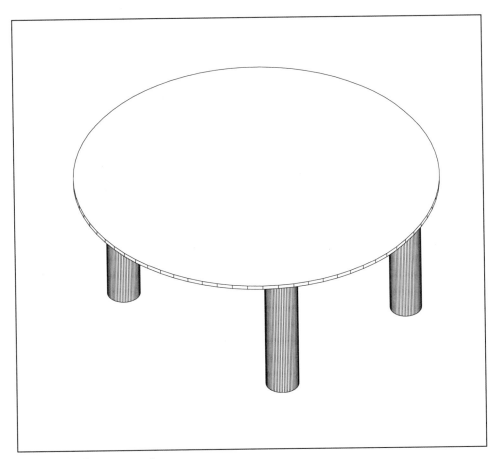

Figure 9-9: 2D line representation

What kind of objects are represented in Figure 9-9 anyway? They are lines, just lines, lots and lots of little lines that represent the hidden line view. But there's no need to hide the lines. They were hidden when you plotted this drawing.

So that there is no misunderstanding, the drawing in the figure is not a 3D drawing. You can turn it to an Isometric view to see what it looks like. Figure 9-10 illustrates an Isometric view of a 2D line drawing. As you can see, there are no 3D coordinates to this drawing at all.

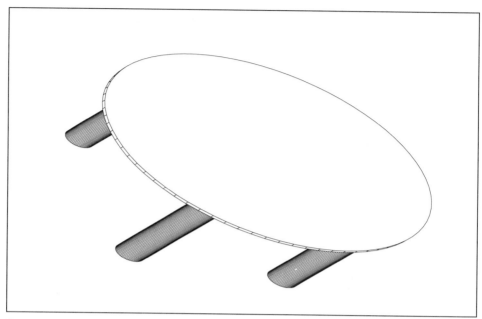

Figure 9-10: Isometric view of 2D line drawing

This section has simply provided a little tip and trick to help you take something in 3D and create a 2D line drawing out of it. You can even make it a Perspective view by turning Distance on before you plot.

Blocking Rules

As a final recap, review the blocking rules.

1. If you want a true 3D block, then make sure you're set to the World Coordinate System when you block and when you insert the block.

2. Generally, the angle of view at the time the block is created is of no importance—with one exception. You may want the angle of view to be the inserted view into a WCS Plan view of your drawing. If this is the case, make sure that the UCS is set to View before it is blocked. Then when the block is inserted into the WCS Plan view, it will come in at the same viewing angle as it was when you blocked it.

3. You may want a 2D line drawing with a hidden line Perspective view. If this is the case, set up a DXB plotter and plot to a DXB file with hidden lines. Then, in a new drawing without a prototype, DXBIN and the drawing will come in as a 2D line drawing, appearing as though it were in 3D.

Moving On

Because of the extra time it takes to model in 3D, it makes sense to have as many items as possible stored as 3D blocks. This chapter has given you the simple rules necessary to make blocking and inserting blocks in 3D as easy as in 2D.

In Chapter 10, "Paper Space," you'll learn the theory and the mechanics of Paper Space. It will give you the ability to create orthographic projections, assembly drawings, and in general enable you to compose and scale your drawing on the screen exactly as it would appear on your paper. That's why Autodesk calls it Paper Space.

Paper Space

This chapter will take the mystery out of Paper Space and take you step by step through the mechanics and theory of Paper Space versus Model Space.

In this chapter you'll learn the theory behind Paper Space and how AutoCAD has given you the tools necessary to organize and design your presentation drawings. You'll look at an overview of Paper Space, the mechanics and commands involved and then how to work with multiple scales on the same sheet. You'll also learn how to hide lines on only selected parts of your drawing. And, as an added bonus, you'll learn new uses of Paper Space that are really not part of its original intention.

Overview

AutoCAD has two major graphical spaces. They are called Model Space and Paper Space. The concept of Model Space is nothing new. It has always been available within AutoCAD and was the only mode available prior to Release 11. Autodesk just had to give it a name once the new Paper Space was developed.

So that there is no misunderstanding from the very beginning, except for some tricks that I'll show you, you're generally always working with a single model. You're not working with multiple drawings. Therefore, whatever you do to your model while in Paper Space will affect all views and aspects of the model itself.

Autodesk has always had a penchant for renaming traditional methods of working with your drawing when new methods are developed. When the User Coordinate System was developed in Release 10, Autodesk indicated that you had always been working in the World Coordinate System and just didn't know it. When the concept of noun/verb was developed for Release 12, you discovered that you had traditionally been working under the verb/noun concept.

Remember when you were in elementary school and the teacher gave you an assignment to create a poster project? On the poster you pasted various models of the major exports of a country. Well, this concept is similar to the way that Paper Space works. Think of Paper Space itself as being the poster board upon which you are going to put various models.

These models are contained in viewports, and they possibly could be different views of the same drawing.

While working in Paper Space, you can move the models around. But what you're actually moving are the viewports that contain the model. Once you have the models positioned on the screen exactly the way you want them, you can, in essence, "glue" them down. But remember that the models are still on the poster board. And you can write on the poster itself. Of course, whatever you write or draw on the poster doesn't affect the model itself. It's like writing on the background. This is the essence of the concept of Paper Space.

So how does working in Paper Space increase your productivity? Paper Space is designed to let you compose multiple drawing views on the same sheet and then plot them out altogether. Imagine that you need three views of your model. You can create three viewports in Paper Space, and using the other 3D tools I've discussed, such as DVIEW or VPOINT, create in each of the viewports the exact view of the model you want. You can resize, align or arrange the viewports on the screen exactly as you need. This arrangement can represent an Orthographic projection or an assembly drawing.

Once the various items are positioned, you still can draw on the poster board itself to label the items on your model or draw arrows from one item to another. Even the title block itself can be part of the poster board, meaning Paper Space, rather than the model itself. Remember that when you're working in Paper Space, you are working on the poster, not the model. Once everything is exactly the way you want it, you can plot it all out at once for a first-class presentation.

Tilemodes

The entire concept of when you're in Paper Space or Model Space is confusing in AutoCAD. This confusion is brought about primarily by the terminology that Autodesk uses in AutoCAD. The important thing to remember is that when you're working in Paper Space, you're unable to work on the model itself. You can only work on the model while in Model Space.

While in Paper Space, the model is contained within Paper Space viewports. How to work in viewports and how to toggle from one to another has already been discussed in detail. When you were working in these viewports, you were working in Model Space. Even when you had only one view of the model on the screen, you were still working in a single viewport in Model Space. Also, remember the configuration of the viewports. You placed them in a variety of configurations using two, three, four or more viewports. You created multiple arrangements. The one thing that all of the viewports had in common was that they were tiled.

A tiled viewport is one in which the viewports can't overlap. Your tiled viewports looked like the tiles that you might find on your kitchen floor or on a checker board. They were next to each other, but one tile could not overlap the other. Also, once the viewports were set up in the configuration, you couldn't move them around or reshape them; they were fixed.

Whether the tiles are fixed or whether you can move them around is determined by a system variable called TILEMODE. When TILEMODE is set to 1, then the tiles are fixed and can't be moved. When TILEMODE is set to 0, then the tiles are free to be moved and can even overlap each other.

What does TILEMODE have to do with Paper Space? Until you can free the viewports so that they can be moved around and are not as fixed tiles, you can't work in Paper Space. Therefore, the system variable TILEMODE is your gateway to Paper Space. This means that if TILEMODE is set to 1, you can only work in Model Space. If TILEMODE is set to 0 and the fixed tiles restriction is eliminated, then you can work in either Paper Space or Model Space. Now see how this process works.

Look at Figure 10-1, which shows a single view of an object in Model Space. You probably recognize the mouse you drew in Chapter 6, "Viewports." Here, it is placed in a single viewport in Model Space. At this point TILEMODE is set to 1. Therefore, you can only work in Model Space. As a clue, you will know you are working in Model Space when the UCS icon appears normal.

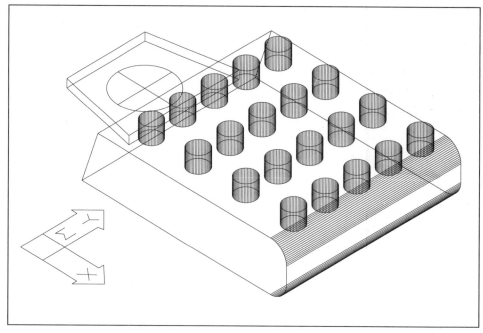

Figure 10-1: Single view in Model Space

 Figure 10-2: The Paper Space icon from the Standard toolbar

From the Standard toolbar choose the Paper Space icon. Or in the command prompt window:

Type: `TILEMODE <Enter>`

Response: `New value for TILEMODE <1>:`

Type: `0 <Enter>`

What happened? Your screen went totally blank. In the lower left-hand corner of the screen, there is a right triangle with an X and Y. This is the icon for Paper Space. The TILEMODE system variable is your gateway to the access of Paper Space features. You have access to Paper Space only through the TILEMODE system variable.

There is one important point that I must emphasize here: you are not necessarily in Paper Space just because TILEMODE is set to 0 (zero). TILEMODE simply determines your ability to manipulate the viewports either as tiled or not tiled. But you can't work in Paper Space if TILEMODE is set to 1.

Setting Up Paper Space Limits & Title Block

Now pick up with the blank screen you read about in the preceding section. What happened to your drawing? It's still there. You can prove it by resetting TILEMODE to 1. And your drawing will appear. But for now, keep TILEMODE as 0.

If you haven't made any changes to the AutoCAD prototype drawing, then changing TILEMODE from 1 to 0 will bring you initially to Paper Space mode. You know you are there when the UCS icon changes from the XY icon to the right triangle.

When you're in Paper Space, it's as though you are in another drawing. The important thing to understand when working in Paper Space is that the size of the drawing area should be equal to the size of the effective drawing area of the actual sheet of paper on which you're going to plot. Therefore, when working in Paper Space mode, your limits should be set to the effective drawing area of your paper.

Take a second to see what that means. You'll use an example of a specific pen plotter with certain limitations. These are not necessarily the limitations of your plotter. Naturally, there are many plotters on the market with different specifications. Some standard plotter specifications are as follows. Figure 10-3 shows Paper Space limits for a plotter.

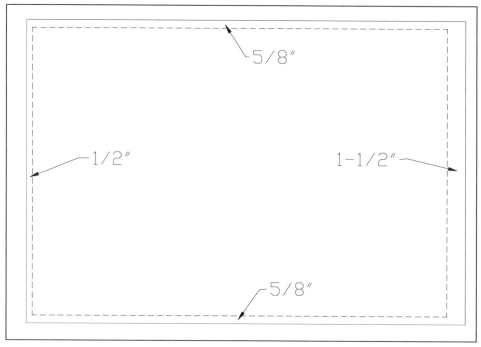

Figure 10-3: Paper Space limits for plotter

The limitations on your plotter might be that you can plot to within 5/8"
on each side of the width of the paper and to within 1/2" at one end and
1 1/2" on the other end. This means that your effective drawing area on the
paper will lose 2 inches lengthwise and 1 1/4" inches on the width.

Assume that your paper physically measures 24" by 36". Your effective
drawing area, therefore, is a width of 22.75 inches and a length of 34
inches. As long as you don't draw anything larger than 22.75" by 34", then
your drawing is guaranteed to fit on the paper. As different plotters have
different limitations, your limits should be set accordingly.

The interesting thing about Paper Space is that you can set up the limits
and units independently from the limits and units used by your model.
Therefore, to facilitate your work, set your units in Paper Space to Engineering with two decimal places of precision. Either use the UNITS command or the Units... dialog box from the Settings pull-down menu.

Now set your LIMITS to 0,0 in the lower left and to 34,22.75 in the
upper right. Then set your GRID and SNAP to .5 each.

Figure 10-4: The Zoom All icon from the Zoom flyout of the Standard toolbar

From the Zoom flyout feature of the Standard toolbar choose the Zoom All icon. Or in the command prompt window:

Type: ZOOM <Enter>

Type: A <Enter>

Type: ZOOM <Enter>

Type: .9x <Enter>

This positions the grid in the middle of the screen. Make a new layer, call it TITLE and make it the current layer.

Figure 10-5: The Layer Control icon from the Object Properties toolbar

From the Object Properties toolbar choose the Layer Control icon. Or in the command prompt window:

Type: LAYER <Enter>

Type: M <Enter>

Type: TITLE <Enter> <Enter>

Your current layer should be TITLE. Now draw your title block and border, beginning with the border. Use either LINE or PLINE to draw a rectangle around the entire limits. Then in the far right-hand block, put in your title block in accordance with the size and shape of the kind of title block you want to use. Figure 10-6 shows the title block sizes and border sizes in Paper Space.

Figure 10-6: Title block and border in Paper Space

At this point you've created the equivalent of a sheet of paper and drawn your border and title block on that sheet. You've made certain that your limits are within the acceptable limits of your plotter.

Now make a new current layer called BORDERS.

Type: LAYER <Enter>

Type: M <Enter>

Type: BORDERS <Enter> <Enter>

You create the BORDERS layer so that the viewports you create while in Paper Space will be on the BORDERS layer. As you will see, the viewports themselves have lines forming their borders. Therefore, when you create the viewports in Paper Space, you want them to be on a layer that you can turn off or freeze. This way, you can later eliminate the viewport borders if you want.

MVIEW

Again, where is the drawing? When you're in Paper Space, you can't see your model until you create a minimum of one viewport using the command called MVIEW. For this example, create one viewport in Paper Space.

Figure 10-7: The Floating Model icon from the Standard toolbar

From the Standard toolbar choose the Floating Model Space icon. The first time you use the command in a new drawing it activates the MVIEW command to let you create floating viewports. Then it lets you switch to MSPACE. Choose the icon or in the command prompt window:

Type: MVIEW <Enter>

Response: ON/OFF/Hideplot/Fit/2/3/4/Restore/<First Point>:

Pick a point at the lower left-hand corner of your border and create a window to the upper right-hand corner. Figure 10-8 shows the single viewport in Paper Space.

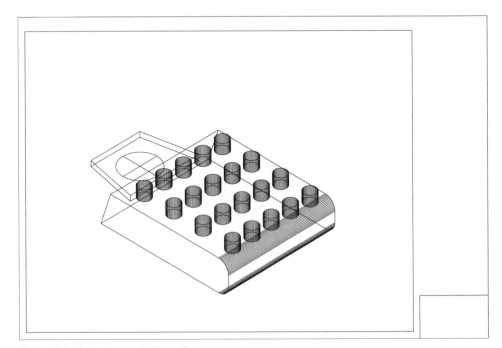

Figure 10-8: Single viewport in Paper Space

Now your Model Space drawing appears in the viewport you created. Move your crosshairs around. Notice that you can't get into the viewport to work on your model because you're still in Paper Space. The viewport itself is the object in Paper Space, not the model in the viewport. If you were to draw at this point, you would be drawing on the equivalent of the poster, not in the model.

Now erase this large viewport and create others.

Figure 10-9: The Erase icon from the Modify toolbar

From the Modify toolbar choose the Erase icon. Or in the command prompt window:

Type: ERASE <Enter>

Type: L <Enter> <Enter>

Here, you issued ERASE last. Because the viewport was the last thing drawn using the MVIEW command, you erased the viewport. Remember that the viewport itself was the object; that's why it disappeared.

Figure 10-10: The Floating Model Space icon from the Standard toolbar

From the Standard toolbar choose the Floating Model Space icon. Or in the command prompt window:

Type: MVIEW <Enter>

Response: ON/OFF/Hideplot/Fit/2/3/4/Restore/<First Point>:

Repeat the preceding command three times by pressing the spacebar; you'll create three smaller windows within the border of the title sheet. See Figure 10-11 for three viewports in Paper Space.

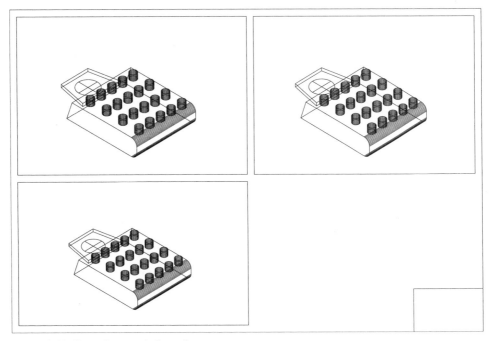

Figure 10-11: Three viewports in Paper Space

Notice how easy it is to freely draw the viewports. Remember that you're still in Paper Space, as indicated by the Paper Space icon in the lower left-hand corner of the screen.

What would happen if you used regular AutoCAD edit commands on the objects while in Paper Space? To find out, try the MOVE command.

Figure 10-12: The Move icon from the Modify toolbar

From the Modify toolbar choose the Move icon. Or in the command prompt window:

Type: MOVE <Enter>

Response: Select objects:

Pick one of your viewports and press Enter to confirm the selection. When you pick viewports, you must pick the border of the viewport.

Response: Base point or displacement:

Now pick a point anywhere on the viewport and move it where it overlaps another viewport. See Figure 10-13 for overlapping viewports in Paper Space.

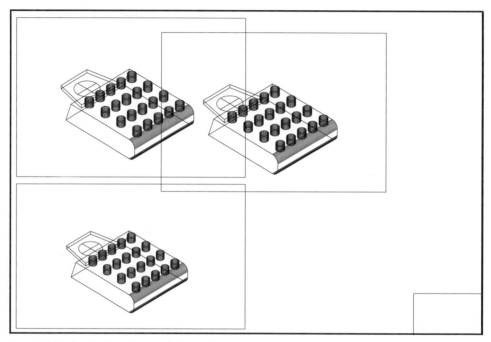

Figure 10-13: Overlapping viewports in Paper Space

As you can see, the viewports themselves are the objects in Paper Space in every sense. You can pick them up and MOVE them around, resize them with the SCALE command, and ERASE them, STRETCH and COPY them. You can use most of the AutoCAD commands on the viewports to properly adjust their size and position on the paper.

The viewports can overlap here because TILEMODE is turned off. The viewports are not restricted to side-by-side tiles.

Now see what is happening in Model Space.

 Figure 10-14: The Tiled Model Space icon from the Standard toolbar

From the Standard toolbar choose the Tiled Model Space icon. Or in the command prompt window:

Type: TILEMODE <Enter>

Type: 1 <Enter>

Notice that the model itself is still exactly as you left it. You could, if you wanted, toggle back and forth between TILEMODE 1 and TILEMODE 0. This way, you could toggle between Paper Space for composition and presentation and Model Space to work on your drawing. As you will soon learn, you don't have to toggle between modes. You have access to Model Space while in TILEMODE 0.

Bringing in Viewports to Paper Space

Because Model Space has its own VIEWPORTS command, wouldn't it be easier if you already had a viewport configuration and brought it into Paper Space instead of trying to line up the viewports in a certain pattern or configuration using the MVIEW command?

Bringing a viewport configuration into Paper Space is not only possible but is also the practical way to do it. Remember that in Model Space you can create tiled viewports in virtually any configuration you want. The only restriction is that the viewports remain tiled to each other. At the same time, you also have the opportunity when you create the viewports to save the viewport configuration. Now create a viewport configuration and see how you can take that configuration in Model Space and transfer it over to Paper Space.

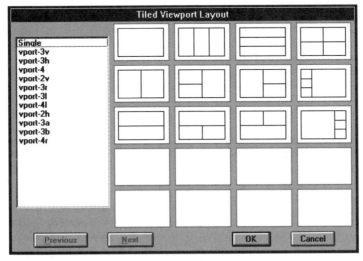

Figure 10-15: The Tiled Viewport Layout dialog box

From the View pull-down menu, choose Tiled Viewports then Layout.... In the Tiled Viewport dialog box choose vport-4. Or in the command prompt window:

Type: `VPORTS <Enter>`

Response: `Save/Restore/Delete/Join/SIngle/?/2/<3>/4:`

Type: `4 <Enter>`

You now have four viewports on your screen. Figure 10-16 shows the four viewports in Model Space.

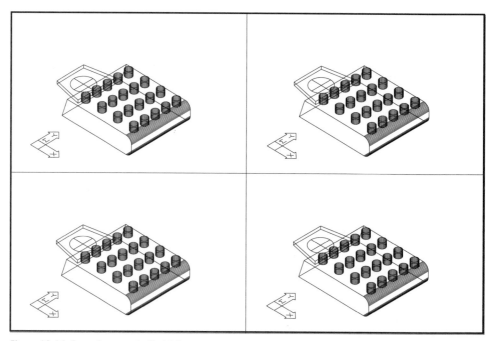

Figure 10-16: Four viewports in Model Space

Pick and make active the upper-left viewport.

Type: `PLAN <Enter>`
          `W <Enter>`
          `ZX <Enter>`

Remember this is the ZOOM Extents AutoLISP ZX.LSP program that is part of your 3D tools. It makes the model the right size in the viewport.

You have simply made the upper-left viewport the Plan view of your drawing. Now pick and make active the upper-right viewport.

 Figure 10-17: The S. E. Isometric icon from the View toolbar

From the View toolbar choose the S. E. Isometric view icon. Or in the command prompt window:

Type: VPOINT <Enter>
      1,-1,1 <Enter>

Pick and make active the lower-right viewport.

 Figure 10-18: The N. W. Isometric icon from the View toolbar

From the View toolbar choose the N. W. Isometric view icon. Or in the command prompt window:

Type: VPOINT <Enter>
      -1,1,1 <Enter>

Pick and make active the lower-left viewport.

Type: DVIEW <Enter>

Response: Select objects:

Type: ALL <Enter> <Enter>

Response: CAmera/TArget/Distance/POints/PAn/Zoom/TWist/CLip/Hide/Off/Undo/<eXit>:

Type: D <Enter>

Type: 10 <Enter> <Enter>

In the lower-left viewport, create a Perspective view similar to Figure 10-19, which shows four views in Model Space.

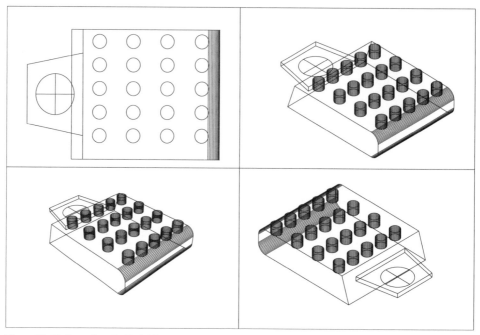

Figure 10-19: Four views in Model Space

At this point, I will assume that you have set up the four views as you want them.

From the View pull-down menu choose the Save option or Tiled Viewports. Or in the command prompt window:

Type:　　VPORTS <Enter>

Response:　Save/Restore/Join/SIngle/?/2/<3>/4:

Type:　　S <Enter>
　　　　　V4 <Enter>

V4 is a name given the viewport configuration. Now return to a single viewport. Pick and make active the lower-right viewport:

Type:　　VPORTS <Enter>

Response:　Save/Restore/Join/SIngle/?/2/<3>/4:

Type: SI <Enter>

Type: ZX <Enter>

Now you'll see how you can transfer the configuration that you saved from the viewports over to Paper Space. First, you must return to Paper Space through the TILEMODE gateway. Either choose Paper Space from the View pull-down menu, or at the command prompt window:

Type: TILEMODE <Enter>

Type: 0 <Enter>

Notice that Paper Space is exactly as you left it. Nothing has changed. Now erase all three viewports that are currently on the screen.

Type: ERASE <Enter>

Now pick each one of the borders of the viewports and press Enter to confirm. The viewports should now be removed. At this point, you're ready to place your viewport configuration from Model Space.

Type: MVIEW <Enter>

Response: ON/OFF/Hideplot/Fit/2/3/4/Restore/<First Point>:

Type: R <Enter>   (This is the Restore option.)

Response: ?/Name of window configuration to insert:

Type: V4 <Enter>

AutoCAD now wants to know where you want to place the viewports. Pick some place in the lower-left corner within the title block border and then the upper-right corner within the border, making sure that you don't overlap the actual title border itself. After you've picked these two corners, the four viewports from Model Space are restored in this area.

Even though these viewports look exactly as they did in Model Space and even though they are currently tiled, the four viewports that were created are independent viewports that can be moved, resized, etc. Using the Restore option of the MVIEW command makes it easier to take viewports that were created in Model Space and bring them over to Paper Space. Refer to Figure 10-20 to see the four viewports in Paper Space transferred from Model Space.

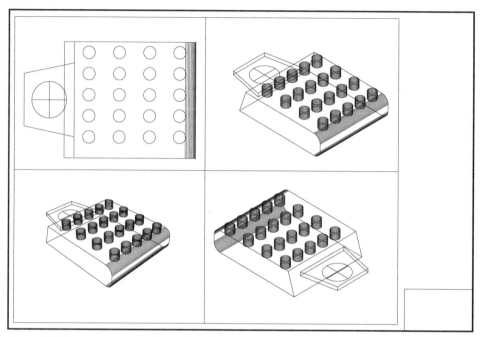

Figure 10-20: Four viewports transferred from Model Space to Paper Space

MSPACE & PSPACE

So far you have learned that one way to work on the model is to be in TILEMODE 1, thus in Model Space, or to be in TILEMODE 0, which gives you access to Paper Space. Remember that while in Paper Space you can't actually work on the model. Even though toggling between the modes is a viable alternative, it's inconvenient. It would be nice if you could simply toggle into Model Space while in TILEMODE 0 and work in the viewports of Paper Space the same as when you were in TILEMODE 1. Well, you can.

While in TILEMODE 0, you can toggle between Paper Space and Model Space with the PSPACE and MSPACE commands. MSPACE places you in Model Space, and PSPACE places you in Paper Space. Both of these commands operate only while in TILEMODE 0. Now see how they work.

Figure 10-21: The Floating Model Space icon from the Standard toolbar

From the Standard toolbar choose the Floating Model Space icon. Or in the command prompt window.

Type: MSPACE <Enter>

Figure 10-22 shows Model Space in TILEMODE 0.

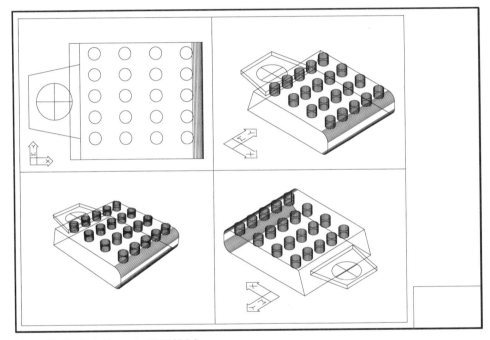

Figure 10-22 : Model Space in TILEMODE 0

Notice how the Paper Space icon disappears and the traditional UCS icon appears in each of your four viewports exactly as it was in Model Space in TILEMODE 1. In reality you are in Model Space; you aren't in Paper Space. This is the Model Space mode of TILEMODE 0. It can get confusing, can't it?

If you try to move from viewport to viewport, the first thing you notice is that Model Space mode operates exactly as you would expect with multiple viewports. You are locked in a single viewport with crosshairs. In the other viewports, you have an arrow. If you want to make another viewport active, pick in that viewport. Then you will have crosshairs in that one and arrows in the others or any place else on your screen. There is no difference in working in MSPACE within TILEMODE 0 and the viewports in TILEMODE 1.

While the MSPACE command is active, you can't work on the Paper Space background. You can't move or resize the viewports; you are totally locked in the active viewport. But this means that here you can work on the actual model itself.

Now you can return from Model Space to Paper Space:

 Figure 10-23: The Paper Space icon from the Standard toolbar

From the Standard toolbar choose the Paper Space icon. Or in the command prompt window:

Type: PSPACE <Enter>

Notice that the UCS icons in each of the viewports now disappear and the Paper Space right-triangle icon appears in the lower-left corner. This icon indicates that you are in Paper Space.

I have created three quick AutoLISP programs to help you move back and forth between MSPACE and PSPACE or to return to TILEMODE 1 regardless of where you are. You can activate them even while in TILEMODE 1. Therefore, if you want to be in Paper Space, simply type the name of the program. PS.LSP takes you to TILEMODE 0 and Paper Space. MS.LSP takes you to TILEMODE 0 and Model Space. MV.LSP takes you to TILEMODE 1.

You can find PS.LSP, MS.LSP and MV.LSP in the AutoLISP section of the book. As with the other 3D programs, make certain that PS.LSP, MS.LSP and MV.LSP are properly loaded. If you have the *AutoCAD 3D Companion Disk* installed properly and have loaded 3DTOOLS.LSP, all you need to do is type in the name of the program.

Now try each of the programs:

Type: MV <Enter>

Notice you are in TILEMODE 1.

Type: MS <Enter>

Here, you are in TILEMODE 0 but in Model Space.

Type: PS <Enter>

Here you are in TILEMODE 0 and in Paper Space.
These three 3D tools make moving from one mode to another very easy.

Hiding Lines in Paper Space

Hiding lines when you plot is generally a function of checking the Hide Lines box in the Plot dialog box. Then the lines will be hidden when you plot. You can still do this if you're hiding lines from Paper Space as well. But one of the real values of Paper Space is to be able to hide lines in one viewport and not another. Obviously, you can't just tell the PLOT command to hide all the lines.

Here is the procedure you use. Assume that you want the lines hidden only in your perspective viewport, which in your case is the lower-left viewport. Don't hide the lines in the other three viewports at the time you plot.

Type: MVIEW <Enter>

Response: ON/OFF/Hideplot/Fit/2/3/4/Restore/<First Point>:

Type: Hideplot <Enter>

Response: ON/OFF:

Type: ON <Enter>

Response: Select objects:

Pick the lower-left viewport and press Enter to confirm. You can perform this procedure from either Mspace or Pspace. Only the viewports that you select using the Hideplot option of MVIEW will hide the lines at plot time.

Another important thing to remember when using this technique is to make certain that the Hide Lines box in the Plot dialog box is *not* checked. Otherwise, AutoCAD will hide the lines in all the viewports.

Controlling Layers in Paper Space

If you were working in Model Space exclusively in TILEMODE 1, you would only be able to control the visibility of layers with ON and OFF or FREEZE and THAW. But the status would be global for all viewports. In Paper Space, on the other hand, using TILEMODE 0 you can freeze layers with FREEZE in some viewports and not in others by using the VPLAYER command.

VPLAYER is viewport-specific, thus allowing you to issue FREEZE and THAW to layers in each viewport independently. In this example, assume that you have changed the buttons on your mouse in your drawing to a layer called BUTTONS:

Type:	VPLAYER <Enter>
Response:	?/Freeze/Thaw/Reset/Newfrz/Vpvisdflt:
Type:	F <Enter>
Response:	Layer(s) to Freeze:
Type:	BUTTONS <Enter>
Response:	All/Select/<Current>:
Type:	S <Enter>
Response:	Select Objects:

Pick one of the viewports and press Enter to confirm. Figure 10-24 shows the BUTTONS layer frozen on only one viewport.

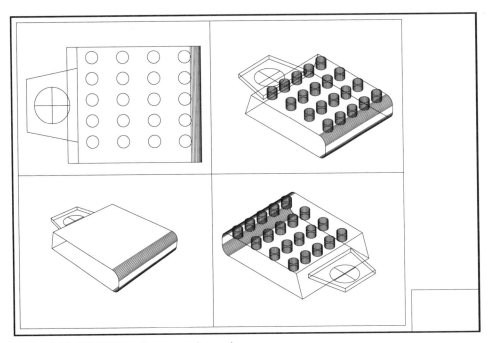

Figure 10-24: BUTTONS layer frozen on only one viewport

Because the primary reason for Paper Space is to give you flexibility in presentations, it is only expected that AutoCAD would give you layer control in each viewport independently.

Erasing Viewport Borders

The creation of viewports places each viewport on the screen with a border. Often, you may find it desirable to erase the borders themselves, leaving the actual viewports.

When you created the viewports for this chapter's example, your current layer was BORDERS. Therefore, the viewports themselves, which are the objects in Paper Space, are on the BORDERS layer. If you want to erase the borders of the viewports, all you have to do is turn off or freeze the BORDERS layer. Turning off the BORDERS layer will not affect what's in the viewports, only the visibility of the borders.

Figure 10-25: The Layers icon from the Standard toolbar

From the Standard toolbar choose the Layers icon. Set Layer 0 (zero) to be current and Layer Borders to be frozen. Or in the command prompt window:

Type: LAYER <Enter>
           S <Enter>
           0 <Enter> <Enter>

This first sets you to the 0 layer.

Type: LAYER <Enter>
           F <Enter>
           BORDERS <Enter> <Enter>

This sequence freezes the BORDERS layer. Figure 10-26 shows the Paper Space viewports without borders.

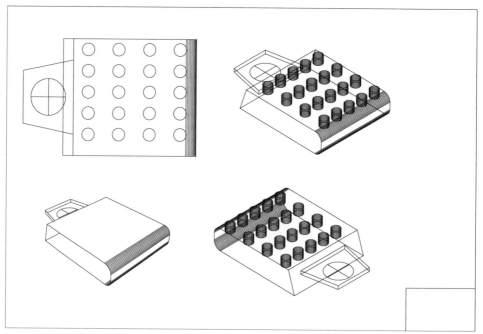

Figure 10-26: Paper Space viewports without borders

Drawing in Pspace Compared With Mspace

Remember that *Pspace* is Paper Space mode. It's like having two drawings in memory at one time. You can draw on the second drawing without affecting the first drawing. This is what you are doing when you are in Paper Space and the viewports are the objects. Any drawing that you create while in Paper Space mode is not part of the model. Label your viewports as an illustration.

Choose the Paper Space icon, or in the command prompt window:

Type: PS <Enter>

This PS.LSP AutoLISP program will assure that you are in Paper Space mode. Using the DTEXT command, place text around your drawing, labeling each one of the viewports. See Figure 10-27 for a view of text drawn in Paper Space.

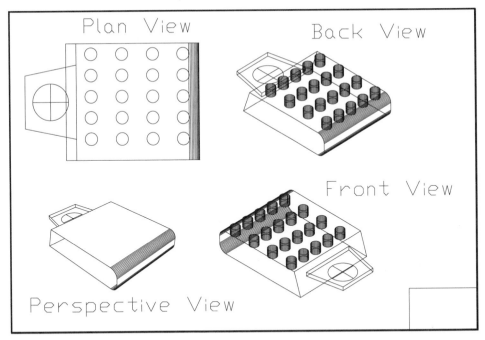

Figure 10-27: Text drawn in Paper Space

Type: MV <Enter>

MV.LSP is the AutoLISP program that takes you back to TILEMODE 1 in Model Space. Notice that the model is not harmed at all. The objects that were created in Paper Space are not part of the model.

Type: PS <Enter>

Later on, if you move the actual viewports, the items that you drew in Paper Space or the text that you placed will not necessarily be aligned with the viewports and thus the model itself. This is why you drew the title border and title block in Paper Space—not Model Space—so that it would not be a part of the actual model itself.

Scaling in Paper Space

One of the most valuable features of Paper Space is the capability to create different scales on the same sheet. In reality, when creating different scales, it doesn't matter whether your drawing is 3D or 2D. This technique works equally well.

Remember that your drawing limits in Paper Space were set to 0,0 and 34,22.75—the actual size of the effect drawing area of your paper for your specific plotter. Therefore, when you plot, the scale will be at 1 = 1. When you enter Model Space with the MSPACE command, you can check your limits. You will see in any viewport that they are still set as they were originally.

Choose the Floating Model Space icon or in the command prompt window:

Type: MS <Enter>

This command makes sure that you are in Model Space.

Assume that this view is a Plan view of a large architectural area. Also assume that this view is to be plotted at 1/4" = 1'-0". Then type **ZOOM 1/48xp** and press Enter.

At this point the drawing will be sized within the viewport at a scale factor of 1/4" = 1'-0". It may or may not fit in the viewport that you have allotted. Or it may be too small for the size of the viewport. But what you have here is definitely a *"what you see is what you get"* plot.

If your drawing limits in Model Space (not Paper Space limits) were initially set at 144',96', then it would take the entire 36" by 24" sheet of paper to fit the drawing at 1/4" = 1'-0". Here, you are trying to get the drawing at that scale on only a portion of the drawing sheet. Remember that the Paper Space outline created by your title block represents the 1 = 1 sheet of 34" by 22.75" effective paper drawing limits. Then you need to rescale the full size of the drawing to fit in the window. But by how much?

First, look at where I got the number 1/48 and the XP at the end. How many quarter inches are there in one foot? The answer is 48 because there are 12 inches to a foot and 4 quarter inches to an inch; therefore, 12 x 4 = 48. When you zoom to 1/48xP, you are telling Paper Space to give you a zoomed view relative to that Paper Space viewport, which is equal to 1/48th of a Paper Space unit. And what is a Paper Space unit? It's the 34" by 22.75" paper you're going to plot on. If this concept is difficult to con–ceptualize, don't worry. You don't have to understand it to use it. Just remember that 1/4" = 1'-0" is 1/48xP. Then what is 1/8" = 1'-0"? It's 1/96xP because 8 x 12 = 96. And a 1/16" = 1'-0" scale would be 1/192xP.

Even though you've used architectural units in these examples, using other units and scale factors is a piece of cake. A 1 = 50 scale factor would be ZOOM 1/50xP while in that viewport. A 1 = 1000 scale factor would be 1/1000xP, etc. In your model, scale the upper-left viewport 3 to 1:

Type: ZOOM <Enter>

Type: 3XP <Enter>

By creating each view you want within each viewport, you can then scale the view as necessary within that viewport. You also will see what scale factor is necessary for the size of the viewport. Ultimately, you have a picture of exactly what your final plot will look like.

Remember that the model does not change size, as would be the case with the SCALE command. The XP at the end of the ZOOM factor scales the image in the active viewport by that ratio. Only the ZOOM view of that object in relation to Paper Space units changes.

There are a few things that you need to keep in mind when scaling in Paper Space:

- If you change the size of the physical viewport itself, go back and issue another ZOOM XP in that viewport.

- If you want a certain view, always create that zoom and view first before you issue the ZOOM XP command. Finding your view is easier that way.

- When you are ready to plot, always change back to Pspace before plotting. That way, you will plot the entire Paper Space. If you are in Mspace and in a viewport model when you plot, then you will get only that one view plotted, the same as if you were in TILEMODE 1.

- Finally, if you don't want the borders of the viewports to plot, then turn off the BORDERS layer where the viewports reside. Only the viewports themselves are on this layer. When the layer is turned off, the borders will disappear.

Moving Objects From One Viewport to Another

Now move away from 3D to learn a practical trick using Paper Space that you can use in 2D or 3D. It's obvious that Paper Space is not strictly a 3D tool. If you want to lay out a presentation in AutoCAD, you can lay out multiple viewports and plot them out at independent scales. But start with the assumption that laying out a presentation is not what you want to do. You want to have two drawings in memory at the same time and copy objects from one drawing to another. Here's how you can do that.

Make sure that your main drawing is in TILEMODE 1 in Model Space. Then, using the PS command, change to Paper Space. Make one small viewport in Paper Space with the MVIEW command. See Figure 10-28 for a view of the main model in one viewport in Paper Space.

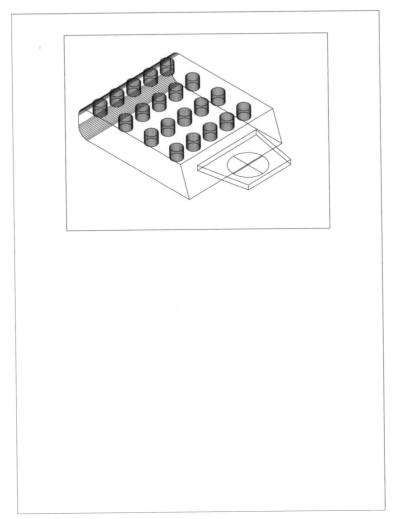

Figure 10-28: Main model in one viewport in Paper Space

Now insert another drawing in the Paper Space area using the INSERT command. Make sure you preface the name of the drawing with an * (asterisk) so that it will come in exploded if you need to copy only parts of this drawing to your model. Figure 10-29 shows a second drawing in the Paper Space area.

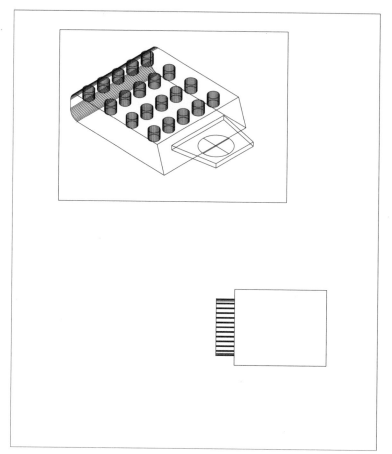

Figure 10-29: Second drawing in Paper Space area

Because you can't actually transfer objects from Paper Space to Model Space, I have created a program called PSCOPY.LSP. This program enables you to select objects in Paper Space and then copy them over and place them into your Model Space drawing.

You can find PSCOPY.LSP in the AutoLISP section of the book. As with the other 3D programs, make certain that PSCOPY.LSP is properly loaded. If you have the *AutoCAD 3D Companion Disk* installed properly and have loaded 3DTOOLS.LSP, all you need to do is type in the name of the program.

Now try PSCOPY.LSP and see how it works:

Type: PSCOPY <Enter>

Response: Select objects to copy:
           Select objects:

Select the object you want to copy and press Enter.

Response: Basepoint:

Pick a base point (pick-up point) for the objects to copy and then move them over to the Model Space viewport and pick. You also can enter a scale factor and rotation angle. Then they are placed in Model Space. See Figure 10-30 for a view of objects moved from Paper Space to Model Space.

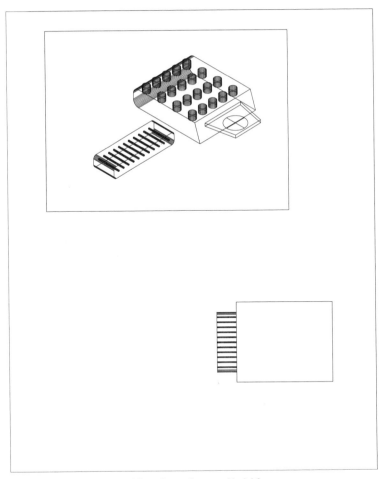

Figure 10-30: Objects moved from Paper Space to Model Space

After you copy the objects from Paper Space to Model Space, erase all of the objects in Paper Space and move completely back to Model Space.

Type: PS <Enter>
       ERASE <Enter>
       All <Enter> <Enter>

This sequence erases all of the objects—including the viewport—in Paper Space only. It does not erase the objects in Model Space.

Type: MV <Enter>

This returns you to TILEMODE 1 and Model Space, where your objects are located. See Figure 10-31 for both objects in TILEMODE 1.

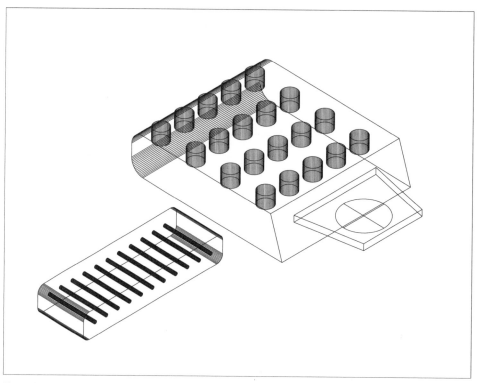

Figure 10-31: Both objects in TILEMODE 1

This exercise, an AutoLISP program, has given you a means of moving objects from one drawing to another using Paper Space. But more important, it has shown you that the two modes are so separate, it is like having two drawings in memory at one time. Therefore, the uses of Paper Space are not strictly limited to presentations and plotting.

Moving On

Paper Space is not part of the exclusive world of 3D. Its application in 3D should be obvious to you by now. Paper Space is an under-used feature of AutoCAD that can serve you well, increasing your productivity. This chapter has taken the mystery out of using Paper Space and given you some examples of the many ways that you can use Paper Space in your work.

Chapter 11, "Shading, Rendering & Animation," takes you one step closer to the world of presentation through shading and rendering. In Chapter 11 you will learn the difference between a simple shade and the more complex render. You will learn what you need to do to properly prepare a drawing for rendering. You will also learn about materials, texture and light and the pros and cons of the different rendering algorithms.

As both computers and software become more and more sophisticated, shading and rendering for presentation are becoming a reality, not just something that might be available in the future. The future is now.

CHAPTER 11

Shading, Rendering & Animation

AutoCAD Release 13 renderer outshines the one introduced with Release 12. However, it's still not AutoVision or 3D Studio. It lacks features such as shadow casting, true reflectivity, a complex materials library, texture mapping and use of true materials such as brick, metals, etc.

It does have a rather sophisticated series of lights, including ambient, distant, point and spotlights. You can control colors of entities as well as the lights using both the RGB and the HLS methods. Although the materials library and materials editor are rather limited by AutoVision and 3D Studio standards, you can control some facets of the material to give it a roughness or shine as well as color.

Rendering can be confusing the first time you pick up the program's reference manual. This chapter gives you an easy step-by-step explanation of the terms and concepts used by rendering packages, including of course the RENDER option that comes with Release 13, AutoVision and 3D Studio. It also shows you how to prepare a drawing properly for rendering. If you don't do the work properly up front in AutoCAD, the results in the rendering program are not satisfactory. At the end of Chapter 13, "The AutoCAD Solid Modeler," is a short tutorial on the Release 13 Renderer.

There are many reasons why you should draw in 3D. You might draw for conceptualization and/or error and conflict checking. Or you might wish to make a drawing more realistic so laypersons can understand it. Many mechanical engineers use a 3D model with CNC machines. The most universal reason for taking the time to model in 3D is visualization and presentation—that is, rendering and animation.

Most of the commands in this chapter are found in the Release 13 Render toolbar. (See Figure 11-1.) You may also use the Tools pull-down menu. All the 3D Surface and Solid models you create in this book may be displayed using the HIDE, SHADE and RENDER commands.

Figure 11-1: The Render toolbar

Shading Versus Rendering

Let's begin by briefly illustrating the differences between hiding, shading and rendering. Then we'll discuss the components of a rendered drawing. We'll expand on these aspects of rendering later in the chapter.

Hiding

Figure 11-2: The Hide icon from the Render toolbar

Choosing the Hide icon lets you create a hidden line image of objects in the current viewport. The results remain visible only until you issue the REGEN command. Basically the HIDE command is similar to SHADE, except that 3D surfaces are filled in with a color instead of being represented by their edges. You can hide both 3D surface and solid models.

TIP: If you have a large 3D model to render, test it first with the HIDE command and check it for the removal of hidden surface normals. If your hide results are satisfactory, you'll save rendering time if you toggle on "Discard Back Faces." (See Figure 11-8, later in the chapter.) You can turn this on with the "More Options..." button option of either the Render dialog box (see Figure 11-7) or the Rendering Preferences dialog box (see Figure 11-24). The time you subseqently save depends upon the total number of faces in your 3D model as compared to the back faces it discards.

Shading

Figure 11-3: The Shade icon from the Render toolbar

AutoCAD introduced the SHADE command in Release 11. It's fast and colorful, yet it's nearly worthless as a renderer. But it does serve a useful purpose.

Unlike the HIDE command, SHADE is a flat coloring system with some considerations of light. When you shade an image, each object uses the color you assigned to it. It assumes a light source shining along a line of sight within the current viewport. The line of sight is the same you specified with the VPOINT and DVIEW commands reviewed earlier.

The SHADE command simply paints color on the image. It operates effectively both with a 16-color palette with a standard VGA card and a 256-color palette with a super VGA card.

The SHADE command also has some minor controls with the system variables SHADEDIF and SHADEDGE. SHADEDIF controls the amount of light, and SHADEDGE controls the visibility of the edges of the faces and whether or not the effect you want is shaded or simply drawn with hidden lines.

Shade Setting Limitations

You can experiment by setting SHADEDGE from 0 to 3 and see what happens each time you shade. Entering a 0 (zero) setting shades the surface of your object but not the object's edges. Entering a 1 setting shades the surface of the object. (The edges of the object use the background color.)

TIP: Use a 0 or 1 setting if you have a 256-color palette and wish to produce a realistic colored image.

If you have a 16-color palette, entering a number 2 setting emulates the hide command. The setting doesn't shade your surface, it simply fills it in with the background color. Finally, entering a 3 setting, which is the default and again used for a 16-color palette, merely fills the surface of the object with its allocated color and again uses the background color to draw the edges.

The SHADEDIF (contrast setting) is defaulted to a setting of 70 and may be set to any value between 1 and 100. A low value provides little contrast, a higher number provides more contrast. The best image contrast is around 70, as it's a medium to high contrast value.

Rendering Versus Shading

Rendering adds three more components to the mix than shading:
Color
Material and texture
Lighting and shadows

Basic Color

A rendering begins with basic colors for each object in the drawing. If you render the object at this stage you don't have much more than a simple shade file. To give a rendered drawing a realistic appearance, most rendering programs enable you to add material and texture. Color serves a dual purpose: first, to supply the color you'd expect; and second, as one way to group objects with the same material and texture.

Material & Texture

Figure 11-4: The Material icon

A material may be something like gold, brick, plastic or marble. It may also have different properties such as dullness, shine, transparency, bumpiness or luminance. These properties give a material the sense of texture. You can assign different materials to different objects in your drawing. Most programs permit you to create your own material as well as use bitmap files. These concepts are covered later in the chapter. The renderer with Release 13 uses a form of materials but is not as full-bodied. For true materials, you need AutoVision or 3D Studio.

Lighting & Shadows

Figure 11-5: The Light icon

Choosing the Light icon lets you add lights to the model. The four types of light are point, distant, spotlight and ambient. Once you add lights to your model, you begin to notice a more realistic view. With light, you begin to add different types of shadows. These shadows may be as simple as a depth shadow where the object appears darker as it is further away from the light source to true shadow casting in all directions. You cannot create shadows in Release 13. To create shadows you should use AutoVision, 3D Studio or a third-party rendering program.

Your ability to add shadows is directly dependent on the sophistication of the rendering program that you're using and the amount of time you're willing to wait for the final rendered product.

The difference between shading and rendering is the difference between night and day. Shading in and of itself is a useful tool as a temporary visualization of the model within AutoCAD. It is quick and effective. On the other hand, rendering is really an artistic endeavor designed to portray a photo-realistic image.

The following section shows you how to set up an AutoCAD drawing.

Preparing a Drawing for Rendering

Figure 11-6: The Render icon from the Render toolbar

Remember, the only things that can be shaded or rendered in AutoCAD are extrusions, faces, meshes and regions. Rendering is strictly a 3D function, which you'll achieve through the Render dialog box. (See Figure 11-7.) You can't render lines, arcs, text or hatch patterns. While this may come as a disappointment to many, you simply can't hatch the side of a 3D object and expect it to render in the form of the hatch pattern. You don't apply the brick in a rendering this way. You will see that there's a much easier way than hatching.

When preparing your drawings, use 3D tools in the Surface and Solids toolbars as much as possible. The 3D objects you create with the toolbars have their surface normals aligned for faster rendering.

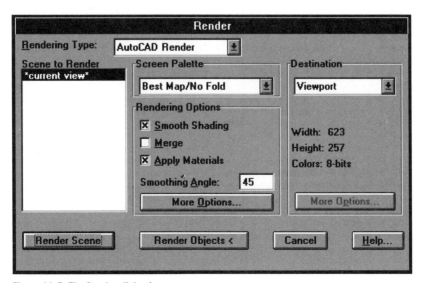

Figure 11-7: The Render dialog box

There are ways to render text, but it must be 3D text. Of course, a software developer even now might be working on a rendering package that will render simple lines, text and hatch. Currently, however, you don't render 2D objects.

Six Quick Steps To Your First AutoCAD Rendering

First, create the model. In earlier chapters, the metaphor of the chicken wire was used to explain what and how lines could be hidden and what could not be hidden. The purpose of that metaphor was to illustrate the reasons for extrusions, faces and meshes. They add a surface so that you can hide lines; they also render these same surfaces. Remember that nothing can be rendered unless it has a surface. And the primary ways of placing a surface on an object are through extrusions, meshes, faces and regions.

Second, create and name your views. This is where the shade command becomes very useful in AutoCAD. If you ever doubt whether an object in a drawing can be rendered, you can always shade the object. Depending on the rendering package you're using, this may not be totally conclusive, but it will give you a good idea of the form and shape of the final product and whether you're missing any surfaces. Remember that if a model won't shade, it won't render.

Third, create and place lights in your drawing. You can accompany each view with any number of light sources. Usually, you include a combination of ambient and point lights. For more dramatic effects you use distant lights and spotlights. See the section on "Lights" later in the chapter for tips on setting up your lighting and colors.

Fourth, save each view with its lights into a scene in order for it to be recalled at a later time. The renderer and AutoVision use AutoCAD-named saved views. See the section on "Setting Scenes & Views," next in the chapter.

Fifth, apply materials to your objects. You also can create and/or import materials for more specialized effects. See "Material by Object" and "Material & Texture" later in the chapter.

Sixth, set up rendering preferences such as Gourard or Phong shading and smoothing parameters. (See Figure 11-8.) Then test render the object. You can then adjust your view, lighting and finish to improve the final appearance and test render again. Finally, save the finished rendering to file. See "Speed Versus Quality" for an in-depth look at rendering preferences.

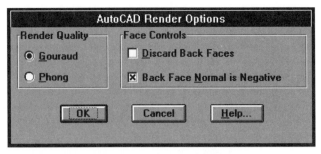

Figure 11-8: The AutoCAD Render Options dialog box

A further step, which may only be achieved on 24-bit devices (as opposed to 256-color), is to merge. For a more dramatic effect, merge rendered objects against a background GIF, TIFF or TARGA image file. To do so, use the REPLAY command to display the image in a viewport, not a render window. Then under the Rendering Options of the Render dialog box (see Figure 11-7) toggle "on" the Merge radio button and then choose the Render Objects button. The resultant rendering merges the edges of the 3D wireframe object against the background image. The 24-bit merge option enhances dramatic effects and realism in your renderings.

Setting Scenes & Views

Figure 11-9: The Scene icon

Choosing the Scene icon lets you add your AutoCAD-created views with embedded lights into rendering scenes prior to the rendering process. You can set and name all your views using the icons in the Views toolbar. Creating scenes saves time. You don't have to set up new viewpoints and new lights each time you render an object. You simply choose a scene. (See Figure 11-10.)

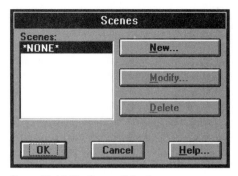

Figure 11-10: The Scenes dialog box

If you are using a rendering package, you can use the dynamic viewing system of that program to change your angle of view. In some rendering packages the dynamic viewer is superior to the AutoCAD DVIEW or VPOINT commands. They almost universally provide more extensive features and the ability to do more and faster dynamic viewing.

Almost all rendering programs let you set your own angle of view. Most rendering packages have their own dynamic viewer. This means that the entire file can be sent without regard to the viewpoint within AutoCAD. Renderer, AutoVision and some other rendering programs work inside AutoCAD and use AutoCAD views.

Third-party rendering programs are convenient because they don't require that a decision on every viewing angle is made in AutoCAD. You can, nevertheless, make these decisions in AutoCAD and transfer the views to most rendering programs. Most packages respect the AutoCAD VIEW command and recognize saved named views, which you can add to the renderer. (See Figure 11-11.) If your rendering program supports this capability, it's a good idea to set up several views. This doesn't mean that you're restricted to only these views. You can still add views in the rendering program.

Now let's look at how AutoCAD sets up scenes.

Setting New Scenes

Below are 5 quick steps to setting up your scenes.

1. From the Render toolbar choose the Scene icon and activate the Scenes dialog box. (See Figure 11-10.)

2. From the Scene dialog box choose "New…", which activates the New Scene dialog box. (See Figure 11-11.) In the Scene Name: enter an eight-character name.

3. In the Views list below it, select either a named AutoCAD view, or *CURRENT*.

4. In the Lights list, select a series of lights or *ALL*.

5. Pick the OK buttons to exit and save the scene.

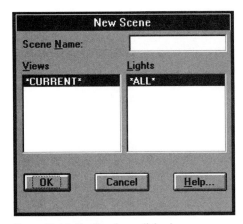

Figure 11-11: The New Scene dialog box

You may also modify a scene by reactivating the Scenes dialog box, then choosing the Modify… button. The Modify Scene dialog box then allows you to rename, change a view and add or remove lights to a scene. Remember the maximum number of lights in a scene is 500.

Material by Object

Figure 11-12: The Materials icon

Rendering programs permit you to add materials to individual objects by selecting the objects themselves. You can set the material by color, by object or by layer. To define a material, you specify the color and any reflective parameters you want the material to have, such as shiny or dull.

Basically you do this in two steps: Define the material with its color, along with its shininess or dullness, and then attach the material to the object in your AutoCAD drawing. The following sections explain this in more detail.

Using Color in a Rendering

Color can play a very important part in preparing the drawing for the final rendering. The AutoCAD rendering package gives you the option of applying color and texture to a block, a layer or an individual object.

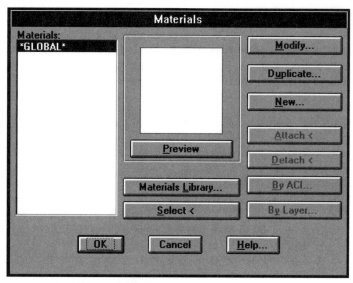

Figure 11-13: The Materials dialog box

One of the nice things in a rendering package is that the actual color you apply to an AutoCAD drawing is totally insignificant. The rendering packages themselves enable you to designate the actual color to be used. In AutoCAD you don't have to worry about what color the object is really going to be. What you need to concern yourself with is the color number.

If you want a different texture or material on a different part of your drawing and you're planning to render by color, then you must have a different color number for the different objects in the drawing. Once you do this, you can change the actual color in the rendering package and apply a unique texture. Just remember that every different material requires a different color number.

Attach Material by Color (ACI)

Here's how you attach materials by the AutoCAD Color Index to objects within your drawing:

1. Choose the Materials icon to activate the Materials dialog box. (See Figure 11-13.) Then select a material from the Materials list. (If you have not placed any materials in the list, you'll pick them from the Materials Library. See "Materials & Texture" later in the chapter.)

2. Apply the material. After you've choosen a material from the Materials list, pick the By ACI... button. This activates the Attach by AutoCAD Color Index dialog box. (See Figure 11-14.) In the Select ACI: column pick a number from 1 to 255, then choose the Attach–> button and the material will pop up in the Select ACI: list next to your chosen number.

3. Pick OK to exit the dialog box. This returns you to the Materials dialog box. You may either pick Attach -> and choose a specific object in your drawing to attach the material to, or pick OK.

   Your material is then attached.

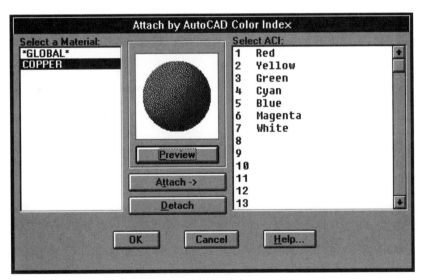

Figure 11-14: The Attach by AutoCAD Color Index dialog box

If you were modeling a lamp, for instance, the base of the lamp might be a different color from the lamp's body—and definitely a different color number from the lamp's shade. In the AutoCAD drawing you don't have to actually concern yourself with the visual color, just the color number. The base might be color 238 and the body 239. This way, the rendering package is able to key in on the different color numbers to apply the material.

If you decide to render by color, then you obviously have limited yourself to the number of materials and textures that can be used in any given scene. Since AutoCAD currently only supports 256 colors, the maximum number of materials that you can have in a given scene is 256. This is not an extreme handicap since most scenes rarely carry that many materials.

In most rendering packages the assignment of the exact shade of color and the assignment of the material are different operations. This means that you have independent control over the actual color of the object and the material used by the object.

Using Layers

Using color is by no means the most advantageous way of organizing your drawing for rendering. This is the main reason why years ago AutoCAD changed the requirement that layers be numbered. When you're in the rendering programs, visualizing the parts of the drawing that need materials is difficult if all you have are different colors. It's hard to remember that color 238 was for the texture on the base of the lamp, for example.

It would be easier to tell the rendering program to apply a wood texture to a layer called lampbase and to place the shade of the lamp on a layer called lampshade.

This way you can apply texture to objects according to their function.

Attaching Material by Layer

Here's how you attach materials by AutoCAD layers to objects within your drawing:

1. Choose the Materials icon to activate the Materials dialog box. (See Figure 11-13.) Then select a material from the Materials list. (If you have not placed any materials in the list, you'll pick them from the Materials Library. See "Materials & Texture" later in the chapter.)

2. Apply the material. After you've choosen a material from the Materials list, pick the By Layer... button. This activates the Attach by Layer dialog box. (See Figure 11-15.) In the Select Layer column pick a layer, then choose the Attach –> button and the material pops up in the Select Layer listing next to your chosen number.

3. Pick OK to exit the dialog box. It returns you to the Materials dialog box. You may either pick Attach -> and choose a specific object in your drawing to attach the material to, or pick OK.

Your material is then attached.

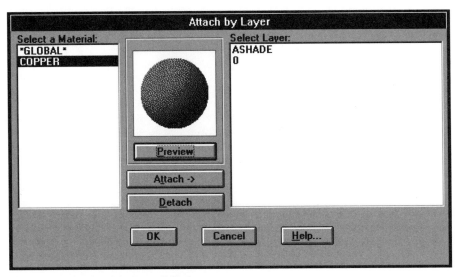

Figure 11-15: The Attach by Layer dialog box

Generally, if you use this layering method, you must tell the rendering package that you'll be rendering layer by layer, not by color. Even if you choose to render by layer, you haven't given up the option of controlling the actual shade of the color itself. At any point you can change the color of any object.

Your task in AutoCAD, therefore, is to make these many decisions ahead of time. You first have to decide whether you'll render by color or by layer and probably what colors and materials you'll use in the final rendered product or, at the very least, which items in your drawing will share the same materials. Rendering the model by layer creates a big departure from your normal layering system because your layering decisions are then governed not by drafting decisions, but by which object might eventually have a certain material. As you can see, layering is a totally different way of thinking about the organization of your drawing. Therefore, you must give much thought to the purpose of the final product when you begin modeling in 3D.

These considerations don't mean that you can't use the actual drawing model in 3D that will be used in traditional drafting for both purposes. Remember that the CHPROP command enables you to change given objects in a traditional 3D model that was drawn with no considerations whatsoever for rendering to the appropriate layers necessary for rendering. Rather than make these decisions up front when you're drawing, simply take the time before you send the drawing to the rendering program to perform some final preparations.

Miscellaneous Drawing Considerations

With the exception of Autodesk 3D Studio, most rendering packages don't permit you to construct geometry in the program itself. This means that you must construct all geometry that is going to be used by the rendering package externally, generally in AutoCAD.

Therefore, when using geometry for any purpose whatsoever, you must include it in the model before sending it to the rendering program. One of the primary ways to send the model to the rendering program is with DXF file transfer. Even Autodesk's 3D Studio itself uses this procedure. Release 13's 3DSIN and 3DSOUT commands insert and export 3D Studio files.

Once you're in the rendering program, you will need to exit the program and return to AutoCAD to make any changes to the geometry. Make your changes there and DXFOUT again. Here programs differ as to whether you have to start over again, or whether the new file will inherit the previous textures, lights, and so on.

All the geometry you will need should be part of the file. It's entirely possible that you want to render several scenes, some scenes with certain objects and other scenes without them. Therefore, all objects need to be brought over to the rendering program in the single DXF file. If the objects are then on separate layers, you can turn those objects on and off in the rendering program just as you can in AutoCAD. But the objects must be there to begin with.

Considering shadows and lights is also important because, as you might realize, you must place objects in front of a light source in order to cast a shadow. Many times it's advantageous to have the shadow cast without seeing the object that is casting it. This will be especially true with a light source coming from outside a window into an interior room.

You have two distinct problems here. The window might require a collection of faces to obstruct the light and cast the shadow in the direction that you want and, at the same time, have a different appearance as a window. Depending on the package you're using, you can solve these problems by creating two different faces on the window with two different layers. Then you can create the shadow using one series of faces and the appearance of the window with the other by hiding the original faces once you've created the shadows.

Again, this book is not meant to be a how-to manual on the different rendering packages. It simply demonstrates the various considerations necessary in the AutoCAD model. You will learn that visualization and appearance is more important than absolute accuracy in the model itself. For a schematic design, you might need to place all of the various parts in the drawing in order for the model to be correct. But in a rendering package, those items may be reduced down to a single pixel, barely visible; so who cares if they are there. Appearance and visualization are paramount.

Creating Colors

Creating colors in a rendering package is quite different from creating colors in AutoCAD. In AutoCAD you are fixed with a 256-color palette, of which each color has a different color number. Therefore, in AutoCAD you simply set the color either by layer or by number. Your graphics driver may enable you to control the shade of the color number, but in AutoCAD itself you are restricted to a color by number.

Rendering programs offer much more control over the shade of any color in the model because color is controlled by either of two methods: RGB or HLS. Your particular program will use one or both of these methods. The better package will use both interchangeably. If you have both, the following sections will explain not only how to use each of these methods, but how to use them in combination to get the exact visual shade you need.

RGB

RGB stands for red, green and blue. By mixing a degree of red, green and blue, you can create a full palette of colors. To find the AutoCAD color wheel options, choose the Light icon to activate the Lights dialog box, then choose Color Wheel…. This activates the Color dialog box where the color wheel is located. It provides slider bars for RGB and HLS.

Most programs give you a slider bar for each of the primary colors. You can move the slider with your mouse from 0 to 255 for each of the colors. There are three important principles to understand when working with RGB sliders. If all three color components are set to 0, you create black. If all three color components are set to 255, you create white. If all three color components are set to exactly the same number, you create gray. The shade of that gray is determined by what number the three components are all set to. The higher the number, the lighter the gray; the lower, the darker the gray.

Using the RGB sliders, you can add or subtract one or more of the primary colors. If you want pure red, then you set red to 255, and green and blue to 0 (zero). The same is true with the other two primary colors. Moving red and green to 255 and blue to 0 (zero) produces yellow.

If you're an artist and have a good background in the mixture of colors, using the slider bar should be a piece of cake. If, on the other hand, you're as color blind and illiterate about colors as I am, this method of creating colors can drive you insane. You may find yourself randomly moving the sliders left and right in the hope of finding a color you can live with. This assumes that your rendering package gives you sliders that will produce the colors dynamically as you move them. Stay away from those packages that require you to input color number combinations from the keyboard. Then you can only see the color you have chosen after you render the model, which can be very time consuming.

HLS

HLS stands for hue, lightness and saturation. This is simply a different way of describing the same thing. Using HLS sliders instead of RGB sliders produces exactly the same color. And in most programs that use either or both, the settings of HLS and the settings of RGB absolutely correlate. In fact, as you move one set of sliders, you see the other set move correspondingly.

You'll find the effectiveness of easily finding the color that you want not in using HLS or RGB independently, but in using the two in combination. But first, see how HLS works.

Hue is simply the color. By moving the slider from 0 to 255, you can move through the basic color spectrum. Notice that you move not by adding red, green or blue, but by simply moving through the 256 basic colors provided by your color palette. If all you had were hue, moving would be similar to using AutoCAD's method of discrete color numbers.

Once you have the basic color (hue), then you can add lightness (sometimes called luminance) and/or saturation. Lightness determines the intensity or brightness of the color. There are 256 possible levels of lightness for each color. If the lightness is set to 255, you have white, regardless of the hue. If the lightness is set to 0, you have black, regardless of the hue.

Saturation, the final component, can be defined as the purity of the color. Imagine you were mixing paint for your house. You had the brightness you wanted, but you wanted to tone it down a bit by adding gray without actually changing the color itself. This is what saturation does. The higher the saturation, the less gray in the color. The lower the saturation, the more gray in the color. This is what purity of color means.

You can go equally crazy trying to get the exact color you want by strictly using the HLS method. Remember that there is a direct one-to-one correlation between the settings of HLS and the settings of RGB. If you're using a program that gives you both methods of creating color, you have the best of all worlds. You can start off using RGB to get as close as you can to the color you want and then lighten it up with lightness and saturation from the HLS sliders. By using these methods together, you have much better control over the selection of color.

Materials & Texture

Figure 11-16: The Materials Library icon

Different rendering programs use different terminology for similar attributes. For all practical purposes the terms *material, texture* and *finishes* are used synonymously. Materials give the rendered drawing a realistic appearance.

Materials fall in roughly two categories; they are *parametric materials* and *bit-map materials*. The following sections describe them in more detail.

Parametric Materials

Parametric materials are the materials and textures that the rendering package itself is capable of creating. They are created internally by the program. Most rendering programs enable you to create your own materials library without the use of texture maps, external files, scanners or any other peripheral devices. (See Figure 11-17.) Parametric materials may go by a variety of names. But they all do about the same thing.

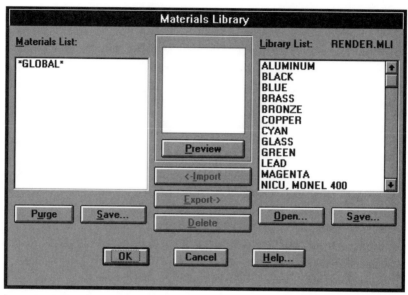

Figure 11-17: The Materials Library dialog box

When building a parametric material, you generally start with the base color of the material and add certain properties to the material. There might be some primitive properties in a materials library already built in to your package, for example, brick, tiles, transparency, stripes, shininess, bumps or reflection. If you combine color and light with any of these materials from the library list along with how the material reacts to light, you can produce almost an infinite variety of materials within the rendering package itself. In AutoCAD the materials library list is in the RENDER.MLI file.

Once you've created these materials, you can save them to a new material library for future use by other models.

Bit Maps

Creating your own materials parametrically from scratch can be a tedious and time-consuming operation. And depending on the limitations of the program, it might be very difficult to exactly match a specific texture or material. Also, it's almost impossible to place background scenes, such as city skylines, mountains, lakes and clouds, strictly using parametric material editors. But if you could take a picture of the particular material you want to use and then apply that picture to an object, then the kinds of textures and backgrounds you are able to produce are actually infinite.

That is exactly what a bit-map material is—a computer graphic reproduction in a graphics file format, generally GIF or TARGA. In most cases applying a bit-map material to an object is as simple as loading the GIF or TARGA file and applying it to the object.

Where do these GIF and TARGA files come from? They come from a variety of places. One program can create these files from videotape. They can be scanned with either a monochrome or color scanner. You can download GIF and TARGA files from various bulletin boards, and you can purchase them from companies that specifically create these files literally by the thousands for sale as bit-map materials. If you have an Internet connection, check the *AutoCAD 3D Online Companion* for free software and art to download.

The rendering program itself has the capability of making a rendering and producing the rendering in the form of a GIF or TARGA file. In turn, this file, in and of itself, can be used as a bit map for another texture. Other ways to produce bit-map files are through Autodesk's Animator and Animator Pro. Each of these programs has that capability, or you can use screen capture programs and save the output as GIF or TIFF files.

There are a couple of things you need to understand about texture files. First, you need to know how big the file is to begin with. This means with what scale and what resolution the file was created. This helps the rendering program figure out how to scale the bit-map file to apply it to the object in your drawing. Scaling is generally done by using techniques such as mapping coordinates or giving the map scale factors. These techniques sound complicated, but they really aren't. In many programs mapping simply amounts to putting a window around the object so that the program can see the appropriate scale. At the very least, some programs allow you to enter a numeric scale factor.

Second, you need to know how often, if at all, the pattern will be replicated over your object and in what direction and format this wrapping will take place. If you want to create a tiled appearance on a floor, you don't want to create one huge tile representing the entire floor. You would want the tiles to be placed similar to an array in AutoCAD. Or if you're wrapping a texture around a sphere or curved area, you don't want it simply to lie flat on the sphere.

All rendering packages that use bit maps for texture files have the capability of defining the format in which the texture file is applied.

Selecting Material to Import Into Your Drawing

Here's how you select materials from the Materials Library and import them into your drawing:

1. Choose the Materials Library icon from the Render toolbar to activate the Materials Library dialog box. (See Figure 11-17.) Then select a material from the Materials List. (If you have not placed any materials in the list, pick them from the Materials Library. The material is simply copied from AutoCAD's RENDER.MLI file.)

2. Select the Materials Library and choose a material from the Library List, then choose <– Import. It appears immediately in the Materials List. Then, either choose another material or pick OK.

3. To apply the material, choose the Materials icon, which activates the Materials dialog box and choose a material from the Materials List. You may either pick Attach -> and choose a specific object in your drawing to attach the material to, or pick OK.

   Your material is then attached.

Lights

Figure 11-18: The Light icon

Working with lights is one of the most confusing aspects to an AutoCAD user beginning to use a rendering program. The AutoCAD drawing doesn't require or use lights. But you must set your lights while working in the drawing. When you draw something in AutoCAD, you can see it immediately. In a rendering program, on the other hand, you conceivably could get a totally black screen if you don't place any lights in the model. The AutoCAD rendering program recognizes this and places one ambient light at all times. AutoCAD provides four types of light: point light, distant light, spotlight and ambient.

Lights serve three purposes in a rendered drawing. First, they produce an ambient light and color to the drawing itself. Second, they are the source of lightness and darkness, adding a degree of realism to the material. And, finally, light casts shadows.

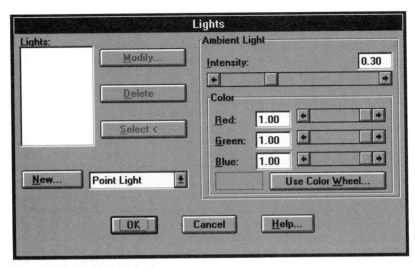

Figure 11-19: The Lights dialog box

Ambient Light

All programs include some form of ambient light. The best way to understand ambient light is to go into a totally dark room. It's almost impossible
to have a room that is totally dark. Once your eyes adjust, you can still see
something. There is still light in the room someplace. But you can't pin-
point it as a beam of light from any given source. If you were to simply
turn up the intensity of this imaginary light so you could see better, the
room would be lit but would not have an identifiable source for the light
and would cast no shadows. There is no direction to ambient light. It
simply illuminates the scene. However, you can control the brightness,
intensity and color of ambient light. AutoCAD sets the intensity of the
Ambient Light at 0.3. Don't set it much higher than this as it produces a
low-contrast washed-out effect in your rendered image. Most programs
don't permit you to have more than one source of ambient light. Ambient
light doesn't require a name in the Lights dialog box, just an intensity level
and a setting for the RGB color slider bars. See the section below on "Adding a Light to a Drawing."

Point Light

An omni or point light is a specific point of light, as the name implies. (See Figure 11-20.) This light, which you can place in a scene, doesn't shine in a specific direction. Again, you can control brightness, intensity (attenuation) and color. Depending on the program, omnis or point lights, may or may not be able to cast shadows. See the section below on "Adding a Light to a Drawing."

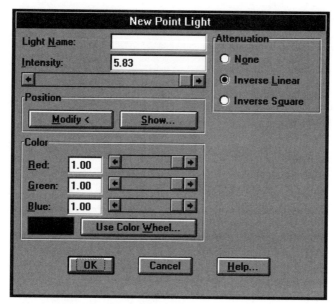

Figure 11-20: New Point Light dialog box

Distant Light

A third type of light is a directional or distant light. (See Figure 11-21.) Directional lights are akin to ambient lights in that the exact point and placement of the light is not critical. What is important is the direction of the light rays. In the Release 13 Renderer these kinds of lights are known as distance lights. Sunlight is an example of a directional light source. The sun strikes the earth uniformly but in a specific direction. These lights can be used to cast shadows, but not in the Renderer. See the section below on "Adding a Light to a Drawing."

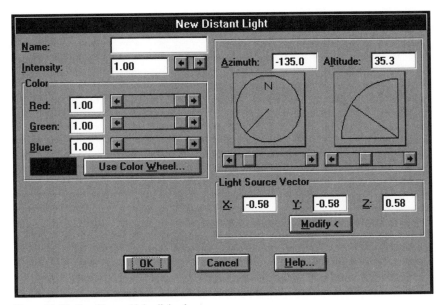

Figure 11-21: New Distant Light dialog box

Spotlight

A fourth type of light is the spotlight. (See Figure 11-22.) It creates a directional, cone-shaped light. With a spotlight you have an inside circle of light that is brighter and an outside circle of light that gradually falls off and is less intense. The spotlight operates in a similar manner to a stage spotlight. It is directional and casts a shadow. See the section below on "Adding a Light to a Drawing."

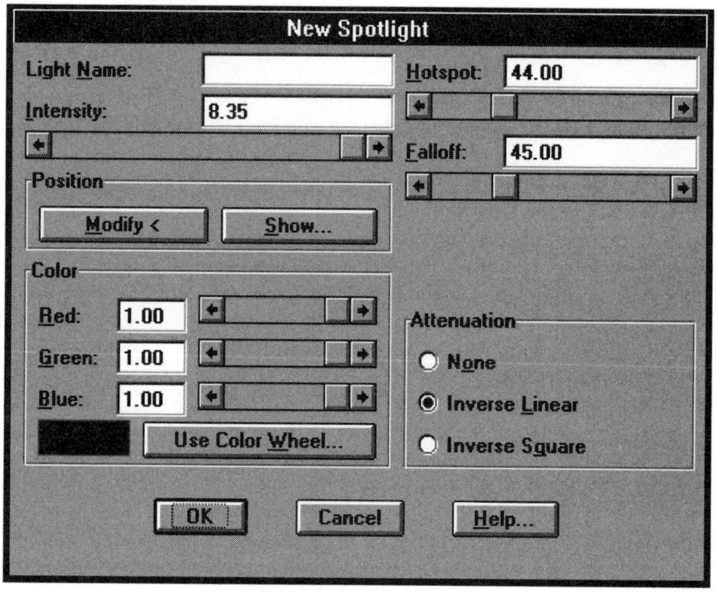

Figure 11-22: New Spotlight dialog box

There are variations on these types of lights. Some programs have track lighting as well as controls over how different forms of light act when they hit reflective or matted surfaces. Generally the reaction of light is considered a property of the material, not of the light itself.

Adding a Light to a Drawing

1. Choose the Light icon, which activates the Lights dialog box. (See Figure 11-19.) Use the Intensity slider bar in the upper right of the dialog box to set the Ambient Light level. The default is 0.3.

2. From the Light pull-down menu, select either Point Light, Distant Light or Spotlight, then click the New... button. This opens the New Light dialog box of your choice. (See Figures 11-20, 11-21 and 11-22.)

   In the New Light dialog box, first enter an eight-character name. Then set the intensity level using the slider bar. Your drawing will have Ambient Light with a preset intensity level and a default location.

3. According to your choice of New Light refer to a section below:

   New Point Light   (See Figure 11-20.) Think of this as a light bulb emitting light in all directions from its location. Objects near to the point light are brighter and objects further away are darker. You'll need to set the Intensity attenuation levels. See "Attenuation" below.

New Distant Light (See Figure 11-21.) A distant light can simulate sunlight. The critical aspect of this light is the direction, not the location, as it emits light in uniform parallel rays in one direction only. In the upper right of the dialog box, you'll set the Azimuth: and Altitude: angles. If you're in the Northern hemisphere you could set the Altitude: to around 70 or 110 to emulate time (before or after noon) and set the Azimuth: angle to emulate the sun's position from the east, the south (180) or the west. Then set the Intensity and color level.

New Spotlight (See Figure 11-22.) In the top right of the dialog box you need to set the Hotspot: and Falloff: angles via the slider bars. If you want a sharp, crisp light circle, set both angles equal. If you want a softer and more dramatic effect to the edge of the cone of light, set the Hotspot: cone angle a few degrees less than the Falloff: angle.

4. To alter the light target and/or light location, choose the Modify <– button to set the X,Y,Z coordinates.

5. Pick the OK button to return to the Lights dialog box, then pick OK again to exit the dialog box or create another light.

Attenuation The New Point Light (see Figure 11-20) and the New Spotlight (see Figure 11-22) have attenuation settings. The attenuation is an intensity level that has a default setting within your drawing. You can reset it in one of four ways:

In the Intensity: space

0 Intensity will turn it off.

1 Intensity sets intensity to none.

With the Attenuation radio buttons

Inverse Linear. The value is half of the extents distance.

Inverse Square. The value is the square of half of the extents distance.

The dramatic and realistic effects achieved by rendering programs are a combination of all the factors discussed thus far. It's not a set of one, two or three rules with the exacting precision found in AutoCAD. Rendering programs are artistic programs aided by an artistic eye.

As with AutoCAD, you can learn many principles and concepts with a rendering program, but in the end, creating a well-lit drawing takes a lot of creativity and a good eye. Once you learn the principles, you can achieve differing results by combining color, material and light and determining how they react with each other. Even if you're not an artist, this can be the most fun part of working in 3D.

Speed Versus Quality

Figure 11-23: The Render Preferences icon

Speed! Speed! Speed! This is the elusive goal of every rendering program. Rendering is an incredibly intensive operation for a computer. The best advice is to get the fastest computer you can afford. And if you can't afford the fastest computer, then put as much memory in your computer as it will hold and you can afford. It's not an exaggeration to say that you can get better than a 50 percent increase in speed every time you double the RAM in your computer. Eventually, you get diminishing returns depending on the size of the model you're rendering. But you can continue to increase speed by having 32 to 64 megabytes of RAM.

Setting Up Render Preferences

Command Line: RPREF

To set up render preferences for the RENDER command use the Renderering Preferences dialog box. To display the dialog box, click on the Render Preferences icon. (See Figure 11-23.)

If you are using a third-party renderer that requires loading, scroll through the Rendering Type: list in the upper left of the dialog box and load your third-party rendering program from the pop-up list.

In the Rendering Options section of the dialog box you may choose to merge images, use smooth shading or apply materials. For more details on the merge option, see the section on "Six Quick Steps To Your First AutoCAD Rendering" at the beginning of the chapter.

In the Screen Palette section of the dialog box, set the screen palette parameters based upon your current screen driver.

In the Rendering Procedure section, determine the rendering procedure such as rendering selected objects or the entire scene. You can determine whether the rendered image is sent to a separate rendering window, to a standard graphics file on disk or to the current viewport. See Figure 11-26 for further options of the AutoCAD Render window. You have choice of viewport size and 8-bit or 24-bit color depth.

If you choose the More Options… button, the AutoCAD Render Options dialog box will appear to provide Gouraud or Phong render quality options and also Face Control options. (See Figure 11-8.) See "Hiding" at the beginning of the chapter on the use of Face Controls.

Finally, if you pick the Reconfigure < button, you can change the configured rendering display driver.

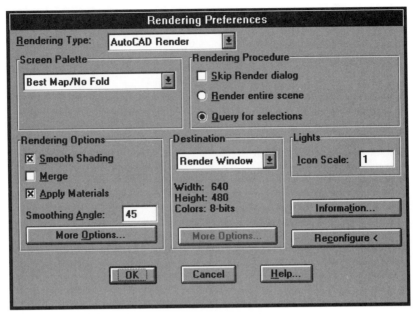

Figure 11-24: The AutoCAD Rendering Preferences dialog box

Types of Rendering Algorithms

Speed levels depend on the algorithm used, the resolution, the number of special effects such as lights, shadows and materials and the type of file to which you're rendering. These are a lot of combinations. Let's start with the algorithm itself.

An *algorithm* is the specific programming code used to render the model. There is a constant swap between quality of the final rendered output and the speed of the algorithm used. While working on and testing the various options of material, color and light, you don't necessarily have to render with the most time-consuming algorithm available on your rendering program. You can always render at a lower resolution using a lesser algorithm to run tests on lights and materials and positions of the objects and view point. Once everything is as you want it, you can perform the final renderings at a higher resolution with a superior algorithm. In the following sections, you'll look at the various algorithms from lowest to highest.

1. **Wireframe Algorithm.** At the absolute bottom of the list is a wireframe algorithm. This algorithm simply shows your model and the placement of the objects in colored wireframe. It is the fastest procedure, but that's not the reason you are using rendering software.

2. **Flat Shade Algorithm.** Next up the ladder is the flat shade algorithm. It is similar to the SHADE command in AutoCAD. It produces a shaded image providing you with some degree of light and material imaging. At this level you wouldn't use it for anything more than fast previews.

3. **Z Buffer Algorithm.** The first level of professional rendering algorithms is known as the Z buffer. It is one of the fastest algorithms created. It has the capability of producing extremely high-quality, award-winning renderings with a relatively low required rendering time.

   The Z buffer algorithm takes a lot of short cuts. It first begins by sorting all of the faces relative to the view point of the user. It identifies only those faces that can be seen from this specific view point, and it throws away any other faces. This concept is where it gets its name. Only the faces that are visible from positive Z will be considered when rendering takes place. As a result, the Z buffer algorithm works on a substantially smaller number of faces than some of the other more accurate rendering algorithms. This algorithm may render at speeds of up to ten times faster than other algorithms.

   There are some drawbacks when using Z buffer. Pure reflections are very difficult to create because if you're going to maintain the speed in a pure Z buffer, then the faces needed to create the reflection are generally discarded. If you find a way to create a true reflection, then it will take substantially longer and will not use a true Z buffer, but possibly will compromise with other algorithms in order to accomplish the effect.

   As you will learn by using programs with Z buffer, adding special effects may slow the process, thus eating away the initial gain.

4. **Gouraud Algorithm.** The gouraud algorithm smooths the facets around a multifaceted surface. Thus it is not as much a full rendering algorithm. The gouraud calculates the intensity of the color at each vertex and interpolates intermediate intensities. In many programs, using gouraud gives you the ability to control the degree of smoothness and the angle at which smoothing will or won't take place. The biggest drawback of gouraud is the limited degree to which you can create specular highlights. These highlights are necessary to produce shiny objects. Therefore, you can't use gouraud exclusively when you want a true reflection.

5. **Phong Algorithm.** Phong is the best compromise for the highest quality rendering and the fastest speed. Phong permits full specular highlights and true reflection mapping. The AutoCAD Renderer has both the gouraud and phong algorithms. To set the algorithm of your choice, choose the Rendering Preferences icon. (See Figure 11-23.) This activates the Rendering Preferences dialog box. (See Figure 11-24.) Choose More Options... and the AutoCAD Render Options dialog box then appears to let you choose either the gouraud or phong algorithms. (See Figure 11-25).

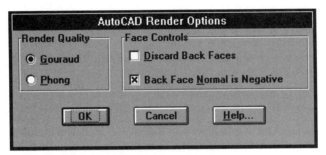

Figure 11-25: The AutoCAD Render Options dialog box

6. **Ray Tracing Algorithm.** The most costly of the algorithms in terms of time is Ray Tracing. Ray Tracing compares every triangular face with every other triangular face. Although it can produce the ultimate in features and functionality, the time costs to render grow exponentially as the size of the model grows.

While performing any given rendering, you will render a scene several times as you adjust light, materials and colors. Most programs offer you a choice of rendering algorithms so you can choose the appropriate one in terms of time and quality to give you the information necessary to make decisions on color, light and material. If you arbitrarily choose the highest rendering algorithm at the highest resolution for each test, the time expense can be intolerable. Therefore, you must understand the relative swap between speed and quality when performing each test.

Screen Resolution

There is more to the quality of rendering and speed than just the algorithm used. Two other factors determine the speed and quality of the rendering. The first is resolution. (See Figure 11-26.) Most of the programs give us a choice of resolution from 320 X 200 to as high as 9999 X 9999. Typical screen resolutions are 320 X 200, 640 X 480, 640 X 400, 800 X 600 and 1024 X 768. For the most part, the higher the resolution you use, the better the quality of the final product and the longer the rendering time.

File Output

The final consideration is the output format of the file—whether the output is 8 bit or 24 bit. 8 bit and 24 bit refer to the number of colors that can be displayed at one time. This is due to the color register in the card and/or file. See Figure 11-26 for further options in the AutoCAD Windows Render Options dialog box. A choice of Viewport Size and 8-Bit or 24-Bit color depth are given.

Bit refers to whether the value of this register is a 1 or 0. Therefore, the color numbers are controlled in binary format.

Without giving into a lesson on binary, here is a quick explanation: If you multiply 2 by 2 eight times, the product is 256. (2 X 2 X 2 X 2 X 2 X 2 X 2 X 2). This is equivalent to eight 1's in binary. If you do the same thing 24 times, the answer is 16,777,216. What this means is that a video card or graphics file that can maintain a color number of up to eight 1's in binary can produce only 256 distinct colors. Therefore, it is called an eight-bit graphics card or an eight-bit graphics file.

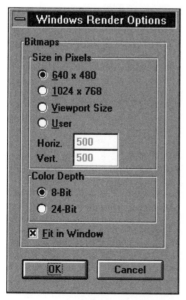

Figure 11-26: The Windows Render Options dialog box

On the other hand, a file or graphics card that can maintain a color number of up to 24 1's in binary can produce sixteen million colors at one time. This type of file or card doesn't need a specific 256-color palette, but instead is called *true color*.

An example of the two types of output files to which you can render is the 8-bit GIF file or the 24-bit TARGA file.

Rendering Statistics

Figure 11-27: The Statistics icon

If you choose the Statistics icon, a dialog box advises you about rendering parameters within your drawing. (See Figure 11-28.) They are scene name, last rendering type, rendering time and total faces and triangles.

The value of the dialog box is self-explanatory. If you forget the scene name, it reminds you. An obvious use is comparison of rendering times. If you are comparing rendering times within different scenes, this is is the best way to time it.

It's also useful if you need to know the number of faces or triangles within the rendering.

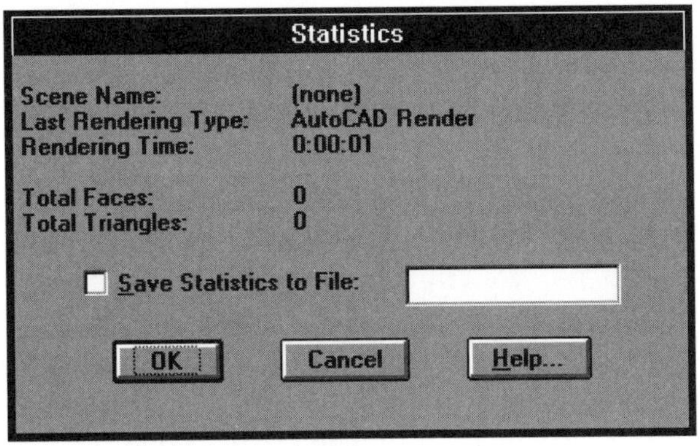

Statistics	
Scene Name:	(none)
Last Rendering Type:	AutoCAD Render
Rendering Time:	0:00:01
Total Faces:	0
Total Triangles:	0
☐ Save Statistics to File:	
OK	Cancel	Help...

Figure 11-28: The Statistics dialog box

Animation

Most rendering programs contain some form of animation as part of their presentation capabilities. There are three basic types of animation available. They are *single path, kinetic* and *key frame*. Animation is nothing but a series of individually rendered frames displayed rapidly one after another. This concept has not changed since the beginning of moving pictures. Therefore, to make your drawings move, you have to create a frame-by-frame rendering that can be displayed back in rapid succession. In the following sections, you'll learn more about each of the different types of animation.

Single Path Animation

The quickest and least complicated form of animation produced by a rendering program is the single path. In single path animation, only one object in the scene moves. In fact, the object that is moving doesn't even have to be in the scene; generally, it's the camera that is moving. This type is the basis of the walk through, walk around, fly by, etc.

To create single path animation, you draw a polyline spline path around and through the model. Each one of the vertices of the polyline becomes a control point. Now you only have to tell the rendering program how many frames it should put between each of the control points. The program then generates the angle of view necessary for each frame equally divided to create a smooth animation. Your only responsibility is to create the path of the camera, the number of control points and the number of frames.

Once the individual scenes creating the animation are done (which only takes a matter of seconds), you can begin to render them. These individual frames are consecutively numbered; therefore, the rendering process is automatic and simply requires time.

Calculating Frames

How many frames do you need? You can create a relatively smooth playback animation in 8 bit with as few as 12 frames per second. Videotape, on the other hand, runs at exactly 30 frames per second. This consideration for videotape is only necessary if you're planning on laying down a frame-by-frame transfer to videotape. If you're going to videotape live from the computer screen, it will record whatever looks good to you.

In any case, recording requires a lot of frames. This means that to do a 10-second animation you have to create and render 300 finished frames. To give you an idea on the time, if you're using the Z buffer algorithm at 320 X 200 resolution and the approximate rendering time per frame is 15 seconds, then it will take about an hour and 15 minutes to create a 10 second animation.

Take a long lunch and your animation will be done. On the other hand, if you're doing a 24-bit Phong rendering at 1024 X 768 to a TARGA file and it takes an average of 10 minutes per frame, then this animation will take 50 hours to render.

Kinetic Animation

Kinetic animation is akin to single path animation in that you set up a path of movement for more than one object. Assume, for example, you're animating a machine and the storyboard requires the camera to move around the machine while one part of the machine moves up and down. This is an example of kinetic animation. If your program supports this type of animation, you would create a path of movement for each of the objects. Again, you would indicate the number of frames between the vertices of the path and let the rendering software create the scenes.

Key Frame Animation

The most sophisticated of the animation procedures is called key framing. This is the traditional method of animation. When you say animation, most people think of the pioneer work performed by Walt Disney. Animation prior to computers was a long, tedious and time-consuming process. To produce a full-length animation, literally hundreds of thousands of hand-drawn images had to be produced.

To expedite this production process, certain principles and techniques of animation such as storyboarding and key framing were developed. Because of the expense of producing all those drawings, mistakes could be costly. Also, Walt didn't want his most talented and expensive senior animators tied to the drawing board. This is what key framing is all about.

Historically, over a given segment a senior animator drew 20 or 30 key frames. These key frames showed how the movement of all of the objects in a scene progressed. Once this movement had been worked out and approved, then the key frames were turned over to junior animators to do the grunt work of drawing all the in-between frames to get to the key frame. That's the way we get the term *key frame animation*.

Advantages of Key Frames

One advantage of key frame animation over single path and kinetic animation is that you're not limited to simply the changes of movement of one object or even multiple objects over a single path. You get to view all changes from one key frame to another.

These changes include changes in movement, rotation, scale and morphing. Morphing is a change of shape. (You might use morphing when you want an object such as a pencil to bend or grow.)

As you can imagine, all of the information that is changed from one key frame to another has to be carefully analyzed to create a smooth transition in the in-between frames. Also, the number of in-between frames is critical not only to the smoothness, but to the timing.

For example, if Mickey were hitting a tennis ball, then the pull back of the tennis racket might be slower than the forward swing and the acceleration past the follow through. At the time the key frame is put into place, the key frame animator doesn't have to take these things into consideration. That movement can be adjusted throughout the work by creating additional in-between frames until the timing is perfected. As you can see, the sophistication of key frame animation is superior to that of single path direction animation.

Key frame animation lends itself nicely to the help of a computer. This technique of animation is the one thing—more than anything else—that separates the animation capabilities of 3D Studio over other rendering programs, because 3D Studio uses key frame animation.

Moving On

Shading, rendering and animation create the ultimate in communication and presentation to your audience. But these capabilities are not necessarily the meat and potatoes in creating a good presentation in 3D.

Chapter 12, "Tips for Composition & Presentation," brings you back down to earth and gives you many of the techniques you will use for composition and presentation of your 3D drawings. Chapter 12 shows you time-saving techniques to set up prototype configurations for Paper Space, line up viewports, create Orthographic projection views, work in perspective and create assembly drawings.

After all, the final presentation is what it's all about.

Tips for Composition & Presentation

In this chapter you'll learn how to use prototypes for Paper Space effectively, line up viewports, create assembly drawings, use Orthographic projection views effectively and work with perspective. You'll also learn the best way to move 3D drawings from one program to another. Along the way you'll also look at some more timesaving AutoLISP programs.

Remember, it's not enough just to be able to draw in 3D effectively. Unless you're working in AutoCAD 3D as a form of therapy generally, you have a given audience to which you need to communicate and present your ideas. Therefore, you must create an effective presentation for your target audience. The following are a series of tips to help you compose and present your drawings more effectively, with the least effort and aggravation.

Using Prototypes & Paper Space

If you have any experience at all working with AutoCAD in a 2D environment, the concept of a prototype drawing and what it can do to save you time when you create a new drawing should not be anything new to you.

Prototype drawings have been used for years in the 2D environment to preset items such as grids, snaps, dimension variables, linetypes, text styles and all of the hundreds of settings that AutoCAD requires to get your project under way. All of these settings are generally created in a drawing. This drawing is then used as the prototype for any new drawings. Anything that is placed in the prototype drawing will be inherited in its totality by the new drawing. In reality, the new drawing begins as a copy of the prototype drawing.

First, look at how you can use Paper Space in a prototype drawing and then look at the concept of a prototype library and the features of Auto-CAD Release 13 that will make a prototype library easy to manage.

Paper Space

As you saw in Chapter 10, "Paper Space," the layout and configuration of Paper Space are vital to not only working in 3D, but creating an acceptable presentation. Following is a review of some of the considerations in Paper Space:

- First, set up your Paper Space limits and your title block depending on the size of the eventual output paper you're going to use.

- Second, determine the number of viewports and their size and spacing where you want them in Paper Space. Remember that you should create viewports using the MVIEW command on a layer called BORDERS.

- Third, consider the view point angle that you want for each of the viewports: whether it should be one of several Orthographic or Isometric views, whether it should be a Plan view and whether any of the viewports should remove hidden lines when they are plotted.

- Fourth, consider any standard text that would appear on the paper next to the viewports. This text is not just limited to the title blocks.

- Fifth, determine the visibility of layers within each viewport.

The preceding considerations lend themselves to being set up ahead of time. If you set up Paper Space and the viewports in advance in a prototype drawing with all of the configurations as previously outlined, then you could begin any new drawing that needed these configurations using this specific prototype in Model Space or TILEMODE 1. You could then use the TILEMODE 1 tiled viewports as explained in Chapter 6, "Viewports," to aid you in the creation of the model.

Remember that these viewports are independent of the Paper Space viewports. And you should use them primarily to aid you in modeling in 3D. Once you've created the model and then changed it to TILEMODE 0 (Paper Space), the model is automatically set up with the different viewports ready for the presentation. At the worst, you may need to adjust the scale slightly within each viewport.

It's obvious that one prototype drawing will not fit all conditions. You'll need a separate prototype any time you're going to change the output size of your drawing media. You'll also need a different prototype drawing if you're changing the viewport position or configuration. In essence you will need a different prototype drawing for any differences whatsoever that are found in Paper Space. Then how do you create and easily control all of these prototype drawings? The easiest way is with a prototype library.

The Prototype Library

In a library most of the items should be in the same place. In versions of AutoCAD before Release 13, placement didn't seem to matter for prototype drawings. When you used the NEWDWG=PROTODWG command,

AutoCAD couldn't find PROTODWG unless it was your default prototype or you gave it the complete drive path specifications.

This is now not the case. You can have a whole library of prototype drawings and keep them in a single directory. For this example, call the directory C:\ACADR13\PROTO and place all of your prototype drawings in this directory.

You must now tell AutoCAD not only where to find your prototype drawings, but which drawing is to be your default prototype. To do this, begin a new drawing. From the File pull-down menu pick New. You are given a Create New Drawing dialog box (see Figure 12-1). Pick Prototype... to bring up a file dialog box. Scroll the Directories List box until you find the C:\ACADR13\PROTO directory and then pick it. This changes the default directory to C:\ACADR13\PROTO. Then pick in the Files box the drawing you want to be your prototype and pick OK. You return to the Create New Drawing dialog box. Now pick the Retain as Default check box. You may give the new drawing a name or not; it doesn't matter. What does matter this first time is that you pick OK in the dialog box.

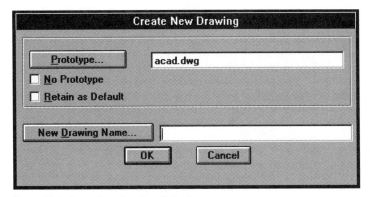

Figure 12-1: Create New Drawing dialog box

You have just created a default prototype drawing. This drawing could be ACAD.DWG or any other drawing you might want to be the default prototype. What is important here is that in creating a default prototype you also told AutoCAD where to find all of your prototype drawings—as long as the default prototype drawing is in the same directory as the rest. From now on you can choose any prototype drawing by only picking Prototype... and picking the drawing. The default directory will contain your prototype drawing library.

Remember that any drawing can be the default if you pick the Retain as Default check box before you pick OK in the new drawing.

Lining Up Viewports

There is no real trick to lining up viewports if you remember that the viewport itself is the object in Pspace. This means you treat the viewport the same as any other object in your drawing. Almost all of the commands available to you in 2D, such as SNAP, OSNAP, MOVE, etc., are available to you when manipulating the position of the viewport in Paper Space. Therefore, if you want one viewport to line up specifically with another viewport and the target viewport is not snapped to a grid point, you might consider drawing a construction from the intersection orthogonally across the screen. See Figure 12-2 for a view of construction lines used to align viewports.

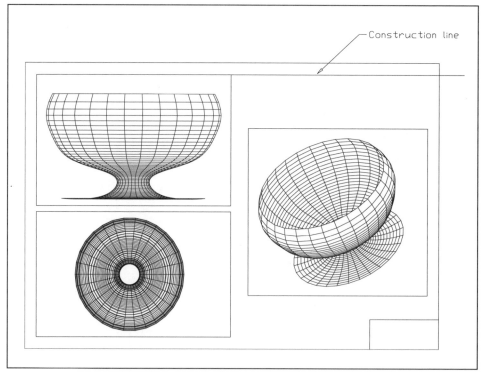

Figure 12-2: Construction lines used to align viewports

Now use the regular AutoCAD MOVE command using object snap intersection and snap on to the intersection of the viewport you're going to move. Pick the second point using object snap perpendicular on the construction line. Now you can erase the construction. This procedure guarantees that the second viewport is absolutely aligned with the first.

By setting ortho to on, you can use the same MOVE commands and make your adjustments left and right as needed. Figure 12-3 shows aligned viewports.

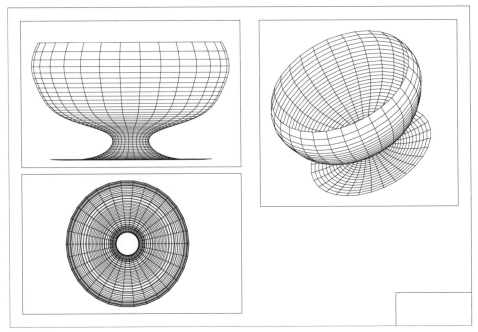

Figure 12-3: Aligned viewports

Two of the AutoLISP programs in the 3D Tools will help you align viewports. VPX.LSP moves the viewport only in the X direction, and VPY.LSP moves the viewport only in the Y direction. The programs ask you to first pick the viewport and then pick some point on the viewport that you want to align. Finally, pick a point on the target viewport. If you're using VPY, then the viewport will only move to line up in the Y direction. The X direction stays constant.

You can find these programs in the AutoLISP section of the book. As with all 3D programs, make certain that they are properly loaded. If you have the *AutoCAD 3D Companion Disk* installed properly and have loaded 3DTOOLS.LSP, all you need to do is type in the name of the program.

You can use this same principle if you want to align the model itself. The only difference is that you can't actually object snap onto the model inside the viewport while in Pspace mode. At the same time, however, while using an orthogonal construction line and using a very deep zoom in Paper Space, you can come very close. You, of course, are required to pick the viewport itself as the object to be moved, but you are permitted to pick a point close to the appropriate part of the model (even though you aren't actually picking the model) as your base point. If you then move that base point with an object snap perpendicular to the construction line, the two objects will line up in Paper Space.

VPX and VPY work well with this method too—except you must pick the base point and the target point on the model.

Using MVSETUP.LSP to Align Objects

Release 13 supplies, among its bonus LISP files, one called MVSETUP.LSP. You may remember it from setting up your initial drawing sheet sizes and drawing limits. One of its functions is to align objects within neighboring viewports, especially while in Paper Space. You load the MVSETUP file through the APPLOAD command and then type **MVS** or **MVSETUP** to use it.

To align an object within a viewport, select Align Viewports. Choose a base point using OSNAP, move to the next viewport and, again using OSNAP, pick a second point that you want to be lined up with the first object. You may choose in turn the Horizontal alignment and Vertical alignment.

Assembly Drawings

There is no real trick to creating assembly drawings; it's very easy to do. The first thing you have to do is to make certain you have each part of the assembly in a separate viewport at the same scale. Each one of the viewports in Paper Space becomes a part of the assembly drawing that you're going to position on the Paper Space viewport.

First, begin by isolating each part in its own viewport. Make sure that each part is rotated at the same angle and is at the same scale. Figure 12-4 shows isolated assembly parts.

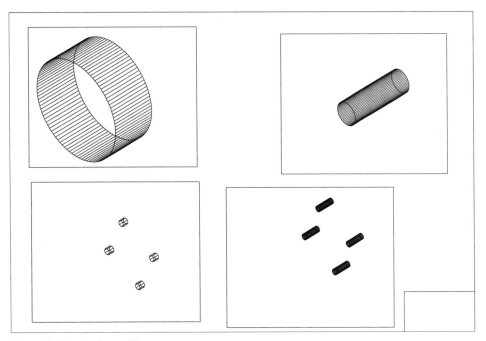

Figure 12-4: Isolated assembly parts

Using a technique similar to the one used in lining up viewports, move in Pspace until you align the various component assembly parts as indi–cated in Figure 12-5. The figure shows the assembly parts in viewports.

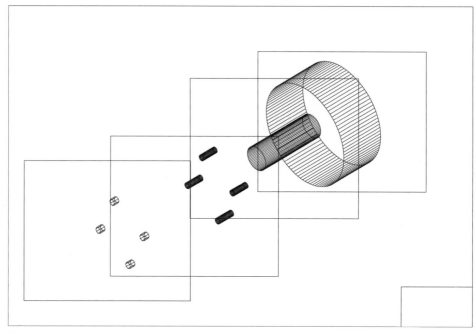

Figure 12-5: Assembly parts in viewports

Figure 12-5 doesn't look like much because all of the viewports are overlapping and visible. Remember that all of the viewports themselves were created with the MVIEW command on a layer called BORDERS. Now watch what happens when you turn off the BORDERS layer. See Figure 12-6 for a view of the assembly drawing without viewport borders.

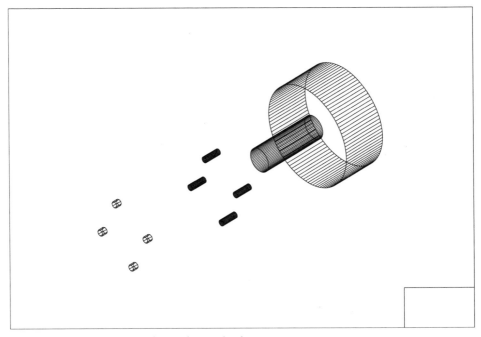

Figure 12-6: Assembly drawing without viewport borders

Because you're still in Pspace mode, you can now use the DTEXT command and label each of the component parts of your assembly drawing.

Orthographic Projection Views

Orthographic projection views can be very useful not only for presentations, but for working in the 3D model as well. Here, you'll learn what an Orthographic projection view is and then learn how you can use it along with several AutoLISP 3D tools that you have created to help you move objects around more easily.

First, what is an Orthographic projection view? Actually, it's easier to describe an Orthographic projection view by first describing an Isometric view. Look at Figure 12-7, which shows an Isometric view.

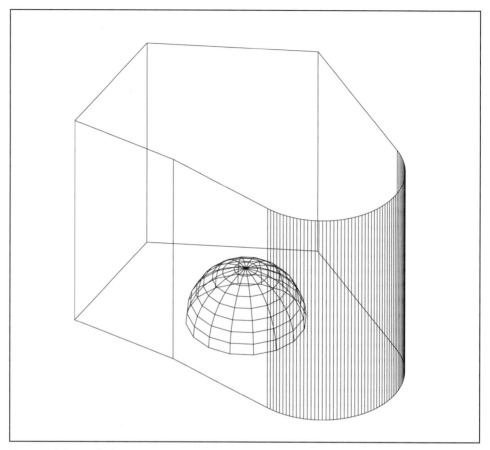

Figure 12-7: Isometric view

An Isometric view is a 2D projection of a 3D model shown from an angle. If the 2D view of the 3D scene is not shown from an angle but "straight on," then it's an Orthographic projection view. This means that if you were to make the UCS parallel to one of the six sides of an object and then go plan to that UCS, you would create an Orthographic projection view.

If you choose the View toolbar, you'll find the orthographic views already created (see Figure 12-8).

There are six main Orthographic projection views possible for most objects. They are the top, left, right, front, back and bottom.

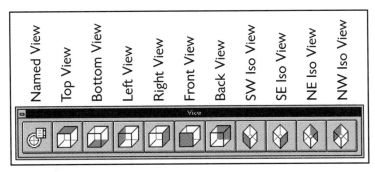

Figure 12-8: The View toolbar

While using an Orthographic projection view, especially if you can rotate your UCS parallel to that view, you can work with the object along a fixed Orthographic construction plane. Working on one plane helps you control the creation and adjustment of geometry in 3D. Also, if you have at least three Orthographic projection views and one Isometric view, you can visualize exactly where the object is in 3D. Look at Figure 12-9 to see Orthographic and Isometric projections.

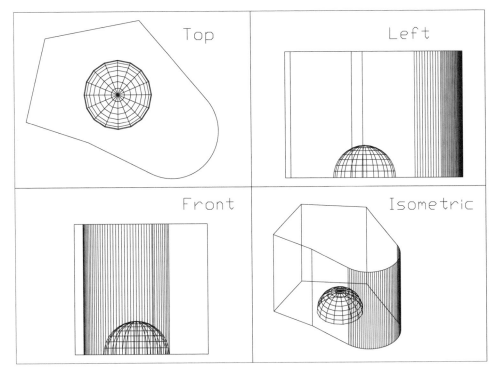

Figure 12-9: Orthographic and Isometric projections

Programs to Work in Orthographic Projection View

The model in Figure 12-9 shows a rounded, dome-like surface. The object here is to make certain that this dome sits squarely on top of the model. As you can see from the figure, from the Top view and the Isometric view, it's difficult to tell if the dome is sitting on top of the model or has fallen into the model. But you can clearly tell in the Left view and the Front view that the dome is clearly inside the model. So what is the easiest way to adjust the dome?

Well, the easiest way to make an adjustment to move the dome "up" is to work in the front or the left viewport. I've created an AutoLISP program specifically to be used with Orthographic projection views to help you move the model. This program, called AV.LSP for align view, assumes that you're active in the viewport you want to manipulate. It then sets your UCS parallel to the view of the Orthographic projection view and sets ORTHO to on. Now it's a simple case of your using the MOVE command. You are forced orthogonally in either left or right or up or down movement. This way, by picking the front viewport and typing **AV**, you can move the dome easily to the top of the model. Once you've moved it to the top, you can see from the other viewports the effect of this movement.

The AutoLISP program PV.LSP, which stands for previous view, will return the UCS to its previous status and return the ortho mode to its previous settings as well.

You can find AV.LSP and PV.LSP in the AutoLISP section of the book. As with all 3D programs, make certain that they are properly loaded. If you have the *AutoCAD 3D Companion Disk* installed properly and have loaded 3DTOOLS.LSP, all you need to do is type in the name of the program.

Additional Programs to Work With Orthographic Projection View

AV.LSP works well if all you want to do is make adjustments up and down or left and right in one Orthographic projection view. Here are three other AutoLISP programs that add even more flexibility: MOVEY.LSP, MOVEXY.LSP and MOVEX.LSP.

Assume that you want to move the dome specifically to the top of the model. You'd need a program that would let you select objects and then pick a base point. Then you'd pick a point on an object of the same Y level to which you want to move. This program is called MOVEY.LSP. Now look at Figure 12-10 to see a dome in the middle of a model.

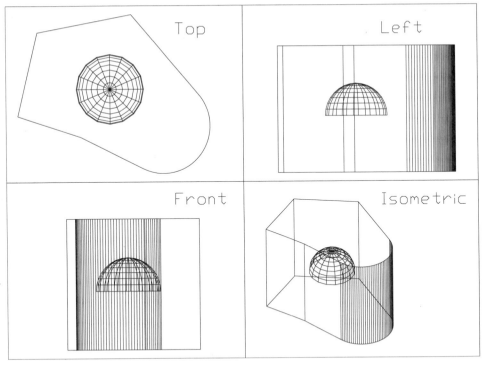

Figure 12-10: Dome in the middle of the model

Make active the left Orthographic projection view in the upper-right viewport and then run MOVEY.LSP. It's important that you first make active one of the Orthographic viewports. The program will set and use a UCS view relative to this initial viewport. Next, select the dome. Pick the bottom of the dome as the base point. Now, using object snap nearest, pick any line on the top of the model. Notice that the dome moves to the top of the model (see Figure 12-11). Notice also that regardless of where you picked for the target point, only the Y value of that point relative to the initial UCS view was changed. Therefore, the dome did not shift left or right.

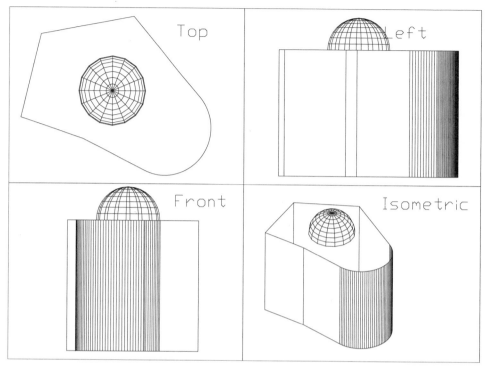

Figure 12-11: Dome at the top of the model

Undo if necessary and begin again. This time, make active the top Orthographic view in the upper-left viewport. Now move the dome to the edge of one of the sides without moving it up or down in the model using the MOVEXY program. This program enables you to move in the X and Y directions relative to the UCS view that is established in the initial viewport, without changing the Z value. Next, select the dome and pick a base point using object snap nearest on the edge of the dome. Again using object snap nearest, place the dome at the edge of the side of the model. Figure 12-12 illustrates the dome moved in the XY direction.

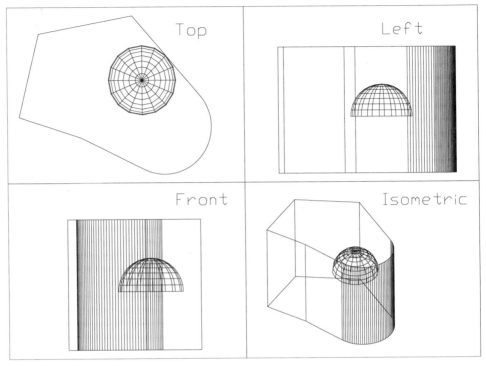

Figure 12-12: Dome moved in the XY direction

MOVEX.LSP works exactly the same way but gives you exclusive control over the X coordinate based on the UCS view of the initial viewport.

You can find MOVEY.LSP, MOVEXY.LSP and MOVEX.LSP in the AutoLISP section of the book. As with all 3D programs, make certain that they are properly loaded. If you have the *AutoCAD 3D Companion Disk* installed properly and have loaded 3DTOOLS.LSP, all you need to do is type in the name of the program.

Working With Perspective

The key to all composition and presentation, as well as many of the tools in working with 3D, is to create a viewport where you can see live and dynamically the creation of your object from any given angle and Perspective view.

One of the main reasons to work with perspective is so that you can see the results of the creation of your model live and in perspective as you're creating it. In many situations you also may want to present the model in perspective at least as one of the views so that your audience can visualize a more life-like model.

One of the major problems of working in perspective, however, is that you are unable to point while perspective is turned on. The easiest way to work around this problem is to create a minimum of two viewports and set your Perspective view in one of the viewports. In the other viewport, make certain that you're not in perspective. Remember that DVIEW Distance, which controls perspective, is independent in each one of the viewports.

As you actually work on the model in one of the viewports, you can see the model take shape in perspective as you're working. From time to time you might need to type **RD** and press Enter (remember that RD.LSP is the AutoLISP program that redraws in all viewports) or even type **REGENALL** to refresh the screen not only in the viewport in which you are working, but also in the Perspective viewport as well.

Another interesting technique is to hide the lines in the Perspective viewport from time to time. These lines stay hidden while you're drawing in the other viewport. However, that is not to say that the new lines you're drawing since you last hid the lines will be hidden from view. But all lines drawn previously will be hidden.

Moving Presentations to Other Programs

In AutoCAD Release 13 there is now an enormous number of file formats that you can use with other programs to enhance your presentation. The major translation format for moving the entire drawing to another program is still the DXF file format. But that's not what I'm talking about here. You can move the presentation, possibly even including the title block and the viewports themselves in Paper Space, to another program such as a desktop publishing program, word processing or even a paint program. It's also entirely possible to take an entire AutoCAD drawing and make it directly a GIF file that can be used as a texture map for render material, as discussed in Chapter 11, "Shading, Rendering & Animation."

One of the keys to moving presentations to other programs is to create a raster file format or a PostScript format of exactly what it is you want on the screen to be presented. This is not an object translation similar to DXF. In fact, you should not even use the new PSOUT, PostScript-out, feature of

AutoCAD Release 13 even though you might want a PostScript file. Using PSOUT will only give you the individual objects. There is no way to hide lines in this file or to create any kind of specific view. On the other hand, you can still do a PostScript-out using the techniques described in the following paragraphs, which are shown not only for PostScript, but also for other raster formats.

The whole theory behind this procedure is that you're going to plot not to paper or to a regular plot file, but a specific raster or PostScript format. To do this, you'll need to create a specific plotter for that purpose. Now see how to create the plotter.

Begin by going into the AutoCAD Configuration menu:

Type: CONFIG <Enter>

Press Enter a couple of times until you get to the Configuration main menu. Now set up a new plotter:

Type: 5 <Enter>

This is the Configure Plotter option of the Configuration menu.

Response: Plotter Configuration Menu
            0. Exit to configuration menu
            1. Add a plotter configuration
            2. Delete a plotter configuration
            3. Change a plotter configuration
            4. Rename a plotter configuration
            Enter selection, 0 to 4 <0>:

Here, add a plotter configuration:

Type: 1 <Enter>

AutoCAD then shows you the plotter drivers available to you. The number beside each plotter driver available will be different depending on your machine setup and its devices. The one you are looking for is:

Raster file export ADI 4.2 - by Autodesk

Choose number 14 on the driver listing.

After you pick this option, you have the following choices of screen sizes. This is the resolution of the output file.

```
1.  320 x 200 (CGA/MCGA color)
2.  640 x 200 (CGA monochrome)
3.  640 x 350 (EGA)
4.  640 x 400
5.  640 x 480 (VGA)
6.  720 x 540
7.  800 x 600
8.  1024 x 768
9.  1152 x 900 (SUN standard)
10. 1600 x 1280 (SUN high-resolution)
11. User defined
```

Let's say that you choose number 1, CGA format, for this example. The following are the raster formats supported:

```
1.  GIF          CompuServe Graphics Interchange Format
2.  XWD          X Window dump
3.  PBM          Portable Bitmap Toolkit Formats
4.  BMP          Microsoft Windows Device-independent Bitmap
5.  TGA          TrueVision Targa Format
6.  PCX          Z-Soft PCX format
7.  Sun Rasterfile
8.  FITS         Flexible Image Transfer System
9.  EPS          Encapsulated PostScript (Adobe-2.0 EPSF-2.0)
10. TIFF         Tag Image File Format
11. FAX Image    Group 3 Encoding
12. Amiga IFF/ILBM Format
```

You will get a choice of several colors:

```
1. Monochrome
2. Color - 16 colors
3. Color - 256 colors
```

You can now choose a color format for the background color. So pick GIF at 320 x 200 with all colors. You can specify the background color to be any of AutoCAD's 256 standard colors. The default of " . " (period) selects a black screen background.

Response `Enter Selection. 0 to 255 <0>:`

Type `<Enter>`

When asked, name the plotter configuration simply GIF File. Continue to press Enter until you are back in your drawing. You are now ready to begin plotting.

Type: `Plot <Enter>`

From the dialog box, pick Plotter Devices and choose the GIF File plotter that you just created. Make sure that the Hidden Lines check box is checked. The GIF File plotter can only plot to a file. That's why that option is grayed out in the dialog box. But you can name the file. You might even take this opportunity to do a full preview of the plot. When everything is as you want it, then pick OK and AutoCAD will begin plotting to the file.

Now you have created a GIF file. See how easy that is. You not only can move your drawing and presentation to other programs and file formats, but you can also bring in other file formats and make them part of your drawing. But don't confuse this conversion with any form of raster-to-vector conversion or the capability to scan an entire drawing. These capabilities are not available as yet from within AutoCAD itself.

Look at a very simple scenario. Assume that you have a scanned image of your corporate logo, and you'd like to place this logo on your title block in Paper Space. This logo could have come from a scanner. It could have been created by your rendering program. Or it could have been created using a paint program or any other method of creating a raster file. You can assume, however, that the logo is in the form of a GIF or PCX file.

The command in AutoCAD to bring in a raster file is GIFIN or PCXIN, depending on the type of file. You also can bring in TIFF files and Post-Script files with TIFFIN and PSIN. For this case, assume that the file is in GIF format:

Type: `GIFIN <Enter>`

Give AutoCAD the name of the file and it will begin loading. The file will be brought in as a block that you can scale. The file actually has been converted by AutoCAD from raster to vector. It no longer is rasters; it is a block within your drawing. The objects contained in the block definition are solids. This term is not to be confused with solid modeling. A solid is an AutoCAD 2D object. The solid is a filled object, filled with whatever color and shape the logo was in. It's not a good idea to ever explode one of these types of blocks. Otherwise, you might have an enormous number of very small solid objects. The fact that they are solid and filled objects will enable you to plot them out with a pen plotter although this process may suck your ink dry.

One final caution when importing raster files into AutoCAD: import files very sparingly. A small logo will be fine, but don't try to bring in an entire drawing. Even on fast machines importing can be a slow, tedious process and make your drawing very large.

Pasting Through Windows

A more efficient way of placing a raster file in your drawing is simply to paste it through Windows. Try this example. Go to your Windows Main group. Press the Print Screen key on your keyboard. Now return to AutoCAD and press Ctrl+V. It pastes right onto the screen. You may also resize the pasted window as with other Windows graphics and it will plot with a raster plotter. See Figure 12-13.

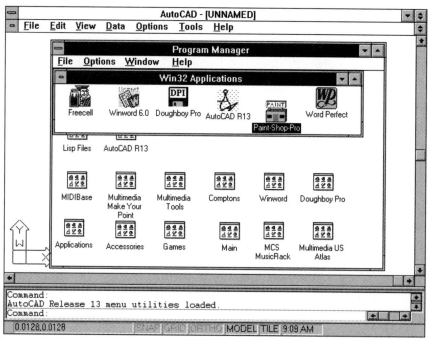

Figure 12-13: RASTER paste

Moving On

Composition and presentation along with shading, rendering and animation are the keys to communicating with your audience. In this chapter and in Chapter 11, you've looked at various techniques and considerations that you can use in creating effective presentations. These things make the investment in working in 3D pay off. Chapter 13 adds new object types for solid modeling. Although it's not the complete modeling extension, it has added functionality that Advanced AutoCAD has needed.

The AutoCAD Solid Modeler

In this chapter you will draw and then render objects using 3D solid commands.

With the metamorphosis of Autodesk's Engineering Works—later called AutoSolid then Advanced Modeling Extension and now Designer—3D information concerning mass properties and even finite element analysis with other programs is now possible. The most universal reason for taking the time to model in 3D is visualization and presentation. This also means 3D modeling and rendering.

The ACIS solid modeler in Release 13 is similar to the Release 12 AME (Advanced Modeling Extension). For all practical purposes AME is not sold anymore and has been replaced by the Designer. Autodesk took the opportunity to include some solid functionality in Release 13 and included the ACIS solid modeler. For those of you who have invested time with modeling in AME, there is an AME convert routine that works most of the time. It's in the Solids toolbar. (See Figure 13-1.) Because of the way solids are expressed in Release 13 as compared to AME, the translation is not always precise.

How a Solid Is Created

Solids are created in one of two ways. First, you can create a solid from one of six basic primitives. (See Figure 13-1.) This simply means there are six basic shapes that AutoCAD has programmed for you. They are the box, sphere, cylinder, cone, wedge and torus. You combine the basic shapes into composite solids by using Boolean operations of Union, Subtraction and Intersection. These commands either combine or cut objects away from one other. The standard AutoCAD commands of CHAMFER and FILLET allow you to edit 3D model edges.

Figure 13-1: The Solids toolbar

The second method of creating a solid is by extruding a 2D object. This object may also be revolved around an axis in a similar manner to REVSURF. Use the EXTRUDE and REVOLVE commands for these 2D operations.

You may also extract a 2D view from a 3D object by using Slice. Or you may extract a 2D Region based upon a section plane of your solid model. Most of the commands, with the exception of Region, are found under the Solids toolbar. During the process you may view a solid model and render it from any angle. You may also determine volume and center of gravity through mass property calculations on the 3D model.

Solid Variables (Isolines & Facetres)

Solids by their very nature are already meshed for you. The number of lines that make up that mesh are controlled by two system variables: Isolines and Facetres.

ISOLINES controls the number of tessellation lines used. But this system variable has no effect on the smoothness of a shade or a render. This is controlled by FACETRES.

FACETRES can go from .01 to 10. This is an algorithm that is a number factor multiplied by VIEWRES. FACETRES set at 2 seems to work well without costing too much time.

For now set ISOLINES to 20. This is roughly the equivalent of SURFTAB1 and SURFTAB2 and has replaced the SOLWDENS command in AME.

Type: ISOLINES <Enter>

Type: 20 <Enter>

Just because you can create basic shapes such as solids doesn't in and of itself make it very useful. The real utility of solids is how you combine these shapes by putting them together or by subtracting one from another.

Creating Solids & Regions

Let's look at an example. Begin by drawing a cube and then a cylinder. Then cut a hole through the cube by subtracting the cylinder from the cube. As you will see, this is easy with solids whereas it is a nightmare with 3D by itself.

Figure 13-2: The 3D Box icon

From the Solids toolbar choose the 3D Box icon or in the command prompt window:

Type: BOX <Enter>

Response: Center of box <0, 0, 0>:

Pick a point representing the center of the box.

Response: Cube/Length/<corner of box>:

Type: Cube <Enter>

As you can see from the varied prompts there are many ways to draw a box. Here we are simply creating a cube.

Response: Length:

Pick two points representing the length of the cube. (See Figure 13-3.) The cube has been rotated to 35,165 to create the view.

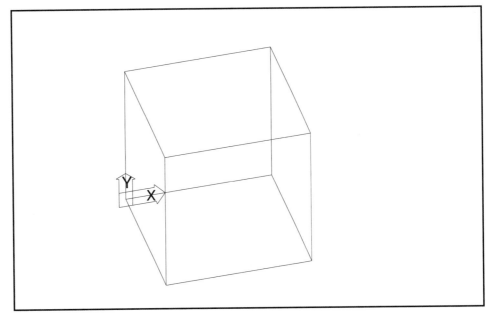

Figure 13-3: Rotate solid cube

Set UCSICON to ORigin

Figure 13-4: The UCS Origin icon.

Now place and rotate the UCS as indicated in Figure 13-3. From the flyout of the Standard toolbar choose the UCS Origin. (See Figure 13-4.) Remember to use osnap intersection or endpoint. When working with solids it's better to work with endpoint object snap if intersection doesn't work.

Figure 13-5: The Cylinder icon from the Solids toolbar

You will now place a cylinder from the back side of the box where the UCS origin is through the front side. From the Solids toolbar choose the Cylinder icon or in the command prompt window:

Type: CYLINDER <Enter>

Response: Elliptical/<center point>

Pick an approximate point for the center of the back side of the cube.

Response: Diameter/<Radius>:

Pick a second point to define the radius as you would in creating a circle.

Response: Center of other end/<Height>:

Pick two points for the length of the cylinder.

It's important to pick a length that is at least as long as the box. It doesn't matter if the cylinder is longer than the box. (See Figure 13-6.)

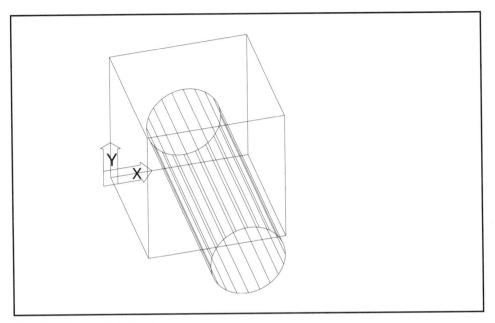

Figure 13-6: Solid cylinder in cube

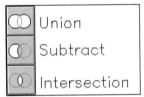

Figure 13-7: The Union, Subtract and Intersection icons from the Modify toolbar

From the Explode flyout of the Modify toolbar choose the subtract icon or in the command prompt window:

Type: SUBTRACT   <Enter>

Response: Select solids and regions to subtract from...
            Select objects:

Pick the cube and press Enter.

Response: Select solids and regions to subtract...
            Select objects:

Pick the cylinder and press Enter.

A hole has now been cut through the cube. (See Figure 13-8.) Here the cube was rotated with DVIEW to 15 degrees so that you could see the hole going completely through the cube.

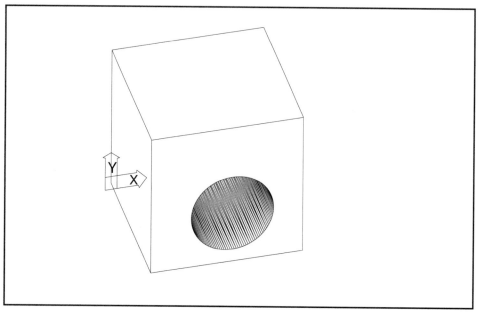

Figure 13-8: Hole in cube.

Just as you can remove mass from a solid, you can also join solids together with the UNION command to make a single solid. Choose the Union icon from from the Explode flyout of the Modify toobar. (See Figure 13-7.)

It isn't necessary to start everything with a primitive. Look at the way a gear with four holes can be drawn. Begin with a large circle and 12 small circles arrayed. (See Figure 13-9.)

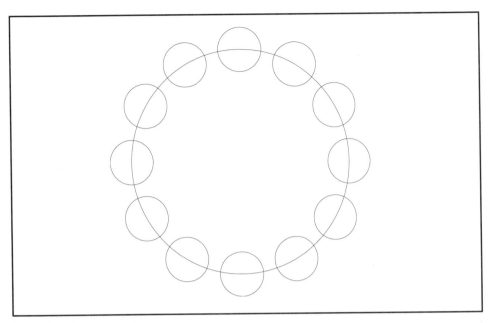

Figure 13-9: Creation of regions

 Figure 13-10: The Region icon

Objects must be regions or solids before they can be subtracted from one another. In this case let's make them regions. From the Polygon flyout of the Draw toolbar choose the Region icon.

From the Polygon flyout of the Draw toolbar choose the Region icon or in the command prompt window:

Type: REGION <Enter>

Response: Select objects:

Select all the circles and confirm. They are now all regions. Use the SUBTRACT command and subtract from the large circle all the smaller circles. (See Figure 13-11.)

Four cylinders are also placed in Figure 13-11. Make sure that the cylinders are extruded more than the eventual gear.

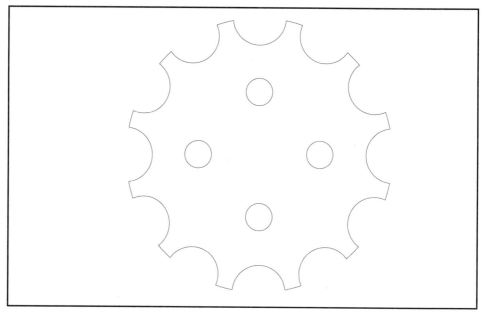

Figure 13-11: Extruded solids

 Figure 13-12: The Extrude icon

You are now ready to extrude the gear.

From the Solids toolbar choose the Extrude icon or in the command prompt window:

Type: EXTRUDE <Enter>

Response: Select objects:

Select the gear and press Enter.

Response: Path/<Height of Extrusion>:

Type in a height that is less than the height of the cylinders.

Now subtract all four cylinders from the gear. You may also use the VPOINT command for the same view as Figure 13-13. Type **ISO**, and yours should now look like Figure 13-13. Other shapes that you draw may also be extruded along pre-determined paths.

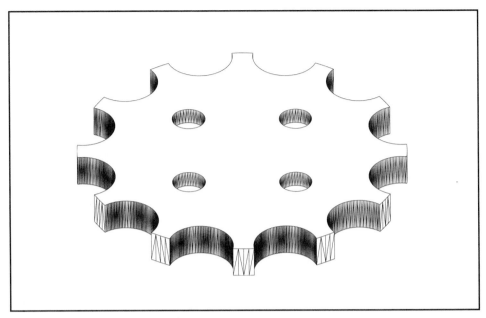

Figure 13-13: Finished gear

Revolving a solid can create just as dramatic effects as using REVSURF. However, you must be certain that the entity is a closed area. You can't just use straight lines.

Figure 13-14: The Revolve icon

Begin with polylines enclosed, as in Figure 13-15. Notice the fillets around all the edges. The straight line will be the axis of revolution just as in a REVSURF. Now, using the REVOLVE command, select the polylines; then select the line as the axis of revolution and choose full circle. Notice that even the prompts are the same.

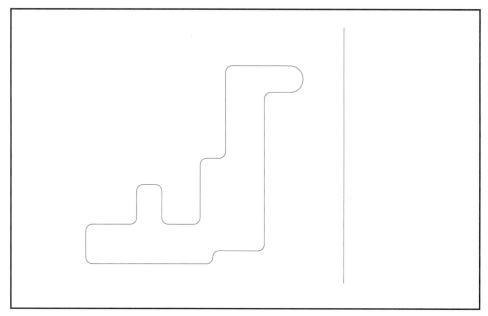

Figure 13-15: Closed polylines

The result is Figure 13-16. It doesn't look like much here. Figure 13-17 shows the image after using the CHSIDE program to move it to the other side and manipulating with DVIEW. You may also want to fillet it as Figure 13-18.

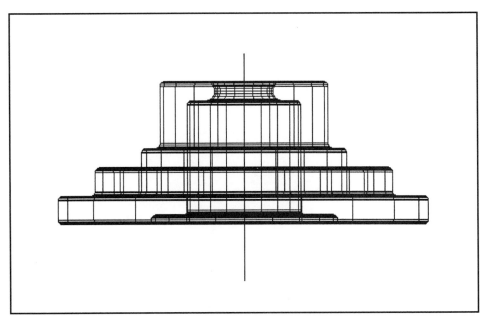

Figure 13-16: Polylines after they've been revolved

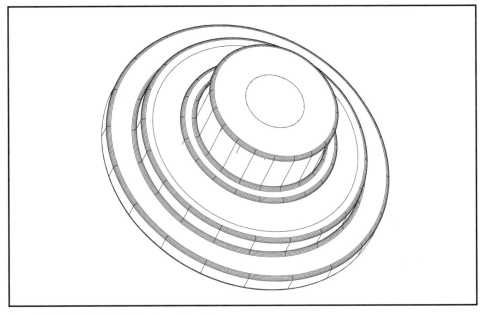

Figure 13-17: ISO of object flipped to other side

Now use the RENDER command. The tutorial at the end of the chapter will help you set lights, materials and render. Look at how nicely it renders with the smooth curved line and the fillets in Figure 13-18.

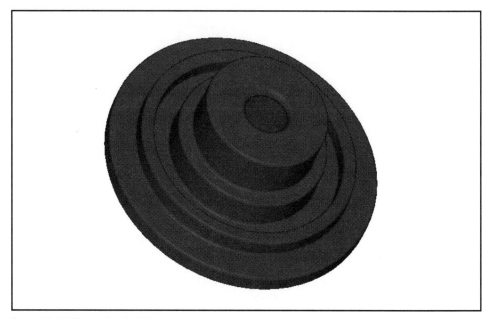

Figure 13-18: The rendered solid

You also can create cross section slices. Use the SLICE command and define a three-point slicing plane. From the Solids toolbar choose the Slice icon or type the command in the command prompt window and then create a cross-section. The result is Figure 13-20. Then render the drawing. The tutorial at the end of the chapter will help you set lights, materials and then render it. The result is Figure 13-21.

Figure 13-19: The Slice icon.

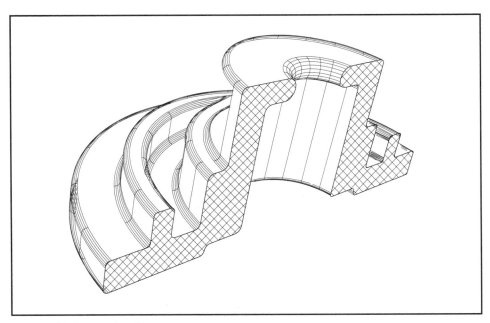

Figure 13-20: Cross section slice

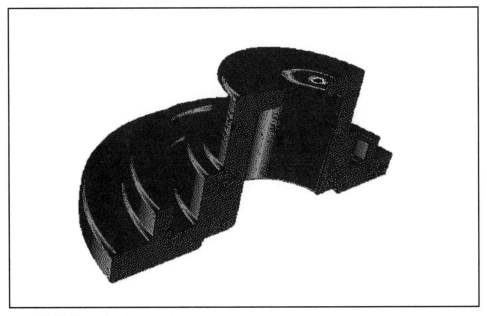

Figure 13-21: The rendered cross section

Because of the fillets, this piece became rather complex. Even though the solids in Release 13 are much faster than AME, this little piece should show you that it's still no speed demon.

Once the solid is created you can use the MASSPROP command to secure some of the mass properties of the object. This is not as extensive as AME was, and you can't add materials.

Rendering Tutorial

The Renderer with AutoCAD Release 13 is more sophisticated than the Release 12 version. Although you can do a lot with this renderer, it is not the equivalent of AutoVision or 3D Studio. It lacks features such as shadow casting, true reflectivity, a complex materials library, texture mapping and the ability to use true materials such as brick and metals.

The Renderer has a sophisticated series of lights, including ambient, distant, point and spotlights. You also have the ability to control colors of entities as well as lights using both the RGB and the HLS methods. Although the Materials Library and Materials Editor are rather limited by AutoVision and 3D Studio standards, you can control some facets of the material to give it a roughness or shine as well as color.

Loading the Renderer

The Renderer loads automatically whenever you issue any rendering command such as RENDER, LIGHT, SCENE or RMAT. It's an ADS program, and you don't have to load it each time you enter a new drawing as long as you stay inside AutoCAD. The loading of the Renderer is transparent to the user, and you'll see the message "Initializing... one time."

You may render any 3D objects without preparation, and AutoCAD will use built-in defaults, although the results may not be satisfactory. To get good results, you need to add lights and materials to the objects in the scene, then adjust them to suit the final rendering.

Adding Lights

The best way to begin is to add lights.

From the render toolbar choose the light icon, or in the command prompt window:

Type: LIGHT <Enter>

This command brings up the Lights dialog box shown in Figure 13-22. There are four types of light: point, distant, spotlight and ambient.

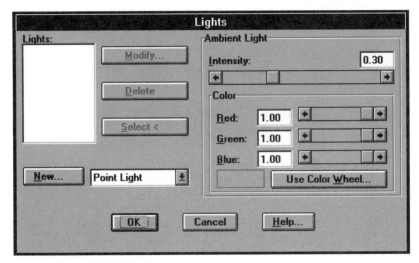

Figure 13-22: The Lights dialog box

Remember that some form of ambient light is always with you. You don't add an ambient light. But you may turn its intensity down to 0.00 and effectively turn it off. On any of the lights you can change the color directly using the RGB method. If you want to use the HLS method and/ or toggle between the two, you first choose the Use Color Wheel... button.

Then you have a choice in a drop box as to whether you want to use RGB or HLS.

By choosing a light from the drop box next to New... button and then picking New... you may add one of the other lights. Pick a new Point Light and then look at Figure 13-23.

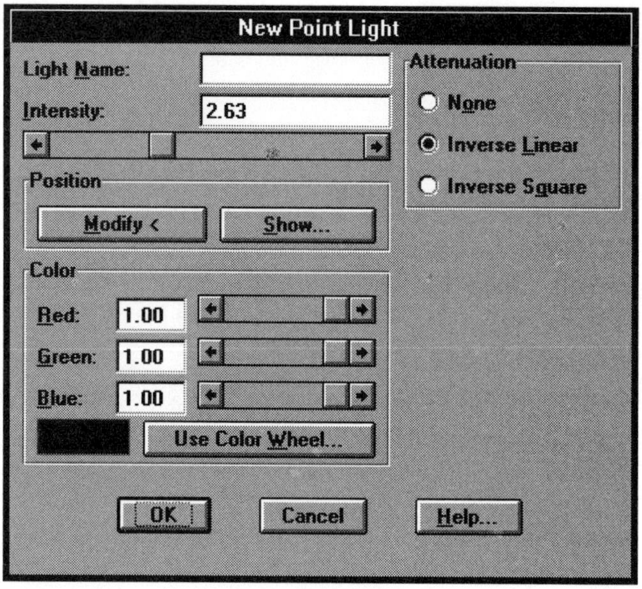

Figure 13-23: The New Point Light dialog box

First, give the light a name. Do this by clicking the Light Name: box. You can control its intensity with a slider bar and change its color in the same manner as with ambient light. You may also position the light by clicking on the Modify < button, located in the Position area of the dialog box.

Positioning a light source is not that easy. It is better if you plan ahead. You have no opportunity to use the regular features of 3D such as changing the UCS. This makes an accurate position for your light difficult at best. An easy way is to position an entity in 3D space ahead of time at a place where you want the light to be. In this way you have the endpoint of a line or a node onto which you can object snap. Later, you can erase this construction line. This is a little more trouble, but it's a lot easier. The AutoCAD manual recommends that you begin by saving your view to a named view. Then use the VPOINT command to set up the angle of the view you want the light to see, and add the new light. AutoCAD places the light at the center of the view. Now you may return to the previous named view. The Show... button only shows the light coordinates.

Attenuation, shown in the center right of the dialog box, simply means how much light reaches the object from its distance in space. This means the closer the objects to the light, the brighter they are illuminated. The farther the objects are from the light, the less light they receive. You may choose None. This means that the attenuation is turned off and all objects receive an equal amount of light.

Inverse Linear and Inverse Square control how light hits the objects. Objects become darker earlier when you use Inverse Square as opposed to using Inverse Linear.

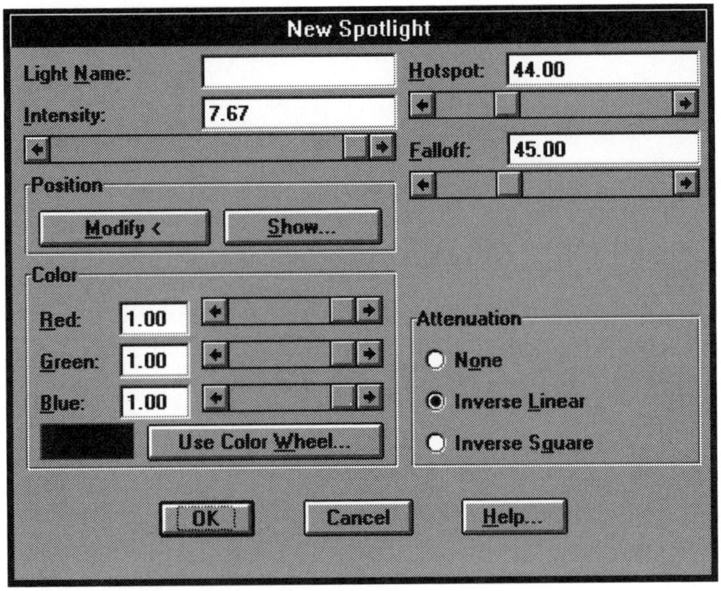

Figure 13-24: The New Spotlight dialog box

Figure 13-24 shows the dialog box for a new spotlight. It is basically the same as for Point Light except for Hotspot... and Falloff.... The hot spot is the size of the inner circle of light, and the fall off is the size of the outer circle of light.

Figure 13-25 shows the dialog box for a distant light. The distant light is generally used for the sun. By using the Azimuth... and Altitude... slider bars, you can easily control the direction and angle of a distant light. The Azimuth controls the direction of the light as in the 360 degrees of a compass, and the Altitude controls the angle of the light from the horizon.

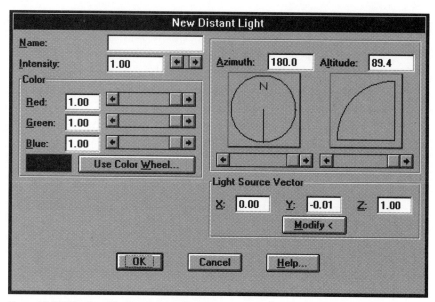

Figure 13-25: The New Distant Light dialog box

Remember that even though the capabilities of adding light seem sophisticated, this renderer does not have the ability to cast shadows. For that you will need AutoVision or 3D Studio.

Adding Materials

From the Render toolbar choose the Materials icon, or in the command prompt window:

Type: RMAT   <Enter>

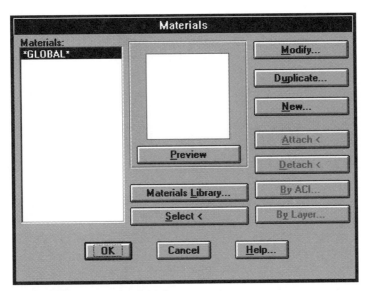

Figure 13-26: The Materials dialog box

Figure 13-26 shows you the Materials dialog box. In order to attach a material to an object in your drawing you must first import a material from the Materials Library. You may have an unlimited number of materials in your library. The file has the extension .MLI. AutoCAD uses the RENDER.MLI file for its default materials library list. To access the Materials Library, click on the Materials Library... button. (See Figure 13-27.)

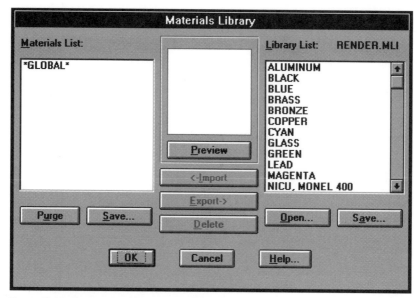

Figure 13-27: The Materials Library dialog box

On the right-hand side is a list of available materials. On the left-hand side is a list of the materials chosen from the library to be used with your objects. Begin by picking a material on the right-hand side and then pick the <-Import button. This copies the material to the left side of the dialog box. You may choose more than one material before you click <-Import. You may save materials from either side to a new file and create a new library. You may also Open other libraries.

Now click on OK to return to the Materials dialog box. (See Figure 13-26.)

You may also create your own materials. The easiest way to do this is to make a duplicate of one that you already have. In the Materials dialog box click on the Duplicate... button. (See Figure 13-26.) Enter a new name at the top of the dialog box and pick OK. You now have a duplicate material under another name. Now pick Modify... You can modify the material while in the Duplicate dialog box as well. (See Figure 13-28.)

You may change the color, ambient color, reflection and roughness of the material. Begin by clicking on Color. If you check By ACI, you have no more color options. It simply uses the color of the object. If By ACI is not checked, you may change the color of the material. Remember that by picking Use Color Wheel... you may toggle also to the HLS as well as the RGB methods. At the top is the slider bar for Value. This determines how much of the color is to be used on the object. You may click Preview at any time and see what a sphere will look like with this material.

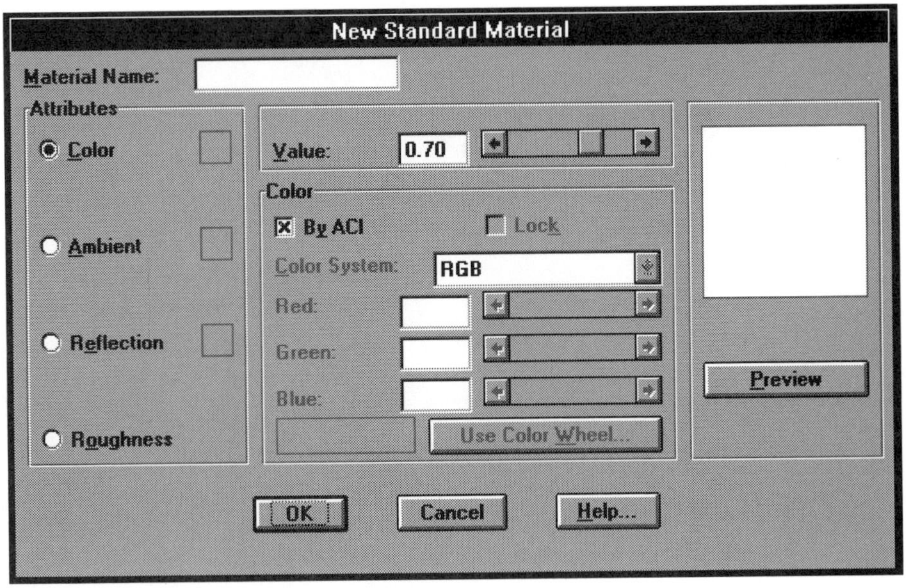

Figure 13-28: The New Standard Material dialog box

Rendering

From the Render toolbar choose the Render icon or in the command prompt window:

Type: RENDER <Enter>

Figure 13-29 shows the Render dialog box. The Screen Palette determines how many and what colors the renderer will choose. Remember, on most machines you may only have 256 colors. The more basic colors available the less it can divide those colors into shades. In this circumstance Best Map/No Fold gives you the optimum number of colors and best look for the render. Fixed ACAD Map forces it to use colors 1 to 256 and, as such, gives you the least desirable palette.

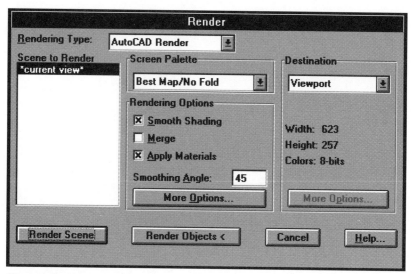

Figure 13-29: The Render dialog box

You may check Smooth Shading, Merge and Apply Materials. Smooth Shading observes the Smoothing Angle and smoothes out any facets where the angle is less than that stated in the Smoothing Angle box.

Merge permits you to merge the rendering with a raster file as a background. This is available only if your graphics card is capable of more than 256 colors. Thus, it is available only in 24-bit color.

The More Options... button permits you to choose Phong or Gouraud rendering quality. You may also choose to discard back faces to save rendering time.

The Destination box determines where the renderer is to render. You may choose Viewport, Render Window or File. The Render Window permits you to change the resolution and the color depth from 8-bit or 24-bit color. Eight-bit gives you 256 colors, and 24-bit 16 million. Rendering to a render window actually renders to a separate screen. You may also render a specific scene or just render certain objects.

If you render to a render window, you may save the rendered object to a file or open a file. The renderer saves to a .BMP file.

Moving On

The Solids addition to Release 13 gives AutoCAD the features to do many things that heretofore were impossible. Release 13's Solid Modeler is not a substitute for those who need true solid modeling. But it does permit you to draw things that were nearly impossible before.

While you work in 3D, not everything you do will go your way. In Chapter 14 "Tips & Tricks" you discover some of the pitfalls you'll encounter and learn how to overcome them. This chapter should help you keep the surprises to a minimum so you won't be completely puzzled when you're faced with one of those "gotchas."

Tips & Tricks

Not everything always comes up roses in 3D Land. Sometimes there is the unexpected. In this chapter I'll try to anticipate the difficulties that you might have and attempt to give you a solution. Obviously, I couldn't possibly cover all of the AutoCAD "gotchas." But learning about some of the more common ones can help you.

Getting Objects to the Right Elevation

From time to time your elevation may be set incorrectly when you create an object. Or you may inherit from someone a drawing in which the elevation is incorrect on some of the geometry. Therefore, you'll want to get everything to the same elevation. But the problem is that you don't know what elevation that is. There are easy ways and hard ways to remedy this problem. You could use the MOVE command, but that is the hardest method of all because to use the MOVE command you must know the elevation of all of your objects.

Another solution would be to list all of the objects and then use the CHANGE command to change the objects to the target elevation. This method will work only if all of the objects were drawn with the same User Coordinate System. Otherwise, they won't change. In this case, the MOVEY.LSP or MOVEX.LSP programs will come in handy.

Not Parallel to the Current UCS

If you're using Release 12, you'll see the "Not parallel to the current UCS" error message often. This message appears whenever you need to edit an object that requires the object to be parallel to the current UCS. The message doesn't keep you from performing the edit; it just advises you that AutoCAD can't make the edit until the object is parallel to the current UCS.

It is impractical to move the object so that it is parallel to the current UCS, but there is nothing to stop you from making the UCS parallel with the object. This is why Autodesk created the UCS Object command. Therefore, to solve the problem indicated by this error message, you should change the UCS to UCS Object and then pick the object on which you want to make the edit. This procedure will temporarily change the UCS to be parallel with the selected object, permitting the edit. After you complete the edit, change back to UCS Previous.

In Release 13, this error does not occur. If AutoCAD can perform the function, it does. If it can't, it doesn't, but gives you no explanation. Use the above suggestions to correct the problem.

Must Be Plan to the Current UCS

The "Must be plan to the current UCS" error message is similar to the message in the preceding section. Using certain commands such as TRIM and FILLET might give you erroneous results if you're not plan to the current UCS. It isn't sufficient to just be parallel. You must be plan to the UCS at the same time.

Again, it's not practical to change the object to be plan and parallel. Therefore, you must change your view and the UCS—a two-step operation. An AutoLISP tool called PVUCS.LSP will do that for you. This program first saves the current view and makes you parallel and plan to the Object Coordinate System. You could do this manually by doing a UCS Object on the object and then go plan to current UCS. But the problem is that there is no view previous. The accompanying program PVRUCS.LSP returns you to the previous view and UCS.

You can find PVUCS.LSP and PVRUCS.LSP in the AutoLISP section of the book. As with all 3D programs, make certain that they are properly loaded. If you have the *AutoCAD 3D Companion Disk* installed properly and have loaded 3DTOOLS.LSP, all you need to do is type in the name of the program.

Using the CHANGE, CHPROP & DDCHPROP Commands

AutoCAD has two change commands that serve two different functions. They are CHANGE and CHPROP (or DDCHPROP). The DDCHPROP and CHPROP commands do the same thing, however, DDCHPROP uses a dialog box. There is one primary additional function using CHANGE. CHANGE gives you the ability to change the elevation of an object. To change the elevation of an object, you must make the object parallel to the current UCS.

In addition to elevation you can change four other properties without the object's being parallel to the current UCS: layer, color, linetype and extrusion. The property's elevation, however, keeps you from using the CHANGE command without a lot of trouble. Therefore, Autodesk simply created the CHPROP command to enable you to go right to changing those properties that did not require any restrictions.

Plot Is Off the Paper

There is only one major thing that you need to remember when plotting in 3D, and that is, you must be in the World Coordinate System before you plot. Using the PLOT command can have unpredictable results if you're plotting while in a UCS other than World. This is especially true if you change the origin of the plot in any way. If you plot, do it from the World Coordinate System.

Rotating a Plot in 3D

You can't use any of the rotation commands in PLOT if you're not in World Coordinate System Plan view. If you do need to rotate the plot, then you must do a physical rotation of your drawing before you plot.

HIDE Hid the Wrong Thing

If you used HIDE and it hid the wrong part of your drawing, there are several issues to address depending on what the problem is. If you were working in Paper Space when you plotted and the wrong items were hidden or they were hidden in one viewport and not in the others, then the problem is that you probably didn't choose HIDEPLOT from the MVIEW command for the appropriate viewport.

Maybe everything was hidden even though you told MVIEW to hide lines in only one viewport. If this is the case, you chose Hide Lines in the Plot dialog box. If you're using the Paper Space HIDEPLOT from MVIEW, then you should not hide lines at the time of the plot.

Another issue is if you told AutoCAD to hide the lines and nothing was hidden, or a portion of the model was hidden and another part was not. This happens because, from a wireframe view, it might look as though you have a surface when you don't. If there is not an appropriate surface, then no lines are hidden.

As another example, you might have some lines hidden, but nothing in your drawing should be hiding the lines. This problem can be caused by a mesh, face or extrusion that is on a layer that is turned off. Remember that when a layer is turned off, the hiding properties of the objects on that layer continue to hide lines even though you can't see the objects. The solution is to freeze these layers using the FREEZE subcommand of LAYER rather than turn them off.

Finally, if the HIDE command doesn't seem to work correctly, the problem could be caused by using the AutoCAD Release 12 algorithm for hiding lines. You can reconfigure AutoCAD in the AutoCAD Configuration menu to use the AutoCAD Release 11 algorithm. This algorithm will take longer but is more complete.

When Everything Turns to Plan

Here is a scenario in 3D that will drive you crazy if you don't know what's going on. Every time you change your UCS, your view point changes to be plan to that UCS. You probably wonder what in the world is going on.

Everything changing to plan is not an accident or a problem in Auto-CAD. It is a feature controlled by a system variable called UCSFOLLOW. When UCSFOLLOW is set to 1, AutoCAD will automatically change each time the UCS is changed to a plan view of the current UCS.

Under normal circumstances, this change is inconvenient. But from time to time you may want to work totally plan to the current UCS as it changes. Then you will set UCSFOLLOW to 1.

Getting to the Other Side

Have you ever tried to use the DVIEW command and no matter which way you move the camera, you can't seem to get to the correct side of the object? This situation happens more often than not.

This is not supposed to happen. But when it does, it's nice to have a solution for getting to the other side of the object. You'll need to use the POINTS command in DVIEW and swap the coordinates for the target and camera. This switch will put you on the other side of the object immediately.

I've created an AutoLISP program called CHSIDE.LSP that will make this switch for you. Just run the program, and the camera and target coordinates are reversed.

You can find this program in the AutoLISP section of the book. As with all 3D programs, make certain that CHSIDE.LSP is properly loaded. If you have the *AutoCAD 3D Companion Disk* installed properly and have loaded 3DTOOLS.LSP, all you need to do is type in the name of the program.

UCSICON Won't Go to Origin

Here's the scenario. You've changed the UCSICON to OR for origin. No matter where you put the origin, however, the UCS icon remains in the lower left of the viewport or screen.

The position of the UCS icon relative to the viewport requires that the icon be visible 100 percent at all times. If the origin is too close to the edge of the screen or viewport so that the icon doesn't fit completely, then it is placed at the lower left of the screen or viewport.

You can solve this problem by zooming out to give the icon room to fit or panning left or right as necessary. Use ZOOM .6x as a start option work-around and try again if it doesn't work immediately.

The Broken Pencil

The broken pencil icon will appear any time that your view point is from positive or negative Y with X going left or right and Z going up and down. Because with most commands that permit pointing you can only select X and Y, the view point makes it difficult to point to anything on the screen with any degree of accuracy.

If you're within one degree either way of this point of view, then you will get a broken pencil. Getting this icon doesn't mean that you can't continue to point, it is simply advising you that if you continue to pick objects, the objects you pick may not be selected accurately.

The cure to this problem is simple. Rotate your UCS at least one degree around X or Y, and the broken pencil will go away. The other alternative is to change your view point.

Using Multiple Viewports

Always work in at least two viewports. And if you aren't simultaneously working in at least two viewports, at least check your work from time to time from two different angles. One of the worst traps you can fall into with AutoCAD is assuming that because the drawing looks right on the screen, it is. You need to use at least one other viewport to check the accuracy of what you're drawing.

No matter how good your work looks on the screen, it's possible that you're drawing in an area that isn't accurate due to your existing view point. By working in at least two viewports at different angles, you can check where you're drawing dynamically while you work.

Quickly Changing the View With UCS

From time to time you may want to rotate your view of the model to an exact angle of view. Using VPOINT or DVIEW many times to get you exactly where you want to be can be very tedious. You have seen how you can make a UCS parallel to a side of the model (refer to Chapter 2, "The User Coordinate System"). Then you can use the PLAN command to move plan to that current UCS. You can also use this procedure to be plan to any current UCS.

The UCS itself doesn't have to be parallel to a side of the model. All you have to do is rotate around X, Y or Z to get the UCS icon at exactly the angle you want and then use the PLAN command to make your view follow. As you can see, this view isn't what you might consider a real Plan view, but you're using the technique to adjust your view point quickly and precisely. Positioning the UCS icon is obviously easier than using DVIEW or VPOINT.

Turning On Distance to Change Camera Target Angle

When you use the Points option of DVIEW, make sure that Distance is turned on. It doesn't matter what the distance is set to. You can give it any distance you want. But using the Points option without an active Distance only changes the angle of view and does not adjust the distance between the camera and the target.

On the other hand, when Distance is active, the Points option not only adjusts the angle of view, but it adjusts the distance between the points picked for the camera and target. Otherwise, you get the effect of being thrown outside of your model.

Correcting Points Option With Distance Off

If you haven't preset a distance with an active Distance option before you use the Points option of DVIEW, all is not lost. You can still adjust the distance. Remember that the Points option sets the angle of view between the camera and target points that you pick. If Distance isn't active, then AutoCAD gives the effect of throwing you outside the model.

But the angle of view is still correct. All you have to do now is take the second step and adjust the distance. If you use the Distance option of DVIEW and give it an appropriate distance, you will be right back inside the model.

Having Too Wide an Angle

If your model looks as if you're looking through the wrong end of a telescope, you probably played around with the Zoom option of DVIEW while perspective was on. This can change the millimeter setting of your zoom lens to something bizarre.

The cure is easy. Use the Zoom option while in DVIEW and change the lens to 50mm. Remember that this situation only occurs when either Distance or Zoom are taken to extremes relative to each other. Here's the really important tip: don't try to use the Distance option to zoom.

Setting Up Viewports Before Drawing

Be sure to set up all of your viewports and any viewport configurations before you draw any objects. You can, of course, do this in a prototype drawing. But even if you don't, you should set up the viewports in Model Space or Paper Space ahead of time. You should do your setup before drawing because any time you change the configuration of any of your viewports, it will cause a regen.

On the other hand, if you set up the viewports and their configurations ahead of time, when you begin drawing, a regen of the large drawing won't occur.

Reducing Regens in 3D

The biggest mistake that most users make is moving around too much in 3D. The DVIEW command is a popular and visually effective command, but it requires multiple regenerations while in use. Remember that any time the view point of the drawing is changed, a regen will occur.

Working in 3D without a strategy is what causes multiple regens. You can speed up the use of DVIEW by not selecting any objects when requested and working only on the "house" symbol or by selecting only enough objects to see where you are. Or you could use the VPOINT command instead.

These procedures save you at least one regen going in. But the biggest single thing you can do to stop regens in AutoCAD 3D is to stop changing your view altogether. Instead, make certain that you have preset viewports that permit you to work on any side of your model. Now, rather than changing your point of view to do your work, simply toggle from one viewport to another. This way, there are no regens.

What have you accomplished? By presetting these viewports, you can begin drawing immediately in whatever view you want and can then toggle to any side of your drawing while it's being created.

Each object is automatically regenerated as you draw. Toggling from viewport to viewport can save you an enormous amount of time while you're doing your work.

No matter how hard you try, though, there are still times when avoiding a regen is impossible. These times include when using the HIDE and SHADE commands, turning perspective on and off, and using PLOT and CONFIG when you come back into your drawing.

Getting More Memory

The single most productive thing you can do to speed up your work is to get more memory (RAM) for your computer. It really doesn't matter how fast or slow your computer is, having more memory will make it run faster.

How much your computer will speed up depends on the amount of memory you add. If you begin at 4 megabytes of RAM, then going to 8 megabytes can almost double the speed in AutoCAD. From then on you can expect a 30 to 40 percent increase in speed every time you double your memory. But this speed increase will reach a point of diminishing returns, depending on the size of the drawing that you're working with.

If you're still working with the Advanced Modeling Extension, you should not work with less than 8 megabytes of memory. If you're using Microsoft Windows, you should consider 8 megabytes the minimum. With each of these programs you will be more comfortable with 16 megabytes.

If your drawings are very large, then consider 32 megabytes of RAM. If you're working with a rendering program, the sky is the limit—depending on what you're doing. Some computers can have as much as 128 megabytes right on the motherboard.

Each application is different. But before you think you have to go out and buy a faster machine, putting more RAM in your existing computer might be the cheapest way to get more speed.

Using Polylines With Different Z Vertices

If you ever need to draw a polyline where each of the vertices has a different Z coordinate, you can't use PLINE. Even if you give PLINE an .XY filter and type in the Z, AutoCAD will force the Z coordinate to the same coordinate as the beginning vertex.

There is a way to draw your polyline, however. You must use the 3DPOLY command instead of PLINE. Using 3DPOLY will enable you to have a different Z coordinate for any of the vertices. It will even enable you to perform a special type of SPLINE across the plane.

Using Solid Fills in 3D

When you view your model from any view point other than plan to the World Coordinate System, any fills will not be visible as filled objects. This is especially true with wide polylines, dimension arrows, solids, etc. You'll see the single-line outline of the object the same as if FILL were turned off.

To correct this problem, you can use an old trick from years ago when AutoCAD didn't have a way to create a filled circle. Hatch the inside of the item with a U hatch dense enough to create the fill when you plot. Make sure that the hatch is on a layer you can turn off or freeze. Use the U hatch only when you need to display or plot the item. This trick will force AutoCAD to fill in the area.

Obviously, you can't hatch an arrow when you dimension. But you can create a block for the arrow using regular lines and hatch it. Then tell AutoCAD you want to use this block as your arrow instead of the one it normally uses. You do this with the DIMBLK dimension variable.

Using Lower SURFTAB1 & SURFTAB2

If your primary purpose is to send your drawing to a rendering program, you don't really need to set SURFTAB1 and SURFTAB2 to extremely high numbers to get smooth, rounded curves in your rendering. Most of the rendering programs have smoothing algorithms that enable you to use lower SURFTAB settings and still create smooth curves. This capability can save you a lot of regeneration time in AutoCAD, as well as make the rendering program more efficient.

Using SHADE in a Smaller Viewport

When you issue the SHADE command or the HIDE command, you can speed up the time shading or hiding takes by performing these commands in a smaller viewport because it has fewer pixels to deal with. If the purpose of your shading is to check your view point or see if you have enough faces, then a smaller viewport will do just fine.

Plotting Only When Using WCS

Always make sure you are active in the World Coordinate System before you plot. If you're not and you change the origin of the plot, then AutoCAD can throw you off the page.

Avoiding Overlapping Grids

Make sure you turn off your Paper Space grid if any of the viewport grids are on. If you don't, then both sets of grids will appear and will overlap each other.

Turning Off Grid When out of Plan

You might find it easier to turn off your grid altogether for anything other than a Plan view. Sometimes the angle of view is such that the grid is distracting and serves no useful purpose.

Centering the Grid on the Screen

In any position other than plan to the World Coordinate System, you may not be able to do a ZOOM .5 and see your grid in the center of the screen. In fact, the grid may completely fill your screen no matter how small the zoom area.

Changing Splines to Polyarcs

It is often best if you don't need to decurve splines or fit curve polylines, that you simply turn these lines into polyarcs. The easiest way to do that is to break them at the same point using the BREAK @ command. Make sure you pick very close to the first vertex. This means use the BREAK command and pick a point somewhere on the spline or curved part of the polyline. When AutoCAD asks you for the second point type @ and press Enter. The spline still looks the same, but it is now a series of polyarcs.

Your final step is to rejoin the broken vertex. Use PEDIT and pick the line. Now use the Join option and pick the two lines, and they will become one. The amount of work AutoCAD has to do in 3D is much less if they are polyarcs, rather than having AutoCAD compute the spline each and every time.

Extruding Text

Text causes a variety of problems when working in 3D. To begin with, text will not extrude even if you issue CHPROP on the thickness of the text. At the same time it has an unusual property when hiding lines. The text will bleed through any hidden lines. Therefore, text will not be hidden behind those lines.

There is a way to correct these problems and change the properties of the text. You can't solve these problems as long as the text is text, however. And, of course, depending on the font, tracing over the text would be very difficult. But there is a way around these problems.

Remember the trick of plotting out to a DXB file. Then you brought in the 3D objects as a series of nothing more than 2D lines with the DXBIN command. When you plotted out to a DXB file, the objects ceased to be the objects they were in the original AutoCAD drawing. When you brought them back, they returned as only a series of very small lines. You can also do the same thing with text.

First, plot by window, isolating the text, and plot to a DXB file. Then erase the actual text in the drawing. Issue DXBIN to the file you just plotted out. When the text comes in again, it no longer is text. As a result it will be hidden, and you can extrude it. Remember that once you perform this trick, the text is no longer true text and can't be edited with the DDEDIT command.

When Text Is in Outer Space

If at any point in time your text is somewhere off in left field, the problem is that you didn't align the text with the UCS Object option prior to placing the text. Chances are that you simply typed the text on the screen where it looked good, or you used the UCS View option for labeling text.

Remember that unless you align the text with the UCS Object option, you have no control over where the text is really being created. In this case, when you change the view point, the text could be anywhere in space.

If you do need to align the text with the view of the screen, make sure you save that view along with the name of the layer so that you can turn it off and on and restore the view as necessary.

Moving On

I'm going to give you a little more help and experience in a real-life environment to see how you can put the tools and concepts that you have to use in a real application. Chapters 15 and 16 are complete tutorials designed to take you from the beginning of a plan to completed presentation. But the purpose of these two tutorials is to give you experience in a format that you can refer to from time to time to help you along the way.

Chapter 15 is designed for the mechanical engineering environment. Chapter 16 is designed for the architectural environment. These designs try to reach a happy medium between the complexities of real life that will tax your ingenuity and the concepts presented in this book, while still permitting you to follow along easily without getting lost. I encourage you to try at least one of the tutorials as it applies to your specific discipline.

These tutorials are not meant to be the end-all to mechanical and architectural modeling. They are meant to be a continuing learning experience. Keep in mind that as with most things in AutoCAD there are always at least five ways to do the same task. You should always strive to find the way that works best for you.

SECTION II

INTRODUCTION TO TUTORIALS

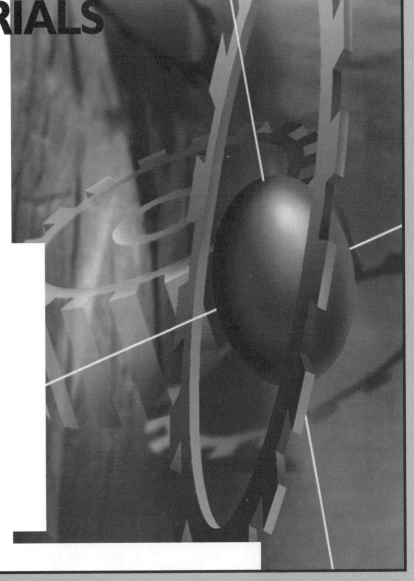

Introduction to Tutorials

It's one thing to learn all of the concepts and tools to work in 3D as you have progressed through the first 14 chapters. It's quite another to face the real problems involved in creating even a simple model. Chapters 15, "Mechanical Tutorial," and 16, "Architectural Tutorial," are tutorials designed to give you experience in creating a model from two different disciplines. Respectively, you'll find a mechanical tutorial and an architectural tutorial.

The tutorials are designed to be completed with the knowledge you gained through working the first 14 chapters. Although it's inevitable that you have some AutoCAD drawing experience, I've kept actual AutoCAD drawing practice in those chapters to a minimum so that I could concentrate on the 3D problems that you'll face and how to solve them.

Throughout the tutorials you'll make extensive use of the AutoLISP programs found in the 3D Toolkit. You learned about these programs in the preceding 14 chapters. They should now be as much a part of your 3D arsenal as any "regular" AutoCAD command. Without them the creation of the models would be much harder. Before beginning the tutorials, make certain that 3DTOOLS.LSP is loaded so that each of the programs is ready for you to use. If you need help with these programs, refer to Appendix A, "AutoLISP & Your 3D Toolkit," and Chapter 17, "The 3D Toolkit," the AutoLISP program section of the book.

In each of the tutorials, you'll encounter various problems. The solutions that I set forth represent only one possible solution in each case. There are many more. How I set up the viewports, create the geometry and work with the UCS is not meant to be the only way or even the preferred way. The preferred way is the way that works. The purpose of these tutorials is to let you see one way a model can be created from beginning to end.

Regardless of your discipline, I encourage you to complete both tutorials. While each tutorial has its own unique problems, how you solve the problems is not limited to the discipline. Each discipline can learn from the solutions of both tutorials.

On the following pages are the fully rendered output of the models drawn in Chapters 15 and 16, as well as other rendered drawings to illustrate the power of 3D AutoCAD and rendering programs.

Good luck as you put together what you've learned!

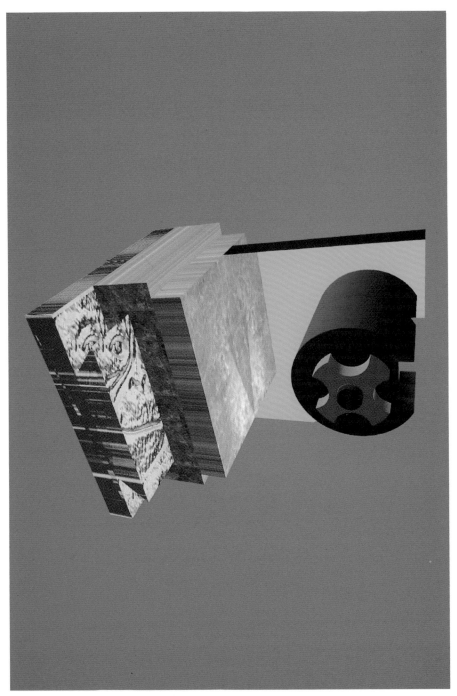

Rendered left view of the milling tool created in Chapter 15, "Mechanical Tutorial"

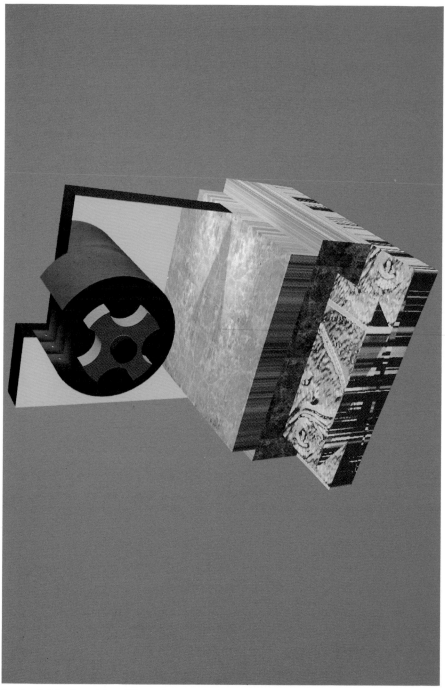

Rendered right view of the milling tool created in Chapter 15

Courtesy of Autodesk, Inc.

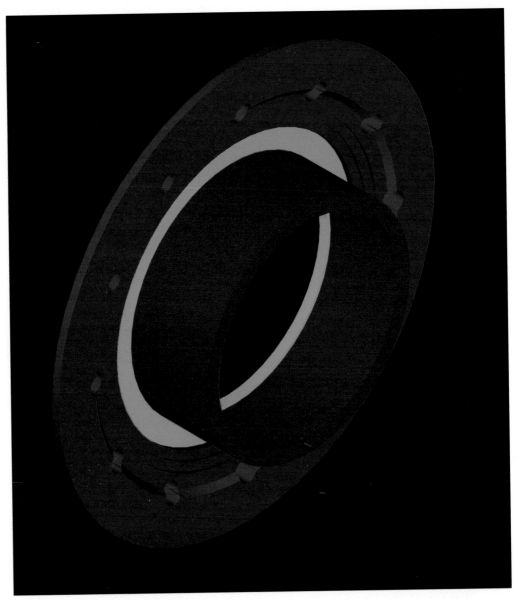

Courtesy of Autodesk, Inc.

Courtesy of Autodesk, Inc.

Courtesy of Autodesk, Inc.

Courtesy of Autodesk, Inc.

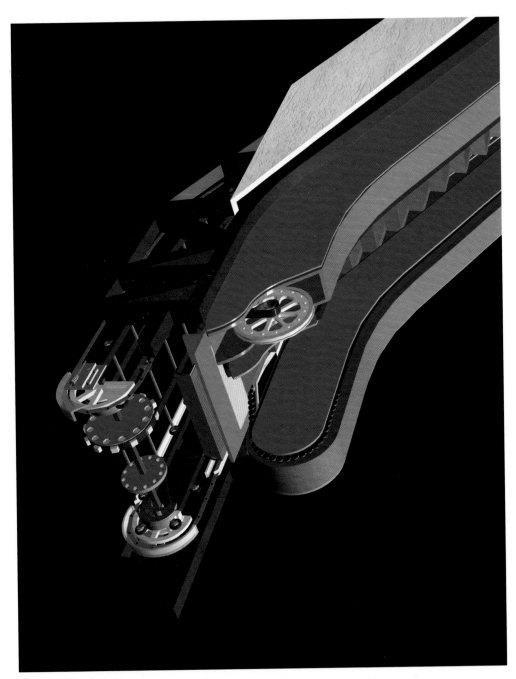

Courtesy of Autodesk, Inc.

Courtesy of Autodesk, Inc.

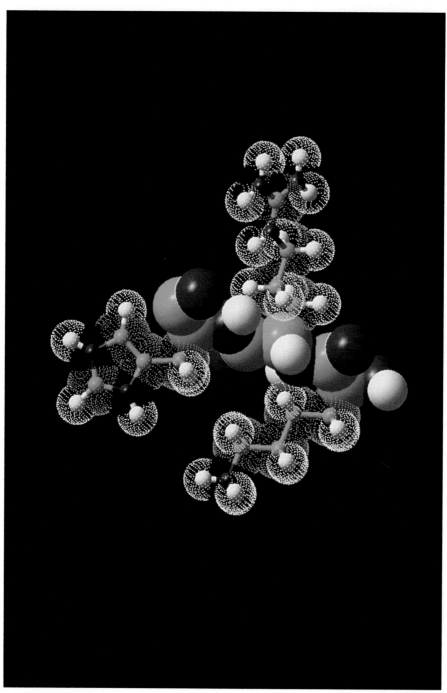

Courtesy of Autodesk, Inc.

Courtesy of Autodesk, Inc.

Courtesy of Autodesk, Inc.

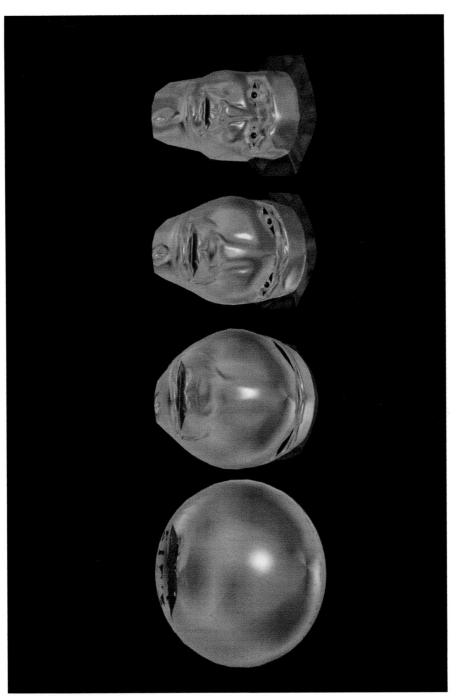

Courtesy of Autodesk, Inc.

Courtesy of Autodesk, Inc.

SECTION III

PRACTICE TUTORIALS

CHAPTER 15

Mechanical Tutorial

In this tutorial you'll create a milling tool. Whenever you approach the creation of a model, it's best that you begin by breaking it down into the necessary steps and parts of the model. You'll see the finished model in Figures 15-35 and 15-36.

There are seven parts to this model. Although the names of the parts may not be technically accurate, I wanted to make them generic enough so that everyone working the tutorial would be able to recognize them readily. The parts are as follow:

- Base 1
- Base 2
- Base 3
- Back Plate
- Notched Spacer
- Shaft
- Collar

Following are the steps you'll perform to create the model:

1. Set up drawing parameters.
2. Draw Base 1.
3. Draw Base 2.
4. Draw Base 3.
5. Set up viewports.
6. Draw a back plate.
7. Draw a notched spacer.
8. Draw a shaft.
9. Mesh the notched spacer.
10. Create and place additional notched spacers.
11. Mesh Bases 1, 2 and 3 and the back plate.
12. Draw and place a collar on the shaft.
13. Extrude the collar.
14. Mesh the collar.

By breaking down the drawing into objects and the steps necessary to create them, modeling in 3D is a simple case of performing each of the steps. Now you can begin with step 1.

Setting Up Your Drawing

Begin a new drawing with the following parameters:

UNITS	Decimal
Precision	4
LIMITS	0,0
Upper right	17,11
GRID	.25
SNAP	.25

After you make the settings:

Type: ZOOM <Enter>

Type: All <Enter>

Drawing Base 1

The next step is to begin your drawing by setting elevation to 0 and thickness to 4.

Type: THICKNESS <Enter>

Type: 4 <Enter>

Now draw a polyline.

Type: PLINE <Enter>

Draw the figure as illustrated in Figure 15-1, which shows the base of the model. Figure 15-2 shows the dimensions of the base along with snap and grid settings to help you draw the figure. Draw your model as a closed polyline.

Figure 15-1: Base of the model

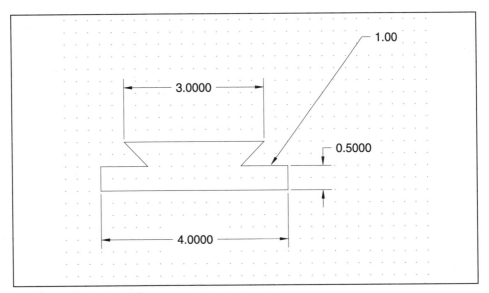

Figure 15-2: Dimensions of the base

Begin on the left-hand side and draw the polyline 4 units to the right. Now draw up .5 unit and then turn left 1 unit. For the angle of the wedge, move two grid dots up and two grid dots to the right to form a 45 degree angle. Turn left 3 units. Now reverse the wedge angle by coming down two grid dots and right two grid dots. Turn left 1 unit and close the polyline. You can close by picking Close from the Screen menu or typing **C** and pressing Enter.

Drawing Base 2

For the third step, change your thickness to 3.

Type: THICKNESS <Enter>
3 <Enter>

Notice in Figure 15-3 that Base 2 sits atop Base 1. Except for Points 2 and 3, all other points of the polyline are object snap intersections of the existing geometry. The distance from Point 1 to Point 2 is 1 unit. The distance from Point 2 to Point 3 is 4 units. With your snap and grid settings, you can conveniently pick those points as well as all other points on Base 2.

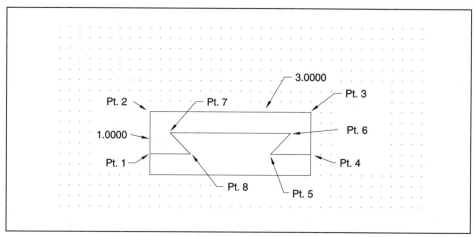

Figure 15-3: Drawing Base 2

To draw Base 2, begin at Point 1, as shown in Figure 15-3, and continue around the base. After you pick Point 8, make sure you close the polyline by picking Close from the Screen menu or typing **C** and pressing Enter. Figure 15-4 shows the completed drawing of Base 1 and Base 2.

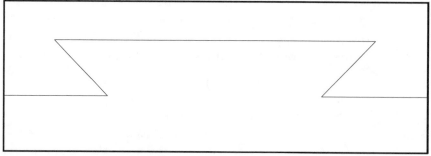

Figure 15-4: Base 1 and Base 2

Drawing Base 3

At this point, leave your thickness at 3 units. Look at Figure 15-5, which shows Base 3 atop 1 and 2. Base 3 is a simple rectangle set in .25 unit or one grid dot from each edge. To draw this base, use a polyline and begin .25 unit to the right of the top left intersection of Base 2. Draw up .5 unit, then to the right 3.5 units, down .5 unit, and finally close the polyline. Don't forget to turn off your grid and snap.

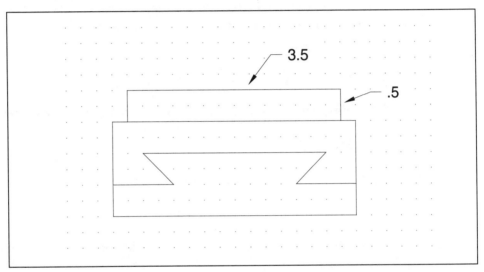

Figure 15-5: Drawing Base 3

Setting Up Viewports

Your next step is to set up four viewports.

Type: VPORTS <Enter>
       4 <Enter>

Pick and make active the lower-left viewport.

Now you'll use the first of the LISP programs. Make sure that they're loaded by using the 3DTOOLS.LSP program.

The ZX.LSP program zooms to 90 percent of the extents within the viewport:

Type: ZX <Enter>

The lower-left viewport will be the front view and, thus, is correct as it is. The upper-left viewport will be the top view of the model.

Begin by picking one time in the upper-left viewport to make it active. You should now have crosshairs in the upper-left viewport and the arrow in the other three viewports indicating that they're inactive.

The following rotates you 270 degrees around X:

Type: RX <Enter> <Enter> <Enter>

The next command creates a Plan view relative to the current UCS.

Type: PLAN <Enter> <Enter>

You are now viewing the model from the top.

Type: ZX <Enter>

Pick and make active the lower-right viewport. Begin with the World Coordinate System.

Type: UCS <Enter> <Enter>

Rotate 90 degrees around Y.

Type: RY <Enter>
        PLAN <Enter> <Enter>
        ZX <Enter>

Now pick and make active the upper-right viewport. This view will be the Isometric view.

Following is an example of some of the problems you may encounter when you try to create an Isometric view. You'll use the ISO program, which is a quick program for VPOINT 1,–1,1.

Type: ISO <Enter>
        ZX <Enter>

Figure 15-6 illustrates an Isometric view shown from the wrong angle.
Even though this model is an Isometric view, it is at an angle relative to
the World Coordinate System. You always draw your model in a manner
so that the extrusions cover the more complex area. But many times you
are forced to begin from an odd angle relative to the World Coordinate
System. The problem is that even if you change the coordinate system,
both the VPOINT command and the ISO program will be relative to the
WCS. Therefore, to solve this problem, the VPOINT 1,–1,1 should be
relative to a User Coordinate System that you can control.

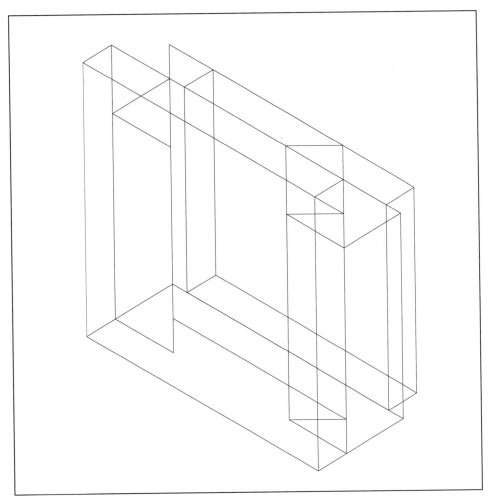

Figure 15-6: Isometric view from a wrong angle

If the system variable called WORLDVIEW is set to 1, then DVIEW and VPOINT are always relative to the World Coordinate System. If you set WORLDVIEW to 0, then DVIEW and VPOINT are relative to the current User Coordinate System.

Type:
```
WORLDVIEW <Enter>
0 <Enter>
UCS <Enter> <Enter>
PLAN <Enter> <Enter>
```

Rotate 270 degrees around X:

Type:
```
RX <Enter> <Enter> <Enter>
ISO <Enter>
ZX <Enter>
```

Always remember to set WORLDVIEW back to 1. It should always remain at 1 unless you have a special need to change it from time to time.

Type:
```
WORLDVIEW <Enter>
1 <Enter>
```

See Figure 15-7 for the correct Isometric view. This figure shows the angle for the Isometric view you need.

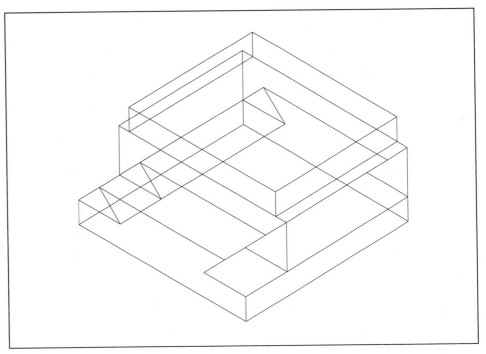

Figure 15-7: Proper Isometric view

Now look at Figure 15-8, which shows all four viewports and their viewing angles.

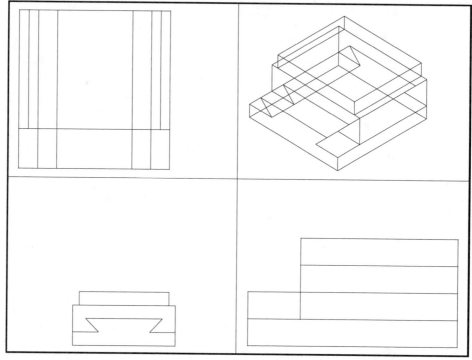

Figure 15-8: Four viewports set up

Now set your UCS back to World.

Type: UCS <Enter> <Enter>

At this point you have drawn the three bases, rotated them correctly and set in place the viewport. Now it's time to set in place the back plate.

Drawing a Back Plate

Now set the back plate forward .75 unit from the back of Base 3. The easiest way to draw the back plate is to change the UCS origin to that beginning point. Many times you'll have a situation where you know the origin must to be set to a specific point, but there is no geometry to attach to. Remember that you can move the UCS origin relative to its current position the same as any other object. Therefore, you will begin by setting the UCS origin to Point 1, as indicated in Figure 15-9. This figure shows the adjustment to the UCS origin so you can draw the back plate.

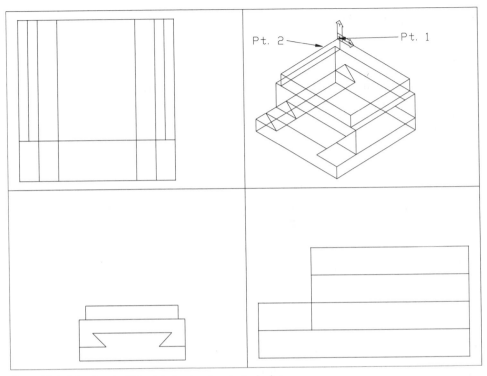

Figure 15-9: Adjusting the UCS origin for drawing the back plate

Type: UCS <Enter>
        O <Enter>

Using object snap intersection, pick Point 1, as shown in Figure 15-9 and rotate the UCS as shown. Once the origin is set at Point 1, move the origin from that point to .75 unit in the direction of positive Z.

Type: UCS <Enter>
        O <Enter>
        0,0,.75 <Enter>

Now the UCS origin is located at Point 2, as shown in Figure 15-9.

Pick and make active the lower-left viewport. Now that the UCS origin is set forward the .75 unit, you can comfortably use snap and grid to draw the back plate from the front viewport. Zoom down to give yourself room to work.

Type: ZOOM <Enter>
        .5x <Enter>

Now pan down so that your lower-left viewport looks like the one in Figure 15-9. Turn snap and grid back on for this viewport only. Then set thickness to .5:

Type: THICKNESS <Enter>
        .5 <Enter>

Turn ORTHO on.
Use the PLINE command to draw a polyline as indicated in the lower-left viewport of Figure 15-10 and draw the back plate.

Type: PLINE <Enter>

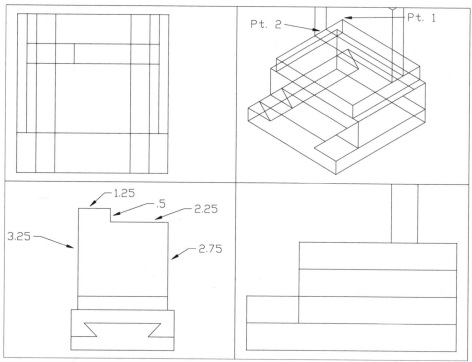

Figure 15-10: Drawing the back plate

Begin your polyline at the left side of Base 3. Don't use object snap intersection; the current UCS origin will control the proper beginning point. Let your snap, grid and ortho work for you. If something is going wrong, you can check it in the other viewports. Draw your first line up 3.25 units, then to the right 1.25 units, down .5 unit, to the right 2.25 units and down 2.75 units. Close the polyline by picking Close from the Screen menu or typing **C** and pressing Enter.

As you are drawing, center the model in each viewport as necessary using the ZX command. Because you have just drawn additional objects, now would be a good time to center the model. First, pick and make active each viewport; then issue ZX.

Type: ZX <Enter>

See Figure 15-11 with each viewport zoomed to 90 percent of the extents.

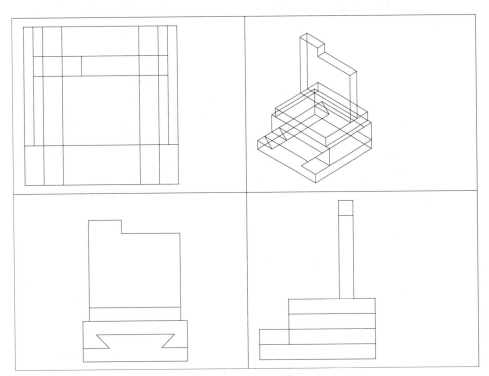

Figure 15-11: Using the ZX command to center the model in each viewport

The back plate is now complete.

Drawing a Notched Spacer

For step 7, you'll add a notched spacer to your milling tool model. First, pick and make active the upper-right viewport. The current UCS origin is on the back side of the back plate. Move the UCS origin to the front side of the back plate.

Type: UCS <Enter>
        O <Enter>

You might want to zoom in temporarily on this intersection to place it accurately at Point 1, as shown in Figure 15-12.

Type: ZOOM <Enter>
        W <Enter>

Place a window around the target intersection. Then use object snap intersection to pick Point 1, as indicated in Figure 15-12.

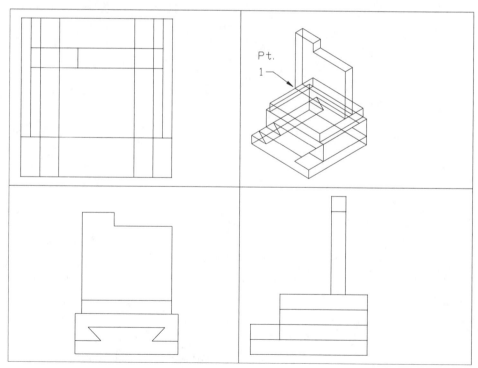

Figure 15-12: Moving the UCS origin to Point 1

Now return to your previous zoom level.

Type: ZOOM <Enter>
        P <Enter>

Next, pick and make active the lower-left viewport. Zoom in on just the back plate so that it will be easier to work.

Type: ZOOM <Enter>
        W <Enter>

Place a window around the back plate and zoom in on the areas indicated in the lower-left viewport of Figure 15-13.

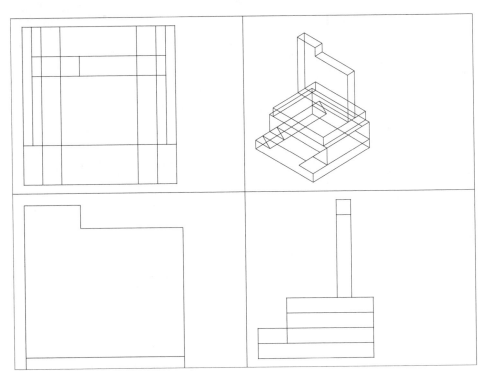

Figure 15-13: Zooming in on the back plate

Now save this view and UCS.

Type: USVIEW <Enter>
        FRONT <Enter>

The FRONT command saves the UCS and a named view by the same name so that you can return to it easily if you need to.
Change the snap and grid to .125.

Type: SNAP <Enter>
        .125 <Enter>
        GRID <Enter>
        .125 <Enter>

Set the thickness to .375.

Type: THICKNESS <Enter>
        .375 <Enter>

Next, use the PLINE command to draw a U-shaped polyline set in .125 unit from the left and .125 up from the top of the right side of the back plate.
Figure 15-14 shows a view of the notched spacer you're going to draw.

Type: PLINE <Enter>

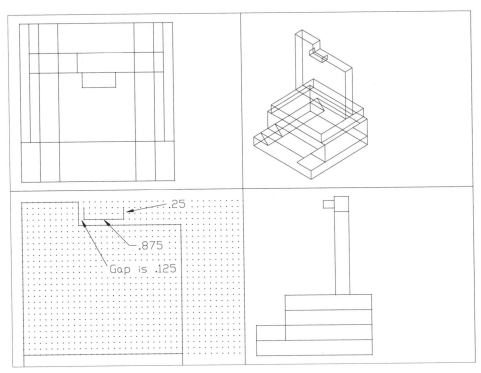

Figure 15-14: Drawn notched spacer

Begin your polyline one grid dot to the right of the side of the back plate and three grid dots from the top of the lower side of the back plate. Draw down .25 unit, to the right .875 unit and up .25 unit; then press Ctrl-C.

To finish the notched spacer, add an arc from each end point of the U-shaped polyline that you've just drawn. To create the arc, you must set a center point. The center of the arc should be .625 unit below the midpoint of the polyline you've just drawn. Therefore, begin by changing the UCS origin to that midpoint.

Turn snap and grid off.

Type: UCS <Enter>
        O <Enter>

Use object snap midpoint and pick the polyline. The lower-left viewport of Figure 15-5 shows Point 1 as the midpoint of the polyline.

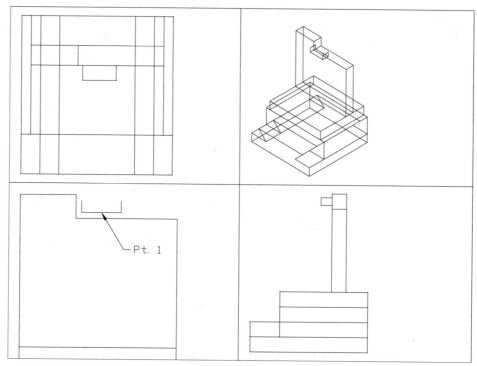

Figure 15-15: Setting UCS origin to the midpoint of the polyline

Now move the origin down .625 unit.

Type: UCS <Enter>
        O <Enter>
        0,-.625,0 <Enter>

See Figure 15-16 showing the new point of origin. This represents the center.

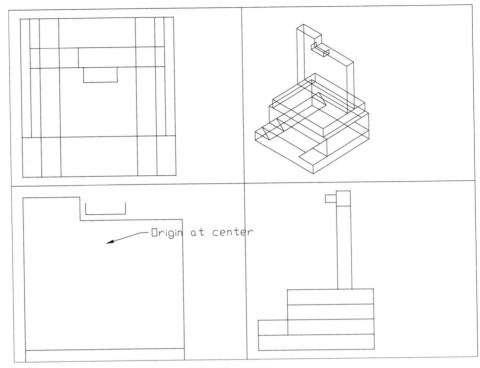

Figure 15-16: Center represented by the UCS origin

Now it's easy to draw an arc from the left end point to the right end point with a center point of 0,0, which is the current origin.

Type: `ARC <Enter>`

From the Draw toolbar, choose the S.C.E. Arc, which stands for Start, Center, Endpoint. Then, using object snap endpoint, pick Point 1, as indicated in Figure 15-17, for the start point.

Response: `Center/End/<Second point>: Center`

Type: `0,0 <Enter>`

Using object snap endpoint, pick at Point 2, as indicated in Figure 15-17.

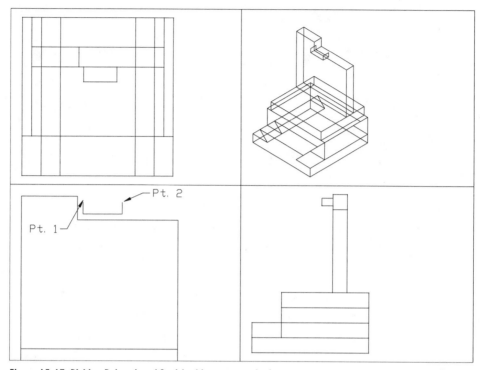

Figure 15-17: Picking Points 1 and 2 with object snap endpoint

See the results of the arc added to the notched spacer in Figure 15-18. Now that you've drawn the initial notched spacers, it's time to draw the shaft.

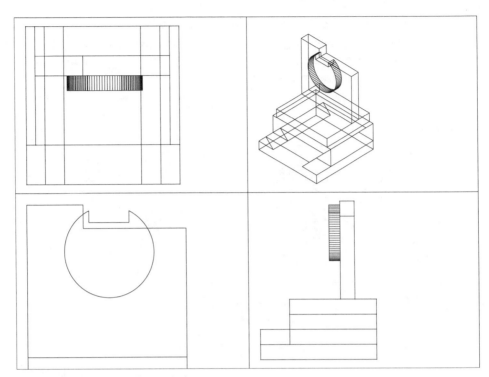

Figure 15-18: Arc added to the notched spacer

Drawing a Shaft

For this step you'll draw a 2-unit shaft in the center of the notched spacer. You know that the center of the arc is at 0,0 of the current UCS. Set the thickness to 2.

Type: THICKNESS <Enter>
2 <Enter>
CIRCLE <Enter>
0,0 <Enter>
.1875 <Enter>

Notice in the lower-right viewport of Figure 15-19 that the circle is not flush with the back side of the back plate. There are many ways that you could move the shaft to that back side, but they all require that you know the exact dimension of the thickness of the back plate. One thing you will notice while working on a 3D model is that you need to keep track of all of the dimensions of the various objects in your drawing. Anything that can help you position objects in your model without having to worry about these dimensions will not only make your work easier, but also will make your drawing more accurate.

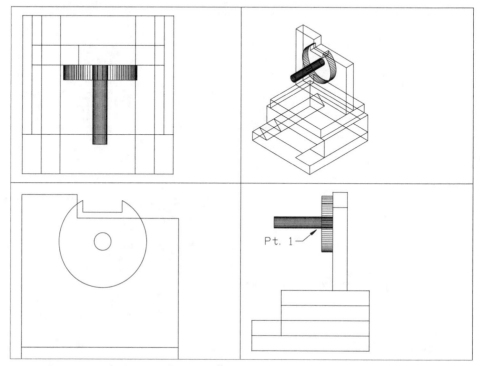

Figure 15-19: Initial placement of shaft

For this example, use the MOVEX.LSP program. Remember that this program will move an object only in the X direction by enabling you to point to an object with the same X coordinate. This means that you can point anywhere on the target object and the shaft will not change the Y and Z coordinates, only the X. (There is also a MOVEY.LSP program for the Y coordinate and a MOVEXY.LSP program, which moves X and Y but maintains Z as a constant.)

To use the MOVEX program, you must adjust the UCS so that X is pointing in the direction you want to move the shaft.

Pick and make active the lower-right viewport.

Type: RY <Enter>

Now your UCS is lined up so that X is pointing to the right in the lower-right viewport.

Type: `MOVEX <Enter>`

Response: `Select objects:`

Pick the shaft and press Enter to confirm.

Response: `Pick the base point`

Using object snap center, pick toward the right half of the shaft, as indicated by Point 1 of Figure 15-19.

Response: `Pick a point for the target X coordinate`

Using object snap nearest, pick any place on the back side of the back plate, as indicated by Point 1 of Figure 15-20. This figure shows the shaft moved to the back of the back plate.

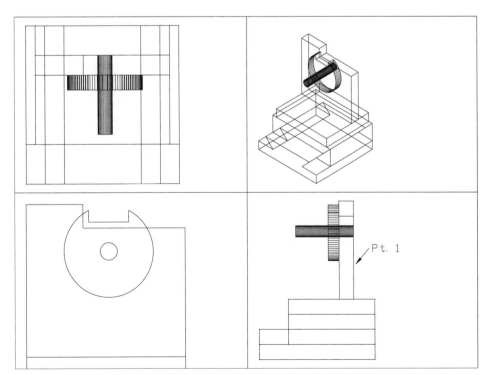

Figure 15-20: Shaft moved to the back of the back plate

Meshing the Notched Spacer

Now you're ready to mesh the notched spacer. For step 9, first pick and make active the lower-right viewport. Save the view and UCS because you'll need to return to it as it is right now.

Type: USVIEW <Enter>
         RIGHTSIDE <Enter>

Pick and make active the upper-right viewport. Then establish the new view and UCS as ISO.

Type: USVIEW <Enter>
         ISO <Enter>

Next, zoom in to the area of the shaft and notched spacer, as indicated in the upper-right viewport in Figure 15-21.

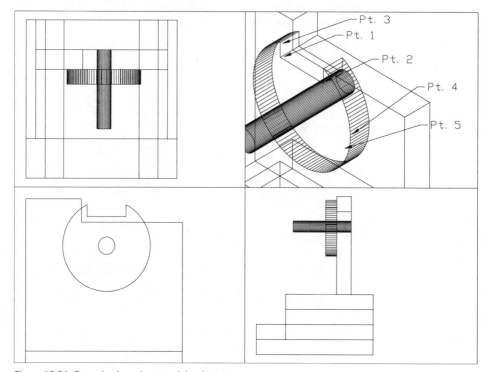

Figure 15-21: Zoom-in view of upper-right viewport

The BMESH13 program is invaluable for placing a mesh on hard-to-define, irregular-shaped objects as you have here. The BMESH 13 program requires that there be no extraneous lines in the view. Therefore, begin by erasing the back plate. You will OOPS it back later.

Type: `BMESH13 <Enter>`

Response: `Select object:`

Pick the arc.

Response: `Pick endpoint or intersection that represents the elevation`

Using object snap intersection, pick the intersection at Point 1, as indicated in Figure 15-21.

Response: `Pick inside area`

Pick anywhere inside the arc, as indicated by Point 2 of Figure 15-21. At this point, the mesh is created.

Type: `OOPS <Enter>` (This returns the back plate.)

You now need to return to the ISO view in the upper-right viewport and then to RIGHTSIDE view and UCS in the lower-right viewport. So first pick and make active the upper-right viewport if it isn't already.

Type: `URVIEW <Enter>`
          `ISO <Enter>`

These commands reestablish the UCS. Next, pick and make active the lower-right viewport:

Type: `URVIEW <Enter>`
          `RIGHTSIDE <Enter>`

These commands ensure the UCS is restored.

It was important to complete one of the notched spacers before creating the other two. In this way, you can copy the completed spacers.

Creating Additional Notched Spacers

Your next task is to place two notched spacers on the shaft. There are several ways you can do this. You could, of course, adjust your UCS and copy the notched spacers in the direction of positive Z, but that would require that you remember the thickness of each of the notched spacers. Try the following technique using MOVEX instead.

To use the notched spacer you created earlier, first pick and make active the lower-left viewport.

Type: COPY <Enter>

Response: Select objects:

Use a window and select both the arc and the U-shaped polyline that make up the notched spacer. Make sure that you remove from the selection set the smaller circle that makes up the shaft. After you've selected the arc and polyline, press Enter to confirm.

Type: M <Enter>   (This puts you in multiple copy mode.)

Response: Base point:

Now pick any point; it doesn't matter where.

Next, pick and make active the lower-right viewport. Turn ORTHO on. Then copy two notched spacers to the right of the back plate, as indicated in the lower-right viewport in Figure 15-22. The upper-right viewport also shows the two notched spacers.

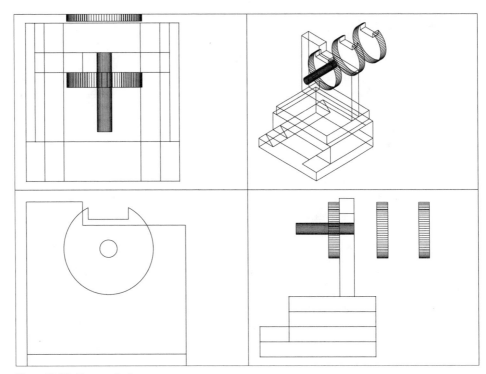

Figure 15-22: Two notched spacers

Don't forget to exit the multiple COPY command.

Type: `<Enter>`

Because you used ORTHO On to place your copies to the right of the back plate in the lower-right viewport, they each have the correct Y and Z coordinates. Now you can use the MOVEX program to adjust each of the new notched spacers in front of the current notched spacer on the shaft without having to know the correction dimensions.

Type: `MOVEX <Enter>`

Response: `Pick the objects you want to move`
`Select objects:`

Select the first of the two new notched spacers by placing a window or crossing around it. You can't just pick the entire notched spacer because it's made up of three objects—the polyline, the arc and the mesh. From this angle you could successfully pick only one of the objects and would, therefore, leave the others behind. After you've selected the notched spacer, press Enter to confirm.

Response: `Pick the base point`

Using object snap center, pick the edge of the arc of the first notched spacer at Point 2, as indicated in Figure 15-23. As you can see, Figure 15-23 shows the points for moving the first new notched spacer.

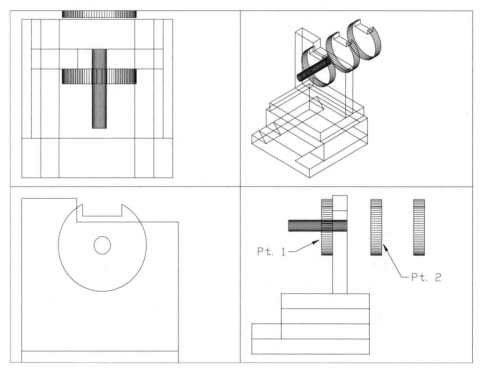

Figure 15-23: Getting ready to move the first new notched spacer

Response: `Pick a point for the target X coordinate`

Using object snap center, pick the point on the edge of the original notched spacer at Point 1, as indicated in Figure 15-23. Picking this point places the first of the new notched spacers in the correct position.

You'll continue using this same process to move the second new notched spacer.

Type: MOVEX <Enter>

Response: Pick the objects you want to move
Select objects:

Using a window or crossing, select the last notched spacer to move and press Enter to confirm. Figure 15-24 indicates the points you use to move the second new notched spacer.

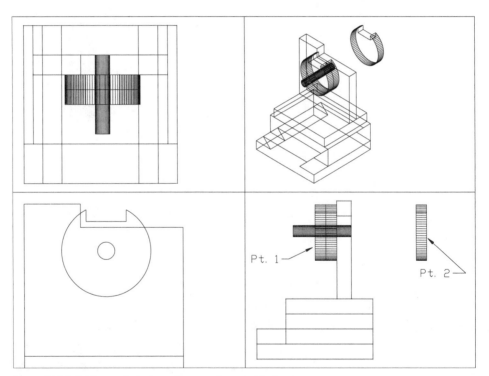

Figure 15-24: Getting ready to move the second new notched spacer

Response: Pick the base point

Using object snap center, pick the edge of the arc on the second notched spacer at Point 2, as indicated in Figure 15-24.

Response: Pick a point for the target X coordinate

Using object snap center, pick the point on the edge of the first new notched spacer at Point 1, as indicated in Figure 15-24. You should now have the three notched spacers correctly positioned on the shaft, as indicated in Figure 15-25.

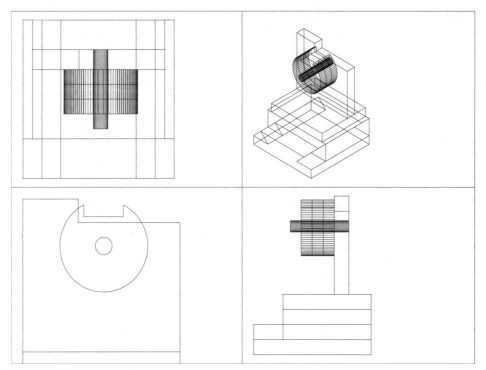

Figure 15-25: Three notched spacers

Meshing Base 1, Base 2, Base 3 & the Back Plate

You now need to place a mesh on each of the bases and the back plate, both front and back. You can start first with the back plate. Pick and make active the upper-right viewport. Then zoom in on the back plate, as shown in the upper-right viewport of Figure 15-26.

Pick and make active the lower-left viewport. Erase the spacers by placing a window around them. Be sure to erase them as a selection set as you will OOPS them back later.

Then pick the upper-right viewport, in the upper-right and lower-left viewports. If this next procedure gives you any problem, then explode the objects that make up the bases.

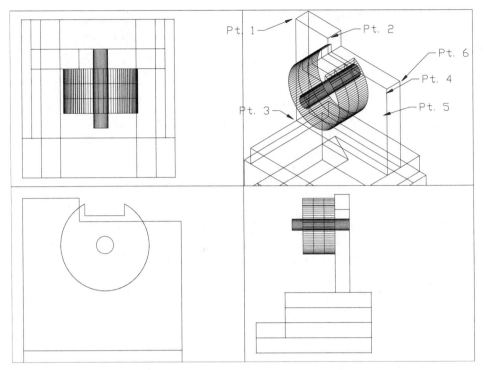

Figure 15-26: Preparing to mesh the back plate

Now you're ready to mesh the back plate as follows.

Type: `BMESH13 <Enter>`

Response: `Select object`

Pick the backplate at Point 1 in Figure 15-26.

Response: `Pick endpoint or intersection that represents the elevation`

Using object snap intersection, pick the intersection at Point 1, as indicated in Figure 15-26.

Response: `Pick inside area`

Pick anywhere inside the back plate, as indicated by Point 2 of Figure 15-26. At this point, the mesh is created for the front of the back plate.

Type: OOPS <Enter>

Rather than create a new mesh for the back side of the back plate, it's easier to copy the mesh to the back side.

Type: COPY <Enter>

Response: Select objects:

Type: L <Enter> <Enter>   (The mesh is the last object created.)

Response: Base point or displacement/multiple:

Using object snap intersection, pick at the intersection near Point 3, as shown in Figure 15-26.

Response: Second point of displacement:

Using object snap intersection, pick at the intersection of Point 4, as shown in Figure 15-26.

Type: URVIEW <Enter>
           ISO <Enter>

This returns you to the original view.

Because you've completed meshing the back plate, you can begin to mesh the bases. Zoom in on Bases 1, 2 and 3, as shown in Figure 15-27.

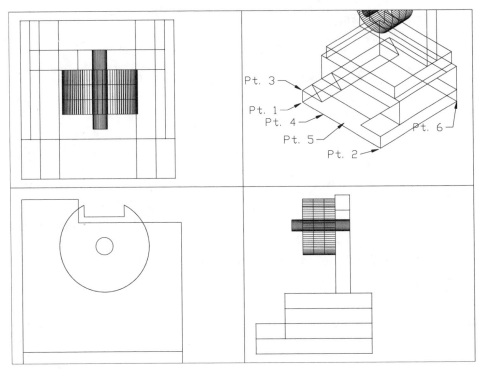

Figure 15-27: Preparing to mesh Base I

To start, mesh Base 1:

Type: BMESH13 <Enter>

Response: Pick the entry to be meshed
            Select object

Pick Point 1, as indicated in Figure 15-27 in upper right.

Response: Pick endpoint or intersection that represents the elevation

Again, pick Point 1. Now pick the lower-left viewport.

Response: Pick inside area

·Pick Point 3. Pick upper-right viewport.
Rather than create a new mesh for the back side of the base, it's easier to copy the mesh to the back side.

Type: COPY <Enter>

Response: Select objects:

Type: L <Enter> <Enter>   (The mesh is the last object created.)

Response: Base point or displacement/multiple:

Using object snap intersection, pick the intersection at Point 4 of Figure 15-27:

Response: Second point of displacement:

Using object snap intersection, pick at the intersection of Point 5 in Figure 15-27. And your mesh of Base 1 is complete.

Next, you'll place the mesh on Base 2, just as you did on Base 1.

Type: BMESH13 <Enter>

Response: Pick the entry to be meshed
          Select object

Pick Point 1, as indicated in Figure 15-28.

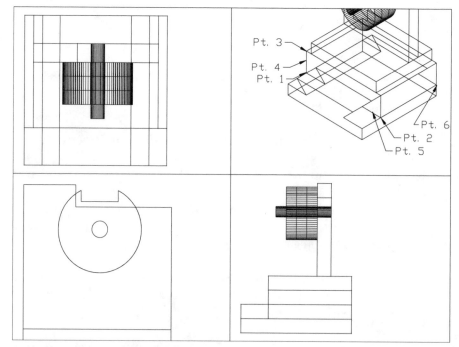

Figure 15-28: Preparing to mesh Base 2

Response: `Pick endpoint or intersection that represents the elevation`

> Using object snap intersection, pick the intersection at Point 2, as indicated in Figure 15-28.
> Pick lower-left viewport.

Response: `Pick inside area`

> Pick anywhere inside the polyline as indicated by Point 3 of Figure 15-28 to create the mesh.
> Rather than create a new mesh for the back side of the base, it's easier to copy the mesh to the back side.

Type: `COPY <Enter>`

Response: `Select objects:`

Type: `L <Enter> <Enter>`   (The mesh is the last object created.)

Response: `Base point or displacement/multiple:`

> Using object snap intersection, pick near the intersection at Point 4 of Figure 15-28.

Response: `Second point of displacement:`

> Using object snap intersection, pick at the intersection of Point 5 in Figure 15-28.
> Finally, you'll place a face on Base 3. Because Base 3 is not irregular, you can use the simpler 3DFACE command.

Type: `3DFACE <Enter>`

Response: `First point:`

> Using object snap intersection, pick the intersection at Point 1, as indicated in Figure 15-29.

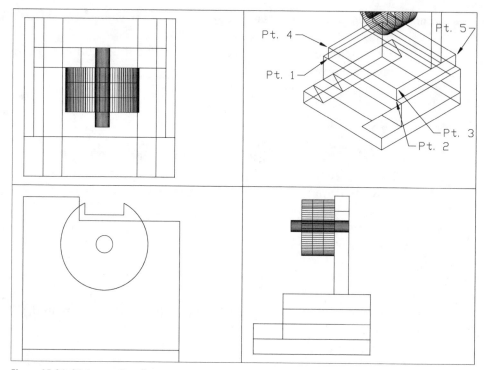

Figure 15-29: 3D face on Base 3

Response: Second point:

      Using object snap intersection, pick the intersection at Point 2 as indicated in Figure 15-29.

Response: Third point:

      Using object snap intersection, pick the intersection at Point 3, as indicated in Figure 15-29.

Response: Fourth point:

      Using object snap intersection, pick the intersection at Point 4, as indicated in Figure 15-29.

Response: Third point:

    Type: <Enter>

Now you've completed the 3DFACE command.

Rather than create a new face for the back side of the base, it's easier to copy the face to the back side.

Type: COPY <Enter>

Response: Select objects:

Type: L <Enter> <Enter>   (The face is the last object created.)

Response: Base point or displacement/multiple:

Using object snap intersection, pick the intersection at Point 3 of Figure 15-29.

Response: Second point of displacement:

Using object snap intersection, pick at the intersection of Point 5 in Figure 15-29. The 3D face is now copied. Return to the Isometric view.

Type: URVIEW <Enter>
            ISO <Enter>

You've now placed a surface on the three faces and the back plate. Also, you've copied these surfaces to the back side of the object.

Drawing & Placing a Collar on the Shaft

Now that you've added meshes to the bases, you're ready to draw and place a collar on the shaft. To do that, first pick and make active the lower-left viewport. You need to restore the UCS and view.

Type: URVIEW <Enter>
            FRONT <Enter>

For this final step in actually creating the model, you'll use the region modeler.

The UCS origin should be at the center point of the outer notched spacer. So pick and make active the upper-left viewport:

Type: UCS <Enter>
            O <Enter>

Using object snap center, pick the bottom edge of the bottom notched spacer, as indicated by Point 1 of Figure 15-30.

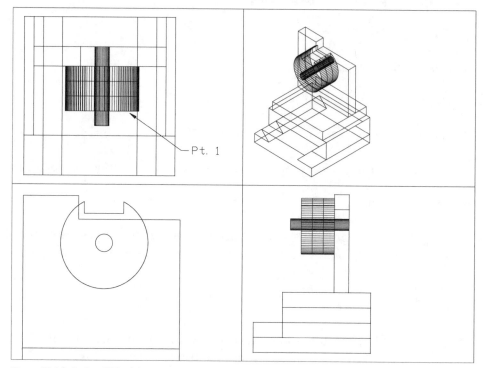

Figure 15-30: Setting UCS origin to the center of the first notched spacer

Now pick and make active the lower-left viewport. Draw a circle with the center at the 0,0 UCS origin.

Type: CIRCLE <Enter>
         0,0 <Enter>
         .625 <Enter>

Next, place a small circle at one of the quadrants of the circle you just drew.

Type: CIRCLE <Enter>

Using object snap quadrant, pick the circle that you just drew.

Type: .3 <Enter>

Array the smaller circle around the larger circle four times:

Type: ARRAY <Enter>

Response: Select objects:

Type: L <Enter> <Enter>

Response: Rectangular or Polar Array (R/P)

Type: P <Enter>

Response: Center point of array

Type: 0,0 <Enter>

Response: Number of items

Type: 4 <Enter>

Response: Angle to fill <360>

Type: <Enter>

Response: Rotate objects as they are copied <Y>

Type: <Enter>

Now create regions.

Type: REGION <Enter>

Response: Select objects

Pick the 5 circles and press Enter.
The lower-left viewport of Figure 15-31 shows a view of the arrayed circles.

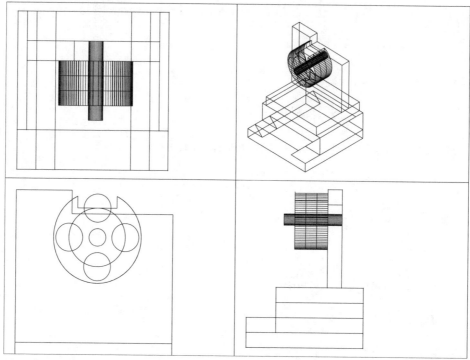

Figure 15-31: Arrayed circles

Now subtract the four smaller circles from the larger circle.

Type: SUBTRACT <Enter>

Response: Select solids and regions to subtract from
              Select object:

Pick the larger circle (this is the circle from which the four will be subtracted) and press Enter to confirm.

Response: Select solids and regions to subtract
              Select objects:

Pick the four smaller circles that were arrayed and press Enter to confirm. See the result of the subtraction in Figure 15-32.

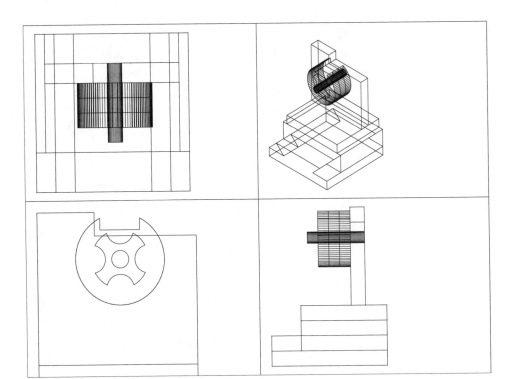

Figure 15-32: Results of using SUBTRACT

You have now created the basic geometry for the collar. Notice how much easier it was to let the region modeler do the work for you rather than try to draw the 2D geometry from scratch.

Extruding the Collar

Type: EXTRUDE <Enter>

Response: Select objects:

Type: L <Enter> <Enter>

Response: Path/ <Height of extrusion>:

Type: .25 <Enter> <Enter>

Meshing the Collar

Because the collar is now a solid it doesn't need to be meshed.

See Figure 15-33 for a front hidden Isometric view and Figure 15-34 for a back hidden Isometric view. Your finished model should look like the one in these figures.

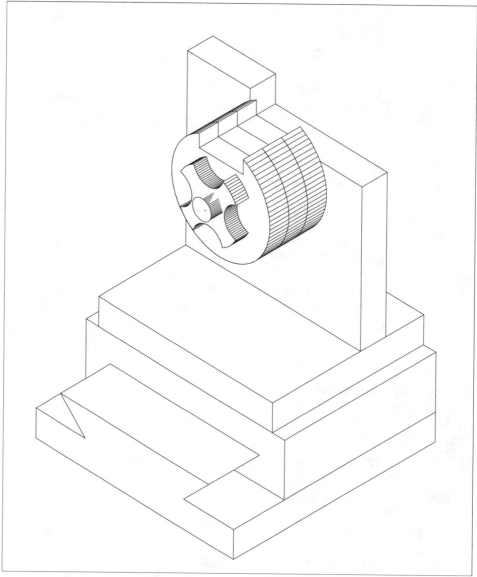

Figure 15-33: Front hidden Isometric view

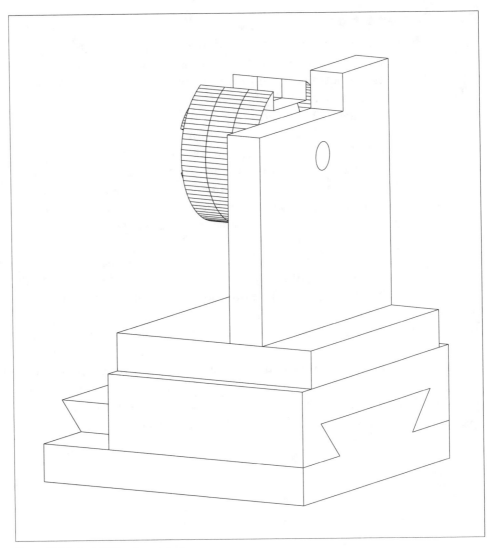

Figure 15-34: Back hidden Isometric view

Final Presentation

Your final presentation will depend on your individual needs. The purpose of your model might be to create individual sheets, assembly drawings, renderings or a multiple-view presentation on the same sheet. You can accomplish each of those from this point.

Notice that you didn't work in Paper Space during this tutorial. Normally, Paper Space is reserved for the actual presentation. You could set up the Paper Space viewports for the view of the actual presentation. Using Paper Space for only the presentation leaves the Model Space viewports available for you to work in different views as needed to facilitate the construction of the geometry—as you did in this tutorial. Therefore, the Model Space viewports and the Paper Space viewports can and probably should be different.

If the final presentation is a rendering, you should make sure that each of the objects that has a different texture or that color is created either on a different layer or with a unique color, depending on the requirements of your rendering program.

Now that you have successfully completed this tutorial, you are encouraged to try your hand at the architectural tutorial if you haven't already done so. If you've completed each of the tutorials, then congratulations. But don't stop learning. Every new model will bring with it new challenges; you'll find better and easier ways to accomplish your goals. And each time, working in 3D gets easier and easier.

CHAPTER 16

Architectural Tutorial

In this tutorial you'll create a house. Whenever you approach the creation of a model, it's best that you begin by breaking it down into the necessary steps and parts of the model. Figure 16-1 shows you the completed model of a house that you'll create.

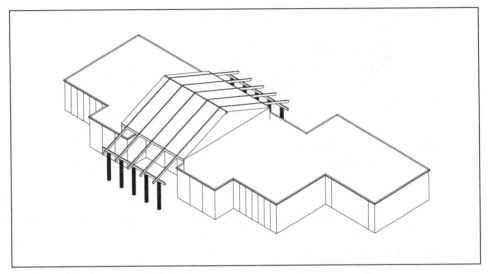

Figure 16-1: The completed model you'll draw.

Following are the eleven major steps to the creation of this model:

1. Set up the drawing parameters.
2. Draw the floor plan.
3. Draw the interior walls.
4. Clean up the wall corners.
5. Construct the columns.
6. Break openings for doors and windows.
7. Construct the beams.
8. Construct a raised roof.
9. Construct a flat roof.
10. Draw side roof faces.
11. Draw door and window faces.

If you break down the drawing into the steps necessary to create each part, modeling in 3D is a simple case of performing each of the steps. So now you can begin with step 1.

Setting Up Your Drawing

Begin a new drawing with the following parameters.

UNITS	Architectural
Precision	1/16
LIMITS	0,0
Upper right	144',96'
GRID	3'
SNAP	3'

After you make the settings:

Type: ZOOM <Enter>

All <Enter>

Begin your drawing by setting the elevation to 0 (zero) and the thickness to 12 feet. Then create and set a new layer called FLOORPLAN.

Type: ELEV <Enter>

0 <Enter>

12'

Layer <Enter>

M <Enter>

FLOORPLAN <Enter> <Enter>

Drawing the Floor Plan

Your next step is to draw the floor plan. Begin with the PLINE command and draw a polyline beginning near the lower left-hand corner of your screen. Draw a layout similar to Figure 16-2, which shows the fully dimensioned floor plan. (Everything in this tutorial is set to even grid and snap units to make it easy to draw.) You should draw your model as a closed polyline. Therefore, when you draw your next-to-last line, you can either close it manually, pick Close from the Screen menu or type **c** to close.

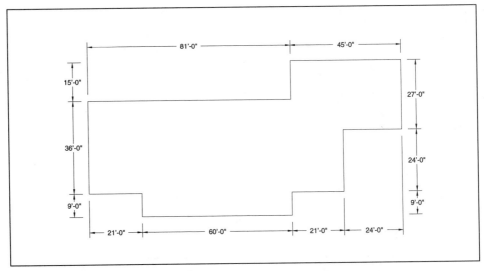

Figure 16-2: Basic floor plan with dimensions

Now offset the closed polyline by 8 inches.

Type: OFFSET <Enter>

Response: Offset distance or Through:

Type: 8 <Enter>

Response: Select object to offset:

Pick the polyline.

Response: Side to offset?

Pick the interior side of the polyline. See Figure 16-3 for a view of the completed double polyline of the walls.

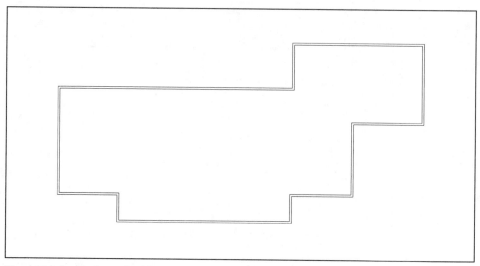

Figure 16-3: Double-line walls of floor plan

Type: <Enter>

Now that you've drawn the floor plan with double-line walls, you're ready for the next step—drawing the interior walls.

Drawing the Interior Walls

Using Figure 16-4 (which shows the large interior room) as a guide, draw a construction line from the midpoint of the bottom wall line to the top line. This line will be a polyline from Point 1 to Point 2. Each of these points is located on a grid/snap point.

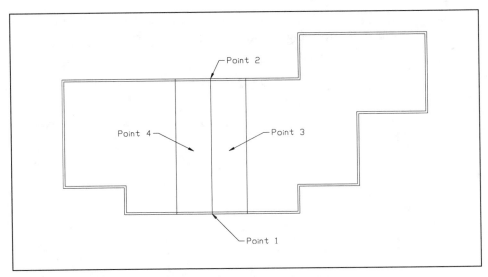

Figure 16-4: Beginning a large interior room

Continue using Figure 16-4 and offset the line you've just drawn to the right and left, as indicated by Points 3 and 4. The offset distance is 12 feet. After you've offset the two lines, erase the center construction line. Figure 16-5 shows the finished center room.

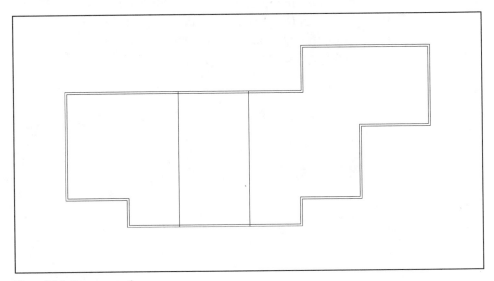

Figure 16-5: Center room drawn

The next step is to offset each of the center room lines 8 inches to create walls. Refer to Figure 16-6, which shows how you achieve this effect of offsetting the room lines.

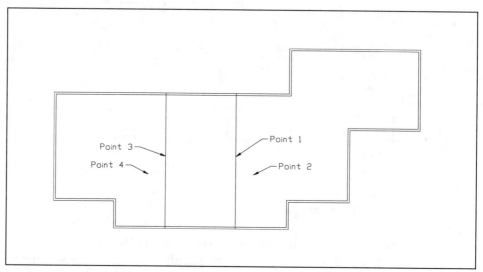

Figure 16-6: Offsetting room lines 8 inches

For the right line, pick the line at Point 1, as indicated in the figure, and offset the line in the direction of Point 2. For the left line, pick the line at Point 3 and offset the line in the direction of Point 4. Figure 16-7 shows the room lines offset and the finished room.

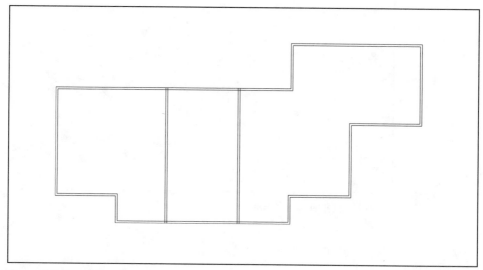

Figure 16-7: Room lines offset

Next, using Figure 16-8 as your guide, draw from left to right a polyline 9 feet from the outside bottom line connecting the two interior room lines. Drawing this line is easy because the grid/snap is still set to even 3-feet intervals. Next, offset the line you just drew 8 inches to the inside, as indicated by Point 1 in Figure 16-9.

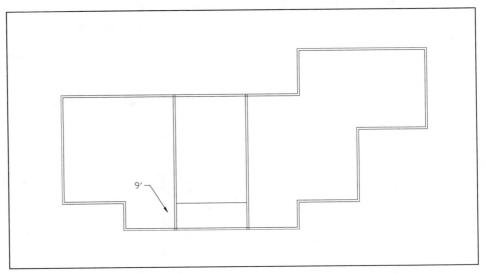

Figure 16-8: Drawing a room boundary line

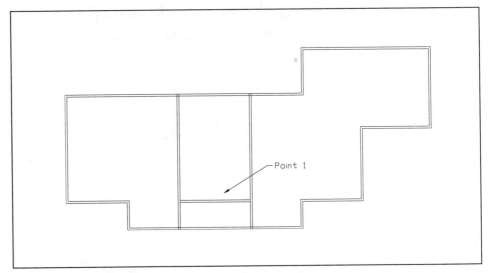

Figure 16-9: Offsetting the line 8 inches to the inside

Now you'll draw some of the rooms on the right side of the floor plan. Begin with a polyline at Point 1, as shown in Figure 16-10. Draw the polyline toward the top of the model until you're even with the first room line, as indicated by Point 2 of Figure 16-10. Continue the polyline to the right to Point 3 and then up to Point 4. Each of these points is on an even grid/snap location.

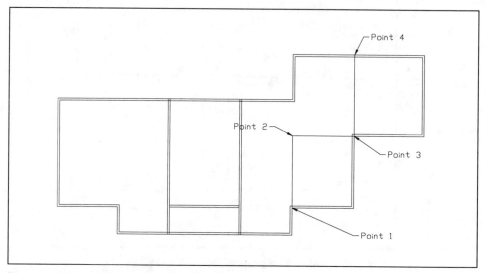

Figure 16-10: Drawing rooms on the right side of the floor plan

You'll now offset 8 inches to the left side the polyline you just drew, as indicated on the right side of Figure 16-11. Then start the room on the left side of the floor plan as shown in the figure.

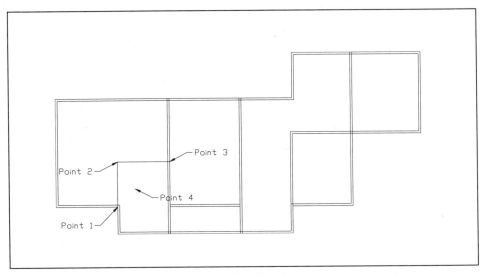

Figure 16-11: Beginning the room on the left side of the floor plan

Using Figure 16-11 as a guide, draw a polyline from Point 1 to Point 2 (which is 15 feet) and then from Point 2 to Point 3 (which is 18 feet). Offset the polyline you just drew 8 inches to the right, as indicated by Point 4.

Next, draw the upper room and hallway, as indicated in Figure 16-12. First, draw a polyline from Point 1 to Point 2. This line is 3 feet away from the lower room line, thus creating a hallway 3 feet wide. Offset the polyline you just drew by 8 inches on the side indicated by Point 3. Figure 16-13 shows the completed interior walls.

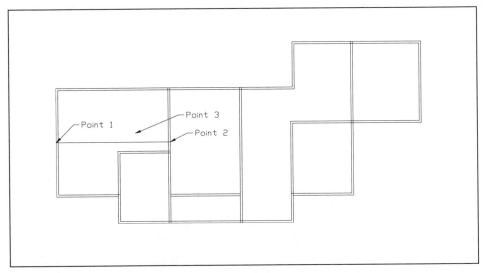

Figure 16-12: Upper room and hallway

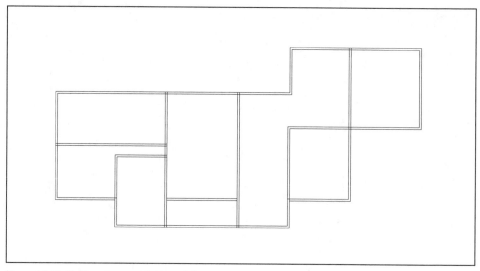

Figure 16-13: Outline of rooms of the model

Cleaning Up Wall Corners

The next major process is to trim the various interior room intersections. For this step you must zoom in on sections of the drawing. The circle in Figure 16-14 indicates the general zoom area, and Figure 16-15 shows a close-up of the zoomed area. Use the TRIM command to trim areas 1 through 6, as indicated in Figure 16-16.

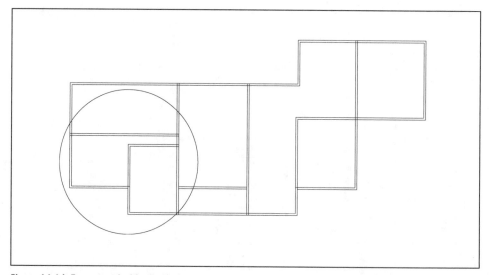

Figure 16-14: Zoom area inside the circle

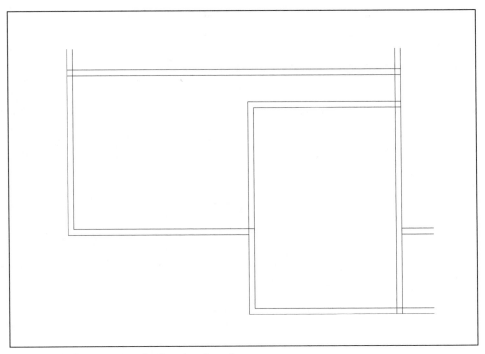

Figure 16-15: Close-up zoom of walls to be trimmed

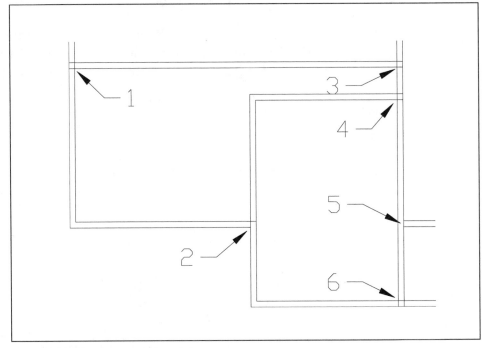

Figure 16-16: Trimming areas 1 through 6

The results of the trim are shown in Figure 16-17, which shows the trimmed interior walls.

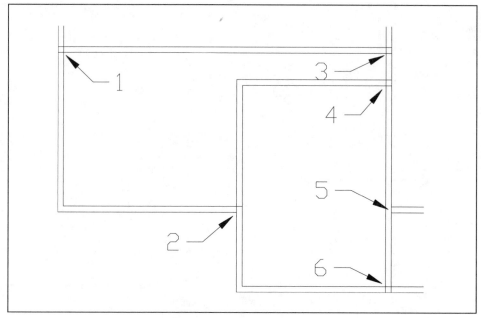

Figure 16-17: The trimmed interior wall areas 1 through 6

Now zoom to the previous view. Figure 16-18 shows the next zoom area in the circle. Trim areas 1 through 4, as shown in Figure 16-19. Then refer to Figure 16-20 for the final view of how these areas are trimmed.

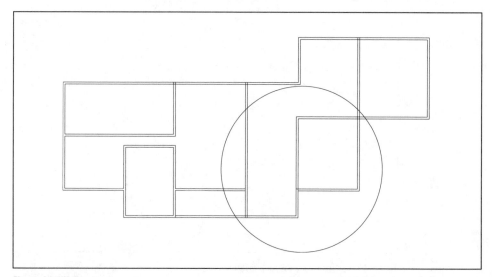

Figure 16-18: Zoom area

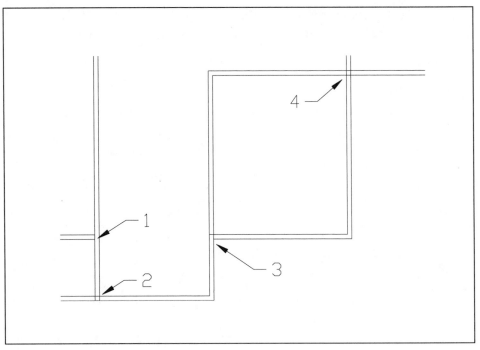

Figure 16-19: Trimming areas 1 through 4

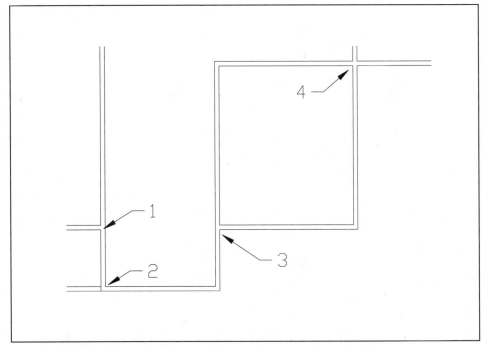

Figure 16-20: The trimmed interior walls

Again, zoom in to the previous view. Figure 16-21 shows the next zoom area in a circle. Then, as shown in Figure 16-22, trim area 1. Figure 16-23 shows the trimmed area.

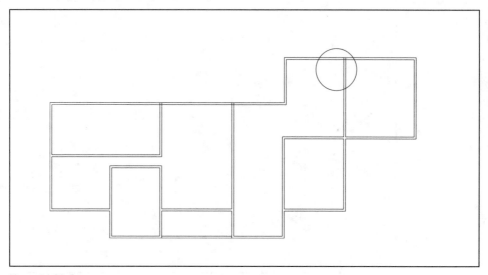

Figure 16-21: Zoom area

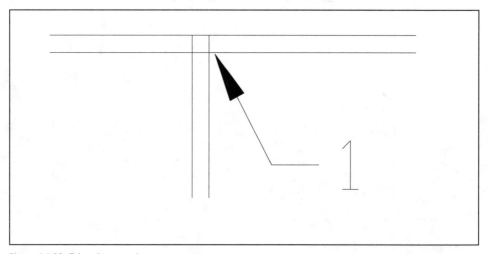

Figure 16-22: Trimming area 1

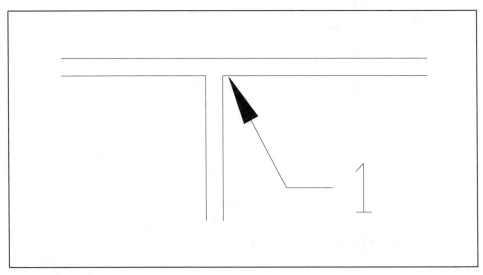

Figure 16-23: The trimmed interior walls

Zoom again to the previous view and zoom to the next zoom area as circled in Figure 16-24. Then, as shown in Figure 16-25, trim areas 1 and 2. Figure 16-26 shows how these areas are to be trimmed.

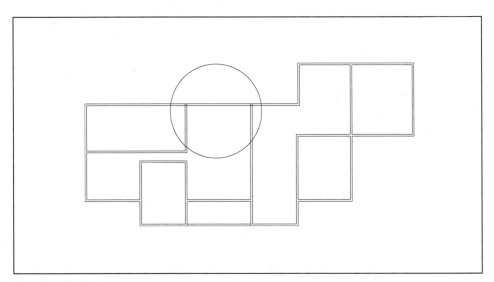

Figure 16-24: New zoom area

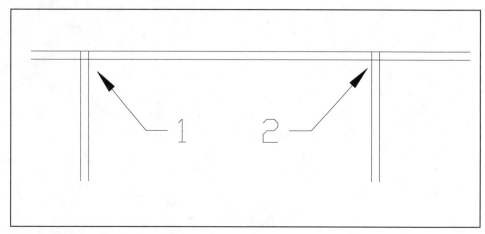

Figure 16-25: Trimming areas 1 and 2

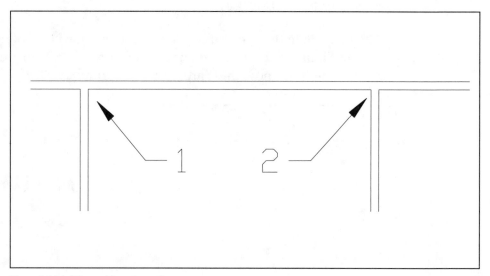

Figure 16-26: Trimmed interior wall areas

Once more, zoom to the previous view. Using the TRIM command, remove the two lines indicated in Figure 16-27. Figure 16-28 shows the lines removed and the completed plan.

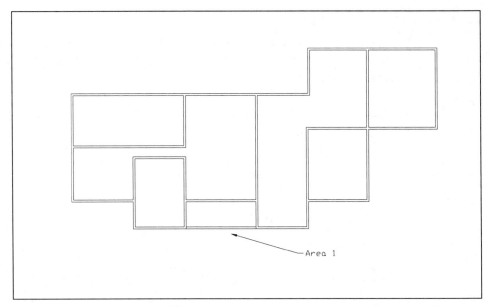

Figure 16-27: Removing the two wall lines

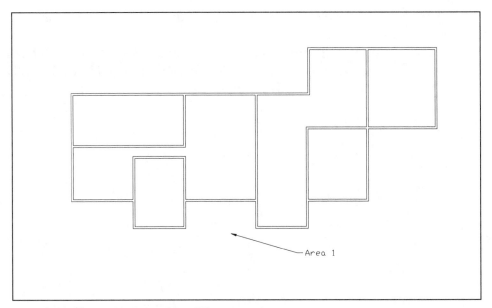

Figure 16-28: The completed plan with wall lines removed

You have now completed the interior walls.

Constructing Columns

For step 5, you'll create columns for your model house. To do that, first make and change to a new layer called COLUMN. Make the COLUMN layer yellow.

Type: LAYER \<Enter\>

         M \<Enter\>

         COLUMN \<Enter\>

         C \<Enter\> (This refers to color.)

         YELLOW \<Enter\>

         \<Enter\>   (Defaults on COLUMN layer.)

         \<Enter\>

Next, change your thickness to 11'2.

Type: THICKNESS \<Enter\>

         11'2 \<Enter\>

If you've turned your snap off during the trim sequence, turn it back on now.

To actually create a column, begin by placing a circle 9 feet below the face of the front wall, as indicated by Point 1 of Figure 16-29. Draw the circle at Point 1 with a radius of 7 inches.

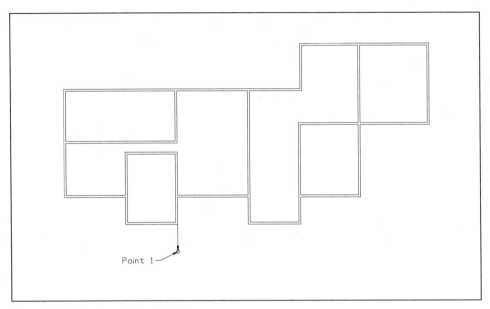

Figure 16-29: Drawing a circle at Point 1

Copy the circle you just drew four times to the right. The distance of each circle is 6 feet from center to center. You should now have five circles 6 feet apart, as shown in Figure 16-30, which shows the five columns.

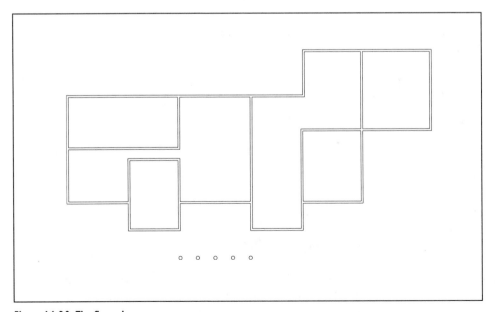

Figure 16-30: The five columns

Breaking the Openings for Doors & Windows

One of the biggest problems faced in architectural drafting is the need to break parallel lines to insert doors and windows. Of course, there is a wealth of third-party software for architectural design that provides the necessary AutoLISP programs. But most of these programs are for the complete insertion of doors and windows.

BRKPAR.LSP is designed simply to break the parallel lines. The program asks for only two things: the distance of the offset of the two parallel lines and the angle of the second parallel line.

You can find BRKPAR.LSP in the AutoLISP section of the book. As with the other 3D programs, make certain that BRKPAR.LSP is properly loaded. If you have the *AutoCAD 3D Companion Disk* installed properly and have loaded 3DTOOLS.LSP, all you need to do is type in the name of the program.

Now see how this program works. First, place a door area in the middle of the entrance way, as indicated by Points 1 and 2 in Figure 16-31. The figure shows in finer detail where to break the walls for the entrance.

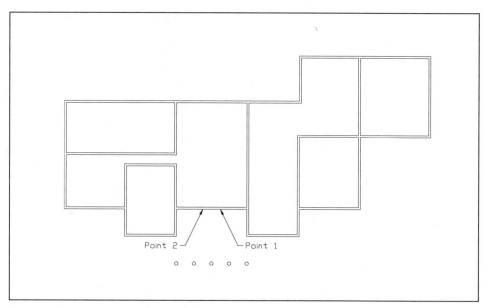

Figure 16-31: Breaking the wall for an entrance

CAUTION: If both lines don't break, your pick box is larger than the distance between the lines. Either reduce the size of the pick box or zoom in a little closer.

Type: BRKPAR <Enter>

Response: Enter offset distance <nil>:

Type: 8 <Enter>

Response: Enter angle of offset <>:

    Because the line that is parallel to the one that you want to break is above, the angle is 90 degrees.

Type: 90 <Enter>

Response: Pick line to break
    Select object:

    Pick the line indicated by Point 1 in Figure 16-31.

Response: Pick first break point

    Pick the actual point indicated by Point 1.

Response: Pick second break point

    Pick the point indicated by Point 2. Notice that in Figure 16-32 both parallel lines of the wall are broken at once.

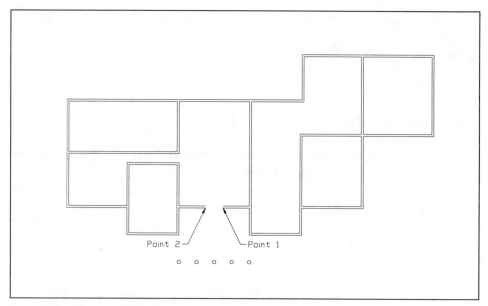

Figure 16-32: The broken entrance

Now you're ready to try another example. Place a door as indicated by Points 1 and 2 in Figure 16-33.

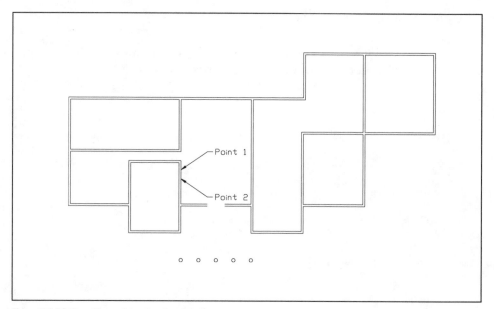

Figure 16-33: Breaking a door area in a room

Type: `BRKPAR <Enter>`

Response: `Enter offset distance <8.0>:`

    Notice that the program defaults to the previous offset.

Type: `<Enter>`

Response: `Enter angle of offset <90>`

    Because the line that is parallel to the one you want to break is to the left, the angle is 180 degrees.

Type: `180 <Enter>`

Response: `Pick line to break`
    `Select object:`

    Pick the line indicated by Point 1 of Figure 16-33.

Response: `Pick first break point`

    Pick the actual point indicated by Point 1.

Response: `Pick second break point`

    Pick the point indicated by Point 2. Notice that in Figure 16-34 both parallel lines of the wall are broken at once.

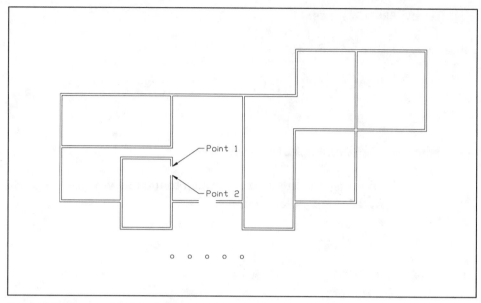

Figure 16-34: The second broken door area

Now, using the BRKPAR.LSP program, continue to break into the walls for the various doors and windows, as indicated in Figure 16-35. This figure shows all the door and window areas to be broken for the complete plan.

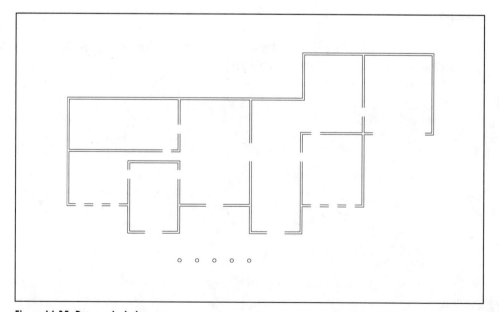

Figure 16-35: Door and window areas

Constructing Beams Over the Columns

For the seventh step of this tutorial, you'll create beams to set atop the columns in the model. Before you do that, however, set up three viewports.

Type: VPORTS <Enter>

   3 <Enter>

   <Enter>

See Figure 16-36 for the three basic viewports layout.

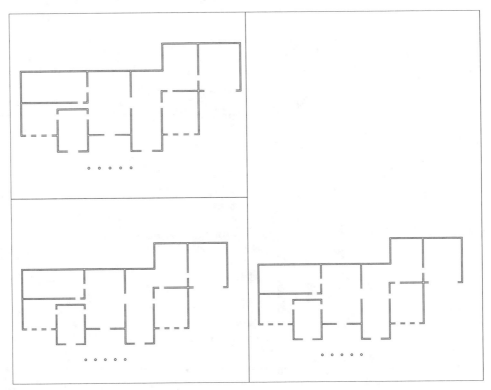

Figure 16-36: Three basic viewports layout

Pick and make active the upper-left viewport. Then change its view point to 1,–1,1.

Type: VPOINT <Enter>

   1,–1,1

   ZX <Enter>

Here, the ZX.LSP program zooms to the extents of the viewport.
Next, pick and make active the lower-left viewport. Also change its
view point to the same as the upper-left viewport.

Type: VPOINT

1,−1,1

Finally, zoom in on the columns, as shown in Figure 16-37.

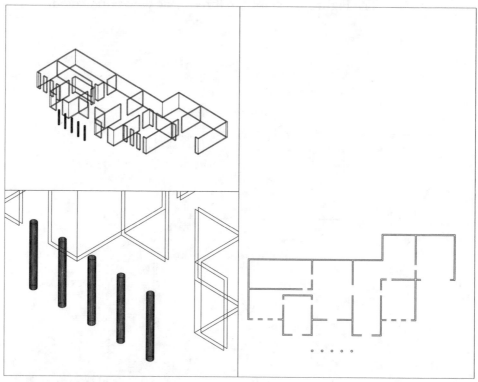

Figure 16-37: Zooming in on columns in the lower-left viewport

To begin constructing the beams, pick and make active the lower-left
viewport if it isn't already active. At this point make a new layer called
BEAMS and make it magenta.

Type: LAYER ⟨Enter⟩

M ⟨Enter⟩

BEAMS ⟨Enter⟩

C ⟨Enter⟩

MAGENTA ⟨Enter⟩ ⟨Enter⟩ ⟨Enter⟩

You're now active on the BEAMS layer. But you need to change the elevation and thickness:

Type: ELEV <Enter>

11'2 <Enter>

10 <Enter>

From the left column to the right column, draw a polyline with a width of 3 inches. Make sure that your snap and grid are still active and still set to 3 feet.

Type: PLINE <Enter>

Response: From point:

Pick the top of the first column on the left.

Response: Arc/Close/Halfwidth/Length/Undo/Width

Type: W <Enter>

Response: Starting width:

Type: 3 <Enter>

Response: Ending width:

Type: 3 <Enter>

Now continue the polyline to the far right column, placing the endpoint on the grid/snap point at the top of the column.

Type: <Enter>   (This ends the polyline.)

See Figure 16-38, which shows the completed cross beam over the top of the columns.

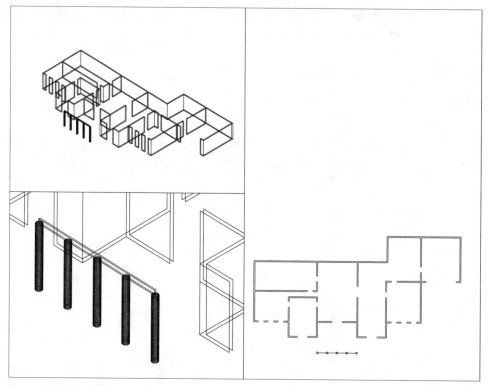

Figure 16-38: Cross beam over the top of the columns

You'll now need to extend the beam you just drew by 3 feet on each side. With Release 13 the easiest way to extend a line is to use grips. You must make sure that grips are enabled; you control the grips by picking Grips... from the Settings pull-down menu.

Now pick the beam. After you pick the beam, the grips are turned on. Next, pick the grip at the right end of the beam. The grip changes color to indicate that it is active.

Extend the line 3 feet at an angle of 0 (zero) degrees, as follows:

Type: @3'<0 <Enter>

Now pick the end grip on the left end of the beam. The grip changes color to indicate that it is active.

Extend the line 3 feet at an angle of 180 degrees on the left end.

Type: @3'<180 <Enter>

See Figure 16-39 to view the beam extended beyond the columns.

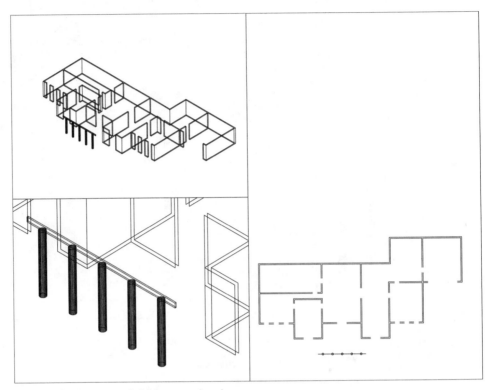

Figure 16-39: Beam extended 3 feet at each end

For the next part of the process, pick and make active the right viewport. Zoom in on the area indicated by Figure 16-40, which shows you a close-up view of where to zoom.

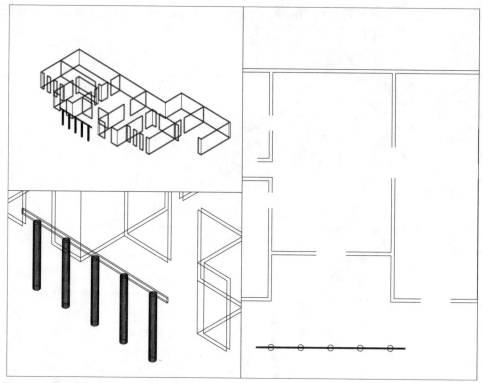

Figure 16-40: Zooming in on the right viewport

Now use the COPY command to copy the beam and columns 6 feet in the Y direction beyond the back wall. Figure 16-41 shows the completed beam and columns copied in the correct direction.

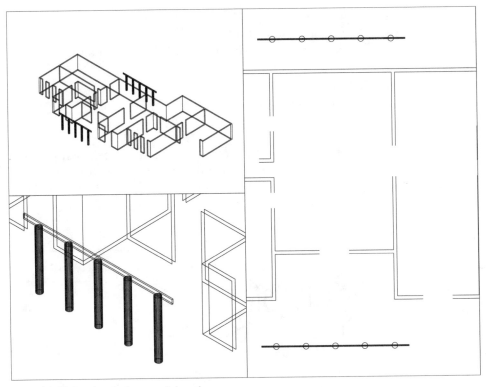

Figure 16-41: Copying the beam and the columns

One of the problems that you're faced with now is using a polyline where one end of the polyline is at one elevation and the center vertex is at another elevation. If you try to use the polyline in the existing World Coordinate System, your polyline won't work because a polyline can't have differing Z coordinates. Only the 3DPOLY can have differing Z coordinates. But the problem with the 3DPOLY is that the polyline can't have a width. So what's the solution?

Here's a little trick to help. First, begin by rotating the UCS 90 degrees around X and Y.

Type: RX <Enter>

RY <Enter>

Then change thickness to 3 inches.

Type: THICKNESS <Enter>

3 <Enter>

Because you've changed the direction of the UCS, you'll invert the width of the polyline and the thickness.

Now you're ready to begin the PLINE command.

Type: PLINE <Enter>

Response: From point:

Pick and make active the upper-left viewport. Using object snap center, pick the upper end of the middle column, as indicated by Point 1 in Figure 16-42.

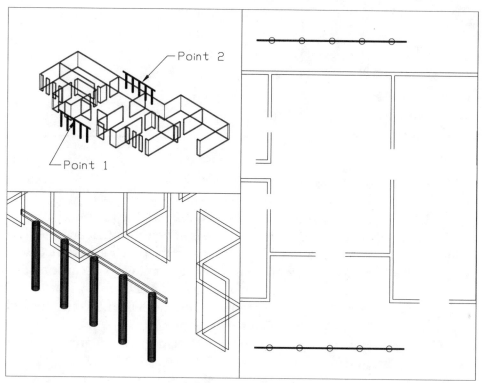

Figure 16-42: Drawing a beam across the house

Response: Arc/Close/Halfwidth/Length/Undo/Width

Type: W <Enter>

Response: Starting width:

Type: 10 <Enter>

Response: Ending width:

Type: 10 <Enter>

Again using object snap center, pick the top part of the center beam on the back side of the model, as indicated by Point 2 in Figure 16-42. See Figure 16-43 for an illustration of the basic beam to be placed across the house.

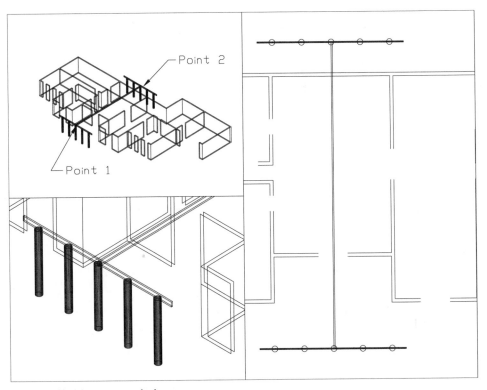

Figure 16-43: A beam across the house

Now extend the beam you just drew by 3 feet in each direction, in a manner similar to the way you extended the beam across the columns. To start, pick and make active the right viewport. When you pick the long beam, the grips will turn on. Next, pick the grip at the bottom, as indicated by Point 1 in Figure 16-44. The grip changes color to show that it is active.

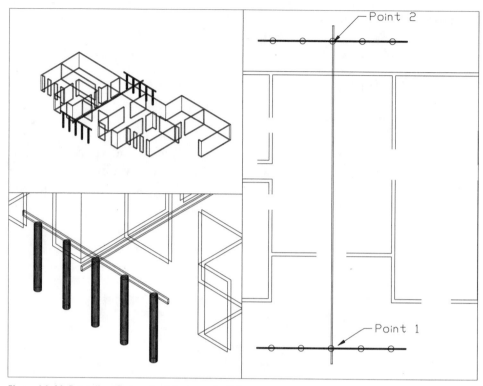

Figure 16-44: Extending the length of the beam by 3 feet

Type: @3'<180 <Enter>

    Now pick the grip at the top end, as indicated by Point 2 in the figure. Again, the grip changes color to show that it is active.

Type: @3'<0 <Enter>

    Now that you've extended the beam 3 feet beyond the columns in each direction, save the current view and UCS.

Type: USVIEW <Enter>
         SIDEVIEW <Enter>

    Then change to UCS World.

Type: UCS <Enter> <Enter>

Now you'll copy the bottom cross beam to the midpoint of the longer beam. Therefore, you're going to copy the bottom beam from Point 1 to Point 2, as indicated in Figure 16-45.

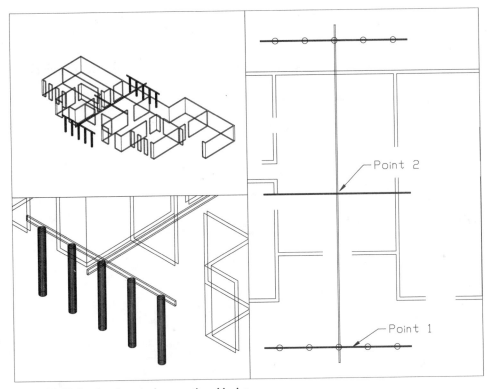

Figure 16-45: Copying the cross beam to the midpoint

Type: COPY <Enter>

Response: Select objects:

Pick the bottom cross beam at Point 1, as shown in Figure 16-45. Confirm the selection by pressing Enter.

Response: Base point or displacement/Multiple

Using object snap intersection, pick the intersection of the two beams to the left of Point 1 and near the center of the column.

Response: `Second point of displacement:`

Using object snap midpoint, pick Point 2, as shown in Figure 16-45.
Your next step is to move the long vertical beam 10 inches higher than where it is now so that it doesn't cross through the other two beams.

Type: `MOVE <Enter>`

Response: `Select objects:`

Pick the longer vertical beam and confirm the selection by pressing Enter.

Response: `Base point or displacement`

Type: `@ <Enter>`

Response: `Second point of displacement`

Type: `@0,0,10 <Enter>`

Now return to the previous UCS.

Type: `URVIEW <Enter>`
`SIDEVIEW <Enter>`

Finally, position your drawing plan to the current UCS.

Type: `PLAN <Enter> <Enter>`

See Figure 16-46, which illustrates a side view of the vertical beam and the correct UCS view.

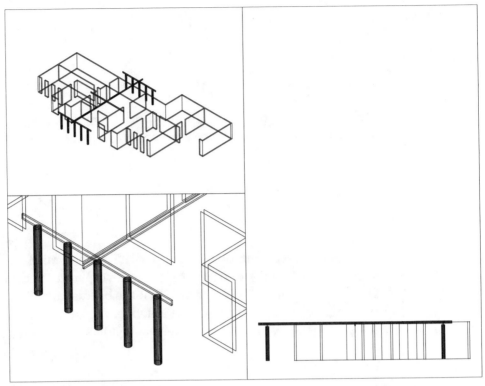

Figure 16-46: Side view of the vertical beam

The roof beams you've constructed are lying flat across the house. Your next step will be to raise the center of the beams to support a raised roof.

Constructing a Raised Roof

Before constructing the raised roof to cover the beams, you must take some additional steps. You must break the long vertical beam in half to create two separate beams.

Type: BREAK <Enter>

Response: Select object:

Pick and make active the upper-left viewport; then pick the longer vertical beam.

Response: Enter second point (or F for first point):

Type: F <Enter>

Response: Enter first point:

   Pick and make active the right viewport. Using object snap midpoint, pick near the midpoint of the beam that you've just selected. Be careful not to pick any other line.

Response: Enter second point:

Type: @ <Enter>

   Now that you've split the beam in two, it's time to raise the roof. Pick at both ends of each of the two new beams that you've created to turn on their grips. Then pick the center grip that the beams have in common. The grip changes color to indicate that it is active.
   Now raise the two beams by 14 feet, as follows.

Type: @0,14',0 <Enter>

   Figure 16-47 illustrates the two raised roof beams.

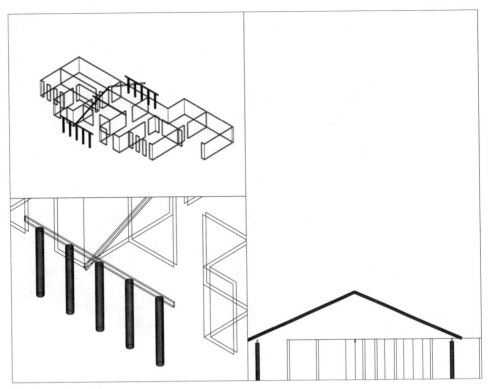

Figure 16-47: Raised roof beams

Next, zoom in on the intersection of the beams, as shown in Figure 16-48. The figure shows the separated beams.

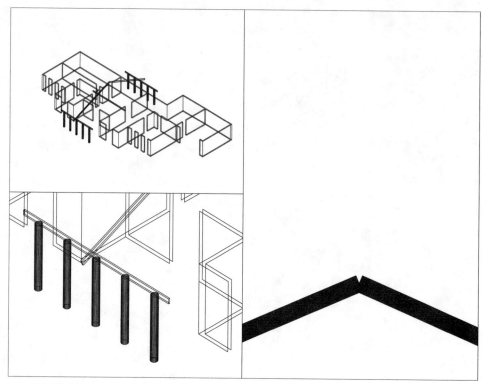

Figure 16-48: The two separated beams

Because the two beams don't come together, you can join them with a PEDIT Join command.

Type: PEDIT <Enter>

Response: Select Polyline:

Pick either of the polylines.

Type: J <Enter>

Now pick both polylines and press Enter to confirm. Press Enter again to exit the PEDIT command. See Figure 16-49 for the results.

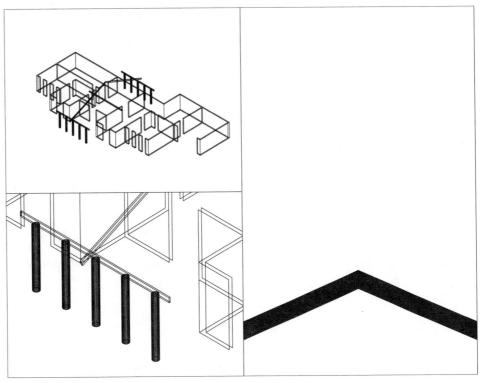

Figure 16-49: Joined beams

Notice in the upper-left viewport you still have a problem. The center cross beam is still lying on the ground. You need to elevate it 14 feet. To solve this problem, first pick and make active the upper-left viewport.

Type: MOVE <Enter>

Response: Select objects:

Pick the center beam and confirm by pressing Enter.

Response: Base point or displacement:

Type: @ <Enter>

Response: Second point of displacement:

Type: @0,14',0 <Enter>

The center cross beam should now be in the correct position. Pick and make active the right viewport.

Type: URVIEW <Enter>

          SIDEVIEW <Enter>

          UCS <Enter> <Enter>

Now you can make multiple vertical roof beams to connect to each column.

Type: COPY <Enter>

Pick the long beam and confirm the selection by pressing Enter.

Response: Base point or displacement/Multiple:

Type: M <Enter>

Response: Base point:

Using the grid/snap, pick at the grid of the lower center column where the beam and the column intersect. Then simply place the beams across by using the multiple COPY command. You should have a beam on each one of the columns, as shown in Figure 16-50.

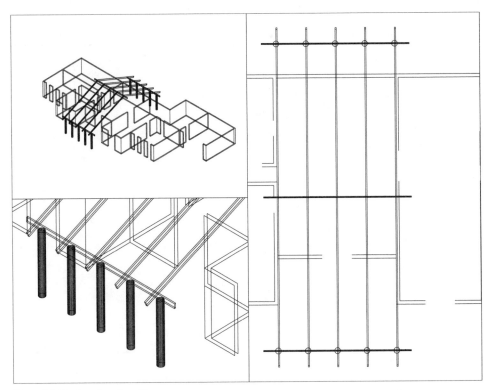

Figure 16-50: Completed roof beams

Now that you've constructed the beams for your raised roof, it's time to place a roof on the beams. To make this task as easy as possible, turn off all layers except your current layer. A good trick is to freeze all layers with an *, and the current layer will not freeze.

Type: LAYER <Enter>

       F <Enter>

       * <Enter> <Enter>

See Figure 16-51, which shows only the BEAMS layer activated.

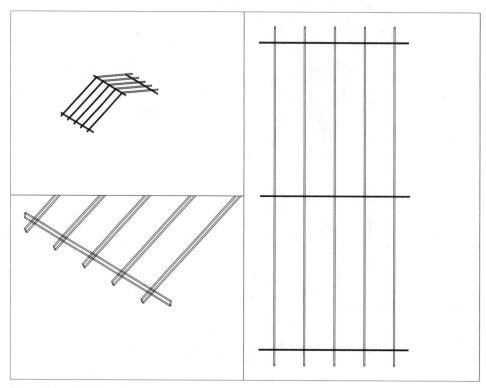

Figure 16-51: BEAMS layer only

Before you can add a covering to your raised roof, you'll need to copy the center cross beam down from Point 1 to Point 2, as indicated in Figure 16-52.

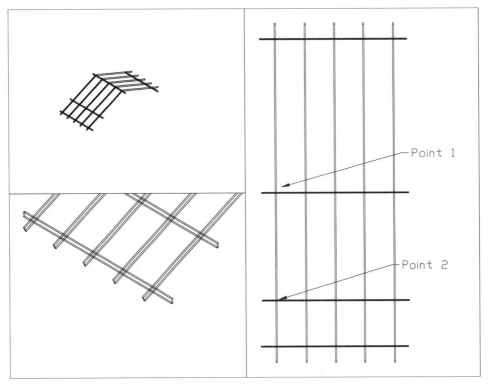

Figure 16-52: Copying the center beam

Type: COPY <Enter>

Response: Select objects:

Pick the center cross beam and confirm by pressing Enter.

Response: Base point or displacement/Multiple:

Using object snap intersection, pick Point 1, as shown in Figure 16-52.

Response: Second point of displacement:

Using object snap nearest, pick a point approximately at Point 2, as shown in Figure 16-52. Then repeat the COPY command to copy the center cross beam from Point 1 to Point 3, as indicated in Figure 16-53. (Remember to use object snap intersection for Point 1 and object snap nearest for Point 3.)

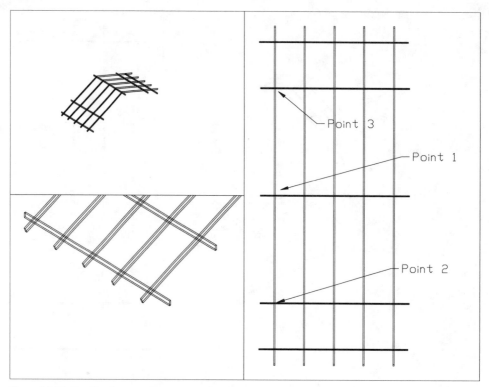

Figure 16-53: Copying the second center cross beam

At this point you're ready to make a new layer called ROOF. Make it green.

Type: LAYER <Enter>
        M <Enter>
        ROOF <Enter>
        C <Enter>
        GREEN <Enter>
        <Enter> <Enter>

Use the 3DFACE command to connect the object snap endpoint of each of the four points of the center cross beam and the lower cross beam, as in Figure 16-54. Repeat the operation to place another 3D face on the top side.

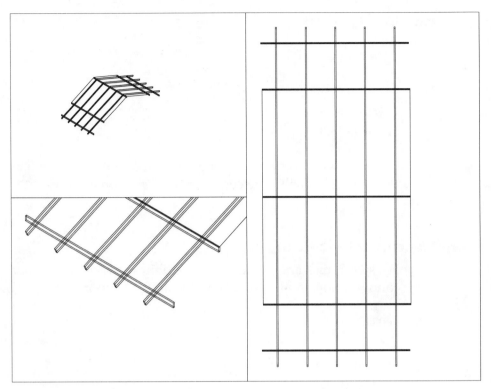

Figure 16-54: Adding a roof

Each of the 3D faces is connected to the bottom of the beams; therefore, you'll need to move the 3D faces up 10 inches to the top of the beams. To do so, pick and make active the upper-left viewport.

Type: MOVE <Enter>

Response: Select objects:

Pick each of the two 3D faces and confirm the selection by pressing Enter.

Response: Base point or displacement:

Type: @ <Enter>

Response: Second point of displacement:

Type: @0,0,10 <Enter>

   Next, thaw all layers:

Type: LAYER <Enter>

   T <Enter>

   * <Enter> <Enter>

   You've now finished creating the raised roof on the center of the house. Your next step will be to construct a flat roof on each side.

Constructing a Flat Roof

For step 9, pick and make active the right viewport. Save your viewport configuration and then change to a single viewport.

Type: VPORTS <Enter>

   S <Enter>

   V1 <Enter>

   VPORTS <Enter>

   SI <Enter>

   ZX <Enter>

   Next, freeze all layers except the FLOORPLAN layer.

Type: LAYER <Enter>

   S <Enter>

   FLOORPLAN <Enter>

   F <Enter>

   * <Enter> <Enter>

   Now make a new layer called FLATROOF.

Type: LAYER <Enter>

   M <Enter>

   FLATROOF <Enter>

   C <Enter>

   RED <Enter> <Enter> <Enter>

Change elevation to 12 feet.

Type: ELEV <Enter>

12' <Enter>

0 <Enter>

Now, using a polyline and grid/snap, outline the right side of the house with a closed polyline and then the left side of the house with a closed polyline. Do not include the center living area (see Figure 16-55).

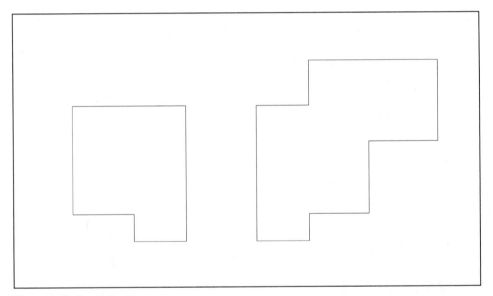

Figure 16-55: Flat roof outline

When you begin the PLINE command, make sure you change the width to zero. Figure 16-55 shows the two polyline areas with all other layers frozen.

Type: LAYER <Enter>

F <Enter>

* <Enter>

<Enter>

Now you'll use the BMESH13.LSP program to mesh both of the roof areas. First, turn off the hatch pattern with the SOLHPAT variable.

Next, begin the BMESH13 program.

Type: `BMESH13 <Enter>`

Response: `Pick the entity to be meshed`
          `Select object:`

Pick the polyline on the right of Figure 16-55.

Response: `Pick endpoint or intersection that represents the elevation`

Pick any intersection on the polyline on the right.

Response: `Pick inside area`

Pick any point inside the polyline on the right. Now the flat roof on the right side should be meshed.
You're ready to repeat the procedure for the left polyline.

Type: `BMESH13 <Enter>`

Response: `Pick the entity to be meshed`
          `Select object:`

Pick the polyline on the left, as shown in Figure 16-55.

Response: `Pick endpoint or intersection that represents the elevation`

Pick any intersection on the polyline on the left.

Response: `Pick inside area`

Pick any point inside the polyline on the left. Your model now has a flat roof covering on both sides of the house.

Drawing Side Roof Faces

At this point the roof of your model is nearly complete, but you must add side roof faces to the raised portion of your roof. Before you can do that, however, you must get back to the original view point of your model.

First, thaw all the layers.

Type: LAYER <Enter>

T <Enter>

* <Enter>

S <Enter>

ROOF <Enter>

F <Enter>

BEAMS <Enter> <Enter>

Next, restore the V1 configuration.

Type: VPORTS <Enter>

R <Enter>

V1 <Enter>

Now pick and make active the right viewport.

Type: URVIEW <Enter>

SIDEVIEW <Enter>

PLAN <Enter> <Enter>

ZX <Enter>

Then pick and make active the lower-left viewport. Zoom in on the 3D face roof area, as shown in Figure 16-56.

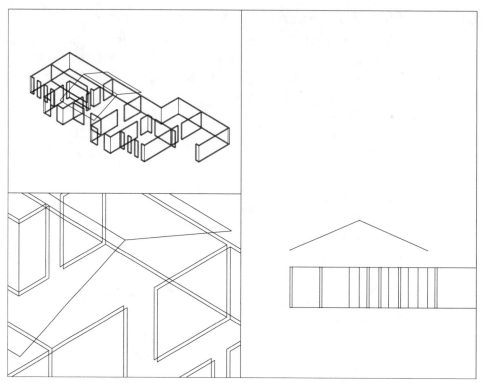

Figure 16-56: Zooming in on the roof area

Use the 3DFACE command and object snap intersection to pick the three points of the triangle, as indicated in Figure 16-57. After you pick the third point, press Enter twice to terminate the 3DFACE command.

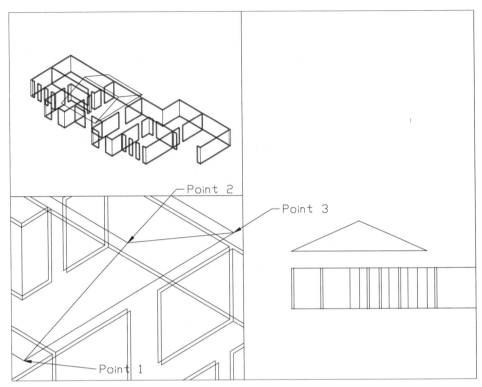

Figure 16-57: Side of the raised roof

Notice the gap from the bottom of the triangle to the wall area. The problem is that you can't just draw a 3D face over the area with the gap because you don't have anything to snap on. To solve this problem, you'll use the regular LINE command to draw two construction lines. Use object snap intersection and begin the lines at the vertex of the triangle. Just use ORTHO On and drop the lines down; it doesn't matter how far (see Figure 16-58). You might want to begin the line in the lower-left viewport and pick the second point in the right viewport.

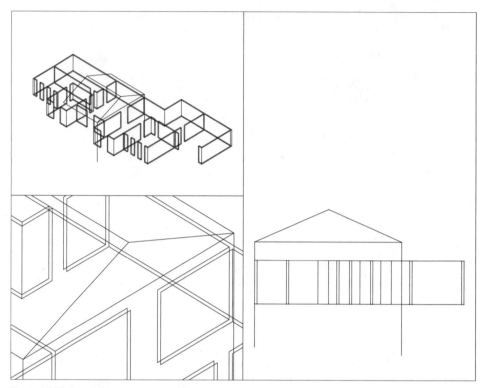

Figure 16-58: Drawing two construction lines

Now pick and make active the right viewport. Draw a horizontal construction line from the object snap nearest to the first construction line, as indicated by Point 1 of Figure 16-59, to the object snap perpendicular to the other construction line, as indicated by Point 2. Make sure that this third construction line is in the open and not near the top of the walls. You'll lower the construction line shortly.

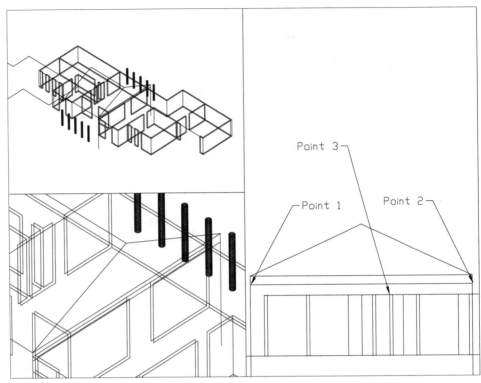

Figure 16-59: Horizontal construction line

Now make use of the MOVEY.LSP program to lower the horizontal construction line. Remember that this program will move an entity to be equal to the Y coordinate of another entity without changing the XZ.

Type: MOVEY <Enter>

Response: Pick the objects you want to move
Select objects:

Pick the horizontal construction line and confirm the selection by pressing Enter.

Response: Pick the base point

Using object snap intersection, pick Point 2, as shown in Figure 16-59.

Response: Pick a point for the target Y coordinate

Using object snap intersection, pick Point 3 or pick any intersection on the top of the walls. The construction line is now moved down to the same elevation as the top of the walls without changing the X and Z coordinates of the construction line.

Freeze all but the current ROOF layer.

Type: LAYER <Enter>

          F <Enter>

          * <Enter> <Enter>

All that is left is the outline of the roof, the side 3D face of the roof and the construction lines (see Figure 16-60).

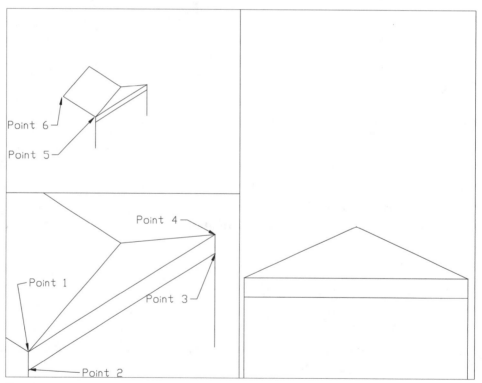

Figure 16-60: Side of the roof

Pick and make active the lower-left viewport. Using object snap intersection, draw a 3D face from Point 1 to Point 2 to Point 3 to Point 4 (see Figure 16-60). Then terminate the 3DFACE command by pressing Enter. Erase the two vertical construction lines.

Next, pick and make active the upper-left viewport. Copy the two 3D faces from Point 5 to Point 6 on the roof, as shown in Figure 16-60.

Then thaw all layers.

Type: LAYER <Enter>
        T <Enter>
        * <Enter> <Enter>

Finally, pick and make active the lower-left viewport. For this part of the tutorial, return to a single viewport.

Type: VPORTS <Enter>
        SI <Enter>
        ZX <Enter>

Drawing Door & Window Faces

All that is left is for you to place 3D faces on each of the window and door areas. So, for step 11, zoom in on one of these areas, as shown in Figure 16-61.

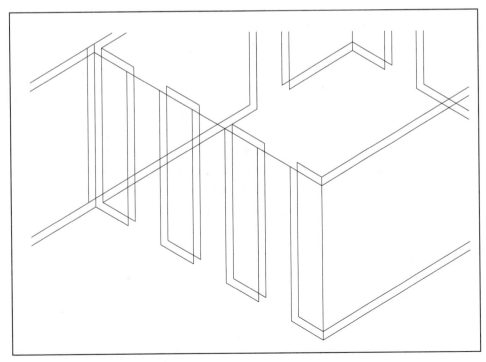

Figure 16-61: Zooming in on a window area

Make DOOR and WINDOW layers. Obviously, you'll use the DOOR layer when you're placing the doors and the WINDOW layer when you're placing the windows. All you'll need to do for the windows and doors is cover the openings with individual 3D faces, as shown in Figure 16-62.

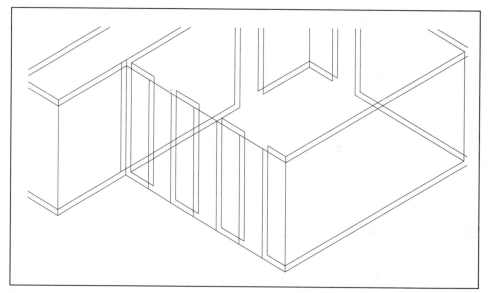

Figure 16-62: 3D faces over openings

Final Presentation

Figure 16-63 shows the finished hidden line view of the house. You might ask why you placed 3D faces only on the openings of the doors and windows in this tutorial. The answer to that question depends on what you want to do with the model. If the presentation of the model is through AutoCAD only, as indicated in Figure 16-63, then you might want to make the doors and windows more elaborate. You could create a more elaborate model by drawing finished 3D door and window parts and inserting them in the drawing.

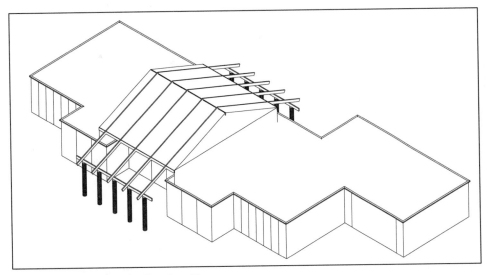

Figure 16-63: Finished hidden line view of house

On the other hand, you could use this model as the geometry for a rendering program. If this is the case, then the 3D faces that you drew are more than sufficient. When the geometry gets to the rendering program, you'll apply a texture map in the form of a GIF or TARGA file to each of the 3D faces. This file will be a picture of the appropriate door or window. Therefore, as you can see, you don't actually have to draw doors and windows or other intricate parts of your model if you have a texture file that can do the work for you. All you need to do is provide a 3D face on which the texture file can be applied.

Now that you've successfully completed this tutorial, you're encouraged to try your hand at the mechanical tutorial if you haven't already done so. If you've completed each of the tutorials, then congratulations. But don't stop learning. Every new model will bring with it new challenges; you'll find better and easier ways to accomplish your goals. And each time, working in 3D gets easier and easier.

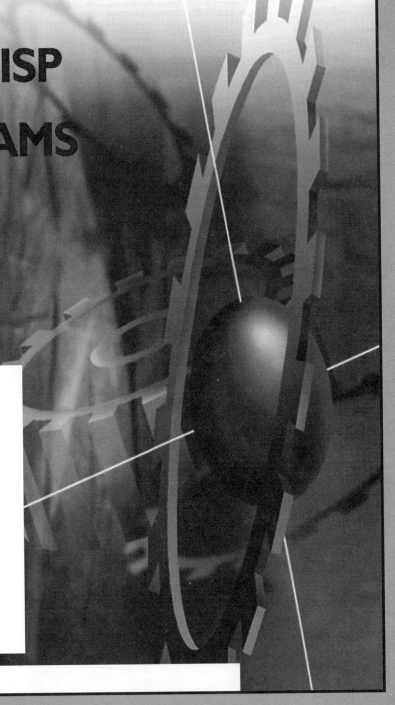

SECTION IV

AUTOLISP PROGRAMS

CHAPTER 17

The 3D Toolkit

AutoCAD was never meant to be run as a totally stand-alone program. AutoCAD's popularity is primarily due to its open architecture and ability to be customized. The 3D tools created in this book afford you the ability to dramatically increase your productivity and to do some things with AutoCAD that are extremely difficult to perform without the help of AutoLISP.

This chapter gives you a complete AutoLISP source listing of each program found in this book as well as detailed instructions on the purpose of the program and how it's used. Beside the name of each program is the chapter in which it was originally introduced so that you can go back to that chapter to see how the program was used throughout the tutorial.

If you have not done so already, you are encouraged to read Appendix A, "AutoLISP & Your 3D Toolkit." This appendix explains the fundamentals of AutoLISP, how AutoCAD finds your AutoLISP program files and the workings of the quick load feature of 3DTOOLS.LSP. There is also the 3D Toolkit Recap which gives you a quick and short explanation of each of the programs.

3DTOOLS.LSP

Rather than trying to control all of your AutoLISP program files at once, it's easier to control one file and let it control the loading and executing of the others. That's what the 3DTOOLS.LSP program does. Once 3DTOOLS.LSP is loaded, all you have to do is type the name of the program you want to run and 3DTOOLS will load and execute the program for you.

Listing:
```
; This utility is used to automatically load any AutoLISP program.
; To use add the name of the program as a C: (command level)
; function. The program should have two statements, the first loads
; the real program and the second executes the real program.
; In this way you only have to load 3DTOOLS.LSP or have the
; ACAD.LSP startup function load 3DTOOLS.LSP and all programs
; will be available.
```

```
(defun C:rx ()(load "rx")(C:rx))
(defun C:ry ()(load "ry")(C:ry))
(defun C:rz ()(load "rz")(C:rz))
(defun C:uslview ()(load "uslview")(C:uslview))
(defun C:usview ()(load "usview")(C:usview))
(defun C:urview ()(load "urview")(C:urview))
(defun C:ubase ()(load "ubase")(C:ubase))
(defun C:rside ()(load "rside")(C:rside))
(defun C:lside ()(load "lside")(C:lside))
(defun C:fside ()(load "fside")(C:fside))
(defun C:bside ()(load "bside")(C:bside))
(defun C:tside ()(load "tside")(C:tside))
(defun C:cplayer ()(load "cplayer")(C:cplayer))
(defun C:pon ()(load "pon")(C:pon))
(defun C:poff ()(load "poff")(C:poff))
(defun C:bsview ()(load "bsview")(C:bsview))
(defun C:rview ()(load "rview")(C:rview))
(defun C:lview ()(load "lview")(C:lview))
(defun C:bview ()(load "bview")(C:bview))
(defun C:fview ()(load "fview")(C:fview))
(defun C:vpd ()(load "vpd")(C:vpd))
(defun C:iso ()(load "iso")(C:iso))
(defun C:zx ()(load "zx")(C:zx))
(defun C:rd ()(load "rd")(C:rd))
(defun C:tcopy ()(load "tcopy")(C:tcopy))
(defun C:iface ()(load "iface")(C:iface))
(defun C:sface ()(load "sface")(C:sface))
(defun C:bmesh ()(load "bmesh")(C:bmesh))
(defun C:bmesh13 ()(load "bmesh13")(C:bmesh13))
(defun C:rmesh ()(load "rmesh")(C:rmesh))
(defun C:hidemesh ()(load "hidemesh")(C:hidemesh))
(defun C:divcir ()(load "divcir")(C:divcir))
(defun C:ucsx ()(load "ucsx")(C:ucsx))
(defun C:3ddim ()(load "3ddim")(C:3ddim))
(defun C:qdist ()(load "qdist")(C:qdist))
(defun C:ms ()(load "ms")(C:ms))
(defun C:ps ()(load "ps")(C:ps))
(defun C:mv ()(load "mv")(C:mv))
(defun C:pscopy ()(load "pscopy")(C:pscopy))
(defun C:vpx ()(load "vpx")(C:vpx))
```

```
(defun C:vpy ()(load "vpy")(C:vpy))
(defun C:av ()(load "av")(C:av))
(defun C:pv ()(load "pv")(C:pv))
(defun C:movey ()(load "movey")(C:movey))
(defun C:movex ()(load "movex")(C:movex))
(defun C:movexy ()(load "movexy")(C:movexy))
(defun C:pvucs ()(load "pvucs")(C:pvucs))
(defun C:pvrucs ()(load "pvrucs")(C:pvrucs))
(defun C:chside ()(load "chside")(C:chside))
(defun C:chthk ()(load "chthk")(C:chthk))
(defun C:brkpar ()(load "brkpar")(C:brkpar))
(defun C:cpext ()(load "cpext")(C:cpext))
(princ "\n   ")
(princ "\n   ")
(princ "\n   ")
(princ "\n3D Tools loaded")
(princ "\n   ")
(princ)
```

RX.LSP Chapter 2

The RX.LSP program rotates the UCS around X 90 degrees. Rather than having to go through the UCS command, this program rotates around X by 90 degrees each time the program is run. Since this is an AutoCAD command line program it can be typed from the command line and repeated with the Enter key, space bar or the button assigned as Enter.

Type: RX <Enter>

Notice how the icon rotated around X 90 degrees. If you need another rotation then press Enter and the command will be repeated. Continue to press Enter until the icon is pointing in the correct direction.

Listing:
```
(defun C:rx (/ ce)
; This program rotates the ucs around X 90 degrees.
; To continue rotating around X press <Enter> for each
; additional 90 degrees.
  (setq ce (getvar "cmdecho"))
```

```
(setvar "cmdecho" 0)
(command "undo" "m")
(command "ucs" "x" "90")
(setvar "cmdecho" ce)
(princ)
)
```

RY.LSP   Chapter 2

The RY.LSP program rotates the UCS around Y 90 degrees. Rather than having to go through the UCS command, this program rotates around Y by 90 degrees each time the program is run. Since this is an AutoCAD command line program it can be typed from the command line and repeated with the Enter key, space bar or the button assigned as Enter.

Type: `RY  <Enter>`

Notice how the icon rotated around Y 90 degrees. If you need another rotation then press Enter and the command will be repeated. Continue to press Enter until the icon is pointing in the correct direction.

Listing:
```
(defun C:ry (/ ce)
; This program rotates the ucs around Y 90 degrees.
; To continue rotating around Y press <Enter> for each
; additional 90 degrees.
  (setq ce (getvar "cmdecho"))
  (setvar "cmdecho" 0)
  (command "undo" "m")
  (command "ucs" "y" "90")
  (setvar "cmdecho" ce)
  (princ)
)
```

RZ.LSP Chapter 2

The RZ.LSP program rotates the UCS around Z 90 degrees. Rather than having to go through the UCS command, this program rotates around Z by 90 degrees each time the program is run. Since this is an AutoCAD command line program it can be typed from the command line and repeated with the Enter key, space bar or the button assigned as Enter.

Type: RZ <Enter>

Notice how the icon rotated around Z 90 degrees. If you need another rotation then press Enter and the command will be repeated. Continue to press Enter until the icon is pointing in the correct direction.

Listing:
```
(defun C:rz (/ ce)
; This program rotates the ucs around Z 90 degrees.
; To continue rotating around Z press <Enter> for each
; additional 90 degrees.
  (setq ce (getvar "cmdecho"))
  (setvar "cmdecho" 0)
  (command "undo" "m")
  (command "ucs" "z" "90")
  (setvar "cmdecho" ce)
  (princ)
)
```

USLVIEW.LSP Chapter 2

The USLVIEW.LSP program saves the current view, layer and UCS by the same name. If the view or UCS already exists then they are replaced.

Type: USLVIEW <Enter>

Response: Name of view, UCS and layer to save:

Type: V1 <Enter>

Obviously here you have the option of naming your view and UCS anything that you want. Notice that what the program does is first to make a layer called V1 if one doesn't already exist then sets you to that layer. It then saves the current UCS as V1 and saves the current view also as V1.

Listing:
```
(defun C:uslview  (/ ce v)
  ; This program saves the view, layer and ucs by the same name.
  ; If the view or ucs already exists then they are replaced.
  ; The ucs should be set before executing this program.
  (setq ce (getvar "cmdecho"))
  (setvar "cmdecho" 0)
  (command "undo" "m")
  (setq v (getstring "\nName of view, UCS and layer to save:  "))
  (if (= nil (tblsearch "UCS" v))
    (progn
      (command "layer" "m" v "")
      (command "ucs" "s" v)
      (command "view" "s" v)
    )
    (progn
      (command "layer" "m" v "")
      (command "ucs" "s" v "y")
      (command "view" "s" v)
    )
  )
  (setvar "cmdecho" ce)
  (princ)
)
```

USVIEW.LSP   Chapter 2

The USVIEW program saves the view and UCS by the same name. If the view or UCS already exists then they are replaced.

Type: USVIEW <Enter>

Response: Name of view and UCS to save:

Type: V1 <Enter>

The view and UCS are now saved by the name of V1.

Listing:
```
(defun C:usview  (/ v ce)
  ; This program saves the view and ucs by the same name.
  ; If the view or ucs already exists then they are replaced.
```

```
; The ucs should be set before executing this program.
  (setq ce (getvar "cmdecho"))
  (setvar "cmdecho" 0)
  (command "undo" "m")
  (setq v (getstring "\nName of view and UCS to save:  "))
  (if (= nil (tblsearch "UCS" v))
    (progn
      (command "ucs" "s" v)
      (command "view" "s" v)
    )
    (progn
      (command "ucs" "s" v "y")
      (command "view" "s" v)
    )
  )
  (setvar "cmdecho" ce)
  (princ)
)
```

URVIEW.LSP   Chapter 2

The URVIEW program restores the view and UCS at the same time if they have the same saved view and UCS name.

Type: URVIEW   <Enter>

Response: Name of view and UCS to restore:

Type: V1   <Enter>

If a view and UCS exist by the name of V1 then they are now restored together.

Listing:
```
(defun C:urview  (/ v ce)
  ; This program restores the view and ucs by the same name.
  (setq ce (getvar "cmdecho"))
  (setvar "cmdecho" 0)
  (command "undo" "m")
  (setq v (getstring "\nName of view and UCS to restore:  "))
  (if (= nil (tblsearch "UCS" v))
```

```
     (princ "\nUCS not found. ")
     (command "ucs" "r" v)
   )
   (if (= nil (tblsearch "VIEW" v))
     (princ "\nView not found. ")
     (command "view" "r" v)
   )
   (setvar "cmdecho" ce)
   (princ)
)
```

UBASE.LSP   Chapter 2

The UBASE program establishes the base point UCS for RSIDE.LSP, LSIDE.LSP, BSIDE.LSP and FSIDE.LSP programs. Those programs change the UCS to the appropriate side relative to the base point established by UBASE.

To begin with you have to have a constant base from which to begin. In order to use the programs you must first establish this base. Begin by creating a UCS generally on the top of the model.

Type: UBASE   <Enter>

There are no additional parameters. The UCS base is now created.

Listing:
```
(defun C:ubase (/ ce)
; This program establishes the base point UCS for RSIDE, LSIDE,
; BSIDE, FSIDE programs.
; Those programs change the ucs to the appropriate side
; relative to the base point.
  (setq ce (getvar "cmdecho"))
  (setvar "cmdecho" 0)
  (command "undo" "m")
  (if (= nil (tblsearch "UCS" "BASE"))
  (command "ucs" "s" "base")
  (command "ucs" "s" "base" "y"))
  (setvar "cmdecho" ce)
  (princ)
)
```

RSIDE.LSP   Chapter 2

The RSIDE program changes the UCS to the right side of the model relative to the base created by the UBASE program.

Type: RSIDE   <Enter>

From the base the UCS icon is rotated to the right side of the model.

Listing:
```
(defun C:rside (/ ce pt1)
; Before running this program ubase.lsp should be run to
; establish the base point.
; This program changes the ucs to the right side relative
; to the base point.
  (setq ce (getvar "cmdecho"))
  (setvar "cmdecho" 0)
  (command "undo" "m")
  (setq pt1 '(0 0 0))
  (setq pt1 (trans pt1 1 0))
  (command "ucs" "r" "base")
  (command "ucs" "x" 90)
  (command "ucs" "y" 90)
  (setq pt1 (trans pt1 0 1))
  (command "ucs" "o" pt1)
  (setvar "cmdecho" ce)
  (princ)
)
```

LSIDE.LSP   Chapter 2

The LSIDE program changes the UCS to the left side of the model relative to the base created by the UBASE program.

Type: LSIDE   <Enter>

From the base the UCS icon is rotated to the left side of the model.

Listing:
```
(defun C:lside (/ ce pt1)
; Before running this program ubase.lsp should be run to
; establish the base point.
; This program changes the ucs to the left
```

```
; side relative to the base point.
  (setq ce (getvar "cmdecho"))
  (setvar "cmdecho" 0)
  (command "undo" "m")
  (setq pt1 '(0 0 0))
  (setq pt1 (trans pt1 1 0))
  (command "ucs" "r" "base")
  (command "ucs" "x" 90)
  (command "ucs" "y" -90)
  (setq pt1 (trans pt1 0 1))
  (command "ucs" "o" pt1)
  (setvar "cmdecho" ce)
  (princ)
)
```

FSIDE.LSP   Chapter 2

The FSIDE program changes the UCS to the front side of the model relative to the base created by the UBASE program.

Type: FSIDE   <Enter>

From the base the UCS icon is rotated to the front side of the model.

Listing:
```
(defun C:fside (/ ce pt1)
  ; Before running this program ubase.lsp should be run to
  ; establish the base point.
  ; This program changes the ucs to the front side relative
  ; to the base point.
  (setq ce (getvar "cmdecho"))
  (setvar "cmdecho" 0)
  (command "undo" "m")
  (setq pt1 '(0 0 0))
  (setq pt1 (trans pt1 1 0))
  (command "ucs" "r" "base")
  (command "ucs" "x" 90)
  (setq pt1 (trans pt1 0 1))
  (command "ucs" "o" pt1)
  (setvar "cmdecho" ce)
  (princ)
)
```

BSIDE.LSP   Chapter 2

The BSIDE program changes the UCS to the bottom side of the model relative to the base created by the UBASE program.

Type: BSIDE   <Enter>

From the base the UCS icon is rotated to the bottom side of the model.

Listing:
```
(defun C:bside (/ ce pt1)
; Before running this program ubase.lsp should be run to
; establish the base point.
; This program changes the ucs to the bottom side relative
; to the base point.
  (setq ce (getvar "cmdecho"))
  (setvar "cmdecho" 0)
  (command "undo" "m")
  (setq pt1 '(0 0 0))
  (setq pt1 (trans pt1 1 0))
  (command "ucs" "r" "base")
  (command "ucs" "y" 180)
  (setq pt1 (trans pt1 0 1))
  (command "ucs" "o" pt1)
  (setvar "cmdecho" ce)
  (princ)
)
```

TSIDE.LSP   Chapter 2

The TSIDE program changes the UCS to the top side of the model relative to the base created by the UBASE program. This also is the same as the original base created by the UBASE program.

Type: TSIDE   <Enter>

From the base the UCS icon is rotated to the top side of the model or rather returns it to the base.

Listing:
```
(defun C:tside (/ ce pt1)
; Before running this program ubase.lsp should be run to
; establish the base point.
```

```
; This program changes the ucs to the top side or base point.
; The origin is not changed.
  (setq ce (getvar "cmdecho"))
  (setvar "cmdecho" 0)
  (command "undo" "m")
  (setq pt1 '(0 0 0))
  (setq pt1 (trans pt1 1 0))
  (command "ucs" "r" "base")
  (setq pt1 (trans pt1 0 1))
  (command "ucs" "o" pt1)
  (setvar "cmdecho" ce)
  (princ)
)
```

CPLAYER.LSP Chapter 3

The CPLAYER program copies the selected objects to the layer of your choice. If the layer does not exist then the layer is created.

Type: CPLAYER <Enter>

Response: Enter target layer name:

Type: Ceiling <Enter>

Response: Select objects:

Select any objects and confirm the selection set by pressing Enter. You have made a copy of the base plan and placed it on a layer called CEIL-ING.

Listing:
```
(defun C:cplayer  (/ v a ce)
  ; This program copies the selected objects to the layer of
  ; your choice. If the layer does not already exist then
  ; the layer is created.
  (setq ce (getvar "cmdecho"))
  (setvar "cmdecho" 0)
  (command "undo" "m")
  (setq v (getstring "\nEnter target layer name:  "))
```

```
(if (= nil (tblsearch "LAYER" v))
(command "layer" "n" v "")
)
(setq a (ssget))
(command "copy" a "" "@" "@")
(command "chprop" "l" "" "la" v "")
(setvar "cmdecho" ce)
(princ)
)
```

PON.LSP   Chapter 3

The PON program turns perspective on. The distance must already be set. The current angle of view is not changed.

Type: PON   <Enter>

This is the only command needed. Wherever the distance was previously set, the distance will be turned on.

Listing:
```
(defun C:pon (/ ce)
; This program turns perspective on. Distance must already be set.
; The current angle of view is not changed.
  (setq ce (getvar "cmdecho"))
  (setvar "cmdecho" 0)
  (command "undo" "m")
  (command "dview" "" "d" "" "")
  (setvar "cmdecho" ce)
  (princ)
)
```

POFF.LSP   Chapter 3

The POFF program turns perspective off.

Type: `POFF   <Enter>`

This quickly turns perspective off.

Listing:
```
(defun C:poff (/ ce)
; This program turns perspective off.
  (setq ce (getvar "cmdecho"))
  (setvar "cmdecho" 0)
  (command "undo" "m")
  (command "dview" "" "off" "")
  (setvar "cmdecho" ce)
  (princ)
)
```

BSVIEW.LSP   Chapter 4

The BSVIEW program establishes the base view for RVIEW.LSP, LVIEW.LSP, BVIEW.LSP and FVIEW.LSP. Those programs change the view to the appropriate side relative to the base view.

Type: `BSVIEW   <Enter>`

The base view has been established and you can now move around your model by typing each of the other program names.

Listing:
```
(defun C:bsview (/ ce)
; This program establishes the base view for RVIEW, LVIEW,
; BVIEW, FVIEW programs.
; Those programs change the view to the appropriate
; side relative to the base view.
  (setq ce (getvar "cmdecho"))
  (setvar "cmdecho" 0)
  (command "undo" "m")
  (command "ucs" "w")
  (if (= nil (tblsearch "UCS" "BASEVIEW"))
  (command "ucs" "s" "baseview")
  (command "ucs" "s" "baseview" "y"))
```

```
(command "view" "s" "baseview")
(command "ucs" "p")
(setvar "cmdecho" ce)
(princ)
)
```

RVIEW.LSP   Chapter 4

The RVIEW program changes the view to the right side of the model relative to the base view established by the BSVIEW program.

Type: RVIEW   <Enter>

The angle of view of the model is now rotated to the right side relative to the base view.

Listing:
```
(defun C:rview (/ ce wv p1 p2 p3 pt1)
; Before running this program bsview.lsp should be run to
; establish the base point.
; This program changes the view to the right
; side relative to the base point.
  (setq ce (getvar "cmdecho"))
  (setq wv (getvar "worldview"))
  (setvar "worldview" 0)
  (setvar "cmdecho" 0)
  (command "undo" "m")
  (command "view" "r" "baseview")
  (command "ucs" "r" "baseview")
  (setq pt1 (getvar "viewdir"))
  (setq p1 (car pt1))
  (setq p2 (cadr pt1))
  (setq p3 (caddr pt1))
  (command "ucs" "z" "90")
  (setq pt2 (list p1 p2 p3))
  (command "vpoint" pt2)
  (command "ucs" "p")
  (command "ucs" "p")
  (setvar "cmdecho" ce)
  (setvar "worldview" wv)
  (princ)
)
```

LVIEW.LSP   Chapter 4

The LVIEW program changes the view to the left side of the model relative to the base view established by the BSVIEW program.

Type: LVIEW   <Enter>

The angle of view of the model is now rotated to the left side relative to the base view.

Listing:
```
(defun C:lview (/ ce wv p1 p2 p3 pt1)
; Before running this program bsview.lsp should be run to
; establish the base point.
; This program changes the view to the left
; side relative to the base point.
  (setq ce (getvar "cmdecho"))
  (setq wv (getvar "worldview"))
  (setvar "worldview" 0)
  (setvar "cmdecho" 0)
  (command "undo" "m")
  (command "view" "r" "baseview")
  (command "ucs" "r" "baseview")
  (setq pt1 (getvar "viewdir"))
  (setq p1 (car pt1))
  (setq p2 (cadr pt1))
  (setq p3 (caddr pt1))
  (command "ucs" "z" "-90")
  (setq pt2 (list p1 p2 p3))
  (command "vpoint" pt2)
  (command "ucs" "p")
  (command "ucs" "p")
  (setvar "cmdecho" ce)
  (setvar "worldview" wv)
  (princ)
)
```

BVIEW.LSP   Chapter 4

The BVIEW program changes the view to the back side of the model relative to the base view established by the BSVIEW program.

Type: BVIEW   <Enter>

The angle of view of the model is now rotated to the back side relative to the base view.

Listing:
```
(defun C:bview (/ ce wv p1 p2 p3 pt1)
; Before running this program bsview.lsp should be run to
; establish the base point.
; This program changes the view to the back
; side relative to the base point.
  (setq ce (getvar "cmdecho"))
  (setq wv (getvar "worldview"))
  (setvar "worldview" 0)
  (setvar "cmdecho" 0)
  (command "undo" "m")
  (command "view" "r" "baseview")
  (command "ucs" "r" "baseview")
  (setq pt1 (getvar "viewdir"))
  (setq p1 (car pt1))
  (setq p2 (cadr pt1))
  (setq p3 (caddr pt1))
  (command "ucs" "z" "180")
  (setq pt2 (list p1 p2 p3))
  (command "vpoint" pt2)
  (command "ucs" "p")
  (command "ucs" "p")
  (setvar "cmdecho" ce)
  (setvar "worldview" wv)
  (princ)
)
```

FVIEW.LSP   Chapter 4

The FVIEW program changes the view to the front side of the model relative to the base view established by the BSVIEW program. This is actually a return to the BSVIEW angle of view.

Type: FVIEW <Enter>

The angle of view of the model is now rotated to the base view side.

Listing:
```
(defun C:fview (/ ce)
; Before running this program bsview.lsp
; should be run to establish the base point.
; This program changes the view to the front side
; relative to the base point.
  (setq ce (getvar "cmdecho"))
  (setvar "cmdecho" 0)
  (command "undo" "m")
  (command "view" "r" "baseview")
  (setvar "cmdecho" ce)
  (princ)
)
```

VPD.LSP   Chapter 4

The VPD program asks you for the angle of rotation and elevation then the distance. If you don't want to change the angles then press Enter at those prompts. This program is a shortcut program for most of the rotational features commonly found in DVIEW, including distance.

Type: VPD <Enter>

Response: Angle of rotation:

Type: 45 <Enter>

Response: Angle of elevation:

Type: 30 <Enter>

Response: Distance:

Type: 20 <Enter>

Listing:
```
(defun rtd (a)
   (/ (* a 180.0) pi))
(defun C:vpd (/ ce a1 a2 d1)
; This program asks you for the angle of
; rotation and elevation then the distance.
; If you don't want to change the angles then
; <Enter> at those prompts.
  (setq ce (getvar "cmdecho"))
  (setvar "cmdecho" 0)
  (command "undo" "m")
  (setq a1 (getangle "\nAngle of rotation:  "))
  (setq a2 (getangle "\nAngle of elevation:  "))
  (setq d1 (getdist "\nDistance:  "))
  (if (/= a1 nil)(setq a1 (rtd a1)))
  (if (/= a2 nil)(setq a2 (rtd a2)))
  (if (and (/= a1 nil)(/= a2 nil))(command "vpoint" "r" a1 a2))
  (if (and (/= a1 nil)(= a2 nil))(command "vpoint" "r" a1 ""))
  (if (and (= a1 nil)(/= a2 nil))(command "vpoint" "r" "" a2))
  (if (/= d1 nil)(command "dview" "" "d" d1 ""))
  (setvar "cmdecho" ce)
  (princ)
)
```

ISO.LSP   Chapter 4

The ISO program sets an Isometric view. This particular isometric view is the view point 1, −1, 1.

Type: ISO <Enter>

There are no other parameters. It takes you directly to an Isometric view.

Listing:
```
(defun C:iso (/ ce)
; This program sets an Isometric view.
  (setq ce (getvar "cmdecho"))
  (setvar "cmdecho" 0)
  (command "undo" "m")
  (command "vpoint" "1,-1,1")
```

```
(setvar "cmdecho" ce)
(princ)
)
```

ZX.LSP   Chapter 6

The ZX program first performs a ZOOM Extents followed by a ZOOM .9x. This will zoom your drawing almost to the edge of the screen.

Type: ZX   <Enter>

There are no other parameters.

Listing:
```
(defun C:zx (/ ce)
; This program will perform first a ZOOM Extents followed
; by a ZOOM .9x. This will zoom your drawing almost to the
; edge of the screen.
  (setq ce (getvar "cmdecho"))
  (setvar "cmdecho" 0)
  (command "undo" "m")
  (command "zoom" "e")
  (command "zoom" ".9x")
  (setvar "cmdecho" ce)
  (princ)
)
```

RD.LSP   Chapter 6

The RD program redraws all viewports at one time.

Type: RD   <Enter>

There are no other parameters. All viewports are redrawn.

Listing:
```
(defun C:rd (/ ce)
; This program will perform a REDRAWALL
  (setq ce (getvar "cmdecho"))
  (setvar "cmdecho" 0)
  (command "undo" "m")
```

```
    (command "redrawall")
    (setvar "cmdecho" ce)
    (princ)
)
```

TCOPY.LSP   Chapter 7

The TCOPY program changes most extruded lines to ordinary lines, maintaining the extruded appearance, but removing the extrusion.

The TCOPY program will ask you to select objects and you will select and confirm all of the objects you want to be copied "up." It will ask for the thickness distance. Then you are to pick each intersection for the connecting lines. That's all there is to it. The finished product will look much like extruded lines, but you won't have any surfaces at all.

Begin with an extruded model.

Type: TCOPY <Enter>

Response: Select objects:

Select the objects to be copied and press Enter to confirm.

Response: Enter distance:

Type: 4 <Enter>   (This assumes 4 is the original distance.)

Response: Pick all intersections then <Enter> to quit:

Object snap intersection should be turned on. Pick each intersection in the drawing. When all intersections have been picked then press Enter and the objects will be copied up and the connecting lines will be automatically drawn.

Listing:
```
(defun C:tcopy (/ ce th p1 a)
; This program permits you to replace an extrusion with individual
; line segments. Enter the extrusion distance and then pick the
; intersections where you would want the extrusion lines.
  (setq ce (getvar "cmdecho"))
  (setvar "cmdecho" 0)
  (setq os (getvar "osmode"))
```

```
(command "undo" "m")
(setq a (ssget))
(setq th (getdist"\nEnter distance:   "))
(command "chprop" a "" "T" "0" "")
(setvar "osmode" 33)
(setq cntr 0)
(princ "\nPick all intersections:")
(while (setq p1 (getpoint"\nPick intersection:   "))
  (setq cntr (+ cntr 1))
  (if (= cntr 1)(setq p3 p1))
  (command "line" p1 ".xy" p1 th "")
)
(setvar "osmode" os)
(setq p2 (list (car p3) (cadr p3) th))
(command "copy" a "" p3 p2)
(setvar "cmdecho" ce)
(princ)
)
```

IFACE.LSP   Chapter 7

The IFACE program will make any combination of the sides of a 3DFACE invisible. The program uses the following codes for each side of the face.

Code	Side
1	Side 1
2	Side 2
4	Side 3
8	Side 4

For each side you want to make invisible, use the appropriate code. If you want to make more than one side invisible at a time then add the respective codes together. Code 0 will make all of the sides visible again.

Type: IFACE <Enter>

Response: Enter sum of the sides to make invisible:

Type: 3 <Enter>

Response: `Select object:`

Pick the 3DFACE. The appropriate sides will be made invisible.

Listing:

```
(defun C:iface (/ ce i e d d1 e1)
; This program will make any combination of the sides of a
; 3DFACE invisible using the following codes:
; 1  Side 1
; 2  Side 2
; 4  Side 3
; 8  Side 4
; If you want to make a combination of them invisible add the
; respective code numbers together.
; 0 will make them all visible again.
  (setq ce (getvar "cmdecho"))
  (setvar "cmdecho" 0)
  (command "undo" "m")
  (setq i (getint "\nEnter sum of the sides to make invisible:  "))
  (setq e (entget (car (entsel))))
  (setq d (assoc 70 e))
  (setq d1 (cons (car d) i))
  (setq e1 (subst d1 d e))
  (entmod e1)
  (setvar "cmdecho" ce)
  (princ)
)
```

When typing this program there is one line that does not fit completely on one line. That line ends with a + sign. Do not type the + sign, continue the line that follows on the same line.

SFACE.LSP   Chapter 7

The SFACE program will show you in order which of the sides of a 3DFACE are sides 1 and 2. You must know this information in order to correctly use the IFACE program.

Type: `SFACE <Enter>`

Response: `Select object:`

Pick the 3DFACE you want to know about.
Side 1 will disappear.

Type: `<Enter>`

Side 2 will disappear.

Response: `<Enter>`

All sides will be visible again. By watching the sides as they disappear you can see which is side 1 and which is side 2. Therefore you will know the direction each side was drawn and be able to derive sides 3 and 4.

Listing:
```
(defun C:sface (/ ce i e d d1 e1 s)
; This program will show you sides 1 and 2 so that you will be
; able to properly use the IFACE program. Pick the 3DFACE you
; want to know about. Side 1 will disappear.
; <Enter> one time and Side 2 will disappear.
; <Enter> once again and the 3DFACE will return.
; In this way you can see Sides 1 and 2 and the direction they
; are going so that you will also derive Sides 3 and 4.
  (setq ce (getvar "cmdecho"))
  (setvar "cmdecho" 0)
  (command "undo" "m")
  (setq e (entget (car (entsel))))
  (setq i 1)
  (repeat 2
    (setq d (assoc 70 e))
    (setq d1 (cons (car d) i))
    (setq e1 (subst d1 d e))
    (entmod e1)
    (prompt "\nThis is side ")(princ i)
```

```
    (setq i (+ 1 i))
    (setq s (getstring))
  )
  (terpri)
  (entmod e)
  (setvar "cmdecho" ce)
  (princ)
)
```

BMESH.LSP   Chapter 7

The BMESH program creates a region and meshes the region automatical-ly. This is very useful in creating a surface on very complex areas.

This program may not be used with Release 13, use BMESH13 instead.

Type: BMESH   <Enter>

Response: Pick the object to be meshed:
Select object:

Pick any line on the surface to be meshed.

Response: Pick endpoint or intersection that represents the elevation:

Using object snap intersection or end point, pick an intersection or end point on the surface to be meshed. The reason for this is to establish the elevation of the mesh.

Response: Pick inside area:

Pick any inside point within the area to be meshed.

Listing:
```
(defun C:bmesh (/ ce el th os e el e2 p1 p3 bpe bpel)
  ; This program creates a region and meshes the region.
  ; Pick first one of the objects to be meshed. Now pick an
  ; intersection to set the elevation. If the UCS does rotate
  ; correctly or there are too many stray lines try RMESH
  (setq ce (getvar "cmdecho"))
```

```
(setvar "cmdecho" 0)
(command "undo" "m")
(if (not region1)(setq region1 (xload "region")))
(setq el (getvar "elevation"))
(setq th (getvar "thickness"))
(setvar "elevation" 0)
(setvar "thickness" 0)
(setq os (getvar "osmode"))
(princ "\nPick the object to be meshed:  ")
(setq e (entsel))
(setq el (cadr e))
(setq e2 (car e))
(command "ucs" "e" e2)
(setvar "osmode" 33)
(setq p1 (getpoint"\nPick endpoint or intersection that+
represents the elevation:  "))
(setvar "osmode" 0)
(command "ucs" "o" p1)
(setq el (getpoint "\nPick inside area:  "))
(setvar "osmode" os)
(setq bpe (C:bpoly el))
(setq bpe1 (solidify bpe))
(solmesh bpe1)
(command "erase" bpe "")
(command "redrawall")
(command "ucs" "p")
(command "ucs" "p")
(setvar "elevation" el)
(setvar "thickness" th)
(setvar "cmdecho" ce)
(princ)
)
```

When typing this program there is one line that does not fit completely on one line. That line ends with a + sign. Do not type the + sign, continue the line that follows on the same line.

BMESH I3.LSP   Chapter 7

This program is to be used only with R13. It will not work with R12. It works the same way as BMESH.LSP for Release 12. This is very useful in creating a surface on very complex areas.

Type: `BMESH13  <Enter>`

Response: `Pick the entity to be meshed:`

Select: Pick any line on the surface to be meshed.

Response: `Pick endpoint or intersection that represents the elevation:`

Using object snap intersection or end point, pick an intersection or end point on the surface to be meshed. The reason for this is to establish the elevation of the mesh.

Response: `Pick inside area:`

Pick any inside point within the area to be meshed.

This program works with Release 13 Only. The program creates a region and meshes the region. Pick first one of the entities to be meshed. Then pick an intersection to set the elevation. If the UCS does rotate correctly or there are too many stray lines try RMESH13.

Listing:

```
(defun C:bmesh13 (/ ce el th os e el e2 p1 p3 bpe bpe1)
(setq ce (getvar "cmdecho"))
(setvar "cmdecho" 0)
(command "undo" "m")
(setq el (getvar "elevation"))
(setq th (getvar "thickness"))
(setvar "elevation" 0)
(setvar "thickness" 0)
(setq os (getvar "osmode"))
(princ "\nPick the entity to be meshed: ")
(setq e (entsel))
(setq el (cadr e))
(setq e2 (car e))
(command "ucs" "e" e2)
(setvar "osmode" 33)
```

```
(setq p1 (getpoint"\nPick endpoint or intersection that represents+
the elevation: "))
(setvar "osmode" 0)
(command "ucs" "o" p1)
(setq el (getpoint "\nPick inside area: "))
(setvar "osmode" os)
(setq bpe (C:bpoly el))
(command "region" bpe "")
(command "change" "l" "" "p" "e" "0" "")
(command "redrawall")
(command "ucs" "p")
(command "ucs" "p")
(setvar "elevation" el)
(setvar "thickness" th)
(setvar "cmdecho" ce)
(princ)
)
```

RMESH.LSP   Chapter 7

The RMESH program creates a mesh from a boundary. The previous
BMESH program will only work if AutoCAD is not confused by extra lines
and if the UCS is rotated at the correct angle even though it may be parallel to the surface to be meshed. The RMESH program will work in all
cases. RMESH uses the UCS 3POINT to set your origin and UCS. Once this
is done then RMESH asks you to select objects that bound the area you
want to mesh. Now pick an interior point. It's only a few more steps, and it
works well.

This program may not be used with Release 13.

Type: RMESH <Enter>

Response: Select origin and elevation:

Using object intersection or end point, pick an intersection or end point
that will represent the origin and the elevation of the surface. Remember
you are also creating the 3 point UCS.

Response: `Select point for direction of positive X`

   Pick a point to define the X axis.

Response: `Select point for direction of positive Y`

   Pick a point to define the Y axis.

Response: `Select boundaries`
   `Pick inside point`

   Pick a point inside the area to be surfaced.
   The surface is created.

Listing:
```
(defun C:rmesh (/ ce os el th x1 x2 x3 a p1 bpe bpe1)
; This program creates a mesh from a boundary.
; You must have the UCS set parallel to the boundary.
(setq ce (getvar "cmdecho"))
(setvar "cmdecho" 0)
(command "undo" "m")
(if (not region1)(setq region1 (xload "region")))
(setq os (getvar "osmode"))
(setq el (getvar "elevation"))
(setq th (getvar "thickness"))
(setvar "elevation" 0)
(setvar "thickness" 0)
(setvar "osmode" 33)
(setq x1 (getpoint "\nSelect origin and elevation  "))
(setq x2 (getpoint "\nSelect point for direction of positive X+
"))
(setq x3 (getpoint "\nSelect point for direction of positive Y+
"))
(command "ucs" "3p" x1 x2 x3)
(setvar "osmode" 0)
(princ "\nSelect boundaries  ")
(setq a (ssget))
(setq p1 (getpoint "\nPick inside point  "))
(setq bpe (C:bpoly p1 a))
(setq bpe1 (solidify bpe))
(solmesh bpe1)
```

```
(command "erase" bpe "")
(command "redrawall")
(setvar "elevation" el)
(setvar "thickness" th)
(setvar "cmdecho" ce)
(setvar "osmode" os)
(command "ucs" "p")
(princ)

)
```

When typing this program there are two lines that do not fit completely on one line. Those lines end with a + sign. Do not type the + sign, continue the line that follows on the same line.

HIDEMESH.LSP   Chapter 7

The HIDEMESH program will make meshes invisible. It does this by first exploding the mesh, then making the 3DFACES invisible.

Type: HIDEMESH   <Enter>

Response: Pick mesh to make invisible:
Select object:

Pick anywhere on the mesh. It will now turn invisible.

Listing:
```
(defun C:hidemesh (/ ce e a n i b1 b c b2)
; This program makes meshes invisible by first exploding the
; mesh, then making invisible the 3Dfaces. When running the
; program all you have to do is to pick the mesh.
  (setq ce (getvar "cmdecho"))
  (setvar "cmdecho" 0)
  (princ "\nPick mesh to make invisible:  ")
  (setq e (car (entsel)))
  (command "explode" e "")
  (princ "\nThe mesh is now a series of 3dfaces. ")
  (princ "\nSelect the entire mesh area to make invisible:  ")
  (setq a (ssget))
  (setq n (sslength a))
```

```
        (setq i 0)
        (repeat n
          (setq b1 (entget (ssname a i)))
          (setq i (+ 1 i))
          (setq b (assoc 0 b1))
          (if (= "3DFACE" (cdr b))
            (progn
              (setq c (assoc 70 b1))
              (setq b2 (subst '(70 . 15) c b1))
              (entmod b2)
            )
          )
        )
        (setvar "cmdecho" ce)
        (princ)
)
```

DIVCIR.LSP   Chapter 7

The DIVCIR program will divide a circle into two arcs. Begin with a circle.

Type: DIVCIR <Enter>

Response: First break in circle

  Pick the first break point on the circle.

Response: Second break in circle

  Pick the second break point on the circle. The circle still looks like a circle, but it's two arcs.

Listing:
```
(defun C:divcir (/ ce os pt1 pt2 a pt3)
; This program divides a circle into two arcs.
  (setq ce (getvar "cmdecho"))
  (setvar "cmdecho" 0)
  (command "undo" "m")
  (setq os (getvar "osmode"))
  (setvar "osmode" 512)
```

```
(setq pt1 (getpoint "\nFirst break in circle: "))
(setq pt2 (getpoint "\nSecond break in circle: "))
(setq a (entget (ssname (ssget pt1) 0)))
(setq pt3 (cdr (assoc 10 a)))
(command "break" pt1 pt2)
(command "arc" pt1 "e" pt2 pt3)
(setvar "cmdecho" ce)
(setvar "osmode" os)
(princ)
)
```

UCSX.LSP   Chapter 8

The UCSX program permits you to point to and adjust the direction of positive X. All you have to do is pick the origin and the direction. The UCS will stay parallel.

Type: `UCSX  <Enter>`

Response: `Pick origin:`

Pick the point of origin.

Response: `Direction for X:`

Pick a point which represents the direction of positive X. The UCS will be rotated pointing X in the correct direction.

Listing:
```
(defun C:ucsx (/ ce os pto ptx)
; This program adjusts the direction of positive X.
; Pick the origin and the direction.
  (setq ce (getvar "cmdecho"))
  (setvar "cmdecho" 0)
  (command "undo" "m")
  (setq os (getvar "osmode"))
  (setvar "osmode" 33)
  (setq pto (getpoint "\nPick origin:  "))
  (command "ucs" "o" pto)
  (setq ptx (getpoint "\nDirection for X:  "))
  (command "ucs" "3POINT" "" ptx "")
```

```
        (setvar "osmode" os)
        (setvar "cmdecho" ce)
        (princ)
    )
```

3DDIM.LSP   Chapter 8

The 3DDIM program dimensions automatically and correctly in 3D. It sets the UCS and the correct direction of X by the order you pick the points.

Type: `3DDIM <Enter>`

Response: `Select object:`

Pick the line you want to dimension.

Response: `First point:`

Pick the first point of the line being dimensioned.

Response: `Second point:`

Pick the second point of the line being dimensioned. Remember to pick these points in the direction you want the text to go.

Response: `Dimension line location:`

Pick a point where you want the dimension to be located. The proper dimensions are placed.

Listing:
```
(defun C:3ddim (/ ce os e pt1 pt2 pt3 a b c)
; This program dimensions automatically in 3D. It sets the
; Object Snap to INTersection, sets the UCS and direction of
; X by the order you pick the points.
  (setq ce (getvar "cmdecho"))
  (setvar "cmdecho" 0)
  (command "undo" "m")
  (setq os (getvar "osmode"))
  (setq e (car (entsel)))
  (command "ucs" "e" e)
```

```
(setvar "osmode" 33)
(setq pt1 (getpoint "\nFirst point:  "))
(setq pt2 (getpoint "\nSecond point:  "))
(setvar "osmode" 0)
(setq pt3 (getpoint "\nDimension line location  "))
(command "point" pt1)
(setq a (entlast))
(command "point" pt2)
(setq b (entlast))
(command "point" pt3)
(setq c (entlast))
(command "ucs" "3point" pt1 pt2 "")
(setq pt1 (cdr (assoc 10 (entget a))))
(setq pt2 (cdr (assoc 10 (entget b))))
(setq pt3 (cdr (assoc 10 (entget c))))
(setq pt1 (trans pt1 0 1))
(setq pt2 (trans pt2 0 1))
(setq pt3 (trans pt3 0 1))
(command "dim" "hor" pt1 pt2 pt3 "" ^c)
(command "erase" a b c "")
(command "ucs" "p")
(command "ucs" "p")
(setvar "osmode" os)
(setvar "cmdecho" ce)
(princ)
)
```

QDIST.LSP   Chapter 8

The QDIST program quickly lets you check the distance to verify dimensions in 3D. All you do is pick two points.

Type: QDIST <Enter>

Now pick two points to measure the distance.

Listing:
```
(defun C:qdist (/ ce os)
 ; This program quickly lets you see the distance to check
 ; dimensions in 3D. You are set to Object Snap INTersection.
```

```
; Pick two points.
  (setq ce (getvar "cmdecho"))
  (setvar "cmdecho" 0)
  (command "undo" "m")
  (setq os (getvar "osmode"))
  (setvar "osmode" 33)
  (command "dist" pause pause)
  (setvar "osmode" os)
  (setvar "cmdecho" ce)
  (princ)
  )
```

MS.LSP   Chapter 10

The MS program sets you to Model Space in Tilemode 0. Even if you are in the traditional Model Space as Tilemode 1, this program first changes you to Paper Space and then changes to MSPACE. In Releases 12 and 13 there is an MS abbreviation, but it assumes that you are in Paper Space to begin with. You can either eliminate the ACAD.PGP abbreviation entry or change the name of this program. If the name of this program is changed, then make sure you also change it in the 3DTOOLS.LSP program.

Type: MS <Enter>

You are taken to MSPACE of Tilemode 0.

Listing:
```
(defun C:ms (/ ce)
; This program sets you to model space in TILEMODE 0.
  (setq ce (getvar "cmdecho"))
  (setvar "cmdecho" 0)
  (command "undo" "m")
  (setvar "tilemode" 0)
  (command "mspace")
  (setvar "cmdecho" ce)
  (princ)
  )
```

PS.LSP   Chapter 10

The PS program sets you to Paper Space in Tilemode 0. Even if you are in the traditional Model Space as Tilemode 1, this program first changes you to Paper Space and then changes to PSPACE. In Releases 12 and 13 there is a PS abbreviation, but it assumes that you are in Paper Space to begin with. You can either eliminate the ACAD.PGP abbreviation entry or change the name of this program. If the name of this program is changed, then make sure you also change it in the 3DTOOLS.LSP program.

Type: PS <Enter>

You are taken to PSPACE of Tilemode 0.

Listing:
```
(defun C:ps (/ ce)
; This program sets you to paper space in TILEMODE 0.
  (setq ce (getvar "cmdecho"))
  (setvar "cmdecho" 0)
  (command "undo" "m")
  (setvar "tilemode" 0)
  (command "pspace")
  (setvar "cmdecho" ce)
  (princ)
)
```

MV.LSP   Chapter 10

The MV program sets you to Model Space in Tilemode 1.

Type: MV <Enter>

Listing:
```
(defun C:mv (/ ce)
; This program sets you to model space in TILEMODE 1.
  (setq ce (getvar "cmdecho"))
  (setvar "cmdecho" 0)
  (command "undo" "m")
  (setvar "tilemode" 1)
  (setvar "cmdecho" ce)
  (princ)
)
```

PSCOPY.LSP   Chapter 10

The PSCOPY program permits you to copy objects from Paper Space to Model Space. You can't actually transfer objects from Paper Space to Model Space. Therefore this program permits you to select objects in Paper Space then copy them over and place them into your Model Space drawing.

Type: `PSCOPY  <Enter>`

Response: `Select objects to copy:`

Select the object you want to copy and press Enter.

Response: `Basepoint:`

Pick a base point (pick up point) for the objects to copy and move them over to the Model Space viewport and PICK. You also can enter a scale factor and rotation angle. They are now placed in Model Space.

Listing:
```
(defun C:pscopy (/ ce a pt1)
; This program permits you to copy objects
; from paper space to model space.
  (setq ce (getvar "cmdecho"))
  (setvar "cmdecho" 0)
  (command "undo" "m")
  (prompt "\nSelect objects to copy:  ")
  (setq a (ssget))
  (setq pt1 (getpoint  "\nBasepoint:  "))
  (if (= nil (findfile "xxtempxx.dwg"))
    (command "wblock" "xxtempxx" "" pt1 a "")
    (command "wblock" "xxtempxx" "y" "" pt1 a "")
  )
  (command "oops")
  (command "mspace")
  (command "insert" "*xxtempxx")
  (setvar "cmdecho" ce)
  (princ)
)
```

VPX.LSP   Chapter 12

The VPX program will align one viewport with another along the X-axis. You must be in Paper Space. If you are not in Pspace mode of Paper Space the program will place you there. Pick first the viewport you want to move then the base point on that viewport. Next pick a point on the target viewport with which you want to align. The program will move the viewport only in the X direction.

Type: `VPX  <Enter>`

Response: `Pick the viewport you want to move:`
`Select object:`

    Pick the viewport.

Response: `Pick the base point:`

    Pick the base point of the viewport.

Response: `Pick the alignment point on the target viewport:`

    Pick some point on the target viewport where you want to align the base point. The viewport will be aligned only in the X direction.

Listing:
```
(defun C:vpx (/ ce vp1 p1 p2 p3)
; This program will align one viewport with another along the
; X-axis. You must be in Paper Space. If you are not in Pspace
; mode of Paper Space the program will place you there. Pick
; first the viewport you want to move then the base point on
; that viewport. Next pick a point on the target viewport with
; which you want to align. The program will move the viewport
; only in the X direction.
  (setq ce (getvar "cmdecho"))
  (setvar "cmdecho" 0)
  (command "undo" "m")
  (setvar "tilemode" 0)
  (command "pspace")
  (prompt "\nPick the viewport you want to move:  ")
  (setq vp1 (entget (car (entsel))))
  (setq vp1 (cdr (assoc -1 vp1)))
```

```
    (setq p1 (getpoint "\nPick the base point:  "))
    (command "point" p1)
    (setq p2 (getpoint "\nPick the alignment point on the target+
viewport:  "))
    (setq p3 (list (car p2)(cadr p1)(caddr p1)))
    (command "move" vp1 "" p1 p3)
    (setvar "cmdecho" ce)
    (princ)
)
```

When typing this program there is one line that does not fit completely on one line. That line ends with a + sign. Do not type the + sign, continue the line that follows on the same line.

VPY.LSP   Chapter 12

The VPY program will align one viewport with another along the Y-axis. You must be in Paper Space. If you are not in Pspace mode of Paper Space the program will place you there. Pick first the viewport you want to move then the base point on that viewport. Next pick a point on the target viewport with which you want to align. The program will move the viewport only in the Y direction.

Type: VPY <Enter>

Response: Pick the viewport you want to move:
           Select object:

Pick the viewport.

Response: Pick the base point

Pick the base point of the viewport.

Response: Pick the alignment point on the target viewport:

Pick some point on the target viewport where you want to align the base point. The viewport will be aligned only in the Y direction.

Listing:
```
(defun C:vpy (/ ce vp1 p1 p2 p3)
; This program will align one viewport with another along the
; Y-axis. You must be in Paper Space. If you are not in Pspace
; mode of Paper Space the program will place you there. Pick
; first the viewport you want to move then the base point on
; that viewport. Next pick a point on the target viewport with
; which you want to align. The program will move the viewport
; only in the Y direction.
   (setq ce (getvar "cmdecho"))
   (setvar "cmdecho" 0)
   (command "undo" "m")
   (setvar "tilemode" 0)
   (command "pspace")
   (prompt "\nPick the viewport you want to move:  ")
   (setq vp1 (entget (car (entsel))))
   (setq vp1 (cdr (assoc -1 vp1)))
   (setq p1 (getpoint "\nPick the base point:  "))
   (command "point" p1)
   (setq p2 (getpoint "\nPick the alignment point on the target+
viewport:  "))
   (setq p3 (list (car p1)(cadr p2)(caddr p1)))
   (command "move" vp1 "" p1 p3)
   (setvar "cmdecho" ce)
   (princ)
)
```

When typing this program there is one line that does not fit completely on one line. That line ends with a + sign. Do not type the + sign, continue the line that follows on the same line.

AV.LSP   Chapter 12

The AV program assumes that you're active in a viewport that is an Orthographic projection view. It then permits you to manipulate objects only "up and down" and "left and right" relative to that viewport.

Type: AV <Enter>

You can now use the MOVE or COPY command. You can only move or copy objects "up or down" or "left or right" relative to the viewport.

Listing:
```
(defun C:av (/ ce)
; This program assumes that you're active in a viewport
; that is an Orthographic projection view. It then permits you
; to manipulate objects only "up and down" and "left and right"
; relative to that viewport.
  (setq ce (getvar "cmdecho"))
  (setvar "cmdecho" 0)
  (setq or (getvar "orthomode"))
  (command "undo" "m")
  (setvar "orthomode" 1)
  (command "ucs" "view")
  (setvar "cmdecho" ce)
  (princ)
)
```

PV.LSP   Chapter 12

The PV program resets the ortho and UCS to their previous settings after you have used the AV program.

Type: PV <Enter>

The ortho and UCS are reset. There are no other parameters.

Listing:
```
(defun C:pv (/ ce)
; This program resets the ortho and UCS to their previous
; settings after you have used AV.LSP.
  (setq ce (getvar "cmdecho"))
```

```
(setvar "cmdecho" 0)
(command "undo" "m")
(setvar "orthomode" or)
(command "ucs" "p")
(setvar "cmdecho" ce)
(princ)
)
```

MOVEY.LSP   Chapter 12

The MOVEY program will move a selection set in the Y direction ONLY relative to the base viewport. This viewport is changed to UCS view. You may now use the other viewports to select the objects and the base point. In this way X and Z are held constant and you're able to move the objects in the Y (elevation) direction without changing the X and Z positions.

Type: `MOVEY  <Enter>`

Response: `Pick the objects you want to move:`
`Select objects:`

Make sure you are in your base viewport when you start the program. But you don't have to stay in that viewport. At this point you can use any viewport to select the objects. Select objects you want to move and press Enter to confirm the selection set.

Response: `Pick the base point:`

Pick the base point of the move.

Response: `Pick a point for the target Y coordinate:`

Pick a point that has the Y coordinate you need. Your objects will only be moved in the Y direction.

Listing: `(defun C:movey (/ ce vp1 p1 p2 p3)`
`; This program will move a selection set in the Y direction ONLY`
`; relative to the base viewport. This viewport is changed to UCS`
`; View. You may now use the other viewports to select the objects`

```
; and the base point. In this way X and Z are held constant and
; you're able to move the objects in the Y (elevation) direction
; without changing the X and Z positions
  (setq ce (getvar "cmdecho"))
  (setvar "cmdecho" 0)
  (command "undo" "m")
  (command "ucs" "v")
  (prompt "\nPick the objects you want to move:  ")
  (setq vp1 (ssget))
  (setq p1 (getpoint "\nPick the base point:  "))
  (setq p2 (getpoint "\nPick a point for the target Y coordinate:+
"))
  (setq p3 (list (car p1)(cadr p2)(caddr p1)))
  (command "move" vp1 "" p1 p3)
  (command "ucs" "p")
  (setvar "cmdecho" ce)
  (princ)
)
```

When typing this program there is one line that does not fit completely on one line. That line ends with a + sign. Do not type the + sign, continue the line that follows on the same line.

MOVEX.LSP   Chapter 12

The MOVEX program will move a selection set in the X direction ONLY relative to the base viewport. This viewport is changed to UCS view. You may now use the other viewports to select the objects and the base point. In this way Y and Z are held constant and you're able to move the objects in the X direction without changing the Y and Z positions.

Type: MOVEX <Enter>

Response: Pick the objects you want to move:
Select objects:

Make sure you are in your base viewport when you start the program. But you don't have to stay in that viewport. At this point you can use any viewport to select the objects. Select objects you want to move and press Enter to confirm the selection set.

Response: `Pick the base point:`

      Pick the base point of the move.

Response: `Pick a point for the target X coordinate:`

      Pick a point that has the X coordinate you need. Your objects will only be moved in the X direction.

Listing:
```
(defun C:movex (/ ce vp1 p1 p2 p3)
  ; This program will move a selection set in the X direction ONLY
  ; relative to the base viewport. This viewport is changed to UCS
  ; View. You may now use the other viewports to select the objects
  ; and the base point. In this way Y and Z are held constant and
  ; you're able to move the objects in the X direction without
  ; changing the Y and Z positions
  (setq ce (getvar "cmdecho"))
  (setvar "cmdecho" 0)
  (command "undo" "m")
  (command "ucs" "v")
  (prompt "\nPick the objects you want to move:  ")
  (setq vp1 (ssget))
  (setq p1 (getpoint "\nPick the base point:  "))
  (setq p2 (getpoint "\nPick a point for the target X coordinate:+
"))
  (setq p3 (list (car p2)(cadr p1)(caddr p1)))
  (command "move" vp1 "" p1 p3)
  (setvar "cmdecho" ce)
  (command "ucs" "p")
  (princ)
)
```

      When typing this program there is one line that does not fit completely on one line. That line ends with a + sign. Do not type the + sign, continue the line that follows on the same line.

MOVEXY.LSP   Chapter 12

The MOVEXY program will move a selection set in the XY direction ONLY relative to the base viewport. This viewport is changed to UCS view. You may now use the other viewports to select the objects and the base point. In this way Z is held constant and you're able to move the objects in the X and Y direction without changing the Z position.

Type: `MOVEXY  <Enter>`

Response: `Pick the objects you want to move:`
`Select objects:`

Make sure you are in your base viewport when you start the program. But you don't have to stay in that viewport. At this point you can use any viewport to select the objects. Select objects you want to move and press Enter to confirm the selection set.

Response: `Pick the base point:`

Pick the base point of the move.

Response: `Pick a point for the target XY coordinates:`

Pick a point that has the XY coordinates you need. Your objects will only be moved in the XY direction.

Listing:
```
(defun C:movexy (/ ce vp1 p1 p2 p3)
; This program will move a selection set in the XY direction ONLY
; relative to the base viewport. This viewport is changed to UCS
; View. You may now use the other viewports to select the objects
; and the base point. In this way Z is held constant and you're
; able to move the objects in an omni direction without changing
; the elevation.
  (setq ce (getvar "cmdecho"))
  (setvar "cmdecho" 0)
  (command "undo" "m")
  (command "ucs" "v")
  (prompt "\nPick the objects you want to move:  ")
  (setq vp1 (ssget))
  (setq p1 (getpoint "\nPick the base point:  "))
```

```
   (setq p2 (getpoint "\nPick a point for the target XY+
coordinate:  "))
   (setq p3 (list (car p2)(cadr p2)(caddr p1)))
   (command "move" vp1 "" p1 p3)
   (setvar "cmdecho" ce)
   (command "ucs" "p")
   (princ)
)
```

When typing this program there is one line that does not fit completely on one line. That line ends with a + sign. Do not type the + sign, continue the line that follows on the same line.

PVUCS.LSP   Chapter 14

The PVUCS program will change to the UCS object and makes you plan to that UCS at the same time. This permits you to perform operations such as FILLET where you must be in Plan view. If the view is not correct you can use RX, RY or RZ to adjust. You will stay plan with each of these adjustments. Use PVRUCS.LSP to return the settings to normal and return to the initial view.

Type: PVUCS <Enter>

Response: Select the object to which you want to be plan
           Select object:

Pick the object with which you want to be parallel. The UCS and the view will change to plan to that object.

Listing:
```
(defun C:pvucs (/ ce)
; This program will change to UCS Object and make you plan to that
; UCS by setting UCSFOLLOW to 1. This permits you to perform
; operations such as FILLET where you must be in plan view.
; If the view is not correct you can use RX, RY or RZ to adjust.
; You will stay plan with each of these adjustments. Use PVRUCS.LSP
; to return the settings to normal and return to the initial view.
   (setq ce (getvar "cmdecho"))
   (setvar "cmdecho" 0)
```

```
(setq ucsf (getvar "ucsfollow"))
(command "undo" "m")
(setvar "ucsfollow" 1)
(prompt "\nSelect the object to which you want to be plan:  ")
(command "view" "s" "tempview")
(command "ucs" "d" "tempview")
(command "ucs" "s" "tempview")
(command "ucs" "e" pause)
(setvar "cmdecho" ce)
(princ)
)
```

PVRUCS.LSP   Chapter 14

The PVRUCS program returns the settings created by the PVUCS program to their original settings.

Type: PVRUCS   <Enter>

The settings are now restored.

Listing:
```
(defun C:pvrucs (/ ce)
; This program will return the settings to normal and return to
; the initial settings after using the PVUCS program.
  (setq ce (getvar "cmdecho"))
  (setvar "cmdecho" 0)
  (command "undo" "m")
  (setvar "ucsfollow" ucsf)
  (command "view" "r" "tempview")
  (command "ucs" "r" "tempview")
  (setvar "cmdecho" ce)
  (princ)
)
```

CHSIDE.LSP   Chapter 14

The CHSIDE program reverses the target and camera coordinates and places you on the other side of your model.

Type: `CHSIDE  <Enter>`

Response: `Select objects:`

Select the objects you want considered for DVIEW and press Enter to confirm.

Listing:
```
(defun C:chside (/ ce tx ty tz tar cam)
; This program reverses the target and camera coordinates
; and places you on the other side of your model.
  (setq ce (getvar "cmdecho"))
  (setvar "cmdecho" 1)
  (command "undo" "m")
  (setq tx (+ (car (getvar "target")) (car (getvar "viewdir"))))
  (setq ty (+ (cadr (getvar "target")) (cadr (getvar "viewdir"))))
  (setq tz (+ (caddr (getvar "target")) (caddr (getvar "viewdir"))))
  (setq tar (list tx ty tz))
  (setq cam (getvar "target"))
  (command "dview" "c" pause pause pause "po" tar cam)
  (setvar "cmdecho" ce)
  (princ)
)
```

CHTHK.LSP   Chapter 16

The CHTHK program will extrude all objects selected in the same positive Z direction. When you use the region modeler and then explode the created objects something strange happens. If you were to list each of the objects you would see that half of them have a message that says that the extrusion direction is in a negative Z. What this means is that if you extrude all the objects, half of them will extrude in the direction of positive Z and half will extrude in the direction of negative Z.

CHTHK.LSP is a program created just for this situation. It is used strictly to change thickness regardless of the extrusion direction of the objects. It can be used on any set of objects as a fast way to change the thickness rather than the CHPROP command. But it's especially useful under these circumstances.

Type: CHTHK   <Enter>

Response: Enter thickness:

Type: .25   <Enter>

Response: Select objects:

Put a window around the objects you want to extrude. Press Enter to confirm the selection.

Listing:

```
(defun C:chthk ()
; This program extrudes the thickness of all objects selected
; in the same direction of positive Z.
  (setq th (getreal "\nEnter thickness:  "))
  (setq a (ssget))
  (setq n (sslength a))
  (setq i 0)
  (repeat n
    (setq e (entget (ssname a i)))
    (setq ng (caddr (cdr (assoc 210 e))))
    (if (= ng -1.0)(setq th1 (* th -1.0))(setq th1 th))
    (command "chprop" (ssname a i) "" "t" th1 "")
    (setq i (+ i 1))
  )
)
```

BRKPAR.LSP   Chapter 16

The BRKPAR program will evenly break parallel lines. One of the biggest problems faced in architectural drafting is the need to break parallel lines so that you can insert doors and windows. The program asks for only two things, the distance of the offset of the two parallel lines and the angle of the second parallel line.

CAUTION: If both lines don't break it is because your pick box is larger than the distance between the lines. Either reduce the size of the pick box or zoom in a little closer.

Type: BRKPAR <Enter>

Response: Enter offset distance <nil>:

Type: 8 <Enter>

Response: Enter angle of offset <>:

Enter the angle of the other parallel line relative to the line you are going to pick.

Type: 90 <Enter> (Also this could generally be 0, 180 or 270.)

Response: Pick line to break:
Select object:

Pick the line to break.

Response: Pick first break point:

Pick the point where the first break point should be.

Response: Pick second break point:

Pick the point where the second break point should be.
Both parallel lines of the wall are broken at once.

Listing:
```
(defun C:brkpar (/ ce dst dst1 ang ang1 ang2 e pt1 pt2 pt3 pt4)
; This program breaks two parallel lines at the same time.
  (setq ce (getvar "cmdecho"))
  (setvar "cmdecho" 0)
  (command "undo" "m")
  (princ "\nEnter offset distance <")
  (princ dst)(princ">:  ")
  (setq dst1 (getdist))
  (if (= dst1 nil)(setq dst1 dst))
  (setq dst dst1)
  (princ "\nEnter angle of offset <")
  (if (= ang nil)(setq ang2 "")(setq ang2 (angtos ang)))
  (princ ang2)(princ">:  ")
  (setq ang1 (getorient))
  (if (= ang1 nil)(setq ang1 ang))
  (setq ang ang1)
  (prompt "\nPick line to break:  ")
  (setq e (car (entsel)))
  (setq pt1 (getpoint"\nPick first break point:  "))
  (setq pt2 (getpoint"\nPick second break point:  "))
  (setq pt3 (polar pt1 ang dst))
  (setq pt4 (polar pt2 ang dst))
  (command "break" e pt1 pt2)
  (command "break" pt3 pt4)
  (setvar "cmdecho" ce)
  (princ)
)
```

CPEXT.LSP   Chapter 17

The CPEXT program permits you to quickly and easily change the thickness of selected objects by pointing to another object with the same thickness.

Type: CPEXT <Enter>

Response: Select objects to change extrusion:
            Select objects:

Select the objects you want to change.

CHAPTER SEVENTEEN

Response:
```
Pick an object for target extrusion:
Select object:
```

Pick the object with the target extrusion.

Listing:
```
(defun C:cpext (/ ce e1 e2 thk)
; This program will permit you to select objects then pick an
; object with the target extrusion. The objects selected will
; have their thickness changed to that of the target object.
  (setq ce (getvar "cmdecho"))
  (setvar "cmdecho" 0)
  (command "undo" "m")
  (prompt "\nSelect objects to change extrusion:  ")
  (setq e1 (ssget))
  (prompt "\nPick an object for target extrusion:  ")
  (setq e2 (entget (car (entsel))))
  (setq thk (cdr (assoc 39 e2)))
  (if (= thk nil)(setq thk 0))
  (command "chprop" e1 "" "t" thk "")
  (setvar "cmdecho" ce)
  (princ)
)
```

Section V

Appendices

AutoLISP & Your 3D Toolkit

Throughout this book, there are a series of ready-to-run AutoLISP programs that, when used collectively, become your *3D Toolkit*. These 50 programs dramatically enhance the functionality of 3D. In fact, once you use these programs you'll wonder how you can possibly work in 3D without them and wonder why they aren't part of the basic program itself.

This appendix is designed to help you understand the fundamentals of how AutoLISP works, without your having to become an AutoLISP programmer. And the 3D Toolkit is an open architecture designed to make it easy for you to add your own AutoLISP programs so that they can become as easy to use as the ones I've provided.

The easiest way to work with the 3D Toolkit is to install the *AutoCAD 3D Companion Disk.* This disk contains all of the programs you've used in the book, ready to run. It is also self-installing. This way, you don't have to worry about debugging program code. You can begin working with the programs immediately and get on with your lessons.

AutoLISP Fundamentals

It's not my purpose to teach you AutoLISP in this section. For a beginning and easy-to-understand tutorial on AutoLISP, read *AutoLISP in Plain English,* published by Ventana Press. What follows is an overview of the fundamentals to help you create AutoLISP program files and load them.

You create an AutoLISP program as an ordinary text file. You may use EDLIN.COM, EDIT.COM or your favorite word processor to create the file. If you use a word processor, be sure to save the file in ASCII or as a DOS text file, not a word processor file.

Using the text editor, type in the program exactly as it appears in the book. A plus sign at the end of a line of code indicates that the line continues. Don't type the plus sign; it's simply there because the line of code wouldn't fit on one line. Also, don't press Enter at the end of the line if you see the plus sign; simply continue typing the line.

You should create a separate text file for each program. The text file should have the same name as the name of the program and must use the .LSP extension. For example, each program begins with a (defun) statement:

```
(defun C:rx ()
```

The name of the program in the preceding line is RX. The C: in front of the rx indicates to AutoCAD that this AutoLISP program should be treated as a command-level program. This means that you can type it in from the keyboard at the command line. Therefore, you should create the RX program as a file called RX.LSP.

After you've created an AutoLISP file, you must load it before you can use it. You load AutoLISP files from inside the AutoCAD drawing. As an example you would load the RX program with the following statement:

```
(load "rx") <RETURN>
```

Notice that when you load the program, you don't include the extension. Once the program is loaded, you can use it the same as an ordinary AutoCAD command. Just type its name and press Enter:

Type: RX <RETURN>

Things That Can Go Wrong

If you aren't an AutoLISP programmer, many things can go wrong when you try to type in and execute your own programs. This is why it's much easier to use the *Companion Disk* that accompanies this book.

The most common mistake made when typing programs is an omission of a parenthesis or a quotation mark. When this occurs, the file will not load, and you can get a variety of error messages. Another common error is to confuse the lowercase *l* (letter L) with a *1* (number one). Many times *0* (zero) and *O* (uppercase letter O) are also confused.

Finding Your AutoLISP Files

Many times when you try to load an AutoLISP file, AutoCAD can't find it because of the directory it's located in. There are several ways you can overcome this problem. You could, of course, place the AutoLISP files in the \ACAD\SUPPORT directory or directly in the ACAD directory, but I wouldn't recommend it. Your own AutoLISP programs should be in their own directory, out of the way of AutoCAD itself. Therefore, I recommend that you place all of your 3D AutoLISP programs in a directory called 3DTOOLS.

Now your problem becomes how to get AutoCAD to know where your files are. Actually, it's very easy. In the DOS version, AutoCAD Release 13 creates a batch file called ACADR13.BAT when it's installed. The first statement in this batch file is

```
SET ACAD=C:\ACAD\SUPPORT;C:\ACAD\FONTS;C:\ACAD\ADS
```

This SET ACAD= statement tells AutoCAD where to look for various files it needs. Each drive and directory name is separated by a semicolon. Therefore, you can use a text editor to add the following directory to this SET ACAD= statement:

```
C:\3DTOOLS
```

Thus, your entire line would read

```
SET ACAD=C:\ACAD\SUPPORT;C:\ACAD\FONTS;C:\ACAD\ADS;C:\3DTOOLS
```

The preceding procedure assumes that AutoCAD is installed on your C: drive in the ACAD directory. If yours is installed on another drive or in another directory, your line should reflect that.

This line doesn't have to be in the ACADR13.BAT file. You can instead place all of the SET statements in the AUTOEXEC.BAT file so that they will be available when you boot your computer. Then you would begin Auto-CAD in the more traditional way by typing **ACAD** and pressing Enter.

For Windows users, this should be added to the support statement in the environment setting.

AutoLISP Quick Load

When you're working with many AutoLISP programs or files, it's inconvenient to load each of these programs one at a time when you want to use it. Loading programs individually cuts down on your efficiency dramatically. If you were to place all of the programs in a file called ACAD.LSP in your SUPPORT directory, then every time you went into a drawing, all of the programs would load.

There are, however, two major problems with this method. First, AutoCAD is already incredibly slow every time you begin a new drawing. Using this method adds a considerable amount of time every time you begin a new drawing or open an existing drawing. The second problem is that many third-party software programs require their own ACAD.LSP file, and you may harm this file by trying to add your own programs to it.

Here is a better way to load your programs. Assume you have the following lines in a traditional ACAD.LSP file:

```
(defun C:rx ()
 (load "rx")
 (C:rx)
)
```

You have a loaded AutoLISP function called RX. But this function is not the real RX program; it is only a function by the same name that first loads RX.LSP and then executes the newly loaded RX function. This way, you don't need to have the entire file loaded at all times. You only need enough code to load the larger file any time the name of the file or command is called.

You might ask why you couldn't just include the traditional "if not" AutoLISP statement in the menu. You could, of course, but the statement wouldn't load the file if the command were typed in instead of accessed from the menu. This method does.

For this book I have included a single file that does the same thing. All of the 3D programs are included with a "load" line within the file called 3DTOOLS.LSP. Now all you have to do is make sure that 3DTOOLS.LSP is loaded; then you have access to all of your programs from the AutoCAD command line. 3DTOOLS.LSP loads fast so that there is not an enormous wait time before you can begin your drawing. You could even include the following statement in your traditional ACAD.LSP file to make sure that the 3DTOOLS.LSP file is loaded automatically:

```
(load "3DTOOLS")
```

If you don't have access to your ACAD.LSP file because of a third-party program, you can add the preceding line to the end of the ACADR13.LSP file, which is found in the AutoCAD Release 13 WIN or DOS SUPPORT directory. Adding the line here will do the same thing.

The 3DTOOLS.LSP File

In this section you'll learn how the 3DTOOLS.LSP file works. There is one line in the file for each of the programs in the book. Of course, the 3DTOOLS.LSP file is included on the *Companion Disk.* You can find a complete listing of the file in Chapter 17, "The 3D Toolkit," along with a complete listing of the other 50 programs.

Following is the first line in the program:

```
(defun C:rx () (load "rx") (C:rx))
```

This line is a complete AutoLISP program in and of itself. The name of the program is RX, the same as the real program that is not yet loaded. This first RX program loads and executes the real RX program.

The following line defines the program:

```
(defun C:rx ()
```

This next line loads the real RX program file:

```
(load "rx")
```

Now the definition of the real RX program has replaced the first one. The following line executes the real program that is now in memory:

```
(C:rx)
```

The next line closes the final parenthesis for the beginning (defun) statement:

```
)
```

The first time you type **RX** and press Enter, the real RX program is loaded and executed. From then on, each time you type **RX**, the program doesn't reload because the real program is already in memory. This way, you are loading the programs you need only once as you need them.

As you can see, this program utilizes an open architecture, which permits you to add other programs to it. You'll have other AutoLISP programs of your own that you either write yourself, copy out of magazines or download from bulletin boards. You can easily add any of these programs to the 3DTOOLS.LSP file for automatic loading. Make sure that your program is in a file of the same name as the program itself. Then follow the format and add your program access line at the bottom of the 3DTOOLS.LSP file.

3D Toolkit Program Recap

Although Chapter 17 gives you a complete program listing and directions on the use of each program, having a concise recap of the programs is useful because it reminds you that they're available.

RX   This program rotates the UCS 90 degrees around X. To continue rotating around X, press Enter for each additional 90 degrees.

RY   This program rotates the UCS 90 degrees around Y. To continue rotating around Y, press Enter for each additional 90 degrees.

RZ   This program rotates the UCS 90 degrees around Z. To continue rotating around Z, press Enter for each additional 90 degrees.

USLVIEW   This program saves the view, layer and UCS by the same name. If the view or UCS already exists, they are replaced. Set the UCS before executing this program.

USVIEW   This program saves the view and UCS by the same name. If the view or UCS already exists, they are replaced. Set the UCS before executing this program.

URVIEW   This program restores the view and UCS by the same name.

UBASE   This program establishes the base point UCS for the RSIDE, LSIDE, BSIDE and FSIDE programs. Those programs change the UCS to the appropriate side relative to the base point.

RSIDE   Before running this program, run UBASE.LSP to establish the base point. This program changes the UCS to the right side relative to the base point.

LSIDE   Before running this program, run UBASE.LSP to establish the base point. This program changes the UCS to the left side relative to the base point.

FSIDE   Before running this program, run UBASE.LSP to establish the base point. This program changes the UCS to the front side relative to the base point.

BSIDE   Before running this program, run UBASE.LSP to establish the base point. This program changes the UCS to the bottom side relative to the base point.

TSIDE   Before running this program, run UBASE.LSP to establish the base point. This program changes the UCS to the top side or base point. The origin is not changed.

CPLAYER   This program copies the selected entities to the layer of your choice. If the layer does not already exist, then the layer is created.

PON   This program turns perspective on. Distance must already be set. The current angle of view is not changed.

POFF   This program turns perspective off.

BSVIEW   This program establishes the base view for the RVIEW, LVIEW, BVIEW and FVIEW programs. Those programs change the view to the appropriate side relative to the base view.

RVIEW   Before running this program, run BSVIEW.LSP to establish the base point. This program changes the view to the right side relative to the base point.

LVIEW   Before running this program, run BSVIEW.LSP to establish the base point. This program changes the view to the left side relative to the base point.

BVIEW   Before running this program, run BSVIEW.LSP to establish the base point. This program changes the view to the back side relative to the base point.

FVIEW   Before running this program, run BSVIEW.LSP to establish the base point. This program changes the view to the front side relative to the base point.

VPD   This program asks you for the angle of rotation and elevation and then the distance. Press Enter at each prompt where you don't want to change the angle.

ISO   This program sets an Isometric view.

ZX   This program performs first a ZOOM Extents followed by a ZOOM .9x. This process will zoom your drawing almost to the edge of the screen.

RD   This program performs a REDRAWALL.

TCOPY This program enables you to replace an extrusion with individual line segments. Enter the extrusion distance and then pick intersections where you want the extrusion lines.

IFACE This program makes any combination of the sides of a 3D face invisible using the following codes:

Code Numbers	Side
1	Side 1
2	Side 2
4	Side 3
8	Side 4

If you want to make a combination of sides invisible, add the respective code numbers together. Using 0 will make them all visible again.

SFACE This program shows you Sides 1 and 2 so that you can use the IFACE program properly. Pick the 3D face you want to know about; then Side 1 will disappear. Press Enter one time, and Side 2 will disappear. Press Enter once again, and the 3D face will return. This way, you can see Sides 1 and 2 and the direction they are going so that you can also derive Sides 3 and 4.

BMESH This program creates a region and meshes it. Pick first one of the objects to be meshed. Then pick an intersection to set the elevation. If the UCS doesn't rotate correctly or there are too many stray lines, try RMESH instead.

BMESH13 Used for Release 13.

RMESH This program creates a mesh from a boundary. You must have the UCS set parallel to the boundary.

HIDEMESH This program makes meshes invisible by first exploding the mesh and then making invisible the 3D faces. When running the program, you only have to pick the mesh.

DIVCIR This program divides a circle into two arcs.

UCSX This program adjusts the direction of positive X. You simply pick the origin and the direction.

3DDIM This program dimensions automatically in 3D. It sets the object snap to intersection and sets the UCS and direction of X by the order you pick the points.

QDIST   This program quickly lets you see the distance to check dimensions in 3D. You are set to object snap intersection; then you pick two points.

MS   This program sets you to Model Space in TILEMODE 0.

PS   This program sets you to Paper Space in TILEMODE 0.

MV   This program sets you to Model Space in TILEMODE 1.

PSCOPY   This program enables you to copy entities from Paper Space to Model Space.

VPX   This program aligns one viewport with another along the X-axis. You must be in Paper Space. If you are not in the Pspace mode of Paper Space, the program will place you there. Pick first the viewport you want to move and then the base point on that viewport. Next, pick a point on the target viewport with which you want to align. The program will move the viewport only in the X direction.

VPY   This program aligns one viewport with another along the Y-axis. You must be in Paper Space. If you are not in the Pspace mode of Paper Space, the program will place you there. Pick first the viewport you want to move and then the base point on that viewport. Next, pick a point on the target viewport with which you want to align. The program will move the viewport only in the Y direction.

AV   This program assumes that you're active in a viewport that is an Orthographic projection view. It then enables you to manipulate objects only up and down or left and right relative to that viewport.

PV   This program resets the ortho and UCS to their previous settings after you've used AV.LSP.

MOVEY   This program moves a selection set in the Y direction *only* relative to the base viewport. This viewport is changed to UCS view. You may then use the other viewports to select the objects and the base point. This way, X and Z are held constant, and you can move the objects in the Y (elevation) direction without changing the X and Z positions.

MOVEX   This program moves a selection set in the X direction *only* relative to the base viewport. This viewport is changed to UCS view. You may then use the other viewports to select the objects and the base point. This way, Y and Z are held constant, and you can move the objects in the X direction without changing the Y and Z positions.

MOVEXY This program moves a selection set in the XY direction *only* relative to the base viewport. This viewport is changed to UCS view. You may then use the other viewports to select the objects and the base point. This way, Z is held constant, and you can move the objects in an omni direction without changing the elevation.

PVUCS This program changes to UCS Object and makes you plan to that UCS by setting UCSFOLLOW to 1. This enables you to perform operations such as FILLET where you must be in Plan view. If the view isn't correct, you can use RX, RY or RZ to adjust. You'll stay plan with each of these adjustments. Use PVRUCS.LSP to return the settings to normal and return to the initial view.

PVRUCS This program changes to UCS Object and makes you plan to that UCS by setting UCSFOLLOW to 1. This enables you to perform operations such as FILLET where you must be in Plan view. If the view isn't correct, you can use RX, RY or RZ to adjust. You'll stay plan with each of these adjustments. Use PVRUCS.LSP to return the settings to normal and return to the initial view.

CHSIDE This program reverses the target and camera coordinates and places you on the other side of your model.

CPEXT This program enables you to select objects and then pick an object with the target extrusion. The thickness of the objects selected will change to that of the target object.

CHTHK This program changes the thickness of the objects selected. Although you can use it at any time, its primary purpose is to examine the extrusion direction of an object to see if it is negative and to ensure that all objects will extrude in the direction of positive Z.

The functionality of any AutoCAD command or AutoLISP program is directly dependent on how you use it. There is a natural tendency to not use these programs because they are not inherently a part of the core program of AutoCAD Release 13. Well, the reality is that most of the new features of Release 13 are not inherently a part of the core program. They are either AutoLISP programs or ADS programs written by Autodesk. You load and execute them in a similar manner as the 3DTOOLS.LSP file. The 3D Toolkit is just easier for you to control.

Think of the programs in the 3D Toolkit as well as additional programs that you include as part of AutoCAD itself and use them. The more you force yourself to use them, the more of a habit they become. And it's habit that creates the most efficiency.

About the *Online Companion*

Welcome to the *AutoCAD 3D Online Companion*

Ventana is breaking new ground by offering, through the Internet, the *AutoCAD 3D Online Companion*, a never-ending source of valuable information.

The *AutoCAD 3D Online Companion* is an informative tool, as well as an annotated archive of free AutoCAD programs found on the Internet. It also offers an archive of Ventana AutoCAD utilities for sale and provides links to other Internet AutoCAD references, including newsgroups covering AutoCAD tips and tricks, and e-mail mailing lists where you can meet with other AutoCAD professionals to discuss cool new trends and the latest secrets of the trade.

Perhaps one of the most impressive features of the *Online Companion* is its Software Archive. Here, you'll find and be able to download the latest versions of all the software mentioned in the *AutoCAD 3D Companion* that are freely available on the Net.

The *AutoCAD 3D Online Companion* also links you to the Ventana Library where you will find useful press and jacket information, as well as other Ventana Press offerings. Plus you have access to a wide selection of exciting new releases and coming attractions. In addition, Ventana's Online Library allows you to order online the books you want.

The *AutoCAD 3D Online Companion* represents Ventana Online's ongoing commitment to offering the most dynamic and exciting products possible. And soon Ventana Online will be adding more services, including more multimedia supplements, searchable indices and sections of the book reproduced and hyperlinked to the Internet resources they reference.

To access, connect via the World Wide Web to
http://www.vmedia.com/autocad.html

About the *Companion Disk*

Congratulations on your decision to learn 3D! As you know, the AutoLISP programs listed in Chapter 17, "The 3D Toolkit," are not just a group of programs you use to enhance your productivity, but they are essential to your success in working in 3D. You use these programs throughout this book and will continue to use them from now on as you work in AutoCAD.

One of the most frustrating aspects of working with new AutoLISP programs is trying to debug simple typing errors. I can't tell you how many people have called me to say that they've had as many as five people check their code and know it is perfectly correct. But still the programs don't work. When they fax a hard copy of their code to me, I've found as many as three major errors preventing the programs from working.

The problem is simply that most AutoCAD users are not expert typists. Autodesk has done everything possible to keep you from having to type. Then why impede your progress by typing and debugging the programs in the book and possibly increasing your frustration level?

What's on the *Companion Disk?*

The *Companion Disk* contains ready-to-load programs for all of the programs you find in this book. The disk includes the 3DTOOLS.LSP program, which will automatically load your programs for you. All you have to do is type the name of the program.

With the *Companion Disk*, you can copy the AutoLISP files to your hard disk or use the install program included on the disk. Then you are ready to use each of the 53 programs you've read about. It's a great way to speed your success in learning 3D and enhance your future productivity.

Index

Colophon

This book was produced on Apple Power Macintosh computers using PageMaker 5.0. PostScript files were printed to disk and output directly to film using a Linotronic high resolution imagesetter.

The body text is set in Palatino. Subheads, running heads and folios are set in varying weights of DTC Classical Sans and DTC Classical Condensed Sans. Sample code sections are set in Letter Gothic. Illustrations were produced using Windows screen captures, AutoCAD, AutoScript and Adobe Photoshop.

The AutoCAD Reference Library

AutoCAD: A Concise Guide to Commands & Features, Fourth Edition ⑤

$27.95

696 pages, illustrated, includes companion disk

Everything you need to produce drawings with AutoCAD—all the key commands, features and skills—is at your fingertips. Highlighted by hands-on exercises, forty-four clear, concise chapters lead you from the simple to the complex. The companion disk contains drawings from exercises in the book, productivity-enhancing AutoLISP routines and more!

The AutoCAD Productivity Book, Sixth Edition ⑤

$34.95

400 pages, illustrated, includes companion disk

The world's most turned-to reference on customizing AutoCAD! Extensively rewritten and updated for Windows, it now features more customizable features and introduces Release 13 networking. An expanded "Productivity Library" includes 30 new, ready-to-run AutoLISP programs and macros. The companion disk includes all the AutoLISP programs and drawings from the book. Available March.

The AutoCAD Reference Library™ Deluxe CD-ROM ⑤

$99.95

AutoCAD users spend most of their working days on the computer. Now, that's where the help is! For the first time on CD-ROM, all five books in this Ventana series are online, fully indexed and searchable by topic, title and keyword. Follow references to a given topic from title to title, or page through general subjects. All the programs, routines and support files from the books are included in this innovative digital handbook. Available March.

Internet Resources

The Internet Tour Guides, Second Edition

Mac Edition: $29.95, 432 pages, illustrated
Windows Edition: $29.95, 416 pages, illustrated

Users can now navigate the Internet the easy way: by pointing and clicking, dragging and dropping. In easy-to-read, entertaining prose, the *Internet Tour Guides* lead you through installing and using the software enclosed in the book to send and receive e-mail, browse the World Wide Web, transfer files, search the Internet's vast resources and more! **BONUS**: Free registration with a top national service provider.

Mosaic Quick Tours

Mac Edition: $12.00, 208 pages, illustrated
Windows Edition: $12.00, 216 pages, illustrated

The *Mosaic Quick Tours* introduce the how-to's of hypertext travel in a simple, picturesque guide. Mosaic™, called the "killer app" of the Internet, lets you view linked text, audio and video resources thousands of miles apart. Learn to use Mosaic for all your information hunting and gathering—including Gopher searches, newsgroup reading and file transfers via FTP.

Walking the World Wide Web

$29.95
350 pages, illustrated

Enough of lengthy listings! This tour features more than 300 memorable Web sites, with in-depth descriptions of what's special about each. Includes international sites, exotic exhibits, entertainment, business and more. The companion CD-ROM contains Ventana Mosaic™ and a hyperlinked version of the book, providing live links when you log on to the Internet.

 Books marked with this logo include a free Internet *Online Companion*™, featuring archives of free utilities plus a software archive and links to other Internet resources.

Internet Virtual Worlds Quick Tour 🖱

$14.00
160 pages, illustrated

Learn to locate and master real-time interactive communication forums and games by participating in the virtual worlds of MUD (Multi-User Dimension) and MOO (Mud Object-Oriented). *Internet Virtual Worlds Quick Tour* introduces users to the basic functions by defining different categories (individual, interactive and both) and by detailing standard protocols. Also revealed is the insider's lexicon of these mysterious cyberworlds. Available March.

Internet Roadside Attractions 🖱

$29.95
376 pages, illustrated

Why take the word of one when you can get a quorum? Seven experienced Internauts—teachers and bestselling authors—share their favorite Web sites, Gophers, FTP sites, chats, games, newsgroups and mailing lists. Organized alphabetically by category for easy browsing with in-depth descriptions. The companion CD-ROM contains the entire text of the book, hyperlinked for off-line browsing and online Web hopping.

Internet Chat Quick Tour 🖱

$14.00
150 pages, illustrated

Global conversations in real time are an integral part of the Internet. The worldwide chat network is where users find online help and forums on the latest scientific research. The *Internet Chat Quick Tour* describes the best software sites for users to chat on a variety of subjects and shows users where to take out verbal aggression. Available March.

To order any Ventana Press title, complete this order form and mail or fax it to us, with payment, for quick shipment.

TITLE	ISBN	Quantity		Price		Total
The AutoCAD 3D Companion, 2nd Edition	1-56604-142-2	_____	x	$34.95	=	$ _____
AutoLISP in Plain English, 5th Edition	1-56604-140-6	_____	x	$27.95	=	$ _____
1000 AutoCAD Tips & Tricks, 4th Edition	1-56604-141-4	_____	x	$34.95	=	$ _____
AutoCAD: A Concise Guide, 4th Edition	1-56604-139-2	_____	x	$27.95	=	$ _____
The AutoCAD Productivity Book, 6th Edition	1-56604-185-6	_____	x	$34.95	=	$ _____
The AutoCAD Reference Library Deluxe CD-ROM	1-56604-226-7	_____	x	$99.95	=	$ _____
The Mac Internet Tour Guide, 2nd Edition	1-56604-173-2	_____	x	$29.95	=	$ _____
The Windows Internet Tour Guide, 2nd Edition	1-56604-174-0	_____	x	$29.95	=	$ _____
Mosaic Quick Tour for Mac	1-56604-195-3	_____	x	$12.00	=	$ _____
Mosaic Quick Tour for Windows	1-56604-194-5	_____	x	$12.00	=	$ _____
Walking the World Wide Web	1-56604-208-9	_____	x	$29.95	=	$ _____
Internet Virtual Worlds Quick Tour	1-56604-222-4	_____	x	$14.00	=	$ _____
Internet Roadside Attractions	1-56604-193-7	_____	x	$29.95	=	$ _____
Internet Chat Quick Tour	1-56604-223-2	_____	x	$14.00	=	$ _____
				Subtotal	=	$ _____
				Shipping	=	$ _____
				TOTAL	=	$ _____

SHIPPING:

For all standard orders, please ADD $4.50/first book, $1.35/each additional.
For Internet Membership Kit orders, ADD $6.50/first kit, $2.00/each additional.
For "two-day air," ADD $8.25/first book, $2.25/each additional.
For "two-day air" on the kits, ADD $10.50/first book, $4.00/each additional.
For orders to Canada, ADD $6.50/book.
For orders sent C.O.D., ADD $4.50 to your shipping rate.
North Carolina residents must ADD 6% sales tax.
International orders require additional shipping charges.

Name _____   Daytime Phone _____

Company _____

Address (No PO Box) _____

City_____   State_____ Zip _____

____ Payment enclosed ____VISA ____MC Acc't # _____ Exp. Date_____

Exact Name on Card _____ Signature _____

Mail to: Ventana Press, PO Box 2468, Chapel Hill, NC 27515 ☎ 800/743-5369 Fax 919/942-1140